Robert Mason is Lecturer in International Relations at the British University in Egypt. He holds a PhD in Middle East Politics from the University of Exeter.

FOREIGN POLICY IN IRAN AND SAUDI ARABIA

Economics and Diplomacy in the Middle East

ROBERT MASON

I.B. TAURIS
LONDON • NEW YORK • OXFORD • NEW DELHI • SYDNEY

I.B. TAURIS
Bloomsbury Publishing Plc
50 Bedford Square, London, WC1B 3DP, UK
1385 Broadway, New York, NY 10018, USA
29 Earlsfort Terrace, Dublin 2, Ireland

BLOOMSBURY, I.B. TAURIS and the I.B. Tauris logo are
trademarks of Bloomsbury Publishing Plc

First published in Great Britain 2015
This paperback edition published in 2022

Copyright © Robert Mason, 2015

Robert Mason has asserted his right under the Copyright,
Designs and Patents Act, 1988, to be identified as Author of this work.

For legal purposes the Acknowledgements on p. ix constitute an
extension of this copyright page.

All rights reserved. No part of this publication may be reproduced or
transmitted in any form or by any means, electronic or mechanical,
including photocopying, recording, or any information storage or retrieval
system, without prior permission in writing from the publishers.

Bloomsbury Publishing Plc does not have any control over, or responsibility for,
any third-party websites referred to or in this book. All internet addresses given
in this book were correct at the time of going to press. The author and publisher
regret any inconvenience caused if addresses have changed or sites have
ceased to exist, but can accept no responsibility for any such changes.

A catalogue record for this book is available from the British Library.
A full CIP record is available from the Library of Congress.

ISBN: HB: 978-1-78076-721-5
PB: 978-1-7883-1443-5
eBook: 978-0-85773-898-1
ePDF: 978-0-85772-520-2

Series: Library of Modern Middle East Studies 153

Typeset by Jones Ltd, London

To find out more about our authors and books visit
www.bloomsbury.com and sign up for our newsletters.

In loving memory of my wife, Dr Sherry Sayed Gadelrab, 1979–2013

CONTENTS

Acknowledgements	ix
Introduction	1
1. A Conceptual Framework	4
2. The Shaping Factors of Regional Insecurity and Conflict in the Formulation of Contemporary Saudi and Iranian Foreign Policy	11
The 1979 Iranian Islamic Revolution: The Birth of Resistance Politics	16
The Iran–Iraq War (1980–1988): The Carter Doctrine and the Seeds of US Containment Policy	20
The First Gulf War: The USA as a Local Power and the Subsequent Complexities of Establishing a Pan-Regional Security Architecture	24
The Critical, Comprehensive and Civilizational Dialogues with Iran	28
Saudi–US Relations in the Lead Up to 9/11	32
3. Saudi Foreign Policy: Oil, Wahabism and 'Riyal Politik'	35
The Domestic Environment and Political Economy of Saudi Arabia	36
Saudi Foreign Policies in the Levant and Gulf	45
The Global Relations of Saudi Arabia	59

4. **Iranian Foreign Policy: The Politics of Civilization, Security and Economy** — 84
   The Domestic Environment and Political Economy — 86
   Iran's 'Resistance Axis' and Cold War with Saudi Arabia — 93
   Countering Western Interventions and International Sanctions — 100
   The Dysfunctional International Relationship of Iran and the P5+1 — 117
   The Possibility of Alternative Strategies: Attempting to Reconcile the Resistance and Pro-Western Alliances — 133

5. **The Triangulation of US Foreign Policy towards the Middle East** — 140
   Russia — 140
   China — 146
   India — 150
   Japan — 151
   The Convergence of Western Foreign Policies in the Middle East — 152
   US Policy in the Middle East and Policy Prescriptions — 154

6. **Conclusions: Economic Factors in Middle East Foreign Policies** — 156
   The Relative Weight of Economic and Non-Economic Factors — 156
   Economic Factors in Alliance Building — 159
   Economic Factors in Deconstructing Adversarial Alliances — 160
   Future Trends — 163

Notes — 169
Bibliography — 234
Index — 273

ACKNOWLEDGEMENTS

First of all, I am highly indebted to Professor Tim Niblock whose excellent academic supervision and insights contributed vastly to the quality of this book. I am also grateful to Professor Gerd Nonneman for his guidance and suggestions. In getting the manuscript print-ready I thank Maria Marsh, my Middle East editor at I.B.Tauris, and Hannah Wilks, my copy-editor.

I would like to thank HRH Prince Turki Al-Faisal for the invitation to be a Research Fellow at the King Faisal Center for Research and Islamic Studies in Riyadh. At the same time, my gratitude goes to HRH Prince Alwaleed bin Talal who provided the scholarship that enabled me to travel to Riyadh. I would also like to thank the British Institute of Persian Studies for the travel award and accommodation which allowed me to experience the culture, politics and economics of Iran first-hand. I also appreciate the assistance that Hadi Borhani and my Persian lecturer, Ali Mossadegh, extended to me before my trip.

I am particularly grateful to those individuals who gave up their valuable time to be interviewed for this research, and in many cases for the additional assistance and points of reference they provided. They include: Ambassador Martin Indyk, Ambassador Roberto Toscano, Mr Ruprecht Polenz, Professor Abbas Maleki, Dr Ali Biniaz, Dr Leo Drollas, Sir Richard Dalton, Sir Sherard Cowper-Coles, H.E. Talmiz Ahmad, H.E. Professor Dato' Syed Omar Al Saggaf and

Mr Chris Innes-Hopkins. To the interviewees who preferred to remain anonymous, and to others who have contributed informally to this book, I thank you for your valuable input.

For her unerring encouragement and critical eye, I thank Dr Sherry Sayed Gadelrab. Finally, I will always be grateful to my parents, Chris Mason and Lilianne Thérèse Mason, whose help and support got me to this point and whose early discussions advanced my critical thinking and interest in International Relations.

INTRODUCTION

This book assesses the relationship between economic factors and non-economic factors, and the relative weight of each, in the conduct of Middle East foreign policies but with special reference to Saudi Arabia and Iran. In the Saudi case, economic factors are contextualized within its traditional themes of maintaining security and stability through international alliances and its promotion of stable and long-term energy export markets. In the case of Iran, negative economic factors such as sanctions are put into perspective by other factors such as perceived hostility to the Islamic Revolution, national security issues and emerging splits within the decision-making elite.

The Middle East, defined here as the Arab states plus Turkey, Israel and Iran, is one of the most geo-strategically important regions in the world. Its significance, opportunities and challenges are disproportionate to the size of the region and derive largely from its oil, the Israel-Palestine conflict, terrorism and anti-imperialist foreign policies. Hydrocarbon-based relationships have been important, if not crucial, between the Gulf States, Iran and the West (defined here as the USA, UK, France and Germany). They are also becoming an increasingly important component of relations with Russia and China which, alongside those with the West, function as the main bilateral relations under study and the 'international community' in the following chapters.

Saudi Arabia and Iran have been selected for this research due to their economic and political features, as well as the positions they occupy in the regional and international system. Saudi Arabia has allied itself with the USA, and has a leadership role in the Gulf Cooperation Council (GCC) and across the Islamic world based on its guardianship of the two holy places (Mecca and Medina) and through the influence of Salafism.[1] Saudi Arabia's main economic influence is derived from being the swing producer in the Organization of Petroleum Exporting Countries (OPEC). Iran is included in this research because it pursues a revolutionary political agenda and countering policies against the West through Shi'i and anti-Western allies. It remains heavily dependent on oil and gas revenues for its national budget but is increasingly the subject of unprecedented international sanctions.

Other Middle East states have not been included in this book because they exhibit different characteristics from the states under review, such as not being major oil and gas exporters. Expanding the number of case studies could nonetheless provide an interesting insight into the role of economic factors in 'small states' of the region, states which are less susceptible to the geo-strategic imperatives of these potential regional hegemons, or states which derive a significant part of their budget from economic factors which are not related to the export of hydrocarbons.

The first chapter includes reference to the leading writers on Foreign Policy Analysis (FPA) and the evolution of competing and complementary conceptual frameworks with which to analyse the foreign policies of Middle East states. Chapter 2 provides a background to the pre-9/11 foreign policies of Saudi Arabia and Iran and the events and trends which continue to shape them. It places their respective international relations in historical context, covering events from the oil crisis in 1973, Nasser's attempt at pan-Arabism in the 1970s, the Iran–Iraq War in the 1980s, the collapse of the Soviet Union and the Gulf War in 1991, regional security developments, oil revenue spikes, the emergence of reform and democratization concepts, globalization and increasing interdependence, economic diversification and terrorism.

Chapters 3 and 4 begin with 9/11 and discuss the implementation of US neo-conservative policies towards Saudi Arabia and Iran,

Introduction

and their policies in response. The chapters introduce the foreign policies of Saudi Arabia and Iran respectively, analysing the determinants, decision-making and behaviour at the domestic, regional and international levels. The chapters cover the leading economic, security and geopolitical strands of the foreign policies, attributing relative weight to them and highlighting reasons for the dominance of any single strand. The research ends with Saudi Arabia's responses to the Arab Uprisings and Iran's response to renewed UN Security Council (UNSC) sanctions in 2011.

Chapter 5 discusses the foreign policies of the USA, most notably in the context of China and Russia as members of the BRICS bloc and the UNSC. The foreign policies of other non-aligned states such as India and relatively dependent states such as Japan are also included, showing the extent that the USA can continue to leverage its resources to achieve its foreign policy aims and objectives in the Middle East. The chapter concludes with recommendations for US foreign policy on the Middle East. Chapter 6, the final chapter of the book, compares and contrasts the economic factors of foreign policies across the two states, concluding the role of economic factors versus non-economic factors in Middle East foreign policies and alliances. The findings are placed within the context of an emerging new Middle East.

CHAPTER 1

A CONCEPTUAL FRAMEWORK

The study of FPA, as a sub-discipline of International Relations (IR), emerged during the 1950s and 1960s from the combined works of Snyder, Bruck and Sapin[1] who argued for a conceptual framework that reflected forces at the sub-state level; Rosenau[2] who argued for a multi-dimensional approach to FPA; and the Sprouts[3] who emphasized the importance of perception and interpretation of the global environment by decision-makers. For the first time, FPA challenged conventional IR thinking by attempting to account for all the factors involved in foreign policy making, even those at the sub-system level. FPA, although successful in identifying a range of contributing factors to foreign policy, ranging from individual to group behaviour, was unable to generate a conceptual framework which could easily be reconciled with the dominant IR schools of thought. Therefore, the challenges for FPA remain both conceptual and integrationist.

IR theory made advances in the late 1970s and 1980s when neo-realists such as Waltz[4] and Walt[5] sought to explain the Middle East through the same universally applied conceptual principles as those which explained other regions. It was not until the early 1990s, with the end of the Cold War and the accompanying transition from a bipolar to a unipolar world, that actor-specific FPA gained renewed attention. Constructivism, which focuses on the '(socially constructed) *meanings* of facts and objects they [states] encounter in their domestic and external environments, that inspires their actions', therefore enjoyed a renewed popularity as it was much better than neo-realism at accounting for the onset of globalization.[6] This brought with it the formation of new international relations between states and regions, and an increase in non-state influences on the state (largely through soft power such as international media).

In response, adjusted realism attempted to reconcile the changing balance between soft and hard power approaches to foreign policies aimed at a) national security threats, and b) other national interests during eras less dominated by conflict.[7] However, the conventional neo-realist approach remained a useful theory for explaining the recurrent impact that major conflicts and threats have had on foreign policy. For our purposes, this can be seen firstly in the US perception of the first Gulf War as impinging on its own national interests which led to its subsequent involvement; and secondly in the unusually high level of support that states such as Saudi Arabia gave to the campaign.[8] As the Middle East remains a region prone to conflict, so too are foreign policies implemented with security foremost in mind. However, it is hard to know which other factors beyond security ones influence foreign policy because of a lack of transparency at the state level, also known as the 'black box' of the decision-making process.[9]

The relative weight of constructivist thought, and the unique identity, ideational and ideological factors examined within it, thus point to the necessity to take an 'inside-out' perspective to FPA. Piscatori,[10] Korany and Dessouki all promote this idea when addressing the foreign policies of Arab states.[11] Such a perspective is a useful one when attempting to open the 'black box' of foreign policy to the point of being able to glimpse some of the structures and levers of power within it. Constructivism is particularly useful in reference to states such as Iran, because, as Akbar Rezaei observes, it contends with multiple layers of complexity, including competing factions and interests.[12] It also helps to analyse the important juxtaposition of Islam, pan-Arabism and national sovereignty, and the rivalries associated with ideological and symbolic interpretation and actions.[13]

These actions can be viewed as means by which Middle East states attempt to define their identity, decision-making and policy implementation over the long term. Trying to conceive and communicate policies in this way not only grants more freedom of action to the government as a moral authority, but also bestows greater legitimacy on the government from the people. Hill points out that the belief system of a political leader is a function of both experience and the political system and that, whilst deeply rooted in this structure, it can change.[14] A leader's conception of his/her own role could have important consequences for foreign policy, since it helps shape the national identity (including sub- and supra-national identities), attitudes and strategies which influence decision-making at the domestic, regional and international levels. Indeed, constructivism would hold that this is exactly what forms the basis for international relations.[15]

This debate between structure and identity has been at the heart of conflict in the regional system for decades. For example, pan-Arabism has had insurmountable material obstacles to overcome in the form of penetration in the region by great powers, growing military insecurity and the material consolidation of each state.[16] These issues are still relevant today, especially in the lack of regional cohesion and an over-reliance on great powers for security guarantees instead of a pan-regional operational security framework. Barnett points to pan-Arabism as evidence that struggles do not have to be over territory or 'realist' priorities, but can equally be over legitimacy that stems from a 'normative order of the Arab system' which is predominantly symbolic or ideational rather than strategic.[17] His view is directly opposed to the utilitarian one: a vision of the state which defines its national interests, rather than the material interest of the state which defines its national interest.[18] With the demise of pan-Arabism and collective security, insecurity from a perceived Israeli threat, US domination in the region and unequal revenues from oil and gas, the Middle East remains susceptible to putting national interests above regional ones.[19] Salloukh and Brynen suggest that these issues also make the Middle East a 'permeated' region, due primarily to the influence of non-regional actors such as the USA, and influences as diverse as oil, trade and migration on foreign policy.[20]

These ideas are in fact part of a new swathe of FPA concepts which are rooted in the traditional international relations theories, but

A Conceptual Framework

specify additional forces and dynamics within the Middle East system that could prove to be effective or decisive in the course of foreign policy-making. Even with these additions, a specific and broad-based conceptual framework for the analysis of contemporary Middle East foreign policies remains elusive. Although there have been a growing number of contributions in the field from notable authors such as Nonneman,[21] Hinnebusch[22] and Ehteshami,[23] there is still a wide range of views as to what foreign policy is, what frameworks should be used to set parameters to their study and which determinants prove decisive. The difficulty in definition reflects the extent to which foreign policy is formulated and executed according to both internal and external variables.[24]

In 2004, Holsti defined foreign policy as '... attitudes and commitments toward the external environment, its fundamental strategy accomplishing its domestic and external objectives and aspirations for coping with persisting threats'.[25] Such a definition does not draw on the environment in which such policies are being formulated, the reasoning behind such policies or a classification system. However, Korany and Dessouki have outlined the three basic types of foreign policy as a function of engagement in international politics: isolation, non-alignment and coalition building or alliance construction.[26] Apart from an almost binary 'snapshot' of a state's foreign policy orientation, this still does not explain the reasons for such an orientation. Some of these factors have been captured in other works by Gause (Gulf War),[27] Salloukh and Brynen (regional permeability),[28] and Ansari (US and Iranian relations).[29] The main bar to a conceptual framework which fits Middle East FPA remains the disconnections between such works that are dominated by IR theory, and the over-reliance of FPA on the analysis of the inner workings of states. Constructivism goes some way to bridging this gap by linking the state and system levels through social constructions and 'intersubjective understandings'.[30]

Constructivism is also part of reconciling national identity and state resources in the Middle East as outlined in Rothstein's argument about foreign policy determinants being linked to areas of 'conflict' or 'poverty': conflict is caused by tensions between sub-state identities such as tribal, ethnic, religious or class groups (although it is also true of state relations with supra-state identities[31]). Poverty highlights the gap between foreign policy demands on the state and insufficient resources to meet them. East and Hagen's work found that the more consolidated a state was, (i.e. becoming less exposed to conflict and poverty issues), the greater the capacity and consistency in its actions.[32]

Morgenthau argues Middle East states tend to bandwagon because they lack purpose and resources of their own.[33] Those states which choose to align their interests with the global 'core' can be said to bandwagon, whilst others may choose to 'balance' or 'trade-off' some of their interests in an attempt to gain greater relative autonomy from the West.[34] Bandwagoning is particularly prevalent amongst 'small states', as Clapham notes, not only due to their lack of resources but also as an interim mode while they seek alternative partners with whom to balance.[35] The combination of the Middle East mainly occupying the periphery of the international system and being a 'permeated' region makes it particularly susceptible to bandwagoning tendencies. Threat perception is also an important factor of bandwagoning or balancing, whether with or against states in possession of specific resources, such as Weapons of Mass Destruction (WMD), or more general ones, such as advanced economies.[36]

Evidence from Miller suggests that 'balancing' may be just as attractive to small states since the benefits of bandwagoning could be temporary and ultimately disadvantageous to long-term relations with another power.[37] Walt suggests that bandwagoning is less common than 'balancing' because there is almost always some kind of policy alternative or leveraging mechanism for a developing state.[38] All developing states have some autonomy when making their foreign policy decisions, and particular states, such as Saudi Arabia, may possess a greater degree of autonomy because they have better leverage in the economic sphere.[39] Balancing has thus been termed a 'struggle' by Pranger because a state must use whatever capacities it has in order to ensure its own survival.[40]

In an interdependent world, there is an element of 'bandwagoning' between all states as they develop alliances with partners that best serve their needs. Rather than 'balancing' with one great power, managed multi-dependence is a more complex approach that illustrates the 'balancing' and playing-off that occurs between a state and a series of powers. In so doing, a state is able to carve out greater relative autonomy in the domestic, regional and international environments.[41] 'Relative autonomy' therefore means dependency theory is applicable only some of the time at best, with inter-state relationships much more likely to take a two-way or asymmetrical co-dependent form.[42]

There is, of course, the possibility of an accidental convergence of interests between a developing state and a power patron which is neither planned nor intentional. The 'reductionist' approach outlined by Hinnebusch or the 'coincidence of interests' approach, as outlined by Nonneman, views the foreign policies of developed and developing states as being fundamentally on the same course, seeking the same objectives, whether intentionally or not.[43] The emphasis on alliance building aims, therefore, at reconciling ideological factors which produce discrepancies between comparative foreign policy objectives between states and the environment in which they become distorted or misaligned based on matters of interpretation, principle and aspiration. Hill recognizes this distinction in labelling states as 'anti-core' or 'counter-dependent'.[44]

Nonneman defines the most appropriate conceptual framework for the study of Middle East foreign policies as one which takes the 'multi-level', 'multi-causal' and 'contextual' into account in order to comprehend all possible influences on foreign policy.[45] In recognition of the reality of the domestic, regional and international environments that are sources of threats, resources and opportunities, the concept of 'omni-balancing', as proposed by David and promoted by Nonneman, takes a contextual approach to a constantly changing dynamic between the three environments (domestic, regional and international).[46] It also takes into account the large number of factors which make foreign policies a series of decision-making 'outcomes' in addition to other environmental factors.[47] By reflecting the multi-dimensional aspects of many of the earlier works of FPA, 'omni-balancing' also creates space within the different levels of foreign policy to account for influences attributed to all the major IR theories.

Nonneman states that the following dimensions should be included in considering foreign policy decisions: the external environment (international and regional), transnational identity or ideology, the domestic environment, economic and political policies and interests, state structures and the decision-making process and the leadership's role conceptions.[48] He argues it is necessary to integrate the domestic, regional and international environments into the same conceptual framework, in a necessarily 'complex model of international politics', in order to identify all the potential factors, drivers and determinants in foreign policies.[49] The overall balance may involve 'economic needs, geopolitical imperatives, domestic opinion, and state capabilities'.[50] Omni-balancing is more interested in the intensity of a threat than where that threat comes from, and emphasizes the part played by the decision-making elite, which is expected to perceive the environments in their entirety.[51]

In what Hinnebusch describes as a 'Janus-faced' outlook, foreign policy-making elites simultaneously perceive and reconcile domestic demands with external threats and constraints.[52] It is this recurrent factor of *perception* which, when coupled with threat intensity, is expected to focus attention on the most important factors in foreign policy. This leads to the logical emphasis upon both social constructivism and 'omni-balancing' in this book, in much the same vein as 'neotraditional realism' combines neo-realism with the role of leaders' perceptions.[53] The primary difference is that the conceptual model in this book, which could be called 'constructive-balancing', also takes into account the full range of sub-state factors. This approach is expected to be especially useful in its application to Saudi Arabia, with its strong Islamic identity, domestic vulnerability along sectarian lines and a changing perspective on its most vital regional and international relations. It is useful for the study of Iran as a state with both a strong civilization-based identity and an emphasis on the perceptions of its leadership as its justification for maintaining an anti-systemic/Western stance.

CHAPTER 2

THE SHAPING FACTORS OF REGIONAL INSECURITY AND CONFLICT IN THE FORMULATION OF CONTEMPORARY SAUDI AND IRANIAN FOREIGN POLICY

The Ramadan War, or Yom Kippur War, of 6–22 October 1973, and its aftermath, constituted an important turning-point in the relationship between Middle East oil exporters and the West (i.e. the USA and Europe). Firstly, the boycott of the USA by the Organization of Arab Petroleum Exporting Countries (OAPEC) in retaliation for its support of Israel with military hardware was a watershed in the use of oil as a weapon. Secondly, having wrestled pricing control away from the major oil companies, OPEC gave greater pricing control to the major oil-producing states. At the time, this was perceived as the greatest economic threat to Europe since the Second World War.[1] The embargo followed repeated warnings by Saudi Arabia, delivered directly to the US administration and through ARAMCO, the Saudi state-owned national oil company, that the USA must modify its position to take a more evenhanded approach towards Israel.[2] Since Saudi Arabia had committed itself to a leadership role after the 1967 War, it was no longer in a position to be a passive actor. This episode sets the tone for contemporary Saudi–US relations discussed in Chapter 3 and the role of oil, especially during periods of crisis, over the following decades.

The process leading to an embargo was initiated by Kuwait when it called for a meeting of the six Gulf oil producing states (Kuwait, Saudi Arabia, Qatar, Abu Dhabi, Iraq and Iran[3]) on 16 October 1973 without the attendance of the international oil companies (IOC).[4] The embargo commenced the following day and involved a 5 per cent cut in production, with a further 5 per cent cut planned for each month until Israel withdrew from occupied Arab territories.[5] The 'posted prices' of oil by which revenues were paid to the producing countries were moved much higher than previous negotiations with the IOCs would have suggested, and resulted in a nearly 100 per cent revenue increase almost overnight.[6] '...[T]he oil rent suddenly increased for approximately a decade, from 1973 to 1983, and flooded the entire region, engulfing everybody in the process of rent circulation.'[7] As a result, the Middle East split into rentier and non-rentier states.[8]

The oil embargo was an important event in the global economic system, but it was even more important to the international relations between the primary oil exporters and the primary oil importers. The oil embargo could have been put into effect any time after the formation of OAPEC in 1959, and would have been more effective in 1980 when US dependency on Arab oil was at its peak. The USA had lost its status as 'swing producer' for the first time in the early 1970s, partly as a result of previous boycotts,[9] and had become a net importer of oil by 1973, which itself added upward pressure to oil prices.[10] Therefore the boycott's effectiveness at causing the crisis was as much to do with changing distribution channels as surging demand in the West. Political events and military strategy dictated the terms of oil being used as a weapon. Still, the oil weapon was not the most effective means of getting the USA to compromise on its foreign policy, since all economic weapons take time to take effect. The USA through its high economic development '...would be the last to get hurt...'.[11] However, it did reinforce the efforts of the US Secretary of State, Henry Kissinger, to undertake 'shuttle diplomacy' in order to bring about a timely and effective political solution to the Arab–Israeli war.

On 18 October, Saudi Arabia announced a 10 per cent cut in production. When King Faisal found out that the US Congress was planning to approve a further $2.2 billion in emergency security assistance to Israel, he cut all oil supplies to the USA effective from 20 October.[12] In total, OPEC production was reduced by almost 25 per cent between September and November 1973 and fell from a peak of 3.3 million barrels per day (b/d) in 1972 to 1 million b/d by 1981. By this means, OAPEC countries (Algeria, Bahrain, Egypt, Iraq, Kuwait, Libya, Qatar, Saudi Arabia, Syria, Tunisia and the UAE[13]) continued to exert pressure on the West even after the Arab–Israeli War had ended. On 11 November the European Community issued a joint declaration on Palestine which recognized the rights of the Palestinians.[14] This helped alleviate the additional 5 per cent cut in supply which had affected European states, but would not include the Netherlands or Denmark, which were considered as friendly to Israel.[15] Oil was distributed according to Arab definitions of 'friendly' states, which included the UK and France, the Arab states and most of Africa, and 'neutral' states, including Japan, Portugal and the Netherlands.[16] The difference was meaningful in that 'friendly' states were given assurances that their essential oil requirements would be met, whilst 'neutrals' would be left to pick up the remaining allowances.[17] The differences in oil allocations led to considerable friction between the two groups of states as well as global economic uncertainty, falling stock market prices and rapidly rising international oil prices in the 1970s.

Since there was no real coordinated energy policy within the European Community until after the embargo[18] and no coherent energy strategy between Europe and the USA, each state was left to pursue its own bilateral negotiations with Arab states. This resulted in further breakdown of cohesion within the North Atlantic Treaty Organization (NATO).[19] The UK and France made their bilateral agreements in order to maintain their 'friendly' status within OAPEC and continue to buy oil at the inflated rates. These new agreements had the effect of strengthening the oil policies of the oil-producing states. Oil was set to cost the Organization for Economic Cooperation and Development (OECD) countries an extra $72 billion a year after 1973.[20] Although the extra cost was partially offset by increased exports to the region, the figure was too large an increase for OECD states to maintain, particularly if the revenue accruals continued unchecked.[21]

Putting pressure on the USA through an oil embargo was a novel attempt at applying economic pressure to a political issue. The policy led to oil quadrupling in price just three months after the start of the conflict[22] and to inflation and monetary instability, which were contrary to the interests of both the oil-producing and oil-consuming states.[23] The embargo, which ended on 18 March 1974, succeeded in drawing global attention to the Arab–Israeli conflict as well as to the central role of oil producers in the global economy. Higher international oil prices directly contributed to the budgets of oil exporters and their production and depletion policies. The latter required each state to achieve the highest sustainable economic development before the oil ran out.

The response of the USA to high international oil prices was to place greater emphasis on the 'recycling' of OPEC capital back into the West, and in particular into the USA. The policy was negotiated between US Secretary of State Henry Kissinger, Secretary of the Treasury William Simon and Crown Prince Fahd of Saudi Arabia. The discussions led to the establishment of the Joint Economic Commission, which would oversee capital flows back to the USA and implement the various incentives and rules needed to facilitate such flows. The system worked and established an arrangement that continues to operate. In 1974 when the USA paid $1.7 billion for Saudi oil, Saudi Arabia invested $8.5 billion in the USA, much of it in US military hardware. The arrangement was particularly useful in the late 1970s because Saudi Arabia needed to purchase US arms in order to match Iranian conventional arms proliferation.[24] Furthermore, Saudi Arabia and the USA continued to cooperate on a number of foreign aid programmes designed to secure pro-Western allies during the height of the Cold War.

The 1973 oil crisis and the subsequent increase in oil revenues led to more active diplomacy from Saudi Arabia.[25] Due to the perceived intensity and nature of the Cold War with the USSR, Saudi Arabia maintained a close political relationship with the USA and managed aid programmes with the USA in a very complementary way. These joint aid programmes tended to be focused on the developing world, in the Middle East, Africa and Asia, where Saudi Arabia was able to leverage greater ideological and economic influence than in other regions.

In the post-1973 era, working in tandem with the USA was the main modus operandi of Saudi foreign policy. Saudi Arabia had used financial assistance as part of its foreign policy since the late 1960s,[26] and the Kingdom was able to use some of its new oil windfall on strategic foreign investments, loans and grants. This Saudi policy was implemented to simultaneously finance anti-Soviet operations and the non-alignment movement in Africa, as well as boosting Saudi standing in the Islamic world. Saudi Arabia established a development fund of $2.8 billion for loans to developing nations in 1974[27] and pledged $400 million along with Kuwait and Abu Dhabi to the Islamic Development Bank.[28] Saudi aid has gone to 70 different states, mainly in Africa and Asia, but over 80 per cent of the aid was to Islamic states.[29] Non-Arab states were eligible for low-interest loans but only for specific projects, rather than to cover the costs of oil sales.[30] These generous aid programmes reached $64 billion (around 5 per cent of average Saudi GDP) in technical assistance between 1973 and 1990.[31]

Bilateral aid was also given on the basis of population size and the available economic resources of the recipient state.[32] Except for Syria, in respect to which Saudi Arabia aimed to minimize any potential political threat and confrontation, such aid has been of strategic value to the West.[33] Saudi Arabia has also contributed about a third of the IMF's total Special Oil Facility, which over 50 states have used, including six Western developed states.[34] This, and other aid channelled through the IMF, has directly served US interests.[35] There were limits to Saudi economic aid, and these were illustrated through the cases of improved Egyptian relations with the USA following the 1967 War; Sadat's peace accord with Israel;[36] and South Yemen, which remained ideologically averse to Saudi overtures to cut ties with the USSR.[37]

The Communist advance in the Horn of Africa was of great concern to the White House in the late 1970s and early 1980s because of its geo-strategic location near the Persian Gulf and South West Asia.[38] The USA and Saudi Arabia sent up to $500 million a year to Sudan throughout the 1970s and 1980s.[39] This aid, along with that sent to the opposition in Ethiopia, was thought to be important by both the USA and Saudi Arabia in challenging the Marxist government in Ethiopia as well as the Libyan regime.[40] Saudi Arabia also covertly distributed cash and equipment to Somalia and used its close bilateral relationship with the government to try to break the Somali link with the USSR and to launch an attack against Ethiopia.[41] In other cases, such as Pakistan, 'riyal-politik' was simply expected to induce a better relationship than the one that had existed before. Saudi aid to the Philippines also fell into this category, as Saudi Arabia was attempting to encourage the authoritarian regime of President Ferdinand Marcos to treat the Filipino Muslim minority in a more lenient way.[42]

The USA actively engaged Saudi Arabia on a number of overseas operations where their interests overlapped and in cases which the US Congress was not willing to fund. These notably included the US and Saudi policies of countering Communism in Central America with Saudi funding for the Nicaraguan Contras.[43] As the oil price dropped in the 1980s, and with growing domestic budgetary concerns, Saudi Arabia was in a less favourable position vis-à-vis increasing aid packages. However, Saudi Arabia and the USA remained committed to a range of joint foreign policy initiatives aimed at limiting the expansion and influence of their common Soviet adversary. No joint operation was larger than the $3 billion the USA and Saudi Arabia spent on arming the mujahidin to enable them to repel Soviet forces in Afghanistan in the 1980s, matching each other's spending dollar for dollar. After this operation, the US trend of 'tin cupping' went on throughout the 1990s, making requests to Saudi Arabia that were often sketchy on the details. These US requests culminated in Saudi Arabia underwriting a large portion of the 'Desert Storm' operation in Iraq in 1991.[44]

The 1979 Iranian Islamic Revolution: The Birth of Resistance Politics

The Islamic Revolution in Iran constitutes a vital period for the study of contemporary Iranian foreign policy because it marks the beginning of an independent republic, a non-aligned Islamic state which shortly thereafter severed diplomatic relations with the USA. However, the

Iranian economy did not undergo any such revolutionary redefinition and recalibration. The Iranian economy therefore remained exposed to the international system and to the threat of international sanctions.

Khomeini, the leader of post-revolutionary Iran, did not consider Iran or its foreign policy to be east-focused or pro-West but simply Islamic. At the beginning of the Iranian Revolution he called for 'independence, freedom and the Islamic Republic', words which are still the bedrock of foreign policy decision-making to this day, as provided for by the constitution.[45] 'Independence' was a particularly relevant term given the recent history of Iran's oil industry, which was controlled by the British and Russians throughout the 1970s. The emphasis upon theocracy was rooted in a reaction against the Pahlavi monarchs who had been both authoritarian and secular. Khomeini was also competing against opposition movements such as the secular National Front and various Marxist and Islamist groups which promoted an alternative vision for a new 'Islamic' state.[46] In order to promote itself as a 'hub of Islamism', Khomeini needed to create 'enemies of Islam and Iran', epitomized by the USA and its support for the overthrow of the nationalist Prime Minister Muhammad Musaddiq. The fast-moving events of the immediate post-revolutionary period, including 'internal power struggles, suspicion of American plots, and clerical opportunism' made the US embassy crisis almost inevitable.[47]

Contemporary US–Iranian relations are, in large part, a function of the early days of the Iranian Revolution, and in particular the hostage crisis that started on 4 November 1979 inside the US embassy in Tehran. The Barzagan government was not in favour of breaking relations with the USA but hoped to reformulate its ties into ones based on greater respect. Radical clerics were the ones in control of the embassy and they sought to undermine the provisional government. Therefore, the decision whether Iran would choose to rapidly resolve the situation, as Khomeini had done in February 1979, or to cut diplomatic relations and continue the siege was ultimately in the hands of Khomeini.[48] Instead of having the students who took US personnel hostage arrested, Khomeini gave them a public endorsement. By doing so, he added credibility to their belief that they were involved in a pre-emptive strike against a USA that was bent on destroying the Islamic Revolution. Ultimately, the events were simply a reflection of the domestic political climate and shifting power centres as authority was transferred from the provisional government to a revolutionary one.

The communications problems and mistrust that arose from this incident, as seen from the USA's perspective, have been outlined by Gary Sick, a former Carter administration National Security Council (NSC) staff member. Sick suggests that even now Iran continues to negotiate in bad faith and only pays attention to its domestic environment instead of seeking to balance the resources, energy and prioritization given to its internal affairs with its international relations, especially with the USA. In 1979, the USA was naive about the probable duration of the crisis (52 hostages would be held for 444 days[49]), and had a deficient and superficial understanding of Khomeini.[50] The US government was therefore unable to influence Iranian decision-making through '... sanctions, pleas, intermediaries and threats...'.[51] Finding its usual negotiation strategies had failed, the conclusion was that Iran simply could not be talked to. As a result, perceptions hardened in the US administration, and across the wider public, coming to believe both that Iran was irrational and that it hated the USA.[52] On the other side of the coin, the eventual success of the USA in conducting negotiations through German and Algerian counterparts had no effect on the Iranian perception of the event as a victory against the USA.[53]

The additional shock for the USA of losing eight servicemen during the hostage rescue mission, named *Eagle Claw*, plays a large part in the continued US assessment of Iran as both 'evil' and antagonistic.[54] Events throughout the 1980s continued to reinforce this view and cast a long shadow over US–Iranian relations. These are discussed in more detail with regard to the Iran–Iraq War below.

The Islamic Revolution and the Iranian Economy

Although there was no clear concept of what form an Islamic revolutionary economy should take, the Revolution had an immediate impact upon the structure of the Iranian economy as the state bourgeoisie was removed and exiled. A smaller, more modern, bourgeoisie filled the gap but was still subservient to the state. Nationalization took place under circumstances where properties had been owned and left vacant by the elite or where any firm owed more than 50 per cent of its assets to the banks.[55] Given the circumstances, these options were restrained and the latter was an attempt to assist struggling firms. The Islamic Republic did not form a coherent strategy on the redistribution of wealth, land reform or the control of foreign trade.[56] The political economy dynamic had still not been established, and political instability added more confusion to questions about the economy.

Liberalism in Iran ended in 1981 and the clergy and its allies, in the form of the Moussavi government, took over in February 1982.[57] Greater emphasis was placed upon economic self-sufficiency and self-reliance and a reduction of dependency on the international capital markets. There were also disagreements within the regime, represented largely by the Council of Guardians, as to how revolutionary the Revolution should be in economic terms.[58] Post-revolutionary Iran had two extreme competing factions. One could be classified as free-marketeers who opposed statist policies and advocated a more 'Islamic' approach.[59] The other faction included followers of the Imam who focused on the poor and therefore required higher taxes, redistribution of land ownership and central planning.[60] To overcome the latter approach required the combination of a pragmatic government policy and intervention from the Guardian Council.[61] It was also difficult to contend with Khomeini's pronouncement that '... as long as there is Islam there will be free enterprise also'. The government was committed to this process of free enterprise but after committing $2.5 billion to industrial investment in 1983, it made losses of $3.5 billion. This meant the government was effectively a net subsidiser of poor economic decision-making.

The inherent contradiction of free enterprise, which required integration and cooperation in the international system, and an ideology which spurned partnership with the West, meant that Iran's economy could not be made sustainable over the long term. Ironically, only the international markets could provide the capital necessary for Iran to continue with its revolutionary objectives. In the mean time, the Iran–Iraq War forced the new Iranian political elites to reorientate the economy to serve the war.

The Iran–Iraq War (1980–1988): The Carter Doctrine and the Seeds of US Containment Policy[62]

The Iran–Iraq War – also known in Iran as the 'imposed war', since the USA provided generous assistance to Iraq and organized a pro-Iraqi alliance – was one of the early arenas in which Iran experienced the geo-strategic drawbacks of its revolutionary zeal. Instead of supporting Iran, the USA first tried to balance the power of Iran and Iraq. When Iran failed to respond to a peace treaty in 1982, Western policy subscribed to the idea of an Iraqi bulwark against the possible exportation of the Islamic Revolution to the Gulf monarchies undermining oil supplies and the future of Israel. The war thus confirmed Iran's fear of encirclement, its sense of isolation and containment due to the disproportionate support given to Iraq by the GCC states and the West against Iran. However, even with a new revolutionary government *in situ*, Western support for Iraq in the war was in no way assured. Before the invasion of Iran by Saddam Hussein's Iraq, and even for a while after the invasion had taken place, the USA had no relations with Iraq and viewed it as a radical, pro-Soviet regime with hostile intent towards other US allies in the region (the Gulf States and Egypt).[63]

In contrast, France had relatively normalized relations with Baghdad.[64] These relations were based on deep commercial connections which led France to provide 25 per cent of the total military aid to Iraq and trade some arms illegally.[65] Egypt, Brazil, Spain and the UK also supported Iraq based on perceived commercial opportunities in the region.[66] Although the European states called for a ceasefire at the 1985 Brussels Summit, it was not enough to persuade Iran that Europe was actively searching for a solution to end the war. The UK observed the weapons ban but still exported dual-use components and machine tools to Iraq that could have been used to produce weapons. Iraq received $17.6 billion in aid between 1979 and 1983 whilst Iran only received $5.4 billion ($2 billion was from before the 1979

Revolution). This discrepancy meant that Iran did not have the military capability to close the Strait of Hormuz, and could only manage to interdict shipping there (including Western vessels transporting oil). Meanwhile, Iraq was able to bomb Iranian cities and attack Iran's oil industry, including its tankers. Iran's lack of military assets led to its reliance on the courage of its fighting men in making waves of assaults against Iraq. It was this approach to warfare and Iran's subsequent defeat in the war (180,000 Iraqi dead, 213,000 Iranian dead[67]) that developed, or at least strengthened, Iran's powerful emotional attachment to the concepts of martyrdom and sacrifice. Iran was backed by other 'pariah' states such as North Korea, Libya and Syria.[68] However, many other states sold arms to Iran, including Russia,[69] China, Taiwan, Argentina, South Africa, Pakistan, Switzerland and Israel. China played an important role in the exportation of cruise missiles to Iran during the Iran–Iraq War as well as chemical and nuclear technologies which assisted Iran in the development of its nuclear programme.[70] Israel sold arms to ensure that both sides were weakened through a continued war of attrition, and therefore less of a national security threat to Israel. At the point when Iraq entered Iranian territory, Moshe Dayan, the former Israeli Defence Minister, asked the USA to help Iran reinforce its defences.[71]

The covert Iran–Israel relationship, which comprised mainly an exchange of Iranian oil for weapons, was relatively close for a brief period in the early 1980s, based simply upon Iran pushing aside ideological considerations in favour of national security. The arms trade between Iran and Israel continued until 1982/3, when Khomeini decided Iranian forces should enter Iraqi territory after the Iranian victory in the battle at Khoramshar.[72] Like the USA, Israel wanted two weak states and ongoing division rather than any strong, outright victor in the war.[73] Western positions on the war were confirmed at an early point in the conflict, when Iran did not consider a peace deal in 1982. In the summer of 1982 the USA joined the USSR[74] in its backing of Iraq, and provided intelligence to Iraq, as well as removing it from the State Department's list of 'state sponsors of terrorism'.[75] By doing this, the USA was able to facilitate covert, diplomatic and economic support to Iraq.[76] Western support for Iraq was therefore born from its inability to countenance a victorious Iran, since its foreign policy toward the West had already been confirmed by the US hostage crisis and its stated desire to overthrow regional governments allied to the West.[77]

Furthermore, supporting Iraq was a way of implementing the Carter Doctrine, which provided a political agenda (the protection of 'vital interests' including oil) for US involvement in the Middle East. This was fundamentally about securing energy supplies, but also about maintaining manageable oil prices after a period of particular difficulty under the oil embargo only a decade before. That was not to say that US policy during the war was consistent. The Iran-Contra Affair of 1985 aimed to improve US–Iran relations, advance US interests in Lebanon and secure the release of seven hostages held by Hezbollah (which had connections to Khomeini). Even though 2004 TOW missiles and 200 parts for Hawk missile batteries were shipped to Iran in the so-called 'arms-for-hostages' deal, only three US hostages were released and these were quickly replaced by three more. Arms sales to Iran were only for the purpose of facilitating the release of US hostages and offering a strategic opening in US–Iran relations, and did not constitute an attempt to determine the outcome of the Iran–Iraq War in Iran's favour.[78] The Iran-Contra report found that failure was based on 'too many drivers – and never the right ones – steering in too many different directions'.[79]

Iran finally sought a peaceful solution to the war in 1988 after its economy was significantly weakened, US navy operations in the Gulf had taken their toll and Iraq had begun to regain the advantage on the battlefield.[80] By the end of the war, both Iran and Iraq were economically crippled. It took until 1992 for Iran to recover. Robert Gates, Director of the CIA, stated before a Hearing of the House Armed Services Committee's Defence Policy Panel that: 'While Iraq struggles to recover from the Gulf War, Iran is determined to regain its former stature as the pre-eminent power in the Persian Gulf...'.[81] To achieve these goals, Iran undertook diplomatic measures to end its international isolation and purchased weapons from a variety of foreign suppliers.

Iran also pursued a policy of nuclear proliferation to counter reports of an Iraqi nuclear programme.[82] Until the dream of an Iranian nuclear programme could be realized, Khomeini had to accept that 'liberating Jerusalem via Baghdad' would have to be suspended. Mending fences in the international community, with the Gulf states and then with the USA, was deemed necessary under the Rafsanjani presidency. The USA, in turn, tried to take the opportunity to renew goodwill by ensuring that the World Bank was able to extend its first loan to Iran since 1987. For Iraq, the circumstances provided an economic incentive for the invasion of Kuwait three years later, and may have enabled the unlikely partnership with Iran when it became involved as well.[83] US–Iran relations soured again in 1988 due to an Iranian mine attack against a US frigate, the USS *Samuel B. Roberts*. The US retaliation consisted of the sinking of an Iranian frigate and the shelling of two oil platforms near the Strait of Hormuz.[84] The USA also accidentally shot down an Iranian commercial jet but failed to apologize for the incident.

Such unfortunate incidents have been the hallmark of Iran–US relations in the past few decades and remain so in the contemporary world. This is partly the result of the main candidates in the 2005 Iranian presidential election coming from the 'war generation', having held significant posts during the Iran–Iraq War, ensuring that the conflict continues to have a direct bearing on contemporary Iranian foreign policy. Mahmoud Ahmadinejad occupied a position in covert operations and now drew support from the 'war generation'; Mehdi Karroubi was head of Imam Khomeini's Relief Committee and Martyr's Foundation, and then Chairman of Parliament after the war; and Rafsanjani oversaw the reconstruction and resumption of regional ties in the post-war era.

The Iran–Iraq War informed Iranian political and military strategy significantly and sowed the seeds for an Iranian militarized mindset and nationalist struggle against external domination. These were implemented in the development of Iran's nuclear programme, position and policies in the 'resistance axis'[85] and relations with Sunni states in the GCC. When President Rafsanjani took over in 1989, the same year Khomeini died, the West thought negotiating with a pragmatic conservative would be easier. That did not prove to be the case. Furthermore, as time went on and individuals from the 'war generation' moved up the Iranian political ranks, politicians such as Ahmadinejad were able to draw support from the 'war generation' in the 2005 and 2009 elections. They were also better placed to work with the Islamic Revolutionary Guards Corps (IRGC), and other entities which developed after the war, in their struggle against the West.

The First Gulf War: The USA as a Local Power and the Subsequent Complexities of Establishing a Pan-Regional Security Architecture

The Gulf War was a seminal event in the evolving relationship between the USA, the GCC states and Iran, particularly as it coincided with the demise of the USSR as an opposing force to the USA in the Gulf. The first Gulf War marked the start of increased and direct US influence in the Middle East through new base agreements in the Gulf and as a security guarantor to its GCC allies. The USA, in becoming a 'local power' in the Gulf, also generated renewed Iranian resistance and countering strategies. Iranian actions provocative to the West included the kidnapping of several Western hostages from the mid-1980s, a fatwa against Salman Rushdie (author of *The Satanic Verses*) and the assassination of Shapour Bakhtiar, a former Iranian Prime Minister, in August 1991 in Paris. Therefore it was Iran, not Iraq, which was perceived to be the greater threat before the invasion of Kuwait in 1991.[86]

Prior to the Gulf War, President Rafsanjani had met with King Fahd in Saudi Arabia and re-established diplomatic ties, the first since 1988, which paved the way for better Iran–GCC relations.[87] These relations were still hampered by the unresolved territorial dispute regarding the Tunb islands and Abu Musa. Dialogue nevertheless enabled Kuwait to repair its relationship with Iran immediately after the end of the Iran–Iraq War by apologizing for its support for Saddam Hussein.[88] There was also some hope in the GCC that Oman might be able to bring Iran into a regional security framework to avoid the instabilities of the Gulf War from occurring again. Oman was particularly important since Saudi Arabia, Kuwait and the UAE had lost all credibility with Iran by supporting Iraq in the Iran–Iraq War with $30 billion in grants and loans.[89]

The effects of the war, notably the dissimilar regional policies of the USA and Iran, precluded the reorientation of GCC collective security to include Iran in a broader regional security framework. Saudi Arabia took a similar view to the USA although the government feared the consequences of a build-up of arms after the Gulf War. The Saudis did not support Iran in any regional security framework since the sources of threat (i.e. sectarian, revolutionary, rhetorical and militaristic) had not been resolved.[90] Indeed, the threats posed by these aspects of the Iranian state only worsened, as Iran continued to support terrorism and developed its nuclear programme. Defence was nonetheless discussed at a GCC meeting held in Damascus in 1991 and the subsequent US-brokered 'Damascus Declaration' was expected to ally Egypt and Syria with the GCC to form the 'GCC+2'.[91] The agreement was to include 'friends' but fundamentally it did not provide the inclusive pan-regional agenda Sultan Qaboos, the Sultan of Oman, had hoped for. The Damascus Declaration was shelved in 1992 because it was too expensive ($20 billion over five years), the GCC perceived Syria as untrustworthy (due to its alignment with Iran along the 'resistance axis') and the same applied to Syrian perceptions of the West in the Persian Gulf.[92]

The Gulf War also led to the Madrid Peace Conference. The USA was aware that the Arab–Israeli conflict was divisive and had been used by Saddam to split Arab opinion before the Gulf War.[93] In response to this, and due to Arab cooperation with the USA during the war, the Madrid Peace Process was launched by the USA in 1991. Since Syria and Lebanon were participants in the conference, they could have, at an early stage, undermined the entire 'resistance axis' by signing a peace treaty with Israel each. This did not happen, and given Iran's ability to shake peace with its support of asymmetric warfare, Iran has been relatively free to pursue resistance policies in the Levant. Europe, and particularly France under President Chirac, led a new wave of engagement with the Middle East Peace Process (MEPP) in 1998, in effect taking the Arab stance. Such moves were criticized by the UK and USA, and led to the UK launching the British Initiative in March 1998. The post-war environment failed to deliver the political will or multilateralism that was needed to bridge the inadequacies of regional security and deliver a comprehensive peace in the Middle East. Therefore, rather than directly address the root causes of the 'resistance axis' in the Levant, the USA was left to implement a series of policies that directly targeted an economically weakened Iran.

The US Policy of Dual Containment and Sanctions against Iran in the 1990s

The USA was concerned that the rivalry between Iraq and Iran for regional dominance could destabilize regional security, and exploited their respective economic weaknesses after the Gulf War to implement a policy of 'dual containment' from 1993. The combination of a weakened Iranian economy following conflict and mismanagement in the 1990s, and ongoing Iranian revolutionary rhetoric and terrorist activities, led to the tightening of US sanctions in 1996. Iran has looked upon this policy as provocative and directly linked to Western domination and a US agenda of regime change.

Iran's economy was severely weakened by the legacies of internal and external conflict from the 1970s and 1980s. In the 1990s a sustained fall in the international oil price adversely affected the economy. As a result, by the time Khatami took over as president in 1997 the Majlis (Iranian Parliament) was largely open to Khatami's reformist policies, but its members were the ones taking the initiative on economic decision-making even though they were not qualified to do so.[94] The poor state of the economy, even in a period of high oil prices, was indicative that mistakes were being made and led Khatami to describe the economy before the 2000 presidential election as 'sick'.[95] Questions over how far Khatami was willing to go to '... liberalise politics, open up the country to the outside world and restructure the economy' pointed to the possible need to slow the pace of change in order to maintain unity and stability across all the factions.[96]

At the same time, Iran–US relations hit a series of new lows during this period. This was the result of a number of incidents: the 1992 restaurant bombing in Berlin in which four Iranian Kurdish dissidents died, found in 1997 to have been officially sanctioned by the Iranian regime;[97] the 1994 attack against the Israeli-Argentinean Mutual

Association (AMIA) building in Buenos Aires; Iranian deployment of anti-aircraft missiles, submarine docking stations, chemical weapon artillery and 6,000–8,000 troops on Abu Musa and the Greater and Less Tunb islands, military exercises in the Gulf, and the Iranian nuclear programme;[98] as well as an Iranian-sponsored direct attack against the USA in 1996 when it bombed the Khobar Towers in Riyadh, which were housing US troops.[99] However, the latter incident has since been blamed on al-Qaeda.[100]

The USA responded to this trend of Iranian aggression firstly through a 'dual containment' strategy against Iran and Iraq, promoted by Anthony Lake and Martin Indyk,[101] from May 1993.[102] In 1996 the USA used Iran's economic weakness as political leverage and tightened sanctions through implementing the Iran–Libya Sanctions Act (ILSA).[103] The ILSA increased pressure on Iran by attempting to prevent non-American companies from investing more than $20 million in Iran's oil and gas sector due to its nuclear programme and support for terrorist organizations.[104] This seriously reduced IOC interest in Iran's oil and gas sector.[105] In addition to the ILSA, President Clinton issued two executive orders, one of which barred subsidiaries of US companies from taking part in projects that related to Iran's oil and gas resources. The other barred US individuals from trading, financing or facilitating goods or technology that could benefit the Iranian petroleum sector.[106] In addressing the Iranian nuclear issue, the USA tried, but failed, to thwart the $800 million sale of several nuclear reactors to Iran; the US Secretary of Defence, William Perry, pledged $100 million to the Russian Foreign Minister, Andrei Kozyrev, if Russia did not complete this contract.[107]

Whether the ILSA was coordinated with Saudi Arabia, or whether Saudi Arabia used the opportunity of an economically weakened Iran (struggling with debt repayments and a weak oil sector) to raise its production quotas in OPEC, is debatable. However, the Saudi initiative resulted in a collapse in crude oil prices at the end of 1997.[108] Tehran was infuriated with Riyadh over this policy.[109] The visit of Hashemi Rafsanjani, head of the Iranian Expediency Council, to Saudi Arabia in February 1998 with other senior Iranian ministers, including the oil minister, could not have been more important for the future of Iranian–Saudi bilateral relations. It led to the stabilization of the oil market and an improvement in prices, which would benefit Iran and lead the way for improved regional relations and coordination on regional security.[110]

The Clinton administration kept pressure on the Iranian regime, insisting the country modify its international behaviour before it could be admitted to the 'community of nations'. By April 1995, US policy was suggested by some observers to be leading to the overthrow of the Iranian regime since it was creating regional instability.[111] As early as September 1998 US sanctions were being questioned, since Iranian policy was recognized to be changing under President Khatami. The USA was also urged by the EU and RAND to take a more pragmatic approach, one of engagement.[112] 'Officials have however refused [to reform dual containment and engage in dialogue with Iran], afraid of being seen to be soft on Iran by Congressional opponents and also motivated by classified intelligence that allegedly points to Iranian weapons programmes and support for terrorism.'[113] US sanctions and unilateral actions would come to form the backdrop of its relations with Iran, which are outlined in Chapter 4.

The Critical, Comprehensive and Civilizational Dialogues with Iran

The various dialogues between Iran and the West, during the presidencies of Rafsanjani and Khatami, illustrated the potential for Iran and the West to address the most fundamental questions about the nature of Iranian foreign policy going back to the Islamic Revolution. Their ultimate failure to secure a lasting diplomatic solution to the Iranian nuclear programme and other contentious Iranian foreign policies, however, suggests a more comprehensive effort will be required than those steps already taken.

Iran's Islamic Revolution, anti-Western stance and its pushing for a change in the status quo in the region have all impacted on its relations with the EU.[114] In the eyes of the EU and the USA, Iran has been moving steadily in the wrong direction and as a consequence remained a pariah state during the Clinton administration. The EU did not wholly subscribe to the view that Iran was a pariah state and sought to engage Iran over its most contentious policies in a 'critical dialogue' which was initiated at the Edinburgh Summit in 1992. A year after taking office in 1997, Khatami's call for a 'dialogue of civilizations' was the signal for a gradual normalization of US–Iranian relations. It represented a golden opportunity for the USA to engage Iran. Khatami reached out to the USA at the Islamic Organization Conference Summit in Tehran in 1998, calling for 'thoughtful dialogue' and a 'détente in diplomatic policy'.[115] In a further rapprochement, Khatami sent a Christmas message to the USA in which he said, 'I wish for a new chapter in relations between peoples'.[116] To appear strong and allied to the national interest in order to preserve his power and autonomy, he had nonetheless, to illustrate his lack of 'interest' in negotiating with America by stating that '... we can reach our objectives without American assistance', showing how closely allied his words must be to the national consciousness in order to preserve his power and autonomy.[117]

However, Khatami made all the right indications on all the subjects of US contention with Iranian foreign policy: Khatami stated that Iran was not a nuclear power and that it did '... not intend to become one'. (He clarified this in 2004 by stating that: 'There is a difference between nuclear technology and nuclear weapons ... We do not have the motivation to pursue nuclear weapons. We have not and will not go after them. We do not need a nuclear bomb.'[118]) In addressing terrorism, Khatami stated that 'it [terrorism] must be condemned, and we, in turn, condemn every form of it in the world' and that 'the ugliest form of terrorism in our world is state terrorism'.[119] In addressing the Peace Process, Khatami stated that it 'will not succeed because it is not just' but also said that Iran will not interfere in the peace process.[120]

White House Officials only saw Khatami's statements as part of the continual 'declaratory policy' which only warranted a 'declaratory policy' in response.[121] If Khatami shifted from rhetoric to action, he would have forced the USA to respond in kind, which could have created a significant momentum towards the normalization of relations. In any area such as terrorism, the nuclear programme or the Middle East Peace Process, Iranian action would have most likely been welcomed and supported in a number of concessions and conciliatory steps taken by the USA in response. Instead, US intelligence services stated that ballistic missiles launched by Iran's programme had the potential to reach Israel, Turkey and Saudi Arabia by 1999.[122] Intelligence also pointed out that Iranian agents were monitoring US facilities in the Gulf which could have led to attacks on them. Therefore, even if Khatami was sincere about a rapprochement with the USA, elements in the Iranian political and military system were undermining Khatami's rhetoric with their actions.

Khatami tried to reach out to the USA at the Islamic Organization Conference Summit in Tehran, calling for 'thoughtful dialogue' and a 'détente in diplomatic policy'. Madeleine Albright's response was measured; it referred to the Islamic Republic of Iran, as opposed to a 'rogue state', and also suggested willingness to 'explore further ways to build mutual confidence'.[123] President Clinton also responded positively, stating that Iran 'is changing in a positive way and we want to support that'.[124] Consequently, the USA lifted a ban on some non-oil imports, although this was largely cosmetic as most of Iran's exports are oil-based.[125]

The heads of departments of Iranian and EU foreign ministries met in Brussels in May 1998 to herald a new era of 'constructive engagement', building on some structural changes in the Iranian regime produced by the 'critical dialogue' which had preceded it.[126] The EU called the new process the 'comprehensive dialogue', which was expected to further engage with President Khatami's reform agenda along cultural, economic and political lines.[127] The issues this covered at the under-secretary of state level included the Middle East Peace Process, WMD, human rights and terrorism in addition to talks around energy, trade, investment, refugees and drugs control.[128] Indeed, the 'comprehensive dialogue', within which trade and energy issues were most prominent, led to EU imports from Iran almost doubling between 1999 and 2000 to €8.4 billion. The EU–Iran trade deficit simultaneously decreased six-fold between 1998 and 2000.[129]

Closer relations were planned between the EU and Iran after the 2000 Iranian parliamentary elections, which were based partly on the conclusion of a Trade and Cooperation Agreement (TCA) in 2001.[130] Iran's Five-Year plan for the years 2000–2005 laid out its priorities as removing trade barriers, reforming the economic structure and streamlining rules for production and investment, all of which had the TCA in mind. Khatami's re-election in 2001 and his public diplomatic success with some EU states paved the way in 2002 for the EU to start negotiations on political as well as economic TCA issues. However, so long as political issues were bound to the TCA, trade would only flow as long as political talks continued. The continuation of high-level engagement between Iran and Europe could have paid high economic dividends, which in political terms would have translated into a tangible foreign policy success for Iran.[131]

The combination of Iran distancing itself from the fatwa and £1.5 million bounty on Salman Rushdie's head, and the good working relationship between British Foreign Secretary Robin Cook and Iran's Foreign Minister Kamal Kharrazi, led to a verbal agreement at the UN General Assembly in New York. This resulted in the upgrading of their respective missions to embassies after they had been downgraded in 1997.[132] Such changes in rhetoric did lead European states to recognize an opportunity. Helped by Kamal Kharazi's good relationship with Cook's successor Jack Straw, the UK managed a fresh start for Iranian–UK relations in 2001, particularly after 9/11, ending Iranian isolation and increasing trade and investment between the two states.[133] This fresh start, however, was not mirrored by any such development in the Iran–US relationship. It took until 2000 for the USA to admit its complicity in the 1953 coup and its support of the Pahlavi Shah for 25 years before the Revolution.[134] Instead of creating a blank sheet on which to advance reconciliation and a new era of cooperative relations, Madeleine Albright's speech was received by Khamenei with contempt and scepticism about the role the USA continues to play with regard to Iran.

At about the same time, progress being made by Iran and the EU based on a new TCA was interrupted by 9/11. This tragedy translated into an opportunity to bring Iran and the West together to address vital global and regional issues such as terrorism and the Taliban regime. President Khatami condemned 9/11 on national television but others, such as Ayatollah Emami-Kashani and presidential advisor Mohammad Rez Tajik, were more circumspect about 9/11, preferring to define it in terms related to Israeli state terrorism.[135] This was in contrast to civil society, which defined the event simply as terrorism, as evidenced by the actions of the Deputy Chief of Tehran Fire Department, who publicly declared support for his US counterparts and offered his help in New York.[136] What could have helped thaw relations with the USA was quickly rebuffed by the US Congress as it renewed ILSA for another five years, although it did allow for the president to review it again after two years.[137]

Saudi–US Relations in the Lead Up to 9/11

Before 9/11, there were apparent rifts in Saudi–US relations which were growing and could no longer be finessed in the way they had been during the Cold War. The increased visibility of the USA in the Middle East directly affected the regional security dynamic, which led to growing domestic criticism and threats from violent Islamists, particularly in Saudi Arabia. These had been made all the more real following attacks on US and Saudi targets in the region, including a car bomb at the Saudi National Guard offices in Riyadh in 1995, the Khobar Towers bombing in 1996 and an attack on the USS *Cole* in 2000. Saudi Arabia was therefore under mounting pressure to legitimize its foreign policies in terms which would appeal to the Ulama and secure its vital national security interests.

There were many irritants in the Saudi–US relationship between the mid-1990s and early 2000s, including Saudi authorities refusing to allow the FBI access to the Kingdom in May 1995 to detain a suspected Hezbollah operative called Imad Mughniya.[138] This individual was accused of the 1983 Beirut Marine barracks bombing. However, more important was the massive US presence in Saudi Arabia coinciding with the return of *jihadis* from Afghanistan. Once Saddam Hussein moved Iraqi forces towards the Kuwaiti border again in 1994, after having sparked the Gulf War in 1991 the same way, the USA responded with 'Operation Vigilant Warrior'.[139] This operation left a legacy of US force growth in its Saudi military bases and confirmed the USA as a local power in the Middle East. There were limits to US operations and the continuation of Clinton's dual containment policy, and Saudi

Arabia set these by refusing to grant US forces its territory for use in the lead up to 'Operation Desert Fox' in 1998 to destroy Iraq's 'weapons of mass destruction'.[140] Saudi Arabia was left with constructing a new regional order, absent Iraq and Iran, and formed relations with the Taliban in Afghanistan. Saudi Arabia also continued to be involved in other Muslim states such as Bosnia and Chechnya along the lines of *jihad* ('struggle', although in this sense it is interpreted as 'fighting') and *zakat* ('charitable giving'). However, the Cold War was over and these were no longer Communist states but independent, neutral or pro-Western states with domestic sovereign disputes or challenges.

Furthermore, the degree to which Saudi Arabia could be relied upon by the USA as a staunch supporter was being tested, as was Saudi Arabia's interest in continually underwriting US-led conflicts. It has been estimated that the Gulf War cost Saudi Arabia anywhere between $55 billion, or 56 per cent of its GDP in 1991, and $65 billion.[141] (The true figure would have covered a whole host of 'emergency expenditures' including: '... army mobilisation costs, the local costs of allied forces on Saudi territory, much of the overall cost of USA, UK and French involvement, and loans, grants and debt forgiveness to some other countries to gain their support for the war.'[142]) This was in addition to Saudi Arabia continually being associated with pro-Israeli US foreign policy. There were also irritants between Saudi Arabia/the GCC and the EU since the latter proposed a 'carbon tax' in the 1990s as part of its Energy Charter. Saudi Arabia, amongst others in the GCC, lobbied to have this shelved since it would adversely affect supply and represented a double standard since European states already subsidized their coal industries. The dispute did highlight the different supply–demand priorities of each actor, especially the EU requirement for using oil in a more intelligent and sustainable way. What has been more serious is the ongoing GCC–EU dispute over access to markets, with Saudi Arabia in particular feeling that not enough is being done to open the EU petrochemical market to Gulf competition. This is the single biggest trade barrier to a free-trade area between the GCC and EU.

The main strain in the US relationship prior to 2001 was political, and followed the al-Aqsa Intifada in 2000 which the new Bush administration left for regional actors to solve rather than take a direct stake in. There was therefore space for the EU to take a more active approach but within fundamental constraints imposed by the US-led security dynamic. The fighting was so intense and US interest so little that Saudi Arabia, for the first time, issued the USA with a threat of independence should the situation continue.[143] A meeting to discuss the situation was scheduled for 13 September 2001. 9/11 intervened.

The last 30 years of Middle East history highlight a number of factors that have become pre-eminent in the foreign policies of Saudi Arabia and Iran. The oil producers have become increasingly important in the global economy after 1973. Saudi Arabia, in particular, has used its economic 'structural power' and alliance with the USA to limit the strength of adversaries in the developing world. This chapter has analysed the contentious nature of GCC and Western involvement on the side of Iraq in the Iran–Iraq War, which left a legacy of heightened mistrust in Iran and facilitated Iran's foray into a nuclear programme. After the Gulf War, the Damascus Conference and Madrid Peace Conference were two opportunities for the USA to draw Iran and Iraq back into a comprehensive regional security framework. The MEPP and containment still remain lenses through which other US foreign policies in the region are perceived by Iran. In the lead up to 9/11, many GCC states were attempting to balance their domestic interests with the requirement for US security guarantees. In the case of Saudi Arabia, the way this balance tipped into a renewed emphasis on domestic policy, including dialogue with the Ulama, political consolidation and maintaining security, will be discussed in the following chapter.

CHAPTER 3

SAUDI FOREIGN POLICY: OIL, WAHABISM AND 'RIYAL POLITIK'

Vital regional issues such as the MEPP, Iran and counterterrorism currently serve as opportunities to advance Saudi foreign policies because they tend to be more closely aligned with those of the global powers. At the same time, Saudi foreign policies are being challenged by the implementation of Western foreign policies in the region, particularly during the Arab Uprisings. This is pushing Saudi Arabia to develop close relations with other Sunni states to support its pro-stability agenda (inclusive of its 'Iran Initiative' and perception of the Shi'i threat) and strategic relations with emergent global powers with which it could choose to balance in future.

The following research shows evidence of Saudi Arabia attempting to use its swing status in OPEC to put pressure on the revenues of adversarial oil exporters seeking to maximize oil income, such as Iran. Saudi Arabia also manages its partnerships with major oil importers such as the USA, China and India to assuage their fears about the security and price of their oil supplies, especially during periods of conflict. Maintaining the size of its oil reserves and production is therefore at the heart of its regional and OPEC leadership and its position in a pro-Western alliance, one which is under threat from South American states such as Venezuela.

Finally, the domestic environment is identified as a small but important foreign policy driver. This is due to a change in Saudi economic policy decision-making which tolerated high financial deficits until an increase in surpluses contributed to its transition from a passive to assertive foreign policy posture. Furthermore, the overlapping domestic concerns of securing its oil facilities, its national borders and the status of the regime continue to inform Saudi foreign policies. These received more attention in the 2000s in response to the economic and political reforms demanded during the 'Riyadh Spring' and the Arab Uprisings.

The Domestic Environment and Political Economy of Saudi Arabia

The domestic environment and political economy of Saudi Arabia has played a small but important role in the development of Saudi foreign policy, notably in moving it from a passive stance during an extended period of public deficit in the 1980s and 1990s to a more assertive stance after it had paid off most of the deficits and reined in public expenditures in 2000. At the same time, pressures remain in the national economy that cast into doubt its ability to continue to leverage existing and potential economic resources. The following problems have occurred in the Saudi economy, which could constrain its foreign policies should the oil price fall significantly:

1. The inability to repatriate funds from the foreign holdings of a small number of wealthy Saudi families, forcing the government to look elsewhere for foreign direct investment (FDI).
2. The failure of the Saudi Gas Initiative (SGI) and the resulting need for large-scale FDI into industrial and economic cities.
3. Increasing levels of unemployment in the Kingdom, which have led to calls for economic and political reforms.[1]

The 1970s oil boom led to 40 per cent of the national budget being used on expenditures such as infrastructure. However, once oil revenue peaked in 1980–1982, 1985–2000 remained a turbulent revenue period and could no longer be counted on to fuel a growing economy. Resource-based constraints in Saudi Arabia's economic development became more apparent as the government deficit increased, as did all the disadvantages of the rentier model: a lack of domestic taxation, costs of subsidizing public services and high defence- and policy-related expenditure.[2] One Saudi banker stated the situation simply: 'If the government cut back on its defence spending and all the payoffs that go with it, and sold its basic services even at cost – never mind the profit – its deficits would disappear overnight.'[3] These actions resulted in a government deficit of 25 per cent of GDP in 1987 and more than 14 per cent of GDP well into the 1990s, partly due to Saudi Arabia spending billions of dollars on helping to finance the cost of the first Gulf War.[4] This action represented a necessary delay in increasing Saudi relative autonomy and independence from the USA. Saudi–US strategic relations were still intact and it enhanced another more important foreign policy aim, tying in the USA to increase its national security and ultimately helping Saudi Arabia to punch above its weight in regional affairs after the conflict.

Between 1995 and 1998 state subsidies were beginning to be addressed, with some small increases to expenses such as airfares, illustrating that the Saudi government was heeding advice from the World Bank and IMF to remove subsidies from everyday life. As oil revenues were unpredictable and price rises sudden, wider reform aimed at diversifying the economy has been muted. The status quo was also maintained due to the widespread belief of the business elite that their companies could not withstand foreign competition. Therefore, between 1986 and 2000, oil revenue still accounted for 70 per cent of all income.[5] This has remained the case up to 2011, when oil accounted for 80 per cent of budget revenues and 90 per cent of export earnings.[6] The effect on Saudi foreign policy is that it remains closely tied to oil politics, the international oil price and Saudi economic policy, with few other vested interests being generated by broadening out the sources of GDP. By maintaining its status as a rentier state, Saudi Arabia is forced to continually align with other states that share the same characteristics in OPEC because they have the same pricing requirements. This strengthens its political alliance with other members of the GCC and narrows the common ground with other oil exporters that have different oil and economic policies.

The Forays and Failures to Attract FDI to the Kingdom

The pressure to institute economic reforms started with the oil price crash of 1998, which impacted negatively on the Saudi balance of payments. It also continued in the lead up to the Saudi accession to the World Trade Organization (WTO) in 2005. The Saudi government originally tried to avoid privatization since Saudi holdings abroad stood at $500 billion by the late 1990s, so all that was needed to boost the Saudi economy was a substantial reorientation of investments to the domestic sphere. However, the conditions which would have facilitated long-term domestic investment were not in place between 1985 and 2000 and therefore this idea did not lead to the reorientation of the national economy which was necessary to drive growth. This has been especially disappointing since the wealth of high net-worth individuals has only grown, with some Dubai-based bankers putting the total amount of wealth concentrated in these hands at up to $3 trillion as of 2002.[7] It is precisely the size of these funds that made them more likely to be invested in international markets, since repatriating large amounts from a small number of wealthy families would inevitably lead to difficult political questions being asked.

However, by 2000 the situation had eased temporarily, due to constraint in public spending, higher oil revenues, a reduction in remittances by restricting the use of foreign labour which makes up 80 per cent of the workforce, and the promotion of a new policy of 'Saudization': the process of increasing the number of Saudi nationals in the workforce.[8] This in turn meant that arrears which had been allowed to accumulate over a 17-year period to 115 per cent of GDP could be settled.[9] However, the policy hit a stumbling block soon after it was implemented due to its preference of some groups of Saudis over others for the best jobs, whether due to existing ties or under-the-table inducements, thereby creating artificial divisions in the labour force and adding pressure to reforms sought by the less well-off in society.

Even with lower deficits and new employment policies, Saudi Arabia still needed FDI to address all of its economic issues simultaneously, in particular diversification from oil and gas into the downstream sectors to provide jobs. Therefore what started as Crown Prince Abdullah's meeting with IOCs in Washington in 1998 to discuss upstream investments ideas turned into the Saudi Gas Initiative (SGI) in the early 2000s.[10] In return for upstream investment, but only in non-associated gas production, investors would also have to invest in downstream projects such as power stations, desalination units and petrochemical plants. The difficulties of the plan emerged immediately as many IOCs were not interested in gas and were not prepared to diversify from their core competencies. Although the opportunity was potentially big, the Saudi authorities made sure to limit access to proven gas reserves and concentrate foreign investment in areas which contained very little gas. Had the deal included oil, the situation may have been very different, but since Saudi Arabia already had spare oil production, the emphasis was in developing new projects in underdeveloped industries. The combination of unattractive terms of business and political antipathy in the USA post-9/11 both contributed to the demise and scaling back of the original SGI. In 2001, Saudi Arabia's proven gas reserves were estimated at 204.5 trillion cubic feet, the fourth largest in the world after Russia, Iran and Qatar. The SGI would have realized some of these reserves and boosted the Master Gas System (MGS) which feeds plants in Yanbu on the Red Sea and Jubail on the Persian Gulf. These two plants combined provide 10 per cent of the world's petrochemical production.[11] In 1999, Saudi Aramco invested $45 billion over 25 years in upstream gas development and processing facilities but required further investment and a foreign investment strategy to go with it.[12] The SGI was designed to facilitate that foreign investment, but not only were the proposed acreages and terms unfavourable, IOC shareholders included public institutional investors in the USA and ExxonMobil has many of its top executives based in New York City. It would have been hard to justify, in terms of public relations, their involvement with Saudi Arabia, tainted in the USA so soon after 9/11.

When the SGI failed, it wasn't held against other Western governments such as the UK, since Shell remained involved through a consortium, but it was disappointing to the Saudis and it did mean that they had to turn to the Russians and Chinese.[13] The demise of the SGI has taken away some of the momentum from gas, which was expected to supplement the central role of the oil industry. The pace of development and the one million jobs expected from $100 billion in combined oil and gas projects over ten years from 2000 has dissipated into much smaller and diverse industrial projects.[14] The 'mini' gas initiative signed in 2004, which only included exploration contracts, rather than production arrangements, was so limited and small-scale that it has been called 'cosmetic' by Prince Alwaleed.[15] Instead of facilitating a rapid expansion of downstream industries such as petrochemicals and helping to upgrade power and water infrastructure, the SGI failure has meant that Saudi Arabia must concentrate on other industries to fill these requirements. This has started to be realized as a Malaysian/Saudi group signed contracts for the Shoiba Phase 3 Independent Water and Power Project (IWPP) to supply the regions of Makkah, Jeddah, Taif and Al-Baha, the first IWPP approved by the SEC and valued at $2.4 billion in 2005.[16] In the meantime, the scaling-back of large projects is contributing to a shortage of employment opportunities, short-term internal investments to spark job creation, and the ongoing search for significant FDI.

As matters stand, King Abdullah aims to procure $624 billion inward investment across all sectors of the economy, including 23 per cent in infrastructure development, by the year 2020.[17] However, FDI is highly contingent on being able to attract people to the Kingdom, which is being affected by Saudi Arabia's overriding and largely self-generated security problems. Saudi Arabia believes that it cannot – or does not need to, because of its combination of oil, money and the two holy sites – facilitate business and ensure internal security at the same time. This has only exacerbated the issue of unemployment and efforts aimed at increasing the number of commercial and financial interests of foreign governments.

As well as debates over pro-business policies, slow government decision-making has also been noticeable with regard to the implementation of Sovereign Wealth Funds (SWF). In 2008, Saudi Arabia launched its first SWF. The new fund was launched with $5.3 billion, designed to operate in a similar vein to Norway's General Pension Fund (GPF) which is worth $500 billion, and Singapore's Government Investment Corporation (GIC) which is worth $100 billion.[18] Two more SWFs came online in 2009: the Hassana Investment Company owned by the largest state-run pension fund, with a budget of SR 8.9 billion for 2009, and around 10 per cent of its total investments in the stock market;[19] and Sanabil Al-Saudia, with initial capital of $5.3 billion.[20] Although both funds have a broad mandate across global asset classes, slow decision-making by management appears to have stymied the realization of investments from both investment vehicles. This has mirrored the problems in attracting FDI into Saudi Arabia following the SGI and Economic Cities initiatives, despite the optimism from Western and Saudi sources that they would succeed.[21] The situation is complicated by the Shura Council going through a transformation of its own, whereby it is expected that it will eventually comprise elected representatives, and by 2015 be partly elected by and inclusive of women.[22] The dynamic and growing challenge is to make major decisions rapidly, push through government departmental reforms and develop new government agencies, whilst simultaneously attempting to address the underlying needs of society.

Unemployment and the Pressures to Reform

The scale of the unemployment problem is captured by the figures: the high unemployment rate which stood at 15.3 per cent of a total labour force of 3.3 million in 2001;[23] GDP per capita, which fell from $28,600 in 1981 to $7,000 in 2000;[24] the continued dependence of the private sector on oil and the small size of exports compared to imports (for example, Saudi exports to the USA shrank by 21 per cent between 1999 and 2000, whilst imports from the USA increased by 72 per cent over the same period[25]); and the growing population, which has meant that large numbers of young people are entering the workforce every year. The oil industry is not labour-intensive enough to absorb successive waves of job seekers and so diversification holds the key to employment in the Kingdom. The two biggest companies in Saudi Arabia, Aramco and Sabic, only employ 54,000 people and 16,000 people respectively (of whom 2,000 are Europeans).[26] This demand for a small number of highly qualified Saudis may reduce a 'brain drain' effect from Saudi Arabia, but will not lead to mass employment. In contrast, the number of personnel in the mechanized and infantry brigades and other militia of the Saudi Arabian National Guard (SANG) amounts to 75,000, and the network also provides income for an additional one million Saudis.[27] This is because SANG is a security force that also represents a network of tribal leaders with close historical ties (as descendants of the Ikhwan) to King Abdelaziz Ibn Sa'ud, the founder of the Kingdom.[28] Such ties ensure that employment and other benefits will always be available to them so long as they remain loyal to the King.[29] That is not to say that Aramco and Sabic don't play a role in increasing opportunities for Saudi citizens. The next stage of Saudi economic growth is expected to come from the growth of state-owned enterprises such as Saudi Aramco, Sabic and Maaden (the Saudi Arabian Mining Company) or what Abdullah Dabbagh, President of Maaden in 2002, classified as the 'three legs of the Saudi stool'.[30]

Reacting to the 'Riyadh Spring': National Dialogue, Ulama Disapproval and International Deference

The fundamental barrier to political reform has not only been the government's slow response to domestic pressure, but also the lack of support for it from the Wahabi Ulama. The Saudi political establishment has been forced to make changes in areas such as reforming education for girls only after tragedies such as the Mecca fire in 2002 generated greater domestic pressure for change. The Riyadh compound bombings in 2003 highlighted again that oil money alone couldn't address the root causes of violent extremism. Instead, an emergent civil society put forward a number of reformist-minded manifestos, actions that were collectively dubbed the 'Riyadh Spring'.[31] In response to political grievances from Salafi-Wahabis, the Shi'a, Ismailis and Sufis, Crown Prince Abdullah launched the 'National Dialogue' in 2003. However, because it was not supported by Wahabis, the government was unable to push through its reform. It was also cut short the same year when 11 figureheads of the petitioning movements (Islamist and liberal intellectuals) were arrested and imprisoned by Prince Naif, the Interior Minister, later to be freed by King Abdullah in 2005.[32]

It is likely that privately expressed concerns about human rights from the USA were a factor in this decision to release the imprisoned intellectuals, as it was in the release of three prominent intellectual dissidents who were given six- to nine-year prison terms in 2005 for petitioning the government on constitutional reform. Either way, the issue was not deemed vital enough to stand in the way of rebuilding Saudi–US relations after 9/11 and was not taken up by European states either.[33] This has effectively given Saudi Arabia a free hand to deal with internal issues, including human rights, on its own terms. This enables Saudi Arabia to shore up support from the Ulama and armed forces in a way which may not have otherwise been possible. Thus, there is a very limited foreign policy linkage between the internal politics of Saudi Arabia and external pressure, in contrast to that which exists when it comes to relations between the EU and Iran, for example. As such, the EU is accused of 'double standards' for focusing on human rights with regard to Iran and then taking a 'realist' approach when dealing with Saudi Arabia.[34]

The Arab Uprisings: Securing the Homeland

The Arab Uprisings of 2011 represented, for Saudi Arabia, one of the most comprehensive 'tsunamis' of socio-political change, and possibly one of the most enduring, seen in the Middle East since the Second World War and the advent of Arab socialism.[35] As the rulers of a conservative state and the heads of a Sunni monarchy, the Al-Sa'ud are theoretically at great risk from the challenges posed by the political reforms being demanded by Arab Uprising revolutionaries. Domestically, Saudi Arabia has been shoring up support for the regime through a variety of different methods, which have become more important in the face of greater pressure for reform in the Arab Uprisings: increasing employment, direct payments to Saudis (an extra two months salary was paid in 2011 as part of King Abdullah's cash injection into the national economy) and extending public services.[36] After King Abdullah returned from medical treatment abroad, approximately $40 billion was distributed to Saudis as a range of benefits, including housing, social benefits and small business loans.[37]

The budget surplus enabled the economic package, which functions like an informal stability fund, recognizing that some Saudis still need support.[38] Many of the funds have only partially been distributed, as parts of it are long-term measures which will follow the needs of youth as they grow up. In response to Western criticism that these are 'handouts' or 'bribes', Prince Turki Al-Faisal said that Saudi Arabia has promised a better life and a decrease in the poverty rate and delivered them.[39] However, the money doesn't address the remaining political issues such as the rights of women, as the Women2Drive protests attest.[40] The problem is the concept of *Al-Bai'ah* (meaning 'contract' or 'pledge of allegiance' to God and the people), the social covenant which maintains the position of the ruler (and 22,000 members of the royal family) and upon which the state of Saudi Arabia is based.[41] 9/11 challenged this contract because of the unprecedented amount of pressure for internal reforms which Saudi Arabia was experiencing, largely from the USA. Similarly, the Arab Uprisings have underscored the need for its reinterpretation, particularly in instituting rapid educational and judicial reforms to ensure the Ulama is in sync with the expanding spheres of influence of politics as well as the shifting or evolving will of the people.

The Arab Uprisings have also enhanced anxieties that the Kingdom will suffer from another terrorist attack, possibly a cross-border one, which is rooted in the analysis of Western observers who maintain that the Royal Saudi Land Forces (RSLF) and the Royal Saudi Navy (RSN) are not able to defend the country's vast borders fully.[42] This was a bilateral issue right up to 2005 when Saudi Arabia implemented more robust defensive measures, following US pressure on the GCC states to take more responsibility for their borders.[43] Given the importance of Saudi Arabia to global energy markets, an attack on its installations resulting from the Arab Uprisings could be costly for Saudi relations in terms of undermining its promises of secure energy flows. Some security experts believe that key oil installations could be at risk since the 2003 Riyadh bombings, particularly the larger, more strategic ones including Ras Tanoura and Abqaiq which handle two-thirds of the Kingdom's oil output in the Persian Gulf. The huge territory of Saudi Arabia, its long coastlines, porous borders (especially with Yemen and Iraq), exposed oil facilities, and Shi'i grievances in the east of the Kingdom have all been cited as vulnerabilities. The extent to which Shi'a in the east of the Kingdom have grievances that could threaten the Kingdom is said to be exaggerated since King Abdullah has worked to improve their living conditions since 2005.[44] However, security crackdowns including shootings in the governorate of Qatif are becoming more common.[45] It is also widely known that there are tensions between Saudis, especially the Ulama, who see the Shi'i minority not as a sect of Islam but as deviants from it.[46] If fifth-column or latent separatist tendencies do exist in the Shi'i population, then the survival of the state in the long term is likely to require reforms that go deeper than the short-term measures that high oil revenues are able to supply. This has been of particular concern since trouble flared up amongst the Shi'i community in October 2011, which was followed quickly by Saudi promises to crack down with an 'iron fist' on further trouble.[47] Since Saudi Arabia suspects Iran is key to Shi'i unrest, security concerns are only likely to be heightened by the foiled Iranian attempt to kill the Saudi Ambassador to the USA.[48]

In the meantime, the domestic security budget has risen by about $1.2 billion since 2002 to $8 billion in 2004, so the Saudi authorities can be seen to be acting to protect key sites. This is especially the case with Abqaiq's energy security, which has received $10 billion in investment since the 2006 al-Qaeda attack against it.[49] A 35,000-strong Facilities Security Force which is trained by the USA and guards against internal and external threats, along with Saudi Arabia's Foreign Reserve Initiative, protects oil supplies from the Kingdom from interruption.[50] These are supported by air surveillance from helicopters and F15 patrols. Any pipeline incident is expected to be under control within 36 hours, and whilst tankers could be vulnerable while docked at installations, typically there are just a few giant tankers which transport most of the oil.[51]

Saudi Foreign Policies in the Levant and Gulf

The way Saudi Arabia utilizes economic assets and resources in its bilateral foreign policies illustrates the circumstances and extent to which they both can be advanced to build relations and contain threats. This section outlines Saudi foreign policy in its immediate neighbourhood, in the Levant and the Gulf, where a large number of threats and opportunities are located. It charts the new independent foreign policy course that the Al-Sa'ud has plotted after the second Palestinian intifada and the extent to which it is willing to support a two-state solution. The section goes on to examine how Saudi Arabia underwrites aid to states such as Yemen which could pose a significant economic and political risk should they be allowed to become failed states. Finally, the Saudi–Iranian Cold War is discussed and assessed in terms of the strategies employed by Saudi Arabia to limit Iran's multifarious influences in the MEPP and across the Gulf. Saudi oil policy and aid, the growth and economic development of the GCC and the strength of the Saudi–US relationship can all be contextualized on this basis and within the wider dynamics and developments taking place in the Arab Uprisings, 'Shi'i Crescent' and 'resistance axis'.

Saudi Policy in the MEPP: Supporting Regional Allies and Humanitarianism Whilst Dividing the 'Resistance Axis'[52]

Saudi policy towards regional actors involved in the MEPP highlights the extent to which economic factors are able to influence facts on the ground in Lebanon, Gaza and the West Bank, limit the role of Iran in the peace process and facilitate a lasting two-state solution. The Israel–Palestine conflict has sparked a number of Saudi foreign policy endeavours due to its manifestation as one of the last few remaining pan-Arab causes, the spillover effects of the conflict on regional security and economic development, as well as the Islamic significance of the Dome of the Rock and Al-Aqsa Mosque being located in the Haram Al-Sharif in Jerusalem (the third most important city for Muslims). By taking active measures to secure a fair settlement for the Palestinians, particularly during a period of low interest from the White House throughout the second intifada, Saudi Arabia has been better able to leverage its influence and secure some domestic, regional and international political credit.[53]

Ending the Israel–Palestine conflict is vital to Saudi Arabia for four major reasons. Firstly, it will be a victory for the War on Terror, help make up for the Saudi role in 9/11, and reduce part of the rationale for (and therefore threat from) violent Islamism in the Kingdom and elsewhere. Secondly, it will reduce the political, humanitarian and/or armed resistance roles that Iran and Hezbollah have been able to play. Thirdly, absent direct regional threats, Saudi Arabia could cut back on defence spending, which has prolonged its dependence on the West and drained its national budget. Fourthly, the West could regain stature and deal with related problems in the Middle East, such as the Iranian nuclear programme, and address them in a more robust or proactive way. As an added bonus, the implementation of a two-state solution would contribute positively to Saudi state-building, political consolidation and international image.

Saudi Arabia has not only used economics but also political tools to leverage its interests in the MEPP, signifying its importance in Saudi foreign policy terms. However, unlike the USA, Saudi Arabia is far more limited in how it can leverage its economic and political assets to influence the behaviour of other states or produce new alliances. Saudi Arabia is all too aware of this, with an official stating that 'only the USA can use aid to gain allies'.[54] In political terms too, influencing states suggests that Saudi Arabia is able to change facts on the ground such as returning the Golan Heights to Syria or a cessation of Israeli settlements which, again, only the USA (at best) is currently capable of. Saudi Arabia has emphasized positive political engagement as a facilitating factor to a final settlement in the MEPP. The Arab Peace Initiative in 2002 was a positive message about a final agreement and normalization of relations with Israel from a major regional power, but did not lead to negotiations with Israel. It also served to mitigate some of the pressure the USA was putting on Saudi Arabia post-9/11.

As part of its wider policy in the MEPP, Saudi Arabia has sought to coordinate with Iran between the late 1990s and mid 2000s in efforts to promote stability in Lebanon. However, after the war in Lebanon in 2006, Iran galvanized Arab public opinion in support of Hezbollah, which had managed to take on the Israeli Defence Forces and emerge relatively unscathed. This reflected Saudi policy as being weak, portraying the Al-Sa'ud as being out of touch with the Shi'i community which supported the action along with broader public opinion. As relations broke down between Saudi Arabia and Iran, it has been Hezbollah (and to an extent the Palestine Islamic Jihad, a smaller IRGC proxy[55]), not Hamas, which has been the biggest cause for concern in Saudi circles. Saudi fears have already been realized, since the non-resolution of the Israel–Palestine conflict has meant Hezbollah has been able to supplant the role of legitimate government and advance its own (and Iran's) agenda. The stakes were very high during this period since Hezbollah could have dragged Lebanon into a war against Israel against the will of the Lebanese government. The pressure on Saudi Arabia to prevent another invasion of Lebanon as seen in 2006, a third intifada in Palestine and to keep the MEPP on track dictated its proactive policy to resolve the situation.

The Saudi response was firstly to deposit $1.5 billion in the Banque du Liban (Lebanon's central bank) through the Saudi Fund for Development (SFD) in order to support Lebanon's reconstruction after the 2006 invasion by the Israeli Defence Force.[56] Then, through the 2007 Makkah Accords, and by advocating and supporting the unification of Fatah and Hamas in the Palestinian National Authority (PNA), Saudi Arabia managed to focus on the Islamic concepts of unity, consensus and conflict resolution as a legitimate way to push out Iran and Hezbollah. As the threat remained, Saudi Arabia became increasingly worried about Hezbollah wresting control away from the Fouad Siniora administration in Lebanon, so Sa'ud Al-Faisal proposed an Arab force, backed by NATO and the USA, to intervene in Lebanon and destroy Hezbollah in 2008.[57] This was the only option left to Saudi Arabia since Hezbollah, unlike Hamas, is a Shi'i force and therefore has no links to Saudi funding but plenty of access to funding and resources from Iran and Syria.[58]

In the same vein, King Abdullah was quick to fill the PNA funding void left by the EU after Hamas won its electoral victory in Gaza, leading to indications that Saudi Arabia has spent more on Hamas than Iran has.[59] More sensitive financial aid transfers to groups such as Hamas have been given in coordination and consultation with third parties, such as Egypt, with the simple motive of relieving the consequences of conflict in which Hamas also has experience (e.g. through building schools and hospitals). Thus, Saudi Arabia is said to differentiate between a political stance and humanitarian aid.[60] Saudi Arabia was also one of the few states to go against US demands to cut links with the PNA when Hamas won an electoral victory in Gaza. It was able to do this by using diplomatic engagement with the USA to ensure that its policy of 'waging peace on Israel' could succeed and that supporting the PNA could be maintained.[61]

Saudi policy in the case of Lebanon reflected the need firstly to stabilize and support the Lebanese government, avoiding further conflict and unnecessary humanitarian disaster, and then to implement a comprehensive campaign to remove Hezbollah once it became clear the Makkah Accords would fail. Although Saudi policy towards Hamas is the same as far as humanitarian relief is concerned, it was also easier on two counts: Hamas is a Sunni group and it has existing ties to Saudi Arabia. The implication is that rather than contain or remove Hamas, Saudi Arabia was able to engage with it through intermediaries to contribute to its declaratory Peace Initiative which would align the interests of all regional actors.

There are doubts as to whether the Saudi policy of engagement will continue since some believe King Abdullah is disillusioned after negotiations with Hamas and Fatah failed and Saudi Arabia intervened in Lebanon.[62] However, during the G. W. Bush administration Saudi Arabia was one of the few states to actively pursue a peace treaty with a normalization of relations with Israel on offer. Furthermore, Saudi Arabia put an offer on the table in 2000 to help establish a Palestinian state. The offer, which would become the 2002 Arab Peace Initiative, was renewed again in 2007 (since Bush wanted a Palestinian state established by the end of his presidency in 2009). The plan included a transfer equivalent to $10 billion ($5 billion after the acceptance of the initiative and $5 billion paid over the following three years) from the GCC states to Israel.[63] The evidence therefore suggests that Saudi Arabia does remain committed to the two-state solution, based on the support from the White House and the ability of Egypt to remain able to act as an interlocutor. Since the threat from violent Islamists and the Muslim Brotherhood has risen significantly since 2001, Saudi support may tend to be more behind the scenes than expressed in the form of more overt initiatives that may tempt attacks or undermine the legitimacy of the Al-Sa'ud.

Dominance, Integration and Instability in the Arabian Peninsula

Saudi Arabia is the first state amongst the GCC states, dominating what is theoretically an even platform for consultative decision-making between heads of state. Not only does the GCC have its headquarters in Riyadh but due to its sheer geographical size, the fact it has the largest economy in the GCC, borders every other GCC member,[64] has the largest oil reserves and 'swing' status in OPEC, a close relationship with the USA and custodianship of the two holy places, Saudi Arabia's status within the GCC is unrivalled. In response, smaller GCC States have concluded bilateral free trade agreements (FTAs) with the USA in the 2000s even though trade with the Middle East and North African (MENA) states combined amounts to less than 3 per cent of all US trade.[65] This signifies the political nature of the agreements and the friction within the GCC over Saudi dominance. The UAE government, empowered by high oil revenues, published the online *UAE Yearbook 2006* in which it indicated it wanted to renegotiate its border with Saudi Arabia. Tensions have been apparent with other GCC states such as Qatar, following Qatar's energy minister accusing Saudi Arabia of providing 'no clearance' for a multi-billion dollar project to supply Qatari gas to Kuwait in 2006. Saudi dominance in the GCC therefore includes issues related to intra-GCC trade and investment which require Saudi consent to go ahead.[66]

Borders are largely at the heart of mixed diplomatic relations, but other irritants such Qatar's relationship with Syria, an Israeli trade office in Doha, and comments made by both sides in different Arabic newspapers and Internet posts have also caused consternation.[67] Such comments include Qatar's public statements on dividing Saudi Arabia from Al-Qatif to Al-Sharqiya. More serious are Saudi fears of possible future Qatari attempts ('... at the service of the Zionist entity') to give the Palestinians part of north-east Saudi Arabia, which could be merged with the Palestinian refugee camps in Jordan to create a new

Palestinian state.⁶⁸ This would simultaneously serve to help shrink the Saudi state back to the Hijaz region, equalize influence between the GCC members and give a much-needed boost to Shi'i attempts at secession in the eastern province. However, it should be noted that incendiary statements by the king's brother do not necessarily represent the official view of the Qatari government. Nevertheless, Saudi Arabia and Qatar have had a particularly difficult relationship during the Arab Uprisings because Qatar is home to Sheikh Yusuf Qaradawi, an influential Egyptian Muslim Brother and critic of Saudi Arabia's salafi concepts.⁶⁹

In the period leading up to expected monetary union in 2010, the smaller Gulf States felt it was one of their last few chances to assert their sovereignty and punch above their weight in regional affairs. Whilst monetary union has been delayed, relations have improved, particularly since Iranian influence in the region is perceived to go against the interests of many of the Sunni monarchies. The Arab Uprisings have further tied the interests of the GCC monarchies together as they try to maintain their domestic security and regime legitimacy, and establish a popular trend that supports stability.

Redefining Alliances and Removing Resistance

The Arab Uprisings have highlighted the fact that the Yemeni tribes and political apparatus were loyal to Saudi aid rather than the Saudis per se. Although perceived to be a major force in Yemen by external actors, the actual influence of Saudi Arabia amongst the competing interests of Yemeni political leaders is limited. Saudi Arabia has no interest in defining the course of events in Yemen, but it does have an immediate interest in the preservation of its internal security. If a civil war erupts in Yemen and it becomes a failed state, then the security-related fallout could be considerable, from refugees spilling across the long porous border to increasing poverty rates and the consequent security implications. Whilst few options remain, Saudi Arabia has relied on US drone assassinations launched from an airbase in the Kingdom, and 'dollar diplomacy'.⁷⁰ Saudi engagement is primarily focused on trying to ensure an ordinary transition of power. This would therefore avoid the 'Egyptian model' of uprising, uncertain transition and bloodshed.[71]

Beyond the Arabian Peninsula, if there was a successful conclusion to the MEPP, political change could theoretically be possible between the GCC and Israel, and with Iran, which would have significant consequences for regional peace. By facilitating GCC investments beyond its borders, and increasing the number of economic linkages therein, particularly in utilities and infrastructure, economics could form the basis for improved relations and stability as longer-term interests are generated.[72] The foundations for broadening out economic cooperation across the Middle East have already been formulated in the embryonic monetary union plans currently under study in the GCC.[73] Not only is there a trend of the GCC moving towards coordination and integration, with eventual unification, but given US policy during the Arab Uprisings it is now viewed as the only forum in which Saudi interests will not be compromised.

US and Western interference has had the effect of facilitating internal GCC discussions about a unified military command in the GCC and a rationalization of arms purchases or the establishment of an indigenous arms manufacturing capability.[74] However, the US arms deals such as the F-35 programme still represent incentives for the GCC states not to go ahead with this, through advantages such as offset and co-production deals.[75] The Arab Uprisings have served as a wake-up call for the Saudi government in that it can no longer rely on the USA for its survival and must therefore show greater independence and a greater dexterity regarding its economic resources beyond 'throwing money at the problem'.[76] This has led it to try to establish a new alliance of Sunni monarchies, dubbed Saudi Arabia's 'Iran Initiative', in order to promote a semblance of stability in the Middle East.[77] This culminated in the proposal for Jordan (to which Saudi Arabia has given $400 million and is likely to give more) and Morocco to join the GCC.[78] The plan for enlargement is still being seriously discussed by the respective foreign ministers and could lead to a five-year economic development plan being implemented before their accession.[79] There is no reason why Saudi Arabia wouldn't want to include Egypt in this plan as well, once it becomes more stable (perhaps after presidential elections) since this too would support regional stability, boost Egyptian economic development and deprive Iran of a much-needed regional ally. Saudi Arabia is already encouraging Salafis in Egypt who oppose the idea of a closer alliance with Iran as promoted by the Muslim Brotherhood. In addition, it has also given approximately $4 billion in economic aid to Egypt without strings attached, unlike the conditions of accepting democratic principles set by the USA and IMF.[80] Even without an explicit alliance, this action still includes goodwill and the accumulation of political capital for future use, as part of a counter-revolutionary agenda.[81]

The Arab Uprisings encompass a number of 'top ten' Saudi foreign policy concerns. The uprisings undermine orderly transition in Yemen and encourage Iran to support protestors in Kuwait and Bahrain under its interpretation as an 'Islamic Awakening'.[82] The Saudi response to the crisis in Bahrain has been atypical of Saudi foreign policy reinforced by negative US foreign policies in the region, in particular its action in Iraq. It was one of the most independent and rapid deployments of Saudi troops, sent under GCC auspices to encourage stability, contrary to US pressure to 'remain on the sidelines'.[83] Its mission was to restore law and order and facilitate dialogue with 'mainstream' political parties.[84] Saudi Arabia has also been active with regard to the NATO attacks on Libyan targets, having secured Arab support for the operations, but without taking a real stake in the outcome of events on the Libyan streets.[85]

Iranian influence and traditional alliances with groups in Iraq and Lebanon, as well as with the government in Syria, have new meaning in the Arab Uprisings and at a critical juncture in the MEPP. This makes the regional situation particularly unstable and is less suited to the traditional Saudi approach of engagement and containment. Bashar Al-Assad's reaction to the Arab Uprising in Syria has become unacceptable to Saudi Arabia, which has gone so far as to take the unprecedented step of recalling its ambassador to Syria for 'consultation'.[86] The Saudis expect Syria to stop the bloodshed and institute fast and comprehensive reforms. Saudi Arabia has even explicitly joined a common US–UK–Saudi alliance against Bashar Al-Assad's crackdown on Syrian protests in 2011 which, along with

UN pressure, seems to have (at least temporarily) led him to call a halt to the use of military force.[87] Longer-term Saudi influence may become more apparent if one of its citizens successfully makes the transition from a leading position in the Syrian uprising to take on a position in a new Syrian government. Nofel Marouf Al-Dawlibi is the son of a well-known Syrian figure who worked for King Faisal and died in Saudi Arabia. He is a businessman but is working with the backing of the Saudi authorities to overthrow the regime, and is expected to receive a further boost from the anticipated defection of Syrian ambassadors.[88] It is particularly important for Saudi Arabia to be involved in Syria since any power vacuum left by the sudden removal of President Assad could quickly lead to a de facto victory for the Muslim Brotherhood or a Shi'i group, which would reinforce Syria's close ties with Iran.

The Saudi–Iranian Cold War

The number and range of threats in the immediate neighbourhood of Saudi Arabia have led to different foreign policies in each case. They often reflect the multi-dimensional, interrelated and oscillating intensity of the foreign policy challenges posed by a small number of adversaries. Saudi–Iranian relations have moved from ideological differences after the Islamic revolution and the divisive alliances created by the Iran–Iraq War, to the relatively cordial relations established during the rapprochement of the Rafsanjani presidency, to the Khatami presidency in the late 1990s in the lead up to the UN 'Year of Dialogue Among Civilizations' in 2001.[89] Iran has now risen again to become a central concern and is perceived to be an existential threat to Saudi Arabia on a number of fronts since the removal of Saddam Hussein in Iraq. The Saudi–Iranian rivalry is most clearly illustrated by Saudi Arabia's definition of the 'Gulf' and Iran's definition of the 'Persian Gulf' for the same region, semantics which have led on more than one occasion to diplomatic fallout.[90] Iran's nuclear programme, the leverage of the 'Resistance Axis', 'Shi'i Triangle' (including Iraq and a Pakistan led by President Zardari, whom the Saudis fear is Shi'a) and 'Shi'i Crescent' in the GCC and Levant, and its search for regional dominance, are of primary concern.[91]

The continuing tensions between Iran and the UAE (and the GCC) over sovereignty of the Greater Tunb, Lesser Tunb and Abu Musa Islands remain a barrier to improved relations with Saudi Arabia;[92] relations which could have developed according to Saudi Arabia's role as leading energy producer and Iran's great economic potential.[93] Instead relations have worsened, based on Iran's contribution to smuggling, sectarian strife and involvement with al-Qaeda operations in Iraq which have been perceived by the USA and Saudi Arabia to only deteriorate over time. The Saudi position on Iran is formed on the basis of its role in Iraq in addition to its nuclear programme. King Abdullah has been circumspect about Saudi relations with Iraq since the Maliki government is regarded as being a tool of Tehran. Prince Sa'ud has emphasized the importance of national reconciliation between the Shi'a, Sunnis and Kurds in Iraq, including Saudi impartiality in this process whilst urging Iran to take the same stance.[94] The Saudi Arabian government would have directly intervened in Iraq to protect Sunnis and reduce the Iranian influence had it not been for US pressure and concerns about inflaming sectarian violence.[95] Riyadh is limited as to what it can do, since a clampdown on border security was rendered less effective because the border remains open on the Iraqi side, due to steps not being taken by the Iraqis, British and American forces there. Greater intelligence-sharing was expected to have tangible benefits in this case, particularly since Saudi Arabia caught 2,500 smugglers on the Iraqi border in 2005.[96]

The multifarious WMD-related security dilemmas of Iranian nuclear proliferation were said to be Saudi Arabia's biggest foreign policy concern in 2007, even though Prince Sa'ud said that 'Saudi Arabia is not under any circumstances going to enter into this [nuclear arms] race'.[97] Saudi foreign policy in this area remains unclear and is highly dependent on the actions of other actors in the region. Before any decisions are taken about proliferation, Saudi Arabia remains bound to a Western defence umbrella which aims to reduce tensions in this sphere. It signed NATO's Istanbul Cooperation Initiative (ICI) in 2005 even though there were reservations about Israel's role in NATO's Mediterranean Partnership and perceptions that NATO is dominated by the USA.[98] The nuclear programme has led Saudi Arabia to take its most hawkish stance in advocating a US-led pre-emptive strike against Iranian installations, which has led to increased diplomatic tensions between Saudi Arabia and the USA.[99] Such tensions should be put into perspective, however, since the prospect of an Iran armed with nuclear weapons is one of the Saudi interests that dovetail with those of the USA, keeping them close. Failing a pre-emptive strike by the USA, Saudi Arabia is now opposed to the use of military force against Iran and has considered alternative measures.[100] These have included squeezing Tehran's finances by increasing production to lower global oil prices, (although support from Algeria, Angola, Iraq and Venezuela against what could be seen to be a pro-Western alliance of Saudi Arabia, UAE, Kuwait, and Qatar which voted for an increase in production meant that Iran defeated Saudi Arabia's motion in OPEC).[101] Since then Saudi Arabia has been forced to go it alone in its efforts to use its swing status to unilaterally increase production.[102] This is a prime example of 'resource nationalism' through which state-owned enterprises such as Saudi Aramco are forced to conform to political pressures. These include those associated with '... national pride, competitive inter-OPEC issues [including leadership: the quota system is based on the size of oil reserves, so Saudi Arabia is able to pump more oil than any other state], and a desire to please and reassure customers.'[103]

This move had already been classified by leading economists as a non-starter since Saudi Arabia needs $75 per barrel to pay for its own expenditures,[104] including capital expenditures and reserves of about $5 billion.[105] Since Saudi Arabia earns a bit less than the OPEC average it needs OPEC prices above $80 on average.[106] Saudi Arabia therefore can't afford to reduce the oil price for very long, and coupled with a potential Iranian backlash and Iran being able to adapt to economic pressure with sophistication, increasing production to lower prices would not necessarily be as effective as Saudi Arabia may wish it to be. The only result from the 'worst' OPEC meeting and the failure of its unilateral measures will be to question not only the pre-eminence of Saudi leadership when it comes to oil production quotas, but the *raison d'être* of OPEC itself, since it has been unable to stabilize oil prices or increase production.[107] Since Saudi oil policy needs to simultaneously address its politico-economic needs, its position in the global economy and its relationship with (Western) allies and regional adversaries, it is not surprising that it was left to undertake unilateral measures against a competing oil exporter.

This is especially the case since Saudi Arabia has tried to avoid shaking oil markets in which it has mutual interests with other states, but due to reasons outside of its control they are shaken anyway. If a targeted oil weapon won't work against Iran, these measures could ultimately lead to Saudi Arabia seeking a nuclear deterrence of its own.[108] This is a reflection of the fact that Saudi Arabia not only has the most to lose from an Iran armed with nuclear weapons, but is not generally happy with the effectiveness of the E3 negotiations with Iran.[109]

Alleged Iranian plots such as those to assassinate the Saudi Ambassador to the United States are unlikely to make Saudi Arabia less hawkish on Iran. Prince Turki Al-Faisal has said that Iran must 'pay the price' for its involvement even though Iran denies any such involvement.[110] Such a firm response will no doubt be informed by the seizure of Mecca in 1979, Iran's successful plots to assassinate Saudi diplomats in 1988 and 1989, the Khobar Towers bombing aimed at US military personnel in 1996 for which responsibility was claimed by 'Saudi Hezbollah'[111] (Saudi Shi'a); and the murder of five American soldiers in Kerbala, Iraq, in 2007. However, there are some academics and diplomats who still question the modus operandi of the plot to assassinate the Saudi Ambassador and therefore who the true perpetrator of the attack is.[112]

Interpreting Saudi Arabia's Regional Environment

Saudi Arabia's regional environment should not only be interpreted as the Middle East and North Africa, but as straddling the rest of the Islamic world, defined by loose interconnections with other member states of the Organization of the Islamic Conference (OIC).[113] This alliance tends to include broader issues such as Islamophobia and capacity building rather than just trade, so there is potential for members to select partnerships that work best for them. However, Saudi relations with most members of the OIC are immediately disadvantaged because many members are 'small states', such as Malaysia, which don't cooperate exclusively with Islamic states but all states.[114] Therefore, relations are necessarily rooted in upgrading and helping poor Muslim communities to develop. This might be, in the case of Saudi Arabia, supporting tourism to Malaysia where families feel 'at home' due to the same Islamic way of life, as well as promoting more trade and investment. Saudi aid and support helps countries such as Malaysia to afford more imports and so it is in its interest to develop this relationship through whichever means are most appropriate. The long-term benefits of growing the internal markets of friendly states can only be a good thing and will eventually lead to a point where Saudi Arabia 'gives and takes' more to ensure it keeps its growing customer base.[115] There is also potential for Saudi Arabia to extend counterterrorism training to Malaysia, which has experience of guerrilla warfare but requires preparation to counter the front line of violent extremism in South East Asia. This, along with the traditional leadership qualities of Saudi Arabia, puts it in a dominant position vis-à-vis other OIC members in South East Asia.

Saudi aid has been the highest in the world per capita, at $49 billion over the past three decades.[116] There are no apparent catches to its aid; the only stipulation is that recipient states are friendly states that are undergoing a crisis of some kind, making them deserving of cash or material aid.[117] This was the case with Indonesia, which Saudi Arabia pledged $30 million to following the Asian tsunami in 2004.[118] The SFD has also invested in Africa and Asia, mainly in long-term projects across developing states. The Islamic Development Bank (IDB), of which Saudi Arabia is just one shareholder, takes a similar view but also supports Muslim minorities in non-Muslim states, again mainly in Africa and Asia.[119]

Pakistan represents an aid anomaly which incorporates a very strong bilateral strategic relationship and an important defence thread of Saudi foreign policy. There is the possibility that Saudi interests underwrote up to 60 per cent of the Pakistan nuclear programme as well as some defence (e.g. missile) purchases from the 1970s on the understanding that Pakistan would provide a nuclear deterrent for Saudi Arabia.[120] At minimum, Saudi–Pakistan relations have extended to include a bilateral security umbrella, starting with Pakistani Air Force pilots flying RSAF Lightnings to repulse a South Yemeni incursion across the Kingdom's border in 1969.[121] Up to 15,000 Pakistani troops were stationed in the Kingdom up until the 1980s and cooperation continues to this day. Saudi Arabia discounts and defers payment for oil exports to Pakistan, but this is conditional upon Pakistan implementing bilateral trade agreements in return. During periods of crisis, such as the immediate post-9/11 environment when Saudi Arabia wanted Pakistan to cooperate with the US administration, Saudi Arabia provided Pakistan's daily oil allocation (about 200,000 barrels) free of charge.[122] This reflected the fact that Pakistan is a major oil customer, importing $2 billion of oil each year. Pakistan also supplies the Kingdom with one million expatriate workers.[123] However, instead of sovereign loans which Saudi Arabia extends to other major oil customers, Riyadh generally prefers to focus on building bilateral relations with Pakistan through a joint donor framework. Pakistan remains a major potential market, one in which the Saudi Al-Tuwairqi Group acquired a 75 per cent stake in Pakistan Steel Mills Corporation in 2006.[124] Therefore Saudi Arabia maintains a close bilateral relationship with Pakistan based on a number of important strands in addition to the more common aid transfers, which have included a $573 million pledge for reconstruction following the October 2005 earthquake.[125] The strength of the relationship could therefore extend to giving Saudi Arabia an option to buy a small nuclear arsenal off the shelf should it choose to.[126] In a period dominated by Saudi–Iranian rivalry in global energy markets, (nuclear) antagonism and competing influence in the Levant, such a relationship becomes highly sensitive to Saudi Arabia. This is particularly the case as Saudi Arabia fears the so-called 'Shi'i Triangle' established between Iran, Iraq and Pakistan under President Zardari.[127] Even if such allegations prove to be baseless, it still diminishes Pakistani standing and facilitates Saudi leadership of a Sunni bloc to counter another metamorphosis of the Iranian threat.

The Global Relations of Saudi Arabia

This section examines the seemingly disparate themes of Saudi foreign policy post-9/11, from Saudi dissatisfaction with the USA over its unwillingness to intervene during the second intifada to 9/11 itself and the popular, as well as limited political, backlash against the Saudi regime. The combination of a string of contentions, combined with economic factors such as a high oil price, has forced the Saudi regime to become more pragmatic and persuasive. This section outlines the circumstances under which Saudi Arabia has been able to rebuild its relations with the USA only to see them crumble due to their widely divergent national interests during the Arab Uprisings. A clear pattern emerges which captures the number and nature of the foreign policy contentions and of foreign policy doctrine itself, which is identified as being incompatible. For Saudi 'second-tier' relations, i.e. those below its still predominant relationship with the USA, economic factors are clearly leading Saudi thought towards bilateral consolidation and institutionalization, but again with regionalization as a clear solution to incompatibilities concerning the development of its defence systems. Strategic relations with emerging states in Asia, and with particular reference to China, are found to suffer from China's simultaneous relations with members of the 'resistance axis', albeit on much more preferential terms of non-aligned principles through its 'Five Principles of Peaceful Coexistence'. Therefore Saudi foreign policy towards international actors is often a function of their own policies towards regional competitors and adversaries.

Saudi–US Relations Post-9/11

On 27 August 2001, a message was communicated by Prince Bandar to Condoleezza Rice, then a national security advisor, to express Saudi dismay at President Bush's unwillingness to intervene in renewed fighting between the Israelis and Palestinians. It also expressed Saudi Arabia's willingness to disaggregate itself publicly from US foreign policy with the underlying potential for a new oil embargo or reduced funding for US pet projects.[128] The latter may have included a halt to underwriting costs associated with US military engagement in the Middle East or cutting back on new US defence deals. The US president responded by proposing a high-level meeting, to take place on 13 September 2001. In the intervening period, 9/11 highlighted the sometimes paradoxical and incendiary nature of US–Saudi bilateral relations, particularly with regard to US support for Israel and US military bases on Saudi territory.[129] It would come to dominate the international relations of almost every state, but particularly those in the West and Islamic world, and those who had suffered, or were about to suffer, from terrorism. As an immediate gesture, Saudi Arabia supplied an additional 500,000 barrels of oil a day to the USA to help stabilize the economy and allowed the use of Saudi bases for US intelligence-gathering for the war in Afghanistan.[130]

Nevertheless, there was uncharacteristic pressure on Saudi Arabia from US media interested in drawing lines between the Al-Sa'ud and Islamist terror networks such as al-Qaeda. Crown Prince Abdullah, in an interview with *Time* magazine, expressed his dismay at the negative stories, asking: 'How can a relationship that has been strong and solid for over six decades be questioned like this? ... There is some resentment about the relationship and of the Kingdom that I frankly don't understand.'[131] This confusion reflected the mixed signals sent to the Kingdom due to the internal differences between the stance taken by Congress (and in particular the US Congressional report on terrorism financing) and that taken by the White House. Whilst relations at governmental level remained relatively amicable and accommodating, this did not reflect the increasing gulf between the two societies, and the 'emerging fundamentalism' Prince Sa'ud Al-Faisal observed in the USA in the lead up to the Iraq War.[132]

The subsequent Global War on Terror (GWOT) would come to dominate US relations with most other states, becoming a new international paradigm reflected in politics, diplomacy, commerce[133] and oil,[134] as well as driving new conflicts in Afghanistan and Iraq. The change in US energy policy was of particular and immediate concern to Saudi Arabia since the Kingdom relies on the long-term viability of large and stable markets such as the USA. Reducing US demand for Middle East oil would not only reduce Saudi Arabia's global market share and primary position in the US market from 2002,[135] but also put at risk the close political relationship which has been fundamental to Saudi influence and, to some extent, security in the West. Surprisingly, considering the political climate, Middle East oil producers generally invested $18 billion to $25 billion per year during the 2000s in a mix of US securities, banking products, and in US corporations.[136] There were no wholesale withdrawals and reinvestment of Saudi funds as might have been predicted, since a portfolio approach was already in effect and dictating a broad investment strategy. Although investments have tended to mirror Saudi international relations, there is no overt causal relationship because Saudi wealth is in the hands of private investors which, although they tend to be members of the royal family, invest according to the terms of the deal and with no stated political agenda.

Ironically, the political shock of 9/11 may have only temporarily pre-empted an oil shock which would have had a similarly massive impact on Saudi–US relations. There is an argument which puts a question mark over the actual amount held in the oil reserves of Saudi Arabia and other OPEC members, partly due to 'data transparency' which covers a multitude of reserve issues.[137] Furthermore, Saudi Aramco and the Saudi Petroleum Ministry claimed in 2004 that installing extra capacity would lead to production gains, claims that have not been borne out in Saudi oil exports to the OECD states.[138] In December 2004 Saudi Aramco brought on stream another 800,000 b/d from the Qatif and Abu Safah fields in the Eastern province.[139] Other major projects are the Abu Hadriyah, Fadhili and Khursaniyah (AFK) onshore oil fields which will add another 500,000 b/d.[140] The Khurais field near Riyadh will add another 1.2 million b/d.[141] All this goes some way to alleviating fears about Saudi Arabia's ability to meet rising oil demand, although much of the new production is from ageing fields at a time when there is increasing competition from states such as Brazil. Petrobas, for example, is establishing itself at the cutting edge of offshore exploration, with significant new finds such as Tupi in 2006.[142] In addition, a senior Saudi government oil executive stated in 2007 that Saudi crude oil reserves may have been overstated by as much as 300 billion barrels or 40 per cent of its total reserves.[143] If true, this figure could challenge Saudi pre-eminence in OPEC and, to a lesser extent, in the GCC. It could give Iran confidence in the international oil market and unhinge the hitherto close alliance between the world's largest oil producer and its main customers.

For Saudi Arabia, 9/11 meant a very public persecution and potential prosecution of high-profile Saudis ranging from the so-called 'trillion dollar lawsuit' brought by the families of 9/11 victims to anti-Saudi political campaigns from presidential contenders such as John Kerry.[144] However, the US response could have been more extreme had the suggestions in the briefing given by Laurent Murawiec of the government-funded RAND think tank to the Defence Policy Board been more widely accepted; Murawiec suggested the targeting of Saudi oil resources, financial assets and holy places in response to 9/11.[145] Political measures were taken against Saudi citizens, such as tighter visa restrictions imposed by the Department of Homeland Security, often without specified reasons, which contributed to an 80 per cent drop in Saudi students entering the USA after 9/11.[146] As a counterterrorist measure, it reduced Saudi exposure to post-9/11 US society, not only removing expatriate communities that form vested political interests but also cultural exchange and grass roots dialogue. There was also intense financial scrutiny of both banks and transactions involving, primarily, Saudi charities. This included Riggs Bank, used by the Saudi Arabian embassy in Washington, and the New York branch of Arab Bank, which was the subject of other lawsuits. There were also instances of Saudis with the 'wrong' name having their assets frozen in the USA, and although there was not a massive financial exodus out of the country, Saudi–US banking relationships were certainly more strained.[147] The official charity of the Saudi royal family, Al-Haramain, responsible for the distribution of up to $50 million a year, was pressured and forced to close.[148] Before 9/11 Saudi aid had been free from scrutiny, but after 9/11 there was much more international pressure (mainly from the USA) to curb charitable donations that could end up with militant groups. This 'pressure of evaluation' has served to reign in funding, with much of the financial apparatus dismantled and new regulations introduced by 2004.[149] The USA continued to apply wider pressure on Saudi Arabia into 2003 with an explicit agenda called the Middle East Partnership Initiative (MEPI) which included economic reform, political reform towards democracy, education reform and women's rights.[150] Along with the Middle East Free Trade Initiative, it was subsumed into the Greater

Middle East Initiative (GMEI) in 2004.[151] Apart from mainly being a rehash of existing policies, the momentum to push the agenda came not from regional specialists at the State Department but from US policy-makers, and remained unrealistic due to the conflict between idealism and realism in dealing with existing allies that are undemocratic.[152] Mistakenly, the GMEI was also expected to be the Helsinki Process of the south, mirroring the way the Helsinki Process helped get Warsaw Pact states security based on a political and economic reform agenda.[153]

Such policy failures have meant that bilateral pressure had to be kept up in the Middle East especially during the Arab Uprisings, with the exception of Saudi Arabia.[154] However, the extent to which US concerns about domestic threats in Saudi Arabia had been addressed was outlined in July 2004 when Saudi Arabia was held to be compliant with anti-money laundering standards from the Financial Action Task Force within the OECD.[155] Even after the meeting and high-level 'strategic dialogue' launched by the then Crown Prince Abdullah and President Bush, the USA has continued to accuse Riyadh of its 'unwillingness' to tackle terrorist financing.[156] But Riyadh continues to point to the fact that US intelligence about financial transfers and Saudi support for *madrasahs* in Pakistan is classified, and questions how Saudi Arabia can fight terrorism without access to that intelligence.[157] US pressure and criticism after 9/11 has led to a number of Saudi counterterrorist initiatives, from Prince Sa'ud attending the second Royal United Services Institute (RUSI) conference on transnational terrorism to King Abdullah heading east to put terrorism on the foreign policy agenda and get allies to sign the Riyadh Declaration. This agreement calls for an international anti-terrorism centre which would help make counterterrorism efforts international. Progress in tackling the unintended financing of terrorist cells through charity was underpinned by persuading Saudis to give more to local (Saudi) causes where financial flows could be more easily monitored and controlled.[158] A number of steps were also taken by the government to clamp down on radical clerics in mosques and institute a re-education programme for others. This has been vital, since a large part of Saudi aid is channelled through mosques or clergy, which institutions or individuals therefore played a major role in aid money being diverted to terrorist organizations.

Saudi frustration with US foreign policy started in 2002 with the Arab Peace Initiative[159] after Crown Prince Abdullah had spent significant political capital trying to persuade President Bush to take a more balanced position on Israel and Palestine. As it was seen to detract from the main concerns of the USA post-9/11, the invitation was not taken up by the USA, but it was nevertheless generally welcomed even in parts of the Israeli political establishment precisely because it had come from Saudi Arabia.[160] The MEPP is therefore no longer likely to be a critical element in US–Saudi relations in future. The initiative was not a total loss though and did lead to some agreement on measures to address the Israel–Palestinian conflict from both Saudi Arabia and the USA. The negative response was from Saudi citizens whose largely ineffective boycott of American goods did damage the short-term profitability of a number of US-based companies including Proctor and Gamble.[161]

The Political Imperative for Rapprochement

After the US-led invasion of Iraq, the USA needed Saudi Arabia's relationship with Hamas to at least stabilize the Israeli–Palestinian conflict as another theatre of conflict opened up. At the beginning of the Iraq War, the Saudi oil minister, Ali Naimi, reiterated to the USA and the international markets that oil would not be used as a weapon and emphasized that there would be enough oil to deliver no matter what happened in the war.[162] This was a sentiment that echoed Sa'ud Al-Faisal's position before the war had begun.[163] This was despite the fact that Saudi Arabia was against the invasion, along with many other states in the Middle East.[164] The commitment to keeping oil flowing throughout the war was confirmed again by Adel Jubeir after the meeting between President Bush and Crown Prince Abdullah at Crawford on 25 April 2005.[165] The Iraq War did impact the Saudi economy negatively, through uncertainty. It delayed reforms and legislation and reduced foreign and domestic investments at a time when the economy was gearing up for a more outward-looking era.

Investments have been made; $1 billion out of a total of $2.6 billion in 2002, but the rate was much lower than expected.[166]

The accommodation of Saudi foreign policy to assure the USA that it would continue to pump in difficult conditions reflected its own fear of falling energy demand in the same way that the US fears security of energy supply. It is just as vital to Saudi interests that consumers remain dependent on oil, at least until its contribution to GDP and exports drops further. 'The petroleum sector accounts for roughly 80 per cent of budget revenues, 45 per cent of GDP, and 90 per cent of export earnings', so any downturn in oil demand would have significant consequences for the Saudi economy.[167] On the other hand, on the back of high oil prices, an extra month's salary was paid to Saudis in 2002.[168] Saudi GDP rose by 6.5 per cent in real terms in 2005 leading to the biggest ever budget surplus, which was channelled back into paying off domestic debt, since many Saudis question why the country was amassing such surpluses while still being in debt.[169]

The final temporary measure of rapprochement between Saudi Arabia and the USA wasn't economic but followed the political fallout from the 2003 terror attacks in Riyadh. The Saudis started to cooperate more with the FBI although this only exacerbated anti-US feelings and boosted the cause of the *jihadis* in their recruitment of would-be bombers. Having managed to destroy the home-grown militant campaign, and instituted a late but effective campaign against terrorist financing and religious extremism, Saudi Arabia was able to show the USA and the wider world that it was addressing the issue of terrorism. On 16 October 2005, the former ambassador to the United States, Prince Bandar Bin Sultan Bin Abdelaziz, was appointed as the inaugural head (with ministerial rank) of the Saudi National Security Council.[170] Bringing his experience of international diplomacy and extensive contacts with him, it was an indication to the USA of how serious the Kingdom was about tackling violent extremism.[171] It also meant that King Abdullah could personally take charge of Saudi foreign policy, especially Saudi–US relations, with support from his long-serving and trusted Foreign Minister Prince Sa'ud Al-Faisal.[172]

The Incompatibility of National Interests and International Alliances

It was not just economic policy but the way the GWOT was implemented by the USA that meant it had 'lost the moral high ground' after 9/11. Specifically, Prince Turki Al-Faisal blamed the US administration for its 'negligence, ignorance and arrogance' which served to facilitate the revision of the special US–Saudi relationship into a more normalized relationship.[173] Such arrogance is perceived to be inherent in Saudi fears that the USA will use Saudi Arabia as a 'spearhead of the European-American-Israeli aggression against Iran'.[174] To drive home the consequences of a more normalized relationship, Prince Sa'ud suggested that the USA should no longer be a formal guarantor of Gulf security but that it should be handled by the UN Security Council.[175] By making this suggestion public, Saudi Arabia was instantly downgrading the role of the USA in regional affairs. This has major implications for USA action in the region in future. Previously, in actions against Saddam Hussein for instance, the Clinton administration had relied on King Fahd's dependence on the USA for Saudi security. Saudi willingness to accommodate US interests in the Kingdom, such as the use of Saudi military bases, was also linked to the USA working to bring Syria into the Middle East Peace Process.[176]

Now these Saudi policies have changed based on US policy initiatives or lack thereof, it means that the USA should be seen to be a non-aligned guarantor of the multilateral structures and treaties in place.[177] During the Arab Uprisings, US support for democratization and its unwillingness to take direct action again the growing threat from Iran, including its ability to fuel sectarian divides and instability in states such as Bahrain, Iraq, Lebanon and Yemen, have made the US alliance less relevant to the Saudis.[178] By going it alone, Saudi Arabia could be put in the driving seat of any new security architecture because it can afford to be more independent and innovative in the foreign policies it needs to pursue to create greater stability. This is still likely to be conceptualized in a wider GCC which may bring Yemen in from the cold but certainly Shi'i Iran and Iraq.

Saudi Arabia and the USA have continued to disagree over many US foreign policies concerning the Middle East, which has contributed to diverging foreign policy trajectories. Areas of contention have included the Israel–Palestine conflict, comprising the second intifada and potentially the US non-recognition of a new Palestinian state,[179] Afghanistan in the early stages of the conflict,[180] Iraq,[181] the lack of US support for President Mubarak at the beginning of the Arab Uprisings[182] and how best to tackle the perceived Iranian nuclear threat.[183] Greater tensions are likely to become apparent between Saudi Arabia and the USA as well as European powers due to the speed with which they have recognized and supported rebel uprisings in the Middle East. This is particularly damaging since it not only creates greater instability but harks back to the colonial era of recognition and representation of minority religious and ethnic groups in the security forces and governments across the region. Strong divergence and irritants are also visible in Saudi–Russian relations which range from Chechnya to post-9/11 Russian complaints about violent Islamist groups which prohibit either side from advancing towards an exclusive partnership. Although relations with Russia were buoyed by Crown Prince Abdullah's visit to Moscow in 2003, higher oil prices and strains with the USA (and therefore avenues for joint cooperation with Russia in areas of mutual interest), Saudi Arabia is very anxious about Russia's involvement in Iran's nuclear energy programme and its treatment of Muslims in Chechnya, as well as its status as a military supplier to Hamas. Russia does not therefore represent an obvious alternative for Saudi Arabia to balance with against the USA during the Arab Uprisings and accounts for its choice of the GCC to play a leading role in the future orientation of its foreign policy.

The USA has trained and armed SANG (for example with anti-tank weaponry) over a 30-year period and with combat experience in oil fields threatened by civil disturbances in 1988 and Saudi borders in 1990,[184] against Iraqi mechanized forces at Khafji in 1991 and brigade level operations to secure the Hajj each year.[185] The announcement of a $20 billion arms package which included the Boeing Company's new satellite-guided smart bomb was also an indication that the Bush administration was comfortable with a strategic relationship with Saudi Arabia.[186] To advance the US–Saudi relationship, maintain a strong alliance against Iran and secure up to 75,000 jobs, the USA announced a $60 billion arms deal with Saudi Arabia in 2010.[187] Although complex, subject to change and implemented over up to a decade, the deal is the largest arms sale deal ever.[188] Whilst Saudi Arabia and the USA will continue to have shared strategic energy and security interests, some argue that any Saudi threat to turn away from its alliance with the USA is simply 'blustering'.[189] However, there is evidence that Saudi Arabia will soon have more options to form new political alliances, particularly once the EU adopts a more active foreign policy system following the launch of its External Action Service provided for by the Lisbon Treaty. There is also potential to develop a new alliance with the major energy consumers in Asia, especially China,[190] which overtook the USA as the world's largest energy consumer in 2009.[191] It is in the interests of both the USA and Saudi Arabia to contain and deter Iran, which has had ample opportunity to take advantage of instabilities in the Sunni monarchies in the GCC and beyond.[192] This is the rubric around which post-9/11 US–Saudi relations have been conducted.

Saudi–US relations have been hampered first and foremost by Saudi Arabia's failure to toe the line where the GWOT is concerned and especially in its not being able to support the use of Saudi military bases for US action in Iraq. Many in the Saudi establishment, including Abdulrahman Al-Zamil, a member of the Majlis Al-Shura and former deputy commerce minister, said that the USA and UK were pursuing 'imperialism' with regard to any invasion of Iraq.[193] Prince Alwaleed asked rhetorically that since '... the US had imposed its will on Saddam, why should it not impose its will on Sharon'.[194] Crown Prince Abdullah spoke about a united Arab stance against 'illegitimate' foreign aggression regarding Iraq, but may have been persuaded for the cause if there had been a UN resolution or a WMD 'smoking gun'.[195] The fundamentals of Saudi–US relations are to a large extent housed in the vehicles of US foreign policies concerning Israel, the MEPP, Iraq and Iran, through which they can advance through multilateralism. Oil is literally the lubricant in the relationship as the states shift down gears towards what could potentially become a neutral position in a post-oil era.

Saudi–European Relations Post-9/11

When considering Saudi Arabian bilateral relations with the major European powers, such as the UK, France and Germany, it is important to differentiate these relationships from the EU–GCC relationship which was established through a Cooperation Agreement in 1988. Although this is aimed at strengthening stability and facilitating political and economic relations, and broadening cooperation in energy, industry, trade and services, agriculture, fisheries, investment, science, technology and the environment, it does not reflect the critical dimensions of Saudi foreign relations. These tend to be reflected in bilateral relations on the basis of oil, security and defence, or the MEPP.[196] Furthermore, EU–GCC relations still lack institutionalization, although an annual Joint Council/Ministerial Meeting between the EU and GCC foreign ministers as well as between senior officials at a Joint Cooperation Committee are in the pipeline.[197] Regular contact at the foreign ministerial level and close consultation would inevitably lead to common foreign policy statements regarding regional and international issues.

The main barrier to EU engagement with Saudi Arabia and the GCC is constituted by a combination of factors, including: the good bilateral relations which many of the core EU states have with Saudi Arabia; the particularly high costs should the EU take a harder, more evenhanded and consistent approach with the Saudis and other GCC states (although at the moment the EU only imports 16 per cent of its oil from the Middle East and only 6 per cent or $13 billion from Saudi Arabia[198]); and the EU's lack of any significant capacity to change the political status quo in the GCC without the prior backing of and close coordination with the USA.[199] The EU–GCC FTA is expected to be signed once disagreements over human rights issues have been resolved.[200] Importantly, it could help redress the increasing trade disparities between Europe and Asia where Saudi Arabia exports increasing amounts of its oil.

Growing Bilateral 'Strategic Relationships'

The oil-based development boom in Saudi Arabia has led both the USA and European companies (led by the UK, Italy, Finland and Germany) to invest $1.2 billion and $7.8 billion respectively as of 1998, mainly in joint ventures with an accompanying small but significant expatriate labour force.[201] For EU member states such as the UK, Saudi Arabia has a high profile in terms of its strategic priorities worldwide, including conflict prevention (Iraq, MEPP, Iran, Sudan, Somalia, Syria and Lebanon), climate change, human rights and energy security.[202] Saudi Arabia is a donor, regional leader and political ally of the UK, but it is never engaged at the GCC level by the UK. Because most Muslims in the world pass through Saudi Arabia at some stage in their life, during the Hajj or the Umra, that relationship is of great importance to UK counterterrorism operations. Indeed, counterterrorism after 9/11, particularly with regard to Yemen and al-Qaeda in the Arabian Peninsula (AQAP), has been a major pillar of UK foreign policy and cooperation with Saudi Arabia has been vital to its national interests.[203] The strength and depth of UK–Saudi counterterrorism cooperation is truly extraordinary and in large part this has been attributed to Prince Mohammed bin Nayef, the Counterterrorism Minister.[204] The relationship has been so strong and vital that a UK Serious Fraud Office (SFO) investigation into BAE Systems (the UK defence industry's largest supplier), amid allegations of bribery and corruption in the Al-Yamamah contract, was dropped due to concerns over UK national security expressed by then prime minister Tony Blair.[205] The anger caused by opening up the Swiss bank accounts of the Saudi royal family would have caused it to respond in such a strong way that it has been compared to the row over 'The Death of a Princess'[206] and the huge damage that was done to British economic interests then.[207]

It should be noted that the scale of the Al-Yamamah contract meant that there was also a vital UK jobs dimension to it. British defence-related exports to Saudi Arabia have been largely based on the rolling Al-Yamamah contract which was worth £20 billion when it was signed in 1985.[208] In 1993, 'al-Yamamah II' was signed and at a total cost of £35 billion, became the world's largest oil-for-arms programme, worth 30,000 jobs to the British economy and contributing to a positive balance of trade with the Middle East.[209] It also helped the UK become the third-largest exporter to Saudi Arabia in 1994 after the USA and Japan.[210] The crash in oil revenues in 1997 led to a scaling-back of new Saudi arms purchases although it would continue to benefit from past transactions. However, even without any additional investments in arms, Saudi defence spending was expected to remain at $15 billion per year until 2000 just to maintain and operate the military.[211] This figure monetizes the extent to which Saudi Arabia remains bound into relations with Western governments and is happy to be so; otherwise such long-running contracts could be exchanged for shorter, more tactical ones.

The oil barter agreement that exists in the Al-Yamamah agreement between BAE Systems and Saudi Arabia includes BP and Royal Dutch/Shell and has generated revenues of over $40 billion.[212] BAE has delivered 120 Tornadoes, 90 Hawk jet trainers and 50 PC-9 aircraft to the Saudi military.[213] The programme has been rolling for almost 20 years, and has now moved into the next project phase, called As-Salaam. Although it is 'not the be all and end all' of UK trade with Saudi Arabia as there is a 'big push to other sectors', most notably the large opportunities in education and health and for UK Small and Medium Enterprises (SME) in project management, professional services and design, it nevertheless remains very important.[214] Apart from investments in the non-oil sectors, there are further opportunities to increase bilateral ties through offering official secondments from the EU to ministries and new agencies in Saudi Arabia.[215] Advisors are currently recruited directly to work discreetly in Saudi ministries but there could be practitioner assistance rather than just consultancy.[216] Through this process the EU could not only do more to professionalize the Saudi civil service but develop practices similar to their own, which may lead the Saudi administration to take on a similar mindset in policy-making.

The As-Salaam phase involves a 72 Eurofighter Typhoon contract which is worth £20 billion to BAE Systems, but it is a complex and long-term contract which will require expansion across four different production lines in Germany, Italy, Spain and the UK.[217] The difference between a Typhoon contract with the UK as opposed to a parallel Rafale contract with France comes down to in-Kingdom presence for technical support, training and maintenance.[218] In-Kingdom presence is still a facet of United Kingdom Trade and Investment's (UKTI) message to encourage, among other things, technology transfer and skills transfer to create jobs for Saudis.[219] In 2003, the Saudi–UK relationship had hit a low point. Cabinet ministers in the British government were pressing Riyadh for the release of six British businessmen who had been arrested in connection with a car-bombing campaign.[220] Irritation was reflected when Saudi Ministers accompanying a trade and parliamentary mission to the UK were refused meetings with their British counterparts. Sanctions were also considered against Saudi Arabia, at a time when BA flights stopped on commercial grounds, Saudi dissidents were allowed to continue their activities against the Saudi monarchy from the UK, and Cherie Blair publicly lambasted the Kingdom for its poor image abroad.[221] Bilateral cooperation improved once a deal was worked out for the UK businessmen and on the security side after the attacks in Riyadh.[222] It is this space for effective negotiation that remains a fundamental difference between the foreign relations of Saudi Arabia and Iran. Intense diplomatic activity paid very quick dividends: BA later reinstated its flights to the Kingdom, which is a very important strand in the relationship.[223] HSBC also announced it was to set up an investment bank in Saudi Arabia in early 2005 and there were possibilities for BP and Saudi Aramco to become partners in a new joint venture in Yanbu.[224] The UK government took the opportunity to use its presidency of the EU to improve its relations with Saudi Arabia through supporting its accession to the WTO in 2005.[225]

There was also short-term resistance to UK climate change policies. However, there was a gradual realization in Saudi Arabia that climate change policies in the UK and elsewhere were actually in the interests of Saudi Arabia since they aimed at using oil in a more intelligent and sustainable way over the long term.[226] It could be argued therefore that the UK has been better able to conceptualize its foreign policies in a way which is conducive to the Saudi national interest, unlike the USA. This acceptance of climate change politics is helped by the fact that the UK is a smaller oil market and hence its policies in this area do not impact Saudi Arabia as much as if the equivalent policies were adopted by the USA. Saudi attitudes are also rooted in the realization that oil was is in its third decade of relative decline by the 1990s compared to other forms of energy, whilst the West sought diversification of its energy supplies.[227] A relatively early adoption of climate change policies therefore gave Saudi Arabia time to lead the transitional shift to renewable energy, particularly solar energy, before the globally green economy was finally made explicit by the G20 in April 2009.[228]

At the same time a much more important and strategic dialogue about investment has taken place at the highest levels, particularly after the global recession started to bite.[229] Saudi Arabia had sought to link a UK-led IMF bail out with IMF reform, and yet the G20 summit in April 2009 failed to address such reform. Without much else to tempt Saudi investment into the developed and relatively saturated economies of the West, further funding is unlikely. This represented a missed opportunity to draw Saudi Arabia into the organizations of the global economic regimes dominated by developed states, and therefore this distance is likely to endure. This was the case when the Gulf SWFs accounted for a third of all emergency funding that European governments put in place during the financial crisis in 2008, and yet the restrictions imposed after the cash injection targeted the very same Gulf donors.[230] Global governance is therefore a key issue for Saudi Arabia as it tries to align its existing economic clout more closely with political clout. It is through such realignment, across more institutions than just the G20, that some regional security issues could be resolved, leading to greater regional economic integration and a stronger global economy.[231]

France has had close relations with Saudi Arabia, illustrated by the French Groupe d'Intervention de la Gendarmerie Nationale (GIGN) security force retaking the Grand Mosque after it was seized by 500 dissidents in 1979.[232] Because part of the justification for the seizure was a mindless imitation of the West, it had a bearing on which security forces the Saudi state should rely on. Of Western states, France was seen to be the most neutral and capable of dealing with the new threat of terrorism on Saudi soil, as well as less closely linked to the sources of contention. France is the second largest trade partner with Saudi Arabia amongst European states, after Germany.[233] French exports to Saudi Arabia reached SR 8 billion, whilst Saudi exports to France reached SR 15.24 billion in 2008, based largely on oil exports.[234] The trading relationship experienced a five-fold increase between 2000 and 2008 based largely on greater investments in energy and infrastructure. The largest French investment in the Kingdom is the 400,000 b/d Jubail oil refinery, which is a joint venture between Saudi Aramco and Total and will have cost more than $12 billion once it comes online in 2013.[235]

Crown Prince Abdullah visited President Chirac in Paris in mid-April 2005 on his way to meet with President Bush, and discussed defence cooperation, the Iranian nuclear programme, Iraq, the Hamas victory in Gaza and tensions between Lebanon and Syria.[236] The two leaders reached an agreement on a range of economic and technical issues but did not commit to the Rafale contract, possible contracts with Alstom Transport, or TGV for a high-speed rail network (linking Riyadh with the north) as they were still under consideration by the Saudi Ministry of Interior.[237] However, in November 2009, EADS won its first contract to supply Saudi Arabian Airlines with 58 passenger aircraft and a further five-year contract in July 2009 to enhance Saudi border security which had particularly focused on its border with Iraq.[238] European states such as France have therefore benefited from the trickle-down effects of instability on the Kingdom's doorstep. FREMM multi-mission frigates are also under discussion, but France hasn't supplied any Rafale or other fighters since the late 1990s, although it supplied SANG with 80 French self-propelled artillery systems in 2008.[239] The delay in other contracts may be due to political pressure exerted on behalf of the USA in 2003 for the French to accept war with Iraq, such as freezing an $800 million tank contract.[240] Both France and the UK have close historical, political and defence ties to the Kingdom, and tend to flow more when US deals are constrained by the pro-Israeli lobby and congressional politics. Saudi Arabia's own interests are in balancing relations in favour of other major military powers in Europe. The rolling Al-Yamamah contract has also favoured the UK by tying Saudi Arabia into long-term arms purchases.

In 2006, President Chirac visited Riyadh with most of his ministerial team and top business delegates. Meetings covered a range of topics including terrorism, science and technology, WTO accession and hopes that the EU–GCC dialogue would facilitate trade. This was especially important following a breakdown in the MEPP and the increasing acknowledgement by EU members that the Arab world represented their local neighbourhood as defined by the Euro-Mediterranean Partnership (EMP). The December 2003 European Council paper on strengthening EU relations with the Arab World called for increased bilateral activity which many of its member states, including France, have pushed ever since.[241] In recognition of the increasingly cordial relations between King Abdullah and President Chirac, the latter was afforded the opportunity to become the first foreign leader to address the Majlis Al-Shura. Nicolas Sarkozy got off to a good start in Franco-Saudi relations too following the start of his presidency in 2007, focusing French attention on the Middle East region as one of his four strategic foreign policy priorities based largely on energy considerations and France being able to punch above its weight in the region.[242]

Germany is the Kingdom's largest trading partner in the EU, and third worldwide after the USA and China.[243] Two hundred and twenty German companies are active in the Kingdom and there were approximately 120 joint ventures totalling $3.5 billion, around two-thirds of which are partnerships with Saudi investors.[244] Although German investment throughout the 1990s and early 2000s was level at around SR 1 billion ($266m), it exploded by 1200 per cent in 2006 accompanied by record high exports of $5.4 billion.[245] There are, therefore, strong conventional ties that bind the states together. However, Germany does not import as much oil from Saudi Arabia as many other states (it is more dependent on Russia) and as the Kingdom's economy booms, a trade surplus favouring Germany is likely, although this is somewhat dependent on the oil price. At the time of writing, Germany is debating whether it should sell 200 tanks to the Saudis, a subject which caused concern amongst many of its parliamentarians.[246] Since the tanks can be used for internal and external security operations, the case shows the paradox of different foreign policies in a polarized regional environment.

Saudi Arabia's 'Look East' Policy

A note of caution about Saudi Arabia's 'Look East' policy should be included here before its relations are conceptualized through this policy. All states, whether classified as hegemons or small states, tend to 'look everywhere' since opportunities must first be identified before durable relationships can be established. In the case of isolated states or those which, for various reasons, have been bypassed by globalization, they must also first 'go outside' as China did in the early 2000s with Xiang Zemin's *'zuo chuqu'* policy.[247] Only in areas or with states that represent strategic significance can states adopt a specific policy which simply prioritizes that relationship but nevertheless does not usually close the door on alternatives. China's 'Look Africa' policy and India's 'Look East' policy directed towards South East Asia during the 1990s reflected a content change in their respective relationships in response to the opportunities on offer, but none of these policies could be said to be fixed over the long term.

Saudi Arabia's economic relationship with Japan is indicative of the need for caution when considering its 'Look East' policies. The Arabian Oil Company (AOC) concession highlights the fact that Japanese investment in areas such as infrastructure is critical in keeping bilateral relations on track. In response to the Saudis proposing a $2 billion Japanese investment in a railway project that linked phosphate mines in the north to the city of Jubail, Japan has chosen a new independent path which could have severe consequences for other relationships with Saudi Arabia.[248] Japan has chosen a new path of energy efficiency, i.e. buying oil on the international markets, over energy security, i.e. a strong relationship with key oil producers such as Saudi Arabia. This choice shows that there are developing irreconcilable differences between the massive investment that Saudi Arabia needs to develop areas such as infrastructure, and potential investors such as Japan which perceive this as an unwise investment choice. In the short term, Saudi Arabia's ability to bind in developed economies to the FDI opportunities on offer in its own economy is unlikely to create the same dependent relationship it has with Western defence companies.

The extent to which Saudi Arabia has been found to balance with a range of suppliers can be seen through cases when the USA has not fulfilled its role as exclusive supplier to Saudi Arabia. Saudi Arabia defied the Reagan administration in the USA which would not sell it the ballistic missiles it wanted to counter Iran during the Iran–Iraq War. Instead, Saudi turned to China, which sold Riyadh 36 CSS-2 Intermediate (3000km) Range Ballistic Missiles (IRBM) that were nuclear-capable, but heavily modified to carry only conventional payloads.[249] This deal was arranged between 1986 and 1988 by Prince Bandar Bin Sultan Bin Abdelaziz, then ambassador to Washington and now head of the NSC, signifying the start of much closer Sino-Saudi strategic relations.[250] The USA was rebuffed from inspecting them, and Riyadh chose instead to establish diplomatic relations with China in 1990. Chinese arms sales to the Kingdom have been limited, with the exception of a 2008 contract for China to provide one battalion of artillery pieces.[251] The Saudis deliberately sought to balance its close ties with the USA with the Chinese through increasing bilateral trade and cooperation. Part of that was the Chinese long-range missiles deal but it is also about China wanting to secure resources for itself. It's not just a function of Saudi Arabia; it's also a function of Chinese priorities. Arms sales to the Kingdom are limited for China in the same way that they are for Russia; Saudi Arabia is already tied into long-term US and European arms sale agreements.

Saudi Arabia has been able to consolidate its relationships with the rapidly growing economies and leading oil importers of Asia, notably China[252] and India,[253] in the same way as it had done with Japan and South Korea. King Abdullah's January 2006 royal tour of China, India, Malaysia and Pakistan all indicated potential for long-term economic partnerships.[254] The growth of relations between Saudi Arabia and China have raised anxiety in the USA, which sees China's view of geo-economics as similar to that of imperial Japan during the 1930s with regards to securing its energy needs.[255] Generally, though, although there have been problems related to China's anti-dumping protectionist policy, Saudi Arabia is getting the access it requires in the Chinese market. This makes Saudi Arabia another Chinese conduit for technology transfer from the West since Chinese WTO accession in 2001.[256] Bilateral trade increased from $290 million in 1990 to $40 billion in 2008,[257] but what bonds China and Saudi Arabia the most, both economically and diplomatically, is their combined search for refinery capacity, since most of the sweet crude that China could process is already accounted for by Western markets.[258] Saudi Arabia is therefore helping China source more risky and marginal resources in order to avoid confrontation with other international players.[259]

By 2009, Saudi Arabia exported more oil to China than it did to the USA. This is part of its dual strategy: to use China as a trickle-down oil hub for the Asian markets whilst reducing reliance on the USA. Sa'ud Al-Faisal stated the case for growing the relationship with China simply: 'with China there is less baggage, there are easier routes to mutual benefit'.[260] Saudi Arabia already exports 11.3 per cent of its total to China, a nearly three-fold increase since 2000[261] and since China's oil consumption is expected to grow from 3.5 million b/d in 2006 to 13.1 million b/d in 2030, the oil export-import relationship is only likely to grow stronger over the long term.[262] Such growth could be characterized by more exchanges, such as high-level visits between governments and exchanges of ideas on area-specific as well as global issues.[263] Chinese exports to Saudi Arabia include a $1.8 billion contract given in March 2009 to a Sino-Saudi consortium (which includes China Railway Construction) to build a high-speed rail link between the holy cities of Mecca and Medina.[264] China possesses the combined benefits of being an economic power with associated export and investment opportunities (without the associated human rights dialogue of the USA or EU); a stable and rising military power as a counterbalance to the USA during its perceived withdrawal from the Middle East; and has the long-term potential to supplant the USA as a local security guarantor. Chinese policy looks to remain pragmatic and cautious. Wen Jiabao, the Chinese Premier, toured the Gulf in January 2012, which has been linked with securing alternative oil supplies as well as establishing longer term ties with the region.[265] Deeper ties are also attractive to Saudi Arabia since a closer oil partnership, such as the deal with Sinopec to build a 400,000-barrel refinery in Saudi Arabia,[266] will help to underpin a $100 billion civil nuclear partnership to secure its energy needs and provide a solid foundation of nuclear expertise.[267] China is also forming strong alliances with Iran, Syria and Turkey, and possibly with Iraq, because they are neutral or anti-US regional powers, some with significant oil reserves. This serves to illustrate that China has her own way of dealing with unstable situations in the Gulf, in addition to bilateral diplomatic engagement with Saudi Arabia.[268] China's independence, flexibility to form alliances and lack of political baggage could spell trouble for Saudi Arabia if China continues to tighten its grip on energy supplies, in a similar vein to Russian behaviour over gas supplies to the Ukraine. By working through its regional allies in the Middle East, Africa and South America, it could have access and ownership (through mechanisms such as join ventures) to more reserves than Saudi Arabia.[269] This would again facilitate Saudi Arabia's demise in OPEC and internationally.

King Abdullah's state visit to New Delhi in 2005 was quickly followed by the Delhi Declaration, which provided for an economic partnership between Saudi Arabia and India, and the Riyadh Declaration, which provided for a 'strategic partnership' across all areas from energy to security.[270] The Riyadh Declaration in 2010 was a political agreement, but it is increased economic ties that are crucial in realizing the partnership because they are based on vested interests and the continuing prosperity of the other side.[271] The GCC is India's number one relationship, based on oil, trade and the expatriate community. Indo-Saudi trade increased three-fold over five years to 2010 and India is now the fourth largest trade partner of Saudi Arabia, with bilateral trade at $21 billion between 2009 and 2010.[272] Should an India–GCC FTA be realized, it would create opportunities in a number of areas including: '... food products, pharmaceuticals, machinery and transport equipment, ceramic products, apparels and clothing, cotton and woven fabrics, plastic and rubber products, essential oils, perfumery and cosmetics besides iron and steel articles ...'[273] The FTA issue nevertheless remains skewed in favour of the weight that the petrochemical industry carries in both states, notably India. India has engaged in 'joint ventures, project export, consultancy services, turn-key projects, deferred payment and soft loans ...' at a low level but which formed new economic relations between Saudi Arabia and other Gulf States with India since 2000.[274] The bilateral Saudi–India relationship is still important beyond oil, expatriate labour and trade, since it also encompasses a counterterrorism strand aimed at reducing Saudi exposure to Pakistani terror plots in India (notably the Mumbai bombings in 2008).

With a reduction in state subsidies, measures aimed at reducing unemployment and structural transformation (ranging from the state's capacity to provide electricity, water and health care services[275]), some autonomy and time have been bought by the Saudi government. However, there is little doubt that a deeper understanding of the domestic situation and a new Saudi social contract will be required in future. This will be at a point determined by the convergence between falling oil revenues, FDI continuing to fall below expectations, the government deficit increasing above sustainable levels, and the political demands made by the young in social and decision-making structures above the local level. Already the young have become more visible than government agencies during the Jeddah floods of 2011 because they are better organized.[276] By extending reforms more thoroughly, including limiting the role of government and making it more inclusive; facilitating structural change to speed up decision-making; reducing exposure to princes who have mishandled their portfolios; and consolidating gains to increase the standard of living for all, Saudi Arabia may be in a better position to avoid the kind of overt political disruptions seen elsewhere in the Middle East. It may also avoid the kind of potential reorientation of international alliances that are now considered possible in states such as Egypt.[277]

The Saudi policy of engagement in the MEPP illustrates the extent to which Saudi Arabia can influence various actors but only under a limited set of circumstances. This research shows that only when Saudi Arabia has the right combination of ideological influence, dependency and an absence of intervention in its sphere of influence from major powers can it then optimally leverage its foreign policies. At the point when economic factors and diplomatic engagement are ineffectual, Saudi Arabia has been quick to lobby the USA and NATO into supporting pre-emptive strikes against states that represent a direct threat to its national security. However, current trends show a reappraisal of this approach. The Arab Uprisings and potential threat from a 'Shi'i Triangle' that realigns Pakistan with Iran have served as a wake-up call to Saudi Arabia. Therefore, by working within the GCC and consolidating the institutionalization of the intergovernmental arrangement, Saudi Arabia will have access to more resources from more reliable allies to defend itself. The $100 billion cost to develop a Special Forces Command to unify the Kingdom's Special Forces and deploy abroad if necessary is part of that strategy which could be rolled out across the GCC.[278] By promoting and continuing to dominate the sub-regionalization of foreign policies through a more closely integrated GCC, Saudi Arabia could stand itself in good stead within global governance frameworks.

It is still oil that remains predominant in Saudi Arabia's role in international affairs, in two ways. Firstly, through reassuring the USA that it remains the most reliable energy exporter no matter what the regional conditions or provocations happen to be. Secondly, since OPEC has grown and includes a number of competing economic and political interests and rivalries, the possibility of an oil weapon being used against multiple states as seen in 1973 becomes ever more remote. Manipulating the international oil price on the basis of a foreign policy rationale has been proven to be problematic even for a swing producer because of competing economic pressures. However, in using the oil weapon against Iran, Saudi Arabia recognizes its balance of national interests and is willing to trade diminishing the oil revenues of a regional adversary against a small part of its national budget. This is particularly the case since the cumulative effect of its actions, with international sanctions, payment problems and withering export markets could be enough to push Iran over the edge and force a political change. Its actions vis-à-vis other adversaries remain rooted in a deep calculation of their political, economic and strategic strengths and weaknesses. For Western states, such as the USA which remains independent of any economic pressure, particularly given its recent oil policies in South America, it is likely that any rhetoric about a Saudi oil weapon remains just rhetoric. That is not to say Saudi Arabia could not leverage other resources, particularly in the counterterrorism domain.

The maintenance of Saudi Arabia's position in a pro-Western alliance with a range of economic and Islamic credentials is at the heart of securing a successful conclusion to its key foreign policy issues such as the MEPP and a future for the two-state solution. These could transform its long-term position and therefore requires a commitment to use all of its resources to influence the USA and support regional allies. The Arab Uprisings and the growth of the 'resistance' and Shi'i axes show what is at stake if Saudi Arabia fails to deliver.

CHAPTER 4

IRANIAN FOREIGN POLICY: THE POLITICS OF CIVILIZATION,[1] SECURITY AND ECONOMY[2]

Iran has been under more stringent US sanctions since the ILSA was passed in 1996. The effects of these sanctions have been somewhat counteracted by a period of globalization during which Iran has been able to find alternative markets and divert some exports, as well as circumvent the US trade ban by re-exporting or re-importing through third parties such as the United Arab Emirates (UAE).[3] The wider financial effects are difficult to gauge because a thorough and quantitative examination of its impact has yet to be carried out. The stringent terms of the sanctions have nevertheless been quite successful in preventing significant trade or investment in Iran by US firms and those companies who wished to do business in the USA. Lost FDI is particularly important to the Iranian energy sector at a time when it requires $100 billion to maintain and develop production.[4] The withdrawal of Western companies from Iran's petroleum sector, which generates 20 per cent of its GDP ($870 billion) and 80 per cent of its exports, has simply exacerbated poor relations.[5]

Since 2005, when the conservative Mahmoud Ahmadinejad became president, Iran has become more encircled and ostracized by the Western-dominated international community and negotiation on a range of issues with the West has been increasingly difficult.[6] UNSC sanctions in 2006 meant Iran had to search for alternative states to align with, which has led to a renewed emphasis on regionalism by Iran in the Gulf. However, due to a number of historic irritants between Iran and the GCC states, Iranian attempts at aligning with the GCC have been met with uninterest. Iran has gone on to develop bilateral relationships in Central Asia and with other states that maintain a similar anti-systemic ideological vision. Some states such as Venezuela hold significant oil resources which have contributed to Iran challenging Saudi policy and dominance in OPEC.

Russia and China straddle a number of significant international organizations that represent major threats or opportunities to Iran. Although Russia has fallen into line regarding UNSC sanctions against Iran after the International Atomic Energy Agency (IAEA) referral in late 2009, there still remain a number of opportunities for Iran to develop relations with Russia. Iran and Russia share interests in oil, and the roll back of Western interference from their respective spheres of influence such as the former Soviet Republics in Central Asia and Syria. China is also putting pressure on Iran by showing preference for its political and economic relationship with the USA. However, like Russia, China takes a much more independent view of Iran's nuclear programme and does not favour sanctions. China and Russia continue to supply Iran's energy sector through a US national interest waiver and they could still facilitate Iran's Central Asian regional economic strategy.

Given this context and the historic failure to influence Iran's nuclear and foreign policies of a US containment policy, this chapter advocates active engagement as an alternative UNSC strategy. Instead of the existing negative economic containment through sanctions, it argues for the implementation of a structured agreement with a significant positive economic dimension to it. The agreement may require sizeable economic resources allocated to the venture up front, but the advantages for all sides by broadening the dialogue beyond uranium enrichment could be disproportionate. Such advantages to the West might include establishing the grounds for increased regional and international stability and security. The disadvantages to the current policy approach are clear: whilst sanctions are in place, it is impossible for the West to build any kind of positive bilateral relationship with Iran and the current climate could facilitate a war, which would be costly for all sides.

The Domestic Environment and Political Economy

The Iranian political system is complex and based on disparate sources of power. The decision-making process is split between the state apparatus and a parallel, vertically integrated 'shadow' state system under the direct control of the Supreme Leader. Factionalism has been a part of Iranian politics from the birth of the Islamic Republic of Iran (IRI) in 1979 when there was a provisional government faction headed by Mehdi Bazargan and the Revolutionary Council was dominated by the Islamic Republic Party (IRP). Factions were polarized and, not for the first time, paralysed[7] by the US hostage crisis,[8] although differences emerged between the factions on all the policy issues of substance, particularly the economy. This was the beginning of the split between the reformist and conservative blocs. The only factor that stopped the reformist faction from imploding after their near defeat at the IRP Congress in 1983 was Khomeini's support for the Musavi Cabinet (Musavi was prime minister until 1989).[9] After the US hostage crisis, the Provisional Government was abolished and political power concentrated in the office of the president.

Towards the end of the Iran–Iraq War, factionalism became more prominent. During the 1980s more than 200 factions and political groups formed and incorporated competing but evolving ideological blocs: the left (populist-revolutionary) and the right (elitist-conservatives), which have always remained subordinate to the Supreme Leader.[10] Khomeini's decree on 6 January 1988 reaffirmed *velayat-e faqih*, the concept of an absolute ruler over state affairs and religious law (shari'a) enshrined in the 1979 constitution.[11] Pragmatists had control of the Majlis (Parliament) and the Cabinet, whilst the conservatives controlled the Guardian Council.[12] Pragmatists had a more complex structure to their faction, and major personalities such as Rafsanjani and Velayati (the foreign minister) were in open coalition with political competitors such as Musavi.[13] By 1988, conservative radicals were in control of the Cabinet and the judicial system and derived power from the grass roots of various foundations and districts. These conservatives were in charge of foreign policy from 1981 to 1984 but their isolationist policies were not conducive to winning the Iran–Iraq War. The pragmatists were in charge of foreign policy from 1984 to 2005, and, in contrast to the conservatives, were successful in negotiating peace. Infighting and factionalism burgeoned in the 1980s and led the IRP to be dissolved in 1987.[14] However, pragmatism enabled a reformist agenda to be pursued by President Khatami between 1997 and 2005, when his power base included the Foreign Ministry, the Majlis and the leadership of the armed forces of the IRI.[15] Domestic alliances have spread throughout bazaars and mosques, religious foundations and republican institutions. The right in particular have been able to utilize the clerical establishment (including young mid-level clergy) for its political purposes but still within the parameters of religious edicts.

The Ayotallah is supported in his aims and ambitions internationally and domestically by the IRGC and the Basij respectively. The Basij are a volunteer paramilitary organization under the aegis of the IRGC, totalling 500,000,[16] with duties ranging from security and law enforcement to policing morals.[17] The Leader and the conservatives use these security forces to implement their policies without relying on any other state security forces. The different and sometimes contradictory interests of the reformist and conservative factions resulted in complex strategies by which each faction protected and advanced its interests. The conflict between the reformists and conservatives reached its zenith during the presidency of Sayyid Mohammad Khatami (1997–2005).

As a reformist cleric, Khatami did not wholeheartedly support the absolute powers of the supreme leader.[18] Although Khatami paid basic respect to the Islamic Revolution, he also firmly established the legal authority attached to his office.[19] Khatami's bold approach to the question of political and economic reforms divided the country along reformist and conservative lines.[20] Despite differences of opinion between the factions, Khatami incrementally established an overall majority of reformers in the Majlis which would help sustain stable relations between the president and the Supreme Leader.[21] Towards the end of his presidency, many reformists blamed Khatami for his failure to advance reforms through the concept of *mardumsalari*[22] (Iranian-style democracy) and 'dialogue among civilizations' (including an accommodation and rapprochement with the West).[23]

Khatami was always going to be in a difficult political position with the conservative faction since his programme of political and economic reforms threatened the Supreme Leader's position. By 2002, conservative attempts to defeat the reformist agenda and persecute reformists through 'an intensified judicial campaign' pushed Khatami, his party and his followers to threaten to quit the government.[24] In 2004, the conservatives went on to leverage the Guardian Council into handing a parliamentary election victory to them. Former IRGC members made up one-third of the parliamentary seats after the election, and a member of the Guard was appointed vice-president.[25] At the same time, the Basij was continually used to break up civil society and reformist-led demonstrations in cities across Iran.[26]

In the 2005 presidential election, the conservative factions were able to use the authority of the Supreme Leader's office to institute another campaign against Khatami and his party.[27] The effect that an empowered and coordinated political bloc operating a parallel shadow government had on the election was devastating. By coordinating with the Interior Ministry (responsible for the elections), conservative factions were able to swing the 2005 election result in favour of Ahmadinejad; a feat which was repeated again in 2009.[28] Sir Richard Dalton has since defined this action as amounting to a 'constitutional coup'.[29] From the 2005 presidential election onwards, the conservative political factions have favoured sustaining and developing their respective economic and political advantages across the state.[30] The conservative political elite have employed the IRGC and Basij against the reformists, their political rivals. However, the growing power of the IRGC, coupled with the economic and political consolidation of the conservative elite, has started to contribute to an internal conflict within the government.

The rise of the IRGC in the Iranian economic and political system is intricately linked to their close relationship with the Supreme Leader, their shared desire to maintain the status of the regime and their roots in securing Iranian sovereignty during the Iran–Iraq War. Indeed, the Revolutionary Guard had engaged in direct competition with the regular Iranian armed forces during the war.[31] The IRGC has remained relatively intact since the 1980s, relatively complex and largely independent due to its early defined command structure and a continued lack of civilian oversight or control.[32] The complexity of the IRGC began with the Iran–Iraq War, when a cabinet-level ministry oversaw its wartime expansion and another component oversaw exportation of revolutionary activities.[33] The IRGC considers ideological purity its main source of strength; for example, its headquarters are located in the highly symbolic former US embassy in Tehran. Any reformist policies which place pragmatism before ideological considerations (e.g. pro-Western policies, changes to domestic policies such as Islamic behaviour codes, etc.) will always fundamentally conflict with the IRGC perspective.[34]

The IRGC's budget is extra-governmental, drawing on financing from hundreds of companies and entities in Iran and the Persian Gulf.[35] It has access to large religious endowments such as the Endowment of the Shrine of Imam Reza ($25 billion in net assets) and other umbrella organizations such as the Martyr's Foundation ($20 billion in net assets).[36] Its holdings also span a broad range of Iranian industries including real estate, manufacturing, retail and infrastructure development.[37] The IRGC has contracts with a number of businesses; these contractors include Ghorb, which has a number of active IRGC senior commanders sitting on its board of directors, one of whom is Rostam Ghasemi, who became the Iranian oil minister in August 2011.[38] The IRGC are in the public and private sector, through direct investments, contracts and joint ventures with various domestic and foreign companies including major names in the oil industry (such as Shell, BP and Total), banking (such as HSBC, Deutsche Bank and BNP Paribas) and consumer electronics (such as Mitsubishi, LG and Samsung).[39] The ILSA has been targeting these IRGC interests, which have been partly defined as IRGC interests simply by the large size of their revenues.[40]

Having special status in Iran, IRGC members have been able to go onto privileged positions in the education system or start businesses under the IRGC aegis, but not immediately into government.[41] Under Ahmadinejad, the IRGC's influence (partly through its construction arm, Khatam ul-Anbia) has grown within the NIOC and throughout the Iranian economy.[42] In 2006, Khatam won a contract to develop South Pars phases 15–16 and took over Sadra Yard, a platform builder and submersible oil-rig company operating in the Persian Gulf and Caspian Sea.[43] IRGC investments in oil and gas ventures in South Pars have since been cut back. For example, Ghorb pulled out of a contract to develop a gas field, citing sanctions and their effect on its ability to attract foreign partners.[44] However, the IRGC maintain the capability to operate a covert infrastructure, from 'invisible' piers in the Persian Gulf to control of airports in Iran, which enables it to import everything Iran might need, from consumer goods to nuclear technology.[45] The IRGC has the newest weapons systems and capabilities including intelligence, paramilitary and naval operations.[46] Sanctions therefore empower the IRGC because it is able to profit from them, and this translates into greater political power.

Today, the IRGC is at the very centre of power in the Iranian regime. It is a sort of equivalent of the KGB in the former USSR or FSB in Russia, with the difference that it does not seem to be ready to abandon the present regime.[47] It has now advanced so much, through being close to the Office of the Supreme Leader, and through shared political and economic interests and a common strategic outlook with the conservatives, that it receives the greatest support of all the military units.[48] It is not a political party, but the combination of a praetorian guard of the regime with an economic corporation, or guild.[49] The IRGC are so big and powerful now that they could potentially control the conservative bloc rather than vice versa. Factionalism may prove to be a major challenge or opportunity if it starts to draw elements of the IRGC apart from the Office of the President, in a similar vein to the president and Supreme Leader who are busy consolidating their separate but smaller domains.[50] Hilary Clinton, the then US Secretary of State, said that Iran was becoming a 'military dictatorship' in 2010.[51] This suggests that the ideological and legitimizing forces of Islam that were on display during the Islamic Revolution may no longer be required by the IRGC as it supplants the traditional role of the Iranian government.[52]

Iran's reformist opposition in the form of the Green Revolution was temporarily revitalized in the demonstrations and activities of the opposition Green Movement following electoral fraud in 2009.[53] Although the movement emphasized the issue of 'stolen votes', its major shortcomings were a lack of proposals across the religious domain (i.e. not advancing an alternative system to the *velayat-e-faqih*), the socio-economic system ('crony capitalism') and foreign policy.[54] The post-election environment created new groups of reformists which interacted vertically from elites down to the 'man in the street' and did so in such an atmosphere of confusion that there were concerns that opportunities were being missed for a US–Iranian rapprochement.[55] Repression was the main response from the conservative factions; the same response which has been used each time the reformist movement started to coalesce.[56]

The Institutional Web in Iranian Foreign Policy-Making

Factionalism explains Iranian foreign policy to a large degree, but additional linkages across formal and informal relationships between personalities, networks and state institutions also need to be factored into the Iranian foreign policy-making equation. The Constitution of 1906 provides for the functioning of a modern state, and yet the principle of *velayat-e faqih* continues to institutionalize the ideals of the 1979 Revolution and the dominance of the Leader or Imam.[57] There are seven institutions involved in Iranian foreign policy decision-making:

1. Office of the Supreme Leader: the Supreme Leader is commander-in-chief of the armed forces and with the power to dismiss the head of the IRGC;
2. Office of the President;
3. Foreign Ministry;
4. Head of the Expediency Council;
5. Supreme National Security Council (SNSC): all security forces report to the SNSC,[58] which is headed by Khamenei's direct

representative. This is currently Saeed Jalili, who also doubles as Iran's top nuclear negotiator;
6. Parliament (through the National Security and Foreign Policy Commissions);
7. The recent Strategic Council for Foreign Relations (created in 2006), which oversees Ahmadinejad's foreign policy performance.[59]

The Majlis remains important because it approves all international agreements, contracts and treaties, and the Guardian Council also remains important because it has the power to veto decisions made by the Majlis.[60] In cases where disputes arise, the Expediency Council, which is currently under the direction of Rafsanjani, arbitrates.[61] One of the biggest changes in the 2000s is the way that the SNSC has moved from facilitating decision-making during the Iran–Iraq War to become the principle foreign policy decision-making and policy implementation body.[62] The SNSC includes representatives from the IRGC and senior clerics, and top officials from the ministries of foreign affairs, intelligence and interior.[63] The council deals with issues surrounding the nuclear programme and regional and security policy in particular.[64]

Iran's Economy: Division between Elites

The Iranian economy, like the political system, has been split into two since 1979, along the lines of factions and business alliances between senior clerics. The reformists and conservatives have access to oil and gas revenues, taxes and fees, state enterprise income and municipal income, which the conservatives are able to supplement with additional income from mosques, holy shrines, religious foundations and religious taxes.[65] It is not uncommon for senior clerics, such as Rafsanjani, to run several government bodies and profitable businesses concurrently. Should clerics and oligarchs use this wealth and aspire to threatening political positions they could find themselves denounced by Ahmadinejad.[66] Such was the case between Rafsanjani, the former Iranian president who was angling to be part of the leadership council that could succeed Khamenei, and Rafsanjani's sworn enemy, Ahmadinejad.

The IRGC and the Bonyads – charitable trusts – are answerable only to the Supreme Leader, and their combined wealth could account for between 10 per cent and 50 per cent of the whole Iranian economy.[67] Bonyads were created after the 1979 Revolution, foundations into which the assets of the deposed Shah were channelled in an attempt to establish alternative loci of revolutionary legitimacy.[68] They are not subject to financial audits.[69] The largest is the Foundation of the Oppressed and War Veterans from the Iran–Iraq War (Bonyad e-Mostazafan va Janbazan) with 200,000 employees and 350 subsidiaries, representing $3 billion and 10 per cent of Iran's GDP.[70] Bonyads enjoyed deep discounts on foreign exchange compared with private enterprises in Iran before the reform of the exchange rate system and still benefit from better access and terms of credit at state-owned banks.[71] They also have excellent connections to politicians, which some argue creates corruption and limits reform.[72] Due to the diversity of their activities and geographical reach, some of the Bonyads have been implicated in sourcing dual-use products for Iran's WMD programme.[73]

The factional tensions and split between the political, and to a lesser extent, economic structures in Iran have great significance for the overall direction of Iranian foreign policy outcomes in the regional and international environments. The types of outcomes will be reviewed and analysed in the following sections of this chapter.

Iran's 'Resistance Axis' and Cold War with Saudi Arabia

Regionally, the legitimacy of the Iranian regime is closely connected to its 'resistance' policies that support the struggle against the Israeli occupation of Palestine and against a two-state solution. In contrast, the pro-Western bloc that includes Saudi Arabia defines its regime legitimacy in terms of supporting a two-state solution. A Saudi–Iranian Cold War has developed as a consequence of a number of grievances, both emerging and historic and including those between Iran and other members of the GCC. Tensions across the Persian Gulf make cooperation between Iran and the GCC unlikely and reinforce the negative effects of US-led sanctions against Iran.

The 'Resistance Axis' in the Levant

Iran has relations with Shi'i resistance groups such as Hezbollah, Sunni resistance groups such as Hamas and direct Iranian proxies such as Palestinian Islamic Jihad (PIJ) which, along with Syria, make up the 'resistance axis'. The 'resistance axis' is a relatively loose regional alliance led by Iran and Syria against US dominance in the Middle East, the perceived threat that Israel poses to them, and the leverage it gives both states in Lebanon, particularly during periods of conflict. The central dynamic of the 'resistance axis' rests on subverting efforts towards a two-state solution to the Israeli–Palestinian conflict and the abrogation of the peace treaties signed between Israel and Egypt and Israel and Jordan in order to boost its influence. Iran is an important player in the axis because it supports a range of non-state actors through the Qods (Jerusalem) forces, a unit of the IRGC numbering 15,000 in 2007, which works with Hezbollah in Lebanon and Hamas and PIJ in the Gaza Strip and West Bank.[74] Iran openly challenges Saudi Arabia in a sectarian and ideological struggle over the MEPP, since any possible resolution to the Israeli–Palestinian conflict has major implications for the legitimacy of both the Saudi and Iranian regimes. The USA is also concerned that Iran aims to end its historic vulnerability, boost its domination of the Persian Gulf and transfer WMD to violent Islamist groups operating in the Gulf States and the Levant.[75] Iran's relationship with Hezbollah and Hamas is therefore a significant aspect of the US fears concerning Iranian nuclear proliferation.[76]

Iran's resistance policies in the Levant gain strength from their status as one of the few points of convergence between Shi'i and Sunni public opinion.[77] Atallah suggests that the wider 'Arab public is not only *not* concerned about Iran's regional strength, but thinks it would be better for the region, probably in light of America's perceived weakness vis-à-vis Israel, for that regional strength to continue – unlike the assessment of their rulers'.[78] The rise of Iran can thus be attributed in large part to its being the only available and willing bulwark against perceived Israeli aggression. More specifically, there is evidence to suggest that Iran's policies towards Israel have hardened not only due to Israel's response towards its nuclear programme and the plight of the Palestinians, but specifically regarding the Israeli blockade against Gaza.[79]

Although it has been in Iran's interests to continue to support resistance through proxy groups, questions remain over the extent to which their geopolitical views coincide.[80] As noted in the previous chapter, Hamas is far more willing to consider support from Saudi Arabia and Egypt as two Sunni powers with substantial stakes in the MEPP. Hamas is moving into the Egyptian camp which would complicate Iran's gains from further regional instability, particularly if Iran were to lose its close ties to Al-Assad in Syria.[81] Iran therefore wants to re-establish and shore up its diplomatic relations with Egypt, and Egypt for its part is willing to re-establish diplomatic relations and see Iran playing a significant role in the region, notwithstanding Saudi objections.[82] The vague Iranian offer of economic assistance in case Egypt is pressured by the USA is part of that policy of improving bilateral relations.[83] Diplomatic relations between Iran and Egypt have been severed since 1979 and deteriorated further since Iran treated the assassins of President Sadat as heroes (there is a mural and a street in Tehran dedicated to the assassins).[84] Egypt is vital to Iran in a number of ways: it plays an important role in the MEPP and a balancing role across the wider Middle East, it is the most populous Arab state in the Middle East (with one of the largest armed forces in Africa and the Arab world[85]) and it has a strong sense of civilization which Iran values.[86] In this context, the Obama administration is pushing for unconditional aid from the US Congress for Egypt to counter the attraction of an Egyptian alliance with Iran.[87]

Until Iran can reinforce its 'resistance axis' with other members, and in particular state members, progress in the MEPP will continue to put pressure on Iran. Iran will therefore be more likely to use Hamas and Hezbollah to 'strike out' and disrupt political progress in order to avoid isolation, which has already happened on multiple occasions.[88] The differences in stances taken by Hamas and PIJ towards Israel can be linked to Iran having its 'back against the wall' regionally with specific reference to the ongoing internal conflict in Syria.[89] Were the Al-Assad regime to fall, Iran would lose the conduit through which it channels support to Hezbollah. Iran will also come under mounting US pressure as the only remaining state in the 'resistance axis'. To highlight Iran's anxiety over losing Syria as an ally, Iran has tried to engage the Syrian Muslim Brotherhood through a Turkish intermediary and mediate in the uprisings against Bashar Al-Assad, saying it would support the Brotherhood in government so long as Al-Assad stayed on.[90]

Russia also has a massive stake in maintaining Al-Assad's rule, since Syria is one of the last anti-Western states in the region and is a significant part of the Russian sphere of influence. Therefore, the possibility exists that Iran and Russia will continue to support the Al-Assad regime in order to avoid regime change in Syria and the possibility of a new government opting to join the NATO alliance. An Iranian alliance with Russia would be a fortuitous scenario for Iran, since without such a strong incentive for Russia to ally itself with Iran, the Russian–US relationship is most likely to predominate.

The situation in Syria has only facilitated the erosion of Iran's soft power and credibility amongst Arabs which are disenchanted with the Al-Assad regime, its killing of fellow Muslims and disregard for the collective political will of the Arab League.[91] Although unlikely, Iran could moderate its foreign policies on Syria and Lebanon 'as part of a major deal' with the West.[92] A change in policy of this magnitude would fulfil a large part of Iran's responsibilities as an active member of the international community and contribute to the MEPP rather than detract from it. However, until the West offers the right package of incentives to the Iranian regime, Ahmadinejad will continue to undermine both Western positions and Arab governments.[93]

Iran's Cold War with Saudi Arabia: Causes and Consequences

Iran's resistance policies in the Levant have been supplemented with a broader set of countering policies against threats emanating from the West, including the GCC. The Iran–Saudi acrimony is based on a plethora of antagonisms, but none more relevant than Iran's sense of regional leadership, unresolved territorial claims and nuclear proliferation.

Since the Islamic Revolution, the GCC states have consistently developed a common stance against Iran, notably with Iraq during the

Iran–Iraq War. However, throughout the mid-to-late 1990s Khatami tried to signal to the GCC states and the West that the perceived threat from the Islamic Revolution had subsided and that a new, pragmatic approach could contribute to greater diplomatic engagement. For example, after two decades of cold relations between Iran and Saudi Arabia, a bilateral industrial accord was signed in May 1998 which reflected a desire to move towards a normalization of relations.[94] Saudi Arabia offered a series of potential advantages for Iran: a gateway towards normalized relations with the USA; cooperation on oil pricing and investment in its energy sectors; cooperation on technical, industrial and engineering projects, especially in the copper industry and on the construction of power stations in Iran; and increasing exports to India.[95] In return Iran could help Saudi Arabia access Central Asian markets, confirming Iran's status as a 'lynchpin' between the Middle East and Asia.[96]

By the late 1990s when Iran's Defence Minister, Rear Admiral Ali Shamkhani, promised its security strategy was based on 'removing the causes of tension' and 'building mutual trust', Iran's nuclear programme had only increased regional tensions.[97] Iran has interests in the region which extend to GCC members that have significant Shi'i populations and which fall within Iran's immediate sphere of economic, strategic and political interest. Small GCC members such as Bahrain and the UAE are perceived by Iran to be its potential sovereign satellites, which has led to Iran supporting Shi'i dissidents there.[98] The Iranian claim over Bahrain is due to its having been part of the Persian Empire, and the majority of Bahrainis being Shi'a. The Iranian claim over the UAE rests on Iran's occupation and militarization of three islands in the Persian Gulf: Abu Musa, and the Greater and Lesser Tunb islands.

As part of its anti-systemic stance and a continuation of its claims to Bahrain and the UAE, Iran's 'sabre rattling' and 'threatening language' on the other side of the Gulf have led the way for the GCC states to choose a closer alliance with NATO.[99] There are also bilateral deals being pursued by the smaller Gulf states to enhance their security, such as the agreement between the UAE and France in 2008 to establish a permanent military base with up to 500 French troops.[100] The potential nevertheless remains for a revised pan-Gulf security architecture in which contentious issues such as Abu Musa and the Greater and Lesser Tunb islands could be resolved.[101] Confidence-building measures are unlikely to be successful, however, until the most basic struggles over regional leadership and identity are reconciled. Such was the strength of feeling on the subject of whether the Gulf should be classified as 'Persian' or 'Arabian' before the Islamic Solidarity Games in 2010 that the whole event was cancelled.[102]

Iranian foreign policy in the Persian Gulf to a large degree comprises the 'Saudi factor', which reflects Saudi Arabia's 'posture and pursuits in the region'.[103] Other factors, notably the US factor, are also of central concern to Iran, particularly across its broader sphere of influence, including Afghanistan and Iraq.[104] It is in areas where Saudi and US interests converge – such as a sustainable international oil price, the MEPP and the isolation of Iran – that Iran must counter most effectively if it is to succeed in securing its interests. Iran constantly seeks to exploit any gaps in Saudi policy regarding the MEPP, and has done so again during the Arab Uprisings. For example, Ahmadinejad highlighted the differences he perceived between Saudi Arabia's robust policy approaches to internal conflicts in states such as Yemen and its less robust approach regarding Israel.[105]

Although Iran considers Saudi Arabia a regional adversary, Iran needed to integrate with the GCC in order to avoid the worst impact of sanctions. Iran hoped to use a monetary union to facilitate integration, starting with Iraq, followed by the smaller GCC states, and then expanding to include Saudi Arabia and other states after that.[106] However, inflation in Iran was expected to exceed 20 per cent in 2008, double that of most Middle East and Central Asian states.[107] This created a technical issue, one which Iran was attempting to overcome with the littoral states of the Persian Gulf during the Iran–Kuwait trade committee meeting in February 2011.[108] However, a more formidable and fundamental obstacle to monetary union and, indeed, to integration with the GCC lies in the choices that the GCC member states have made and continue to make in bandwagoning with the West against Iran. These choices effectively prevented the adoption of the suggestion made by Hassan Rowhani, the then Supreme

Leader's representative to the SNSC, for a Persian Gulf Security and Cooperation Organization to develop in 2007 in response to growing concerns about the Iranian nuclear programme.[109] His plan envisaged the inclusion of all the Gulf States; joint security arrangements including a joint enrichment consortium for nuclear energy; a WMD-Free Zone in the Middle East; and the removal of foreign troops, especially US troops in Iraq.[110]

Iran's foreign policies therefore preclude the building of a new alliance with the GCC through renewed cooperation. On the GCC side, until the Iranian nuclear programme has been dealt with comprehensively by the UNSC and IAEA, and Iranian regional ambitions have been clarified and resolved (including Iran's claims over Abu Musa, the Greater and Lesser Tunb islands), no cooperation will take place between Iran and the GCC.[111]

The mutually contradictory oil policies of Iran and Saudi Arabia are also proving to be a barrier to enhanced cooperation, especially as Iran seeks to maximize its returns on oil during sanctions. Iran managed to defeat Saudi Arabia's unilateral oil weapon during the 'worst' OPEC meeting, but it is becoming harder for Iran to compete with Saudi Arabia's oil resources.[112] Iran has oil and gas problems (Iranian capacity is 3.7m b/d, which is a long way from the 6m b/d of the Shah's days), and claims that its oil reserves are greater than Saudi Arabia's are 'exaggerated'.[113] Although oil price rises help Iran, the number of customers has fallen because they are less able to pay in other currencies apart from the US dollar, which is part of the sanctions regime against the Iranian government.[114] Iran is concerned with Saudi economic dominance in the GCC but also the advantage that Qatar has in benefiting from FDI and foreign expertise to extract from the North Dome (6,000km in Qatari territorial waters) at 77 million tonnes per annum.[115] If Iran is able to extract on a similar level to Qatar, Iran could increase its standing in its proposed gas group[116] which might rival Saudi-dominated OPEC, and include Qatar and Russia which are known to be less pro-US than other states in the region.[117] Iran is also looking at the projected increase of EU dependence on gas from 50 per cent to 80 per cent by 2030 and sees an opportunity to regain a major export market through exporting via third-party states.[118]

The Arab Uprisings coincided with a period in which there had been very little economic cooperation and regional integration between Iran and the GCC to result in increased tensions and instability in the Persian Gulf. The 'Saudi factor', particularly in OPEC, has created the preconditions in which any future Western sanctions or interventions will have a disproportionate impact on Iran, contributing to its sense of regional containment and encirclement. The Iranian countering policies against the perceived threats from the West will be discussed in the following section.

Countering Western Interventions and International Sanctions

Iran has felt forced to supplement its central status in the 'resistance axis' with a broader, militant Shi'a countering posture against an infringing Western presence, starting with the war in Iraq in 2003. Since UNSC sanctions were introduced in 2006, and following an existential threat to the 'resistance axis' caused by the Arab Uprisings in Syria in 2012, Iran is stepping up its search for security. Barring any opportunities to balance with the GCC, Iran is recalibrating its internal economic policies and primary trading partnerships in Central Asia, and is attempting to internationalize the 'resistance axis'. Iran has been successful at developing relationships with states that take a similar anti-US perspective, are under sanctions, or are in dire need of economic cooperation. In so doing, Iran appears to be resisting the USA first and foremost through a strategic 'axis of oil' with Venezuela which can also be used against regional adversaries such as Saudi Arabia in OPEC, to boost its oil revenues and attract the interest of major powers such as China and Russia.

Iran and Iraq after Iraq

After the US-led invasion of Iraq in 2003, Iran had the perfect opportunity to retaliate against the USA and increased the pressure on US forces by supporting a rise in sectarian violence. Through this policy, Iran has been able to keep the US forces occupied in Iraq and contain the threat of US-led regime change in Iran. Iran has also ensured that by maintaining active links to the Shi'i militia in Iraq, Iran has the option to apply similar pressure to the new Iraqi government if Iraqi policy becomes too closely aligned with the West.

The removal of Saddam Hussein was a good opportunity for a rapprochement between the USA and Iran and for better regional security. However, a rapprochement was not taken seriously by the USA, so it did not end up as a positive development for Iran.[119] Both the USA and Iran want a democratic and inclusive government in Iraq, but Iran would prefer Iraq to be tied up with domestic concerns rather than becoming a regional threat once again.[120] After the Iraq war, sub-national identities have been increasing tensions, in Iraq and regionally, between Kurds, Sunnis and the Shi'a. Some of the tensions come from the preference that the international community has over its dealings with the Kurds. For example, there are now international negotiations with the Kurds which have led to increasing energy exports, a secure border and foreign trade, all of which is in stark contrast to the negotiations with Shi'i Iran over its nuclear programme.[121]

The main Iranian concern about Iraq is the presence of US troops and military bases and its longer-term alliance with either the USA or Israel or both. It is this which reinforces Iran's cooperation with Shi'i groups in Iraq.[122] Furthermore, Iraq still has not resolved issues related to the Iran–Iraq War. Iran is still expecting $149 billion-$1 trillion in war reparations from Iraq.[123] Iraq ignored the 1975 Algiers Agreement and went to war with Iran less than six years after signing it, so the new Iraqi government needs to make its position clear on this agreement.[124] Iran now views Iraq with mistrust after the removal of Saddam Hussein, based on disproportionate Sunni dominance over Iraq's natural resources, economic strength and geo-strategic position.[125] Despite troubled relations, Iran has also shown readiness to export oil and gas to Iraq as a sanctions-avoidance measure and as a possible pathway that leads to increased Iran–Iraq–GCC cooperation over the long term.[126]

UNSC Sanctions: Renewed Pressure on Iran after 2006

By 2006, more incremental and integrated sanctions were adopted by the UNSC to increase the pressure on Iran. The following section describes what the UNSC sanctions were and how Iran has responded against them with unprecedented countermeasures.

The UN Security Council resolutions on the Iranian nuclear issue highlight the important role that Russia and China have played in moderating the hawkish stance of other Security Council members. UNSCR 1696, which demanded that Iran suspend uranium enrichment by 31 August 2006 or face possible economic and/or diplomatic sanctions, was passed but only under Article 40 which did not authorize military action as a logical next step.[127] UNSCR 1737 centred again on the failure of the P5+1 (another term for the E3+3, referring to the five permanent members of the UN Security Council – the USA, Russia, China, the UK and France – plus Germany) to get Iran to suspend uranium enrichment and led to sanctions on technology that could assist the Iranian nuclear programme, Iranian nuclear- and missile-related corporations and individuals close to them.[128] UNSCR 1747 extended the sanctions on Iran to include more military entities (including IRGC entities and Bank Sepah), banned arms transfers by Iran (aimed at curtailing the trade to Hezbollah in Lebanon and the Shi'a in Iraq) and called for an arms embargo against Iran.[129] UNSCR 1803 increased the pressure on Iran through banning the export of dual-use items to Iran, authorized inspections of shipping to Iran and called for prohibition of financial transactions with Iran's main banks (Bank Melli and Bank Saderat).[130] UNSCR 1929 followed in May 2010 after the failure of the 'Tehran Declaration': a three-way deal between Iran, Brazil and Turkey to send 2,600 pounds of uranium to Turkey in exchange for medical isotopes.

The most recent sanctions are different from all the other sanctions because they are being imposed by a group of nations which includes China and Russia, thereby ratcheting up the pressure on the IRGC. This could, in turn, lead Iran to engage in the tactic of nuclear negotiations to relieve the economic pressure.[131] The united will of the international community is a concern to Iran because its allies, including Brazil, South Africa, China and Turkey, voted for the sanctions.[132]

There is still space for Iran to respond and the 'door remains open' to further engagement.[133] That is perhaps because the West knows that sanctions are a long-term tool, and given Iran's ability to evade and smuggle, it is able to avoid the worst consequences from sanctions or at least ensure that those consequences are limited to the most vulnerable sectors of society.[134] The USA is the only actor capable of breaking the deadlock and has made a lot of progress in cooperating more effectively with China and Russia to put pressure on Iran.[135] Working with the Iranian regime has become more problematic as the Obama administration initially sent letters directly to Khamenei rather than Ahmadinejad. The US administration took some time to realize that the Supreme Leader, not the president, is in charge of the nuclear file.[136] However, by only addressing Khamenei, the US administration embarrassed the Iranian president who not only secured a 'heavy majority' in the 2009 elections but remains an integral part of the foreign policy process.[137] Khamenei has also taken a tough stance against the West, refusing to rule out the use of oil as a weapon as of June 2006 and indicating that shipments of oil from the Persian Gulf could be at risk.[138] Iran's dependence on oil revenue makes this scenario highly unlikely, especially when oil production is down from 6 million b/d in 2002 to 1.6 million b/d in 2006.[139] Instead, Iran has resorted to allegedly directing attacks against the USA, firstly through a conspiracy to blow up fuel tanks at the John F. Kennedy airport in 2007, and then another attempt aimed at Saudi Arabia's representatives in Washington in 2011.[140]

Sanctions, with the potential for escalation to 'crippling sanctions',[141] and a lack of direct contact have continued to be US policy as 201, by which time Iran could possibly have a nuclear weapon, draws closer.[142] The USA has also requested that German does more bilaterally, although the German government has failed to take significant or effective action because it knows that other companies will jump into the void after German companies withdraw from Iran.[143] Nevertheless, sanctions have proven to be more extensive as of November 2011, with France emphasizing 'unprecedented' sanctions aimed at forcing Iran to the negotiating table, the USA focusing on Iran's petrochemical sector and the UK concentrating its sanctions against dealings with the Central Bank of Iran.[144] The UK's actions have subsequently been met by the Iranian Parliament with a vote to expel the British Ambassador and reduce further economic and trade links with the UK.¹⁴⁵ It has also led to Basij forces storming the British Embassy in Tehran, the expulsion of Iranian diplomats from the London embassy and other retaliatory measures expected on the Iranian side.¹⁴⁶ The USA soon followed the UK in sanctioning the Iranian Central Bank.¹⁴⁷ In the lead up to the US presidential elections in 2012, the USA has effectively declared an 'economic war' against Iran, which could become another step down the slippery slope into a full war with Iran.¹⁴⁸ The unprecedented move has had a particularly negative impact on the value of the Iranian rial which dropped to its lowest point in two decades, undermining one of Iran's national symbols and reinforcing its sense of international isolation.¹⁴⁹

By December 2011, Iran's vice-president Mohammad-Reza Rahimi declared that Iran could close the Strait of Hormuz in retaliation for a possible EU oil embargo and US measures to reduce Iran's oil revenue.¹⁵⁰ Such an action is highly unlikely since it would do more damage to Iran's oil exports than those of other oil-exporting states in the region, although it could lead to higher oil prices that benefits Iran in the short term. Furthermore, the European oil embargo is self-defeating since it would negatively affect the fragile economies of Greece, Italy and Spain.¹⁵¹ However, there is evidence that Ahmadinejad is letting sanctions impact negatively on the Iranian economy in order to put pressure on Khamenei to negotiate on the nuclear issue.¹⁵² There is no evidence that Khamenei is responding to this pressure and he will most likely continue to bar serious negotiations on the nuclear issue. There is also the possibility that sanctions could have the positive effect of making Iran's non-oil exports cheaper, therefore enabling Iran able to make up for some of its lost foreign earnings.¹⁵³ Either way, this sequence of declarations, actions and events reinforces the neutral or negative influence that tighter sanctions are exerting on Iranian foreign policy. These influences have generally been channelled into a number of countering strategies which Iran has pursued domestically, regionally and internationally. Each one will be discussed in the following sections.

Iran's Domestic Countering Policies: Reducing Subsidies and Relieving the Pressure to Reform

One of the countering measures adopted by Iran after UNSC sanctions were imposed in 2006 has been a reduction in Iranian state subsidies. These were a quick and easy way for the regime to reduce the pressure from sanctions. The presidential struggle for control of the economic decision-making apparatus followed, as did Khamenei's policy of 'economic *jihad*' in 2011. Although sanctions have put unprecedented pressure on Iranians and Iranian businesses, domestic pressure to address the root causes of sanctions has yet to modify the politics and policies of the regime.

Whether Iran will survive through tighter multilateral sanctions is an ongoing debate in Iran, and the costs of the nuclear programme must be weighed up against the mounting cost of sanctions and state subsidies. Whilst some foreign diplomats believe that the consequences sanctions are beginning to be felt in the Iranian economy,[154] the effect of sanctions has been somewhat offset by strong economic growth (6 per cent) based on rising international oil prices in 2006 and 2007.[155] Much therefore depends on the international oil price and the Iranian government's ability to provide subsidies and investments in social structures from schools to hospitals. Sanctions are hard to counter and if the oil price drops to $80 a barrel and production keeps falling it will create problems, but whilst oil is at $100 per barrel it will relieve pressure along with a reduction in subsidies.[156] The reductions in subsidies are part of a strategy to counter sanctions, but these as yet have not gone far enough.[157] In particular, Iran needs to be able to pay its import bill, cover the costs of social security, support the elite and find markets for its oil.[158]

The situation is deteriorating since Iran is dependent on oil for its budget but cannot attract the FDI required to convert more of its oil into a long-term financial revenue stream. It is clear that Iran's aim of achieving 8.5 million b/d by 2015 at an investment cost of $50 billion is not realistic.[159] In fact, Iran's oil production capacity is falling from its current capacity at 3.7 million b/d.[160] In the short term at least, OPEC[161] and the Arab Uprisings have kept oil prices high and ensured that Iran receives adequate oil revenues.[162] Khamenei has nevertheless called the Islamic year that corresponds with 2011 'the year of economic *jihad*' in recognition that the economy is becoming a serious issue for most Iranians and Iranian businesses across different industries.[163]

Attempting to overcome the effects of sanctions may prove to be an area in which Khamenei and Ahmadinejad come into conflict. Ahmadinejad has already tried to 'maximise his freedom of action' during 2011.[164] He first tried to take over monetary policy-making by firing his central bank governor who favoured tighter monetary policies.[165] In contrast, Ahmadinejad favoured expansionary policies to support the poor, who are his base.[166] He then integrated the Management and Planning Organization (MPO), the main organization responsible for economic planning, into the Office of the President.[167] Ahmadinejad went on to fire his Foreign Minister in signs that he preferred a candidate without such close ties to Khamenei.[168] Ahmadinejad also fired his intelligence minister, only to reinstate him under pressure from Khamenei.[169] Ahmadinejad even took temporary control of the oil ministry as caretaker oil minister just before an OPEC meeting in 2011; a decision that was again quickly reversed by the Supreme Leader.[170]

The Fars News agency, which is close to the IRGC, also published an interview which denounced Ahmadinejad's chief aide Esfandiar Rahim Mashaei for commenting on religion without any theological training.[171] This was an unusual move by a conservative faction which is normally allied with Ahmadinejad. It gives some indication of the sensitivity and discord which comes as a result of the president infringing upon the realm of the Supreme Leader. Ahmadinejad is also under political pressure due to corruption charges against some of his political allies.[172] This has helped Khamenei in his bid to try and dissolve the position of the president and consolidate power under his own authority.[173] Incidents such as speculation fuelled by the privatization process which has led to fraud and corruption to the tune of $2.8 billion (1 per cent of Iranian GDP) could cause a further loss of legitimacy to the presidency.[174]

However, so far Ahmadinejad has been successful at continuing to implement his subsidy reforms and independent economic policies (*iktisadi istiqlal*) from foreign powers, to limit the effect of sanctions. Iran has cut subsidies on most energy and food products since December 2010 in order to save the government up to $60 billion annually.[175] The effect has been an increase in the amount of oil for export, to relieve pressure on state finances whilst trying to cushion the blow for poorer families with a small, yet symbolic, $40 per month government payment.[176] This action was lauded by the IMF in a 2011 press release.[177] However, the reforms are being viewed more circumspectly by Iranian businesses which are finding it harder to stay in business.[178] Protests by Bazaaris in October 2008 (the first since 1979) were some of the first signs of discontent.[179] Store owners in Esfahan, Mashad, Tabriz and Tehran all closed their businesses to protest against the new 3 per cent VAT.[180] Such protests notwithstanding, the initial success of reducing subsidies on flour, water and diesel bolstered Ahmadinejad at a critical juncture of nuclear negotiations with the West in Istanbul in January 2011, making him and his team more assertive in talks.[181] The move was particularly important for the regime because sanctions and high domestic consumption of petroleum were putting great pressure on the country's finances.[182] According to the CIA, the Iranian economy grew by 1.5 per cent in 2009 whilst unemployment was around 20 per cent.[183] Therefore, as long as the Iranian economy is still growing and mismanagement can be contained, Iran should be able to avert a financial crisis which would put significant pressure on the regime.

Iran's Countering Strategy: Supporting and Broadening the 'Resistance Axis'

The combination of Western interventions and the Arab Uprisings have highlighted the fragile state of the traditional 'resistance axis'. Iran's resistance strategy post-2006 has thus focused on a close political relationship with some Latin American states which take an anti-US view, and are therefore more likely to assist Iran with its sanctions avoidance measures. This is a prudent strategy which will provide Iran with some support in order to maintain, and if necessary possibly supplement, its 'resistance axis'.

States in Latin America are particularly susceptible to Iranian diplomatic overtures because they have a similar history of imperialism, anti-US sentiment or non-alignment. They may also lack strong legal systems which could block some Iranian influences.[184] Bolivia could benefit from Iranian assistance to nationalize its oil industry although Brazil prefers to focus on economics rather than politics in its bilateral relations. Ecuador appears to be open to cooperation with Iran, since it needs investment following default on its national debt[185] and has already concluded discussions with Iran on medical cooperation.[186] Ecuador could also potentially launder Iranian money since its currency is the US dollar.[187] Iran's relationship with Argentina has been slow to recover after its alleged involvement in the 1992 bombing of the Israeli embassy, followed by the bombing in 1994 of the Asociacion Mutual Israelita Argentina (AMIA) in Buenos Aires. Originally blamed on Hezbollah in conjunction with the Quds forces and the Ministry of Information and Security (MOIS), the investigation is ongoing.[188] Indeed, a fresh agreement was reached in January 2013 to establish a joint commission to investigate the 1994 incident.[189]

However, it is Venezuela and Cuba, both of which are considered to be pariah states by the USA, and the latter of which is under US sanctions, that gives Iran most cause for optimism about building a complementary 'resistance axis' in Latin America. Venezuela and Cuba were the only states (along with Syria) that voted against the resolution to refer Iran to the UN Security Council.[190] The most troubling development from a Western and Saudi perspective is that the Iranian and Venezuelan 'axis of annoyance' is morphing into a much more threatening 'axis of oil' which could help Iran to counter UNSC sanctions.[191] Iran's bilateral trade relationship with Venezuela has grown exponentially from $1.5 million in 2001 to $20 billion in 2007, based on 181 trade agreements across industries such as steel and oil, auto and ammunition manufacturing.[192] In 2007, Iran and Venezuela set up a $2 billion fund to counter US influence in the developing world and has sought OPEC support for oil to be priced in Euros rather than the US dollar.[193] By taking such an anti-US stance amid allegations of 'US military imperialism', and threatening the pricing policies and dominance of Saudi Arabia in OPEC, the 'axis of oil' has already led to US warnings to Venezuela against becoming too closely involved with Iran.[194] Such warnings may not be necessary if the Venezuelan government post-Chavez chooses a new foreign policy orientation, but for the time being it remains an important relationship in Iranian foreign policy.

Iran is also developing links with other non-Western states. Whereas the rationale may appear to be buttressing the 'resistance axis' in a similar way to the Iranian-Venezuelan relationship, the timing of these trade and cooperation agreements after UNSC sanctions were passed in 2006 illustrates that this is not the case. The relationships are linked to Iran's global search to reduce its isolation and boosting its non-oil trade revenue. Some relationships such as those with the Non-Aligned Movement (NAM) states serve to reduce international pressure. Iran is able to rely on some states which share similar political features or vulnerabilities (e.g. as non-signatories of the NPT), such as India, to appeal against the linkages created between IAEA language against Iran and the possible political or military implications contained therein.[195] Iran has established mining and agricultural trade links with Zimbabwe (another anti-Western state and with which it cooperated during the struggle for liberation[196]). Iran is also expanding trade ties with Japan. For example, the Japanese firm Jaika is engaged in a project to enrich forests in the Chaharmahal-Bakhtiari province of Iran.[197] Japanese Ambassador Kinichi Komano asserts that additional scientific and cultural ties will continue to rise.[198] There was also significant growth of more than 2,000 per cent in two-way trade between Iran and Cote d'Ivoire, the Republic of Niger and Senegal between 2000 and 2010.[199] However, none of these trade relationships has been enough to offset the huge losses in the Iranian oil trade with the EU, so they still represent largely symbolic gestures rather than alternative markets to the West.

Trade Realignment: A New Policy of Regionalism in Central Asia

In addition to developing ideological partnerships, Iran's new trade partners also include neighbouring states which are able to deliver goods across borders associated with smuggling and states which boost Iranian influence regionally and internationally. Such trade realignment away from the West gives Iran room for manoeuvre and as much autonomy as possible in an increasingly hostile international environment.

Iran seems like the quintessential 'small state' as it is looking at all possible opportunities to develop trade ties and generate space in which it can be less dependent on the 'core' states. The permanent sector is energy, so by focusing on oil, gas and renewable energy, Iran can use its central geographical location to boost exports of both goods and technologies.[200] Ironically some of the push factors towards greater regionalism are the same factors which are undermining it, such as US and UN sanctions, US involvement in Iraq and Afghanistan and the subsequent border closures, local corruption and poor infrastructure.[201]

To confirm its commitment to regionalism, Iran hosted a trilateral summit in Tehran on 24 May 2009 with the rationale outlined by the Iranian Foreign Minister: in order to find 'regional solutions to regional problems'.[202] The result was a 24-point 'Tehran Declaration' which provided for cooperation on terrorism, infrastructure development and the creation of 'pull factors' in Afghanistan to encourage Afghans to return home from Iran.[203] Iran, Afghanistan and Pakistan thereafter established a mechanism for regular meetings at either the ministerial or head of state level.[204] It is perhaps no surprise that less than a year later Riyadh would launch its own Declaration with states such as India on the subjects of harnessing energy resources while combating terrorism, drug trafficking and money laundering.[205]

Iran has had three decades to avoid US sanctions and realign its trade ties with states that are less susceptible to direct US pressure. Alarm bells had already rung for Iran in the 1990s when a marked increase in population size met an increase in public expectations about employment, etc.[206] The new round of UN sanctions involves Russia and China (and other UNSC members such as Brazil, South Africa, China and Turkey) so is different from US-led sanctions but designed by the same chief protagonist. So far, decreasing exports of oil can be offset by increases in the oil price and as long as Iran can pay its import bill, take care of social security and the elites then it should not have to worry in 2011.[207] However, a renewed process of trade realignment is prudent since the international oil price may fall and unless Iran spends on hedging against this fall, its revenues could be at risk. In addition, trade avenues need to be continually developed in anticipation that some will be constrained or closed due to US pressure, thereby making trade realignment a continuous process which makes Iran a moving target at which sanctions are aimed. Much of the Iranian economic emphasis is on trade realignment away from the USA and Europe to other markets such as Iraq, Afghanistan, China, Azerbaijan, Turkmenistan, Armenia and Turkey.[208]

However, the most important trade ties are with Iran's immediate neighbours such as the UAE, Qatar, Oman and Turkey.[209] There is approximately $14 billion trade between Iran and the UAE, but this is suppressed by the Office of Foreign Assets Control (OFAC) restrictions which Iran wants removed.[210] Traders and businesspeople in Dubai take the perspective that it is better to ease sanctions through conventional means than to take any other course of action.[211] This is in contrast to the US policy of putting pressure on the Gulf States, especially the UAE, to implement the sanctions.[212] This has had the effect of displacing trade from the UAE to Turkey, which wants to increase trade with Iran as much as possible within the sanctions regime.[213] Cooperation is likely to be of interest to Turkey, which not only presented an alternative plan to UN sanctions with Brazil, but received one million Iranian tourists in 2008 and through such tourism is listed as one of the possible ways to modify the behaviour of the Iranian regime through supporting Iranian hopes for better relations with Turkey and the West.[214]

That was unlikely to be the case since in a *Transatlantic Poll on Iran Nukes* sponsored by the German Marshall Fund, 25 per cent of respondents in Turkey said they preferred living with a nuclear Iran.[215] However, this position is unlikely to be reflected in the Turkish government since the Kurdish attack on the Turkish military[216] can be seen to be a shot across the Turkish bows on its policies regarding Syria and missile defence.[217] The NATO/Turkish anti-ballistic missile system in Eastern Anatolia (on the Turkey–Iran border region) is needed to mitigate not only the Iranian nuclear programme but also the growing Pakistan nuclear programme.[218] Therefore, Iran is losing allies locally for reasons related to its nuclear programme but missile defence could be eliminated across Europe if Iran walks away from its nuclear programme.[219]

On the Iranian side, the Iran Khodro Company (IKCO), Iran's second biggest company by profitability, signed a Memo of Understanding with Turkey to produce a car that will be manufactured in Turkey and therefore give it easy access to European export markets.[220] Iran also wants a new banking relationship with Turkey, which would help it receive oil payments but Turkey has not yet agreed to this.[221] The additional concern with Turkey is the long border between Iran and Turkey which has a tradition of smuggling across it, so there is certainly more activity happening than is known about.[222] Part of such concerns includes Iran's neighbouring countries trading with Iran in strategic goods such as arms and goods for the nuclear programme.[223] For example, Armenia was part of a three-way deal which managed to put an Airbus on Iranian tarmac which breached Airbus' commitment to the sanctions regime.[224] Iran already sources gas from neighbouring Turkmenistan which is becoming increasingly expensive as China is also importing much of this gas.[225] Iranian Commerce minister Mehdi Ghazanfari and Turkmenistan's President Gurbanguly Berdymukhammedov have stressed accelerating the establishment of the Turkmenistan-Kazakhstan railway which would facilitate regional trade and relations between Iran, Oman, Turkmenistan and Uzbekistan.[226]

A Case Study of the Opportunities and Difficulties in the New Iranian Countering Policy: The Iran–Pakistan–India (IPI) Pipeline

The IPI is a good case study in Iran's difficulties in exporting gas and payment problems, primarily due to sanctions and complications arising from the local security environment. The case study also highlights the triangulation that Iran's trade partners need to perform in order to determine whether their interests lie with Iran or the Western alliance of the GCC states, the EU and the USA. The result of such calculations will prove whether Iran's countering policies against sanctions is sustainable over the long term.

In May 2009 during a trilateral summit hosted by Iran, Iran and Pakistan agreed on a natural gas pipeline that would link the two Muslim-majority states.[227] The $7.6 billion agreement for a natural gas pipeline will link the South Fars gas field with Pakistan's Balochistan and Sindh provinces.[228] The so-called 'peace pipeline' was then expected to traverse into India, thereby becoming the Iran–Pakistan–India pipeline (IPI).[229] Since the agreement was formalized, the pipeline has experienced a number of setbacks. Firstly, Australia's BHP withdrew from a $3 billion contract under the threat of US sanctions.[230] Secondly, the pipeline was suspended due to Indian suspicion and doubt regarding the security of pipeline vis-à-vis its relations with Pakistan, although it is a good example of framing a tense relationship in bilateral relations through a new issue.[231] The poor relations between India and Pakistan have put Iran in a quandary because it wants to engage India on the IPI but understands that it is not necessarily the best way to interact with India and Pakistan simultaneously.[232] Thirdly, extending the IPI beyond Pakistan is dependent on US foreign policy in the region, which was not the case in the 1990s when the USA was still a silent player regarding Iran.[233] For the time being at least, Iran and Pakistan are moving ahead with the pipeline on a strictly bilateral basis.[234] Russia's Gazprom has shown interest in financing it, and there is certainly an incentive for China to link to it since it is keen to avoid US dominance of shipping lanes.[235]

Keeping such pipelines on track will help Iran maintain and increase its revenues from oil and gas sales, and make sure that Iran continues to receive a good price for its exports no matter how much pressure it is under by sanctions. The extent to which Iran is sensitive to pricing is found in Ahmadinejad's removal of then oil minister Kazem Vaziri-Hamaneh in 2007 because he had allegedly sold gas to Pakistan and India too cheaply.[236] He then took temporary control as caretaker oil minister just before an OPEC meeting in 2011, a decision that was quickly reversed by the Supreme Leader.[237]

Russian and Indian oil companies such as Indian Oil Corp. are also becoming increasingly important customers for Iran, as IOCs such as Repsol, Shell and Total are divesting from Iran's natural gas sector.[238] However, it is becoming increasingly difficult for India to pay for Iranian oil since Iran has been cut out of the Asian Clearing Union (ACU) which is used to settle regional commercial debts that have been amassed between members.[239] The USA is constraining Iranian trade with companies and states through stopping the recycling of US dollars through its financial system and is blocking its oil trade 'company by company'.[240] This problem is affecting Iranian oil trades with top importers both regionally and internationally, with the most recent case affecting $5 billion worth of oil revenues which has been 'trapped' in South Korean state-owned banks by the sanctions.[241] Chinese companies are 'filling some gaps' with Iran–Chinese trade reaching $28 billion in 2010, but cannot be counted on to fill them all.[242]

Trade and revenue routes still exist between India and Iran. India has paid $100 million out of the $5 billion it owes Iran from its refineries through a state-owned Indian bank and another Turkish bank (EIH, an Iranian bank based in Hamburg, has also been 'blacklisted' by the USA[243]) into the account of the National Iranian Oil Company.[244] Whatever happens, India has three months credit with Iran and both states are confident that a payment solution can be found to maintain the export of oil to India and payments back to Iran.[245] In the meantime, Iran is pursing other pipeline projects, including one dubbed the 'Persian pipeline' which is potentially able to run to Turkey, Greece and Italy into Western Europe.[246] The same difficulties as beset oil exports are likely to arise, as the end of pipeline is susceptible to political pressure from the USA and the UN sanctions that the core Western European states have signed up to. This would not make exports difficult, but would hinder payments made to Iranian banks. In early 2011, Iran announced another pipeline that would link Iran with Syria and Iraq.[247] This is possibly going to take the longest to come to fruition since it would involve a number of issues including uprisings in Syria, possible instabilities in Iraq and Iranian sanctions.[248]

Regional energy dialogue is especially important to Iran due to the upward pressure on prices resulting from the Arab Uprisings and the increasing demand of many states for nuclear energy as an alternative option to burning fossil fuels.[249] Increasing the number of ties across the region on the basis of important economic considerations such as this increases the amount of social capital which can more easily be turned into serious geopolitical discussions which makes disputes easier to resolve.[250] Unfortunately, the GCC/Iran divide is a stumbling block that forces states such as India to choose between the GCC and Iran when it would prefer not to.[251] It throws into relief the different issues, whereby the GCC represents good economic interaction, Iran represents political challenges and Iraq is an unknown.[252] The effect is that Iran and India are 'working as islands', so Iran wants the future to include more cultural and economic cooperation.[253] By boosting bilateralism and cooperation in this way, Iran can secure a position within more established multilateral organizations and perhaps even leverage that position into a more permanent alliance.

The Prospects for Iranian Participation in Regional Economic Organizations

Although Iran has a preference for bilateralism, there are two multilateral organizations in Iran's immediate environment that Iran is trying to develop or join.[254] They are the Economic Cooperation Organization (ECO) and the Shanghai Cooperation Organization (SCO). The ECO is based in Tehran and its members include Afghanistan, Azerbaijan, Iran, Kazakhstan, Kyrgyz Republic, Pakistan, Tajikistan, Turkey, Turkmenistan and Uzbekistan.[255] It is not economically strong but has lasted 50 years.[256] Iran also wants to push tourism cooperation with members of the ECO and the Developing 8 (Bangladesh, Egypt, Indonesia, Malaysia, Nigeria and Pakistan) as a way to ease its international isolation and boost economic growth.[257] An alternative trading and ideological bloc certainly helps Iran, but it is not enough to counter its multifarious problems of Western firms dropping out of its oil market, insurance agents stopping insuring its shipping and the next round of sanctions.[258] Instead, it has also been suggested that the ECO serve as the foundation for a future regional security mechanism.[259]

Because Iran has difficulty paying for goods, some states also function as conduits for goods which are put through the 'back door' which could potentially involve South Africa or Malaysia.[260] This leads to an increased cost of doing business (as front companies might be involved) as well as time delays which is acceptable to Iran for key goods as long as Iran can still get hold of them.[261] This is not troubling in itself, but is when coupled with evidence of a broader black-market trade in nuclear fuel-cycle technology from Pakistani nuclear expert A. Q. Khan beginning in 1987, with a greater focus in March 1999, admitted by the former secretary of Iran's National Security Council and cleric Hassan Rohani through the Expediency Council in 2006.[262]

Iran also wants to join the SCO in which they currently have observer status, but it is unable to join as a full member since it is under UN sanctions.[263] Like the delays to the Bushehr reactor which have given it leverage over Iran in getting it to sign up to the various UN Security Council Resolutions,[264] Russia again seems to be responsible for this delay.[265] However, Russia is not beholden to the USA. The USA had tried to thwart the $800 million sale of several nuclear reactors to Iran, but not even a $100 million incentive to not complete its contract was enough to stop Russia from fulfilling its obligations to Iran.[266] Russia also plans to sell Iran an S-300 air defence system.[267] More worrying to the USA is the accusation that Russia has inadvertently aided the Iranian nuclear programme, through allowing nuclear scientists such as Vyacheslav Danilenko to work in Iran from 1996 to 2002.[268] Iranian–Russian relations have also been boosted by Tehran's cooperation during the Tajik civil war in 1997, its restrained position on Chechnya and their common opposition to the Taliban in Afghanistan, although this is subject to change.[269]

Russia looks to serve both Iran and the USA, as long as it is in its economic and overarching national interests. Russian and Chinese control of the SCO, which incorporates many states with which Iran wants to trade including Russia, China, Kazakhstan, Uzbekistan, Tajikistan and Kyrgyzstan, could put extra pressure on Iran to modify its nuclear stance in favour of good trade, investment and market opportunities. As UNSC members they hold the keys to the effectiveness of sanctions against Iran, particularly in its energy sector. The US Congress therefore wants to increase pressure on the Obama administration to clarify its national interest waiver that permits China and Russia to continue supplying Iran's energy sector.[270] Through their respective demand and supply sides of an 'axis of oil' and their ability to roll back US influence in Central Asia (through Russia's influence over its former Soviet Republics and switching its bilateral oil trades with Iran from the US dollar to the Russian rouble[271]), Iran is given a chance to ally itself with a credible and long-term alternative to the USA.[272] The USA is already asking China to limit its oil supply from Iran and is working with Saudi Arabia to step up its oil exports to China to substitute those of Iran.[273] This has so far been met with resistance from China which does not agree with sanctions against Iran and particularly with linking sanctions with trade.[274]

The Dysfunctional International Relationship of Iran and the P5+1

The relationship between Iran and the West is the multiplied effect of loaded (i.e. historically informed) perceptions of policy-makers in Iran and the West. The current nuclear deadlock is also a function of all the past relations, including missed opportunities and miscalculations, which is hard to break by any members of the P5+1 or Iran.

Loaded Perceptions in Iran–EU3 Relations

An analysis of the observations from former ministers, diplomats and academics in Iran and the EU3 (Germany, France and the UK) form an important prerequisite to the broader analysis of negotiations and relations between Iran and the West. Iran's resistance and countering strategies have led to Western anxieties over regional events, nuclear proliferation and international security. At the same time, Iranian interpretations and anxieties over a lack of cultural and Islamic sensitivity from the EU are a fundamental obstacle to advancing bilateral dialogues along the diplomatic track.

There are some considerable differences of opinion within the EU3 on the most fundamental principle of Iran's rationality regarding international issues. Some Europeans believe that the Iranian government is irrational, that it has no clear strategy and anyone who says 'yes' during a negotiation with the West is always going to be in jeopardy with other factions.[275] Likewise, former prime minister Tony Blair alluded to Iran's irrationality by widely promoting regime change in Iran.[276] However, other European policy-makers contend that Iran's regime is 'not irrational' or reckless.[277] Iran has always been able to show restraint and an ability to pull back in its resistance activities, making Iran deterable.[278] There is still some concern as to the language that Iran employs when discussing the West. To say that the negative language employed by Iran against the UK is 'only for public consumption', as suggested by various Iranian foreign ministers, goes against 'what they [government officials] learned in their revolutionary studies'.[279] However, this must be put into the perspective of historical Iran–UK relations.

The poor state of contemporary bilteral and Iran–EU3 relations can be attributed to the cumulative effect of past Iran–UK relations. Significant contributing factors include the Anglo-Iranian Oil Company taking a disproportionate share of Iran's oil revenues, British support of the Shah and his anti-Islamic policies and the role of British Intelligence and the CIA in supporting the overthrow of the nationalist Iranian prime minister Mohammed Mossadegh. Indeed, it was the British promise that the USA would receive a share in Anglo-Iranian Oil Company (AIOC) interests once it had helped to depose Mossadegh which facilitated US interference.[280]

The French policy towards Iran has varied under President Chirac and Nicholas Sarkozy. The former came out against sanctioning Iran in 2006.[281] However, this policy was quickly reversed under President Sarkozy the following year when he made remarks about Iran which put France back in the same category of poor relations as the UK. European states were generally unwilling to lose Arab support during the Iran–Iraq War by overtly backing Iran.[282] France in particular sees its support of Iraq during the war as a contributing factor to its poor relations with Iran under Ahmadinejad.[283] The impact this has had on the opinions and foreign policies of successive political generations in Iran has been illustrated by presidents Rafsanjani and Amhadinejad, who both have strong links to the Iran–Iraq War.[284] The war cost Iran 213,000 lives[285] and has therefore been 'burned into [Iran's] memory'.[286] It should therefore inform Western foreign policies towards Iran.

Iran also has qualms regarding the EU on a number of other fronts; most recently based on the UK and France trying to shape the Arab Uprisings.[287] As Suzanne Maloney notes, 'no state that watches the international community bombard Libya will ever concede its nuclear advantage in exchange for rapprochement and trade ties.'[288] It is clear that such interventions are again perceived to be encirclement and contrary to Islam.[289] Iran's relationships with the EU3 have been hamstrung by the institutional mismatch of three states (Germany and France having historically had better relations with Iran than the UK has), but also 'values lobbies' operating in both the European Council and European Commission.[290] These bilateral relations (embodied in the 3+3 framework with the USA, China and Russia) represent the best and only option for improved US relations with Iran.[291] Problems with the Iran–EU dialogue have also been attributed to:

1. The EU accusing Iran of not respecting human rights and nuclear conventions;
2. The EU wanting to waive issues of Islamic significance;
3. The EU not having a profound or nuanced understanding of Iran;
4. The EU thinking that it is easy to change the values and culture of a nation – perhaps due to the diversification in the EU.[292]

The counter-argument is that no one understands the culture of a foreign country as much as those living there. The EU believes in the universality of human rights and that these are not culturally specific.[293] Yet there are accepted double standards in EU foreign policy towards Iran and its human rights, one which is known not to strengthen its credibility.[294] However, the general argument that 'you don't understand what is going on in our [authoritarian] country' amounts to a 'firewall against questioning' and is therefore not accepted.[295]

Missed Opportunities for Iranian–US Engagement: 2001–2003

Khatami's election and reform policies validated the EU's Critical Dialogue which was in turn followed by Khatami's 'Dialogue of Civilisations'.[296] This soon became UN's Year of Dialogue Amongst Civilizations in 2001.[297] The USA responded with disappointment that Iran would not go beyond dialogue between peoples to government negotiations which would still include areas of concern to the USA. However, a potential high water mark of US-Iranian cooperation was about to present itself immediately after the beginning of the US-led Afghanistan invasion. Some US objectives against the Taliban and al-Qaeda could not be achieved without cooperation with Iran, particularly with regard to intelligence.[298] Iranian cooperation during Operation Enduring Freedom in Afghanistan was staggering, based on its sympathy for the USA after the 9/11 attacks. Through the 'Geneva Group',[299] Tehran offered the use of its bases in eastern Iran for US transport aircraft; agreed to perform search and rescue missions for US airmen who bailed out over Iran; allowed an American freighter to off-load its cargo of humanitarian supplies at the port of Chah Bahar; and supported US engagement with the ethnic Tajiks[300] that made up the Northern Alliance while pushing for engagement with the Pashtun groups to make the effort against the Taliban and al-Qaeda a pan-Afghan one.[301]

The USA could have been more constructive in its dealings with Iran regarding Afghanistan but Iran received no reward for its early cooperation in the GWOT.[302] Iran has big economic investments in western Afghanistan: Iran is building a railway, supports the bond settlement, supports President Karzai and also supports Shi'i clients through the Second Belt and the Persian speakers of the north, all of which amounts to some quite substantial interests.[303] Iran should therefore have been taken seriously in Afghanistan, and the USA could have facilitated a closer relationship.[304] Instead, opportunities were missed by the USA, such as not rigorously pursuing the Iranian proposal for training 20,000 members of a new Afghan army after the US invasion.[305] The opportunity for bilateral engagement was soon lost after the Afghan government was set up.[306]

US foreign policy was much more dominated by the hostage crisis and a different world view after 9/11. The US attitude in the post-9/11 era was best illustrated by President Bush's 2002 State of the Union address when he labelled Iran part of the 'axis of evil'.[307] Such language has tried to sway the perceptions of the international community into believing that Iran represents a much more dangerous threat to world peace than other states, such as Japan, Brazil, Argentina and Canada, which are far more advanced in their civilian nuclear programmes.[308] It was also at this time that Iran was described by the US State Department as 'the most active state sponsor of terrorism'.[309]

Since 2003, not only were specific political initiatives removed, but space in the American media for debate has also been removed, leaving nothing but caricatures of political figures, extreme op-eds in major publications and a marginalization of the real issues.[310] To counter the negative media commentary, the Iranian Mission to the UN in New York took out an advertisement in *The New York Times* on 18 November 2005.[311] This was designed to outline the allegations against the Iranian nuclear programme and presented a series of justifications for it:

1. The programme is for electricity generation only, given pressures from population which is expected to rise to 105 million by 2050, and oil saving (an estimated 190 million barrels of cruder per year);[312]
2. Iran has the right to enrich uranium under the provisions of the 1968 Nuclear Non-Proliferation Treaty (NPT); it should be noted that the EU3 has never recognised Iran's right to enrich under the NPT;
3. Iran's leaders, including Khomeini, have issued fatwas stating that nuclear weapons are un-Islamic;[313]
4. Over the past 250 years Iran has not waged a war of aggression;
5. Iran's technological development and military capabilities do not support a nuclear deterrence against its adversaries internationally (some Iranian strategists agree with US analysts that a nuclear weapon would facilitate a pre-emptive strike against Iran and additional sanctions and containment);[314]

6. EU3 confidence-building measures, including those on nuclear cooperation and regional security, have not been put into action since 2003.

The US government has been charged with 'malevolent neglect' by the Brookings Institution during the same period because there was no support for the EU3 agenda from the European contact in Washington, John Bolton.[315] This was not as serious as it might have been for Iran–West relations because Iran still looked on EU3 negotiations favourably during 2003–5 with a view to it leading to the inclusion of the USA later on.[316]

The biggest challenge for the EU3 was coming up with the right combination of incentives without substantial US support. There was some US support for the EU3 decision to drop its veto of Iranian WTO membership and allow Iran to buy spare parts for its US fleet of aircraft, but Bush's statements and his 'regime change' State of the Union address in 2005 cancelled out all these economic incentives.[317] A $66 million budget for US broadcasting into Iran was another provocative move which did nothing to strengthen the hand of reformists inside Iran.[318] It is therefore surprising to note that Iran and the USA have tried to communicate at least nine times since the end of the hostage crisis in 1981, starting with the Iran–Contra Affair during the Iran–Iraq War up to direct talks offered by Condoleeza Rice in 2006.[319]

The narrow parameters within which the USA was willing to engage is confusing since the US 2006 *National Security Strategy* stated that the USA 'may face no greater challenge from a single country than from Iran'.[320] The USA and Iran should therefore have plenty to discuss and across a broad range of issues. Instead of diplomatic engagement, 2006 was the year Iran was referred to the UNSC by the IAEA and sanctions were strengthened.

No other opportunity on the scale of Afghanistan has presented itself since and although the Obama administration has tried to be constructive in engaging Iran, the allegations of a rigged 2009 election in Iran has closed the temporary window of opportunity. Iran has been quick to assert its interests in Afghanistan which have led to accusations of corruption regarding its aid transfers.³²¹ Afghanistan, as has been pointed out, is 'not their [Iran's or Pakistan's] back yard to play games in',³²² but without US engagement on the subject, there is little incentive for Iran to do anything else. As long as the USA remains in Afghanistan Iran is likely to pursue a dual strategy: keeping the US troops preoccupied in Eastern Afghanistan by supplying arms to the Taliban,³²³ but also limiting the most destabilizing effects of terrorism.³²⁴

The neo-conservative policies of the USA coupled with the negative Afghanistan experience gave Iran a ready-made template for its countering policies against the USA and its Western allies in Iraq in 2003. These will be discussed further in the following section.

The Iranian Reaction to the US Invasion of Afghanistan: Iran's Role in Iraq, 2003

The US-led invasion of Iraq provided another opportunity for a rapprochement between Iran and the UK, as an interlocutor to the USA and through its ability to shape a new Iraqi government. Following an Iranian offer to cooperate with the USA on Iraq which was subsequently ignored, Iran has been adept at using Shi'i militia groups for two main reasons: firstly, to ensure that the US administration was preoccupied with sectarian conflict and therefore unable to continue with its regime change policy in Iran. Secondly, Iranian connections to Shi'i militia could maintain leverage vis-à-vis the Iraqi government if Iraq once again threatened Iranian national security interests.

The 2003 Iraq War changed Iran–West relations, especially Anglo-Iranian relations, profoundly. Iran initially took the UK more seriously because of its actions in Iraq, the UK's position as an interlocutor to the USA and the UK's ability to help shape the new government in Iraq.³²⁵ The Anglo-Iranian relationship then soured mainly because the USA and UK were not going to leave Iraq quickly or advance Iranian interests.³²⁶ Iran therefore put pressure on the UK in Iraq and started its own embargo against UK exports that lasted four months.³²⁷ In 2004 Iran intensified its campaign of negative media stories against the British Embassy in Tehran, including an accusation that the UK constructed a tunnel underneath the embassy through which it was delivering spies and prostitutes.[328]

The USA should have been engaging Iran on issues that concerned its national security, particularly from 9/11 onwards, and yet there are limited political will and official channels to do so. Furthermore, Riyadh proved to be an obstacle to diplomatic engagement between Washington and Tehran over Iraq.[329] The main leverage that Saudi Arabia held was in the sale of $20 billion worth of US arms to the Kingdom, and the projected sales to Arab monarchies between 2011 and 2015 set to reach $122.8 billion.[330] Nevertheless, there is evidence that there was an Iranian offer on the table to cooperate with the USA regarding Iraq.[331] However, there was no apparent response to the offer and because the USA designated the IRGC a terrorist organization, Iran has therefore felt no compunction in increasing its support for insurgencies in Iraq.[332]

The Qods force allegedly smuggled arms to Shi'i militia such as the Mahdi Army and Badr Brigade.[333] Iran has allegedly supported acts of terrorism against US and Sunni targets through hosting operatives such as al-Qaeda.[334] However, blaming Iran for such incidents may simply be a diplomatic ploy to get other regional states such as Saudi Arabia to engage in Iraq to help contain Iran.[335] The IRGC has also been able to enter Iraq through the hundreds of miles of ill-defended border with Iraq, contrary to what Richard Armitage, then Deputy Secretary of State, said about the USA using Iraqi bases to 'pressurize Iran'.[336] IRGC forces have crossed the border into Iraq because the regime perceives the USA's engagement in Iraq as yet another attempt to use Iraq as a regional counterweight, building and supporting regional alliances against Iran and establishing military bases next to Iran's borders.[337]

US foreign policy favoured the continuation of containment policies over a broad-based dialogue that could make progress on the range of issues that the US administration points to in documents such as the *National Security Strategy*.[338] The main reservation that Condoleeza Rice, then Secretary of State, had about negotiations with Iran from 2003 was that Iran 'wanted a big delegation' and broad-based dialogue which 'was not intended' or planned for by the US administration.[339]

Meanwhile, Iran and the EU3 negotiated the Paris Agreement in 2004 which was designed to provide objective guarantees that the Iranian nuclear programme was benign and therefore allow dialogue to advance between Iran and the West.[340] In return for full disclosure of all past nuclear activities, the ratification of the NPT's 'Additional Protocol' which relates to inspections and temporary uranium suspension, Iran was promised peaceful nuclear technology.[341] The Agreement also offered an 'energy partnership' to assist Iran in modernizing its oil and gas sector, and the inclusion of Iran into a regional security architecture and support for a WMD Free Zone (FZ) in the Middle East.[342]

The USA was not interested in pursuing the Paris Agreement: nor were Iran's Gulf neighbours, which is surprising given that Iranian involvement in Gulf security could be a 'potential game changer', especially if it was offering security at a low level of arms.[343] Instead, the USA appears intent on staying as a 'local power', which has been made clear from its recent arms sales to the UAE and Saudi Arabia.[344] This has left the USA free to extend its sphere of influence unchecked and 'freeze' Iran out of regional issues, thereby undermining Iran's vital interests.[345] The USA does, however, recognize the importance of regional stability and therefore accepts that an increase in Iranian influence is not against US interests.[346] US engagement with Iran would therefore be as beneficial to promoting US interests in the region, if not more so, than the promotion of Iranian interests. US strategic and security interests have grown to include the MEPP, the GWOT and sectarian violence. In each area, Iran could play a decisive role.

An inherent contradiction has existed for some time in US foreign and energy policy: the USA promises a diversification of oil supplies, aiming to secure them and minimize the risk of flow disruptions. Simultaneously, the USA has implemented foreign policies towards Iran, Iraq and Libya which produce the opposite effect, reducing oil supplies and increasing associated costs.[347] It was the deep divisions within the Bush administration, between the hawkish neo-conservatives in the Department of Defense and the Office of the Vice-President who wanted regime change (but did not want to dedicate too many resources to the policy) and the more liberal approach taken by the

State Department that led to the continuation of previous US policy on Iran.[348]

The Nuclear Deadlock: 2005 Onwards

Ahmadinejad's election facilitated the demise of nuclear negotiations between Iran and the West. His decision to remove the seals and start conversion of uranium at an enrichment facility in Isfahan coupled with a lack of nuclear transparency, a diplomatic deadlock and anti-European rhetoric following the 2009 election, provided a new prism through which sanctions have tightened further. These policies appear to be miscalculations by both Ahmadinejad and Khamenei since alternative powers and oil markets such as China ultimately prefer their relationships with the USA to those with Iran.

After Ahmadinejad won the 2005 Iranian presidential election, Iran accused the EU3 of prolonging the process laid out in the Paris Agreement due to pressure from the USA. Iran suggested that the IAEA develop the technical, legal and monitoring processes required to solve the deadlock.[349] The EU3 was split in this case and none of the incentives proposed to Iran were enough to dissuade it from its continuing with its enrichment plans. At this fork in the road, Iran thereafter took a path leading away from the platform of accommodation with the West.[350] Iran started conversion (a step before enrichment) again in August 2005 when it broke IAEA seals at the Isfahan facility.[351] In response to the new Iranian nuclear policy, the EU suspended the TCA and energy charter (overland gas regulation).[352]

The IAEA board then referred the case to the UN Security Council in February 2006, after initial fears expressed by ElBaradei that Iran could face the same kind of US led intervention that Iraq experienced in 2003.[353] In 2003, EU foreign ministers from France, Germany and the UK made a historic visit to Iran to resolve the issues of nuclear transparency regarding the IAEA, and to persuade Iran to sign the Additional Protocol and to suspend enrichment.[354] Iran did suspend enrichment but was expecting EU3 support for its negotiations at the IAEA which did not happen.[355] This disappointment led the way for the Majlis to stop the implementation of the Additional Protocol after the referral of Iran to the IAEA in 2006.[356]

It then became clear that it would be hard to make progress with Iran under the EU3 remit which meant that Iran could exploit gaps between the USA, the EU and Japan over regional and economic issues, especially regarding US sanctions.[357] The nuclear issue was a block and human rights were off the agenda, both of which cast a shadow on the bilateral Iran–UK relationship.[358] There was simultaneously an increase in the number of negative opportunities exploited in the UK–Iran relationship which included the British Institute of Persian Studies director being expelled in 2005; the British Council director being refused a visa in 2006; and threatening British Council staff, in effect closing it down, in 2007.[359] This was accompanied with an increase in the intensity of fighting in Iraq, and an increase in Iranian support for the Shi'a.[360] After the re-election of Ahmadinejad, 2009 was a watershed only in the degree of negative actions taken by Iran: the UK was labelled as the 'ringleader' of international opposition to Iran, and from 2009, there was a thorough deterioration in the UK–Iran relationship.[361]

The foreign policies of the USA – the 'Great Satan' – continue to form the foundations of Iranian foreign policy towards the West in general.[362] The USA, which has gone the longest without contact with Iran – 30 years with only sporadic contact on Afghanistan and the nuclear file – has no feel for Iranian diplomacy or the factors which influence its responses.[363] This has made it far more susceptible to rely on the strategic assessments of Israel which has lobbied the US government according to its own national interests. Israeli Prime Minister Netanyahu calls Iran's nuclear programme a 'messianic apocalyptic cult'. This is an indication of the seriousness with which Israel regards the Iranian nuclear programme after Ahmadinejad publicized his desire to 'wipe Israel off the face of the earth'.[364] Israeli military options towards Iran remain constrained by the US administration which understands that a military strike will serve the interests of the Iranian regime more than their own.[365] Nevertheless, Israel continues to lobby the USA and induce the maximum sanctions from the West through pronouncements of an imminent pre-emptive military attack.[366] The

USA and Israel have cooperated on at least two pre-emptive technological strikes directed against Iran's nuclear programme, most notably using a computer virus called 'Stuxnet'.[367]

American or Israeli covert operations against Iran may have included, amongst other incidents, a plot to assassinate Iran's 'missile king' in 2011.[368] Future covert activity could also theoretically include the US backing the Majahedin e-Khalq (MEK), a US-proscribed organization for its terrorist activities carried out in the 1970s,[369] to put pressure on the Iranian regime.[370] There are already accusations of Israeli Mossad agents impersonating CIA agents in order to recruit MEK operatives against Iran.[371] The Iranian response has also been apparent through attempted Iranian assassinations of Israeli diplomats in Bangkok.[372]

Iranian relations with other actors such as China are therefore a function of these very poor relationships as Iran seeks to find alternative powers with which to balance. As of 2008, Iran's liquefied natural gas (LNG) remains under US control since exporting it requires the participation of the IOCs.[373] Japan imported 18 per cent of Iran's 2.47 million b/d in 2007, with 42 per cent going to the rest of Asia (in total, Asia accounts for 60 per cent).[374] Most of the rest goes to China which leaves 'China calling the shots'.[375] Some of that business includes Sinopec retooling an idled crude distillation plant in its Tianjin refinery and turning it into a condensate splitter to process Iran's South Pars condensate.[376]

China is spending $2.5 billion in developing the South Azadegan oil field that straddles the border with Iraq. Output could reach 600,000 b/d which would be a major boost to Iran's energy sector. China's CNOOC (China National Offshore Oil Corporation) has already signed a $1.76 billion deal in 2009 to develop the North Azadegan field which has reserves estimated at 42 billion barrels.[377] The Sino-Iranian relationship is a function of the regional and international political environment that has led to the alignment of interests between the two states.[378] Iran is seeking new trade partners, and in particular oil markets (Iran was responsible for 23 per cent of China's oil imports in 2009, second only to Saudi Arabia[379]) to counter the sanctions regime, whilst China is exploring new trade opportunities in the Middle East (in everything from shoes to prayer mats).[380] Gas has also been a major linkage between the two states and a $20 billion deal over 25 years was signed in 2004 between Chinese state-owned Zhuhai Zhenrong Corporation and Iran.[381] China will try to forge close links with Iran within the bounds of the international sanctions which it only supports under pressure from the USA.[382]

Although the USA cannot trade on good relations with China and others to begin another dialogue with Iran,[383] China has appeased Washington and avoided sanctions on its big energy firms by reducing oil- and gas-related investment in Iran.[384] This trend confirms that 'China is not ready to lose too many feathers for Iran' because China still has other options for importing oil from suppliers such as Saudi Arabia.[385] China was considered by many leading figures in the Iran government (including Khamenei, Rafsanjani and Ahmedinejad) to be a more reliable partner for Iran than a rapprochement with the West, but China's compliance with sanctions and reduction of investment in Iran demonstrates that this assessment is mistaken and pressure on Iran will increase further.[386]

In May 2008, the original 2006 'energy partnership' presented to Iran by the P5+1 was enhanced by the Bush administration to include political cooperation and enhanced energy cooperation.[387] In response, Iran was interested in a six-week sanctions freeze in return for a six-week enrichment freeze but this proposal did not go anywhere in Geneva in August 2008.[388] Therefore a new confidence-building measure was required in 2009, which was developed by the USA, France and Russia for the Tehran Research Reactor (TRR). The USA had built the Tehran reactor during the Shah's era (who incidentally spent $1 billion on his nuclear programme[389]), allowing Iran to develop isotopes for medical research, but now Iran is now running out of nuclear fuel for this reactor.[390]

The offer made was for Iran to accept the exportation of 80 per cent of its Low Enriched Uranium (LEU) – 1,200 kg at the time – in exchange for fuel for Iran's research reactor.[391] The intention was to recreate dialogue between the USA and Iran, not to replace dialogue on the nuclear programme. The Obama administration eventually opposed the deal even though Iran was more willing to ratify the Additional Protocol after the proposal in 2009 than at any time before.[392] Instead, the USA opted for wider-ranging and rigorous sanctions which would raise the price of the nuclear programme and put Iran in the dock of the world's court (at the UNSC) once again.

Following the Iranian election, the prospect of crippling sanctions brought the Iranian nuclear negotiator Sayed Jallili to meet privately with Under-Secretary of State William Burns in Geneva in October 2009.[393] The tentative agreement reached focused on a number of key areas of contention: IAEA inspections at Qom, reprocessing of 75 per cent of Iran's LEU for medical use (less than had been proposed before because Iran had continued to enrich), and further talks.[394] Although Ahmadinejad 'did not have a problem' with the P5+1 and IAEA proposal, hardliners inside Iran managed to thwart the shipment of enriched uranium and sent counter-proposals.[395] In the end, Iran refused because the offer specified too high an amount of LEU.[396]

In February 2010, Iran (through a meeting between the former Austrian Ambassador to Tehran, Michael Postl, and Ahmadinejad's chief of cabinet, Esfandiar Mashaie, who is acknowledged to have the confidence and backing of the president) allegedly accepted the TRR proposal to export 1,200kg of its LEU.[397] This was because losing 1,200kg was less of a worry than it had been the previous year and because the agreement would be tantamount to international acceptance of the Iranian right to enrich.[398] In addition, the Iranian regime's attitude toward the nuclear issue was said to have changed between the proposal on 1 October 2010 at the UN in Geneva and the IAEA Vienna talks which started on 19 October 2010.[399] The reasons were stated as being due to political friction domestically in Iran over the programme and due to changes to the potential agreement that had been added between the meetings, particularly over where the exchange of LEU would take place (Austria, Switzerland and Turkey were all possibilities) and the transfer of it in a single 'tranche', which caused Iran to question the motives of those involved.[400]

The TRR deal was rejected by 'spoilers' involved in the nuclear negotiations including former Foreign Minister Kamal Kharazi and National Security Secretaries and former nuclear negotiators Ali Larijani[401] and Hassan Rowhani.[402] Mashaie, Ahmadinejad's chief advisor, was quoted as saying that it was the UK that was the 'spoiler' of the P5+1 after the 2009 elections and that Iran would prefer to negotiate directly with the USA rather than France and Russia over the TRR.[403] The USA was sceptical of the accepted proposal and believed it was merely a rouse to confuse or delay sanctions and Iran would be unlikely to go ahead with the proposal if sanctions proceeded.[404] However, Iran's negative stances may be changing as it is running out of the 20 per cent enriched uranium it needs to keep the TRR going and is therefore showing a greater willingness to compromise on this aspect of the nuclear programme.[405]

The deal remained on the table at negotiations in Istanbul in January 2011 (taking into account new enrichment figures) and remains the only confidence-building measure available.[406] An Iranian delegation has been invited to the International Conference on Afghanistan in Bonn conference so there is room for constructive engagement, notwithstanding tensions over the Washington terror plot, particularly on a regional trade agreement, counterterrorism, narcotics[407] and the drug traffickers who kill Iranian law enforcement officials.[408] However, it is the IRGC that the West will need to negotiate directly with, since they control the ballistic missile programme, anti-drug trafficking efforts, border control in sensitive areas such as the border with Kurdistan and cooperation with militias and Basij.[409] The incentive of the TRR proposal for Iran to negotiate with the West and give any concessions on its nuclear programme have also been removed as Russia has shown its readiness to sign a radioactive isotope contract with Tehran.[410]

A nuclear deal such as the 'Tehran Declaration' to send enriched uranium to Turkey, Austria or Switzerland, would be 'seen as significant' and could have been successful if it was over a longer period than just the five years, since it would make it a long-term commitment to the NPT.[411] The West's reward would have been Iran finding it harder to explain enrichment in future but it was too big a step for Iran.[412] This combination of enrichment suspension, an on-shore enrichment joint venture with safeguards and specific made-to-measure IAEA monitoring are still seen as the best way to resolve the Iranian nuclear programme.[413] However 'full supervision' in exchange for lifting sanctions is still not expected to include 'snap checks' provided for in the Additional Protocol.[414]

The deadlock thus comes down to Iran resolving internal tensions within the elite and reconciling its starting point regarding uranium enrichment with the West. The EU3's starting point is an open and honest dialogue and a halt to the enrichment.[415] Iran is said to be in 'heavy' violation of its international obligations primarily because there is no civilian justification for its programme and no plant (including Bushehr) can use the more highly enriched fuel.[416] However, there is actually no formal procedure for determining whether Iran has *violated* its obligations under the NPT. Its referral to the UNSC was due to *non-compliance* with the NPT Comprehensive Safeguards Agreement in 2006.[417] Furthermore, Iran's 164 centrifuges in 2006 were far less than the 50,000 required to enrich uranium to the 90 per cent required for weapons-grade material.[418] Therefore, rather than proscribing Iran as being in violation of the NPT, the EU3 could have continued to provide credible security assurances, ensured the programme was as transparent as possible and assisted Iran with a civilian nuclear programme without preconditions, thereby contributing to a positive partnership. Bushehr is not as much of a concern to the P5+1 since the $800 million plant has been under Russian control from the period of the contract in 1995 to the point it became operational in August 2011.[419] It was the concealment of the Iranian programme first at Natanz (2002) and then at Qom (2009) that led the UNSC to support the tightening of sanctions against Iran in 2010.[420] The same year the US administration updated the Iran Sanctions Act (ISA) with the Comprehensive Iran Sanctions and Divestment Act (CISADA) which rescinded the exemption of Iranian caviar, carpets and pistachios from the ISA.[421]

The Bush administration could have done a deal with Iran in 2003–2004 if it had taken the current 'open hand' policy of the Obama administration.[422] Iranians say that Obama's rapprochement with Iran was immature, since his 'open hand' was quickly taken back after the Iranian election.[423] It is more difficult now because of the highly polarized views of the Democrats and Republicans and the US Senate which wants a 'stick' (as opposed to 'carrot') policy towards Iran.[424] In effect the Senate is continuing the 'Bush Doctrine' of exporting democracy (through support for the Arab Uprisings) which could lead to, and indeed has resulted in, further tensions with Iran.[425]

Finally, Saudi Arabia believed that Western engagement with Iran started out on the wrong foot through the EU3 and its explicit communication of carrots and sticks which no self-respecting state would accept.[426] Germany was responsible for trying to keep this format together in negotiations with Iran as a political solution is only possible through this format (in conjunction with the USA, China and Russia: the 3+3); this is because Iran possibly trusts Germany more.[427] There are no alternatives to this negotiation set-up and without full-fledged war, 'we [the EU3] cannot force our will upon Iran'.[428] The same criticism of the 3+3 being the right institutional framework to negotiate with Iran has also been made, but there is no alternative grouping to lead negotiations, nor is there a new package on the table which could have included different or more creative inspections or monitoring regimes.[429]

The Possibility of Alternative Strategies: Attempting to Reconcile the Resistance and Pro-Western Alliances

The following two sub-sections lay the foundations for a rethinking on the current nuclear negotiations deadlock and pro-sanctions regime. The first details a WMDFZ in the Middle East and the difficulty in bringing all the necessary actors on board in order to achieve its ultimate success. The second proposes a new policy of active engagement which could easily be made operational. It tackles the rationale for the 'resistance axis' head-on by questioning the assumptions of sanctions and containment versus the benefits of literally investing in engagement and dialogue.

A WMDFZ in the Middle East: Redefining Alliances

1. The concept of a WMDFZ in the Middle East is based on extending the 1995 NPT review to include chemical, biological, nuclear and their delivery systems, which itself was an initiative put forward by Egypt in 1990 after calls as far back as 1974 from both Iran and Egypt to avoid WMD in the Middle East.[430] The proposal is important because it could be a way out of the nuclear impasse

with Iran. In order for the proposal to work, it must firstly be guaranteed and thus enforceable by the UNSC, and secondly have a sanctions regime (economic, political and military) and rewards regime (economic and technical aid to encourage states to join), which will ensure that states do not feel threatened by those who try to develop WMD.[431]

There are a number of challenges which need to be overcome before a new WMDFZ in the Middle East can be established. The main one is the Cold War that exists between Iran and Israel.[432] Expecting Iran to give up its enrichment programme and Israel to reduce its arsenal would require counter-intuitive thinking and faith in the UNSC during a period of increasing conflict and uncertainty. Much of that uncertainty stems from the Israel-Palestine conflict. Therefore, although there is a potential positive effect of Palestinian statehood so long as it is done in a way that reduces tensions with Israel, a WMDFZ agreement is unlikely to be reached in the near term.[433] Secondly and on a related point, the WMDFZ would require all actors to cease their respective programmes and/or commit to a phased 'draw down' of nuclear weapons according to an agreed-upon timetable. A WMDFZ across the Middle East would have to include an existing nuclear power, Israel, which does not seem, by any stretch of imagination, willing to give up its nuclear weapons.[434] The lag time required by Israel before it could give up its nuclear weapons is not likely to match the expectations of other actors in the Middle East.[435] Without a WMDFZ agreement as a solution to the Iranian enrichment programme, other solutions must be considered. The future of the Israeli and Palestinian conflict is also at stake since both Israel and the PNA will fail to respect outside pressure if Iran is able to obtain nuclear weapons.[436]

What is encouraging for a WMDFZ in the Middle East is that the rationale for an Iranian nuclear programme appears to be limited. It will take Iran many years to approach the 75–200 nuclear warheads that Israel has and its current nuclear programme is therefore not be enough to tilt the balance of power across the Middle East in Iran's favour.[437] Furthermore, it is 'not plausible' for Iran to give nuclear weapons to Hezbollah and Hamas because Iran would suffer from retaliation from

Israel without having the responsibility for when or why a weapon was used.[438] Although a nuclear Iran might embolden certain groups such as Hamas, functioning under an Iranian nuclear umbrella will be of no use to them because Israel has a second-strike capability.[439] Iran already has a second-strike capability in Hezbollah.[440] Therefore, the Iranian nuclear programme could be categorized in terms related to respect and its sense of place in the international community. Reaching a nuclear agreement should be far easier based on cooperation on these terms and through the exploration of universal themes such as non-proliferation than through sanctions.

The Argument for Active Engagement to Remove Resistance

The belief in the West that tightening sanctions will change Iranian foreign policy is the single greatest barrier to adopting a revised Western foreign policy that includes constructive engagement with the Iranian regime. Sanctions may raise the costs of Iran's nuclear programme in order for it to be no longer in its national interests but these costs will be offset by the Iranian 'economic *jihad*'.[441] The costs could also be transferred from the regime to opposition groups of the government, some of which could be most in favour of a rapprochement with the West.[442] Sanctions have not led to improvements in bilateral dialogue, quite the opposite.[443] They may boost the relative standing of the USA[444] and the UNSC, but they simultaneously depress the standing of Iran and therefore makes it less likely that vital nuclear negotiations will take place.[445] More fundamentally, since the UNSC did not come to a formal conclusion as to whether the Iranian nuclear programme was a 'threat to peace' under Article 39, there are doubts as to whether the use of Chapter 8 to impose 'international obligations on Iran' or sanctions is just.[446] Furthermore, '[s]anctions made no difference to [Iran's foreign] policy'.[447] Since the UNSC imposed sanctions on Iran in 2006, the number of centrifuges has grown in sophistication and increased by a factor of eight.[448] Iran is now enriching uranium to two levels (3.5 per cent and 20 per cent) and developed a second enrichment facility, so sanctions have led to greater resistance against the West, not less.[449]

This has been consistent with the case of Libya. 'As for promoting values and conditions that create a more stable environment, there is no evidence that sanctions did so.'[450] In the case of Sudan, lighter sanctions had more success by showing international disapproval whilst allowing for the possibility of a shift in the regime's policies.[451] Although US policy and UN sanctions have shown disapproval, they have also been heavy sanctions which have reduced the likelihood for a shift in the Iranian regime's foreign policies. As long as Hilary Clinton and the USA takes the self-described policy, '[w]e're not going to keep the window [of diplomacy with Iran on the nuclear issue] open forever', Israel maintains a hawkish stance[452] and IAEA reports[453] escalate civil society buzz around military strikes[454] it is imperative to facilitate dialogue at the earliest opportunity.[455]

Ambassador Indyk believes that given where Iran is in its nuclear programme, its history and the possibility of an Israeli pre-emptive strike, the issue is complicated for the USA. In 2012, there was a more coordinated approach between the USA and the EU for increased sanctions that might avoid such an Israeli strike.[456] In the longer term, the only way Iran and the USA can engage is through a 'road map' of reciprocal moves leading to more constructive relations.[457] Reaching a point of 'high equilibrium' or positive balancing between Iran and the UK, Russia and the USA based on mutual strategic value and no fear on all sides is the ultimate aim.[458] However, the US government needs to know what Iran will do if and when it lifts sanctions and not just pocket concessions as it did during the Khatami era.[459] Iran therefore needs to understand that it must be ready and willing to reciprocate in a timely manner in order to advance relations.

So far what Iran is being offered is not a compromise, but rather the surrender of what it considers (and is) its right to enrich.[460] Insisting on Iran giving up enrichment is legally weak and politically ineffective.[461] The Iranian argument to Brazil that 'today Iran has been denied its rights to enrich under the NPT, tomorrow it will be you' is also getting traction; the non-nuclear states are not so convinced that Iran requires special treatment because it is technically in accordance with the NPT.[462] Iran has to be submitted to IAEA controls, and given the doubts and the ambiguities, it has to be submitted to special controls which should be the object of negotiations.[463] Instead of singling out Iran, an improved IAEA framework could simultaneously tackle nuclear-related and proliferation issues of all the nuclear programmes inside and outside of the NPT, including North Korea, Pakistan, India and Israel. Making the NPT more robust or supplementing it with a mandatory Additional Protocol is especially important since part of the Iranian nuclear programme, through 'nuclear-related activities', already falls outside of the provisions contained in the NPT.[464]

Negotiating only on the nuclear issue with Iran and, worse than that, only on enrichment, is a bad strategy. The EU3 should increase the number of issues, and sometimes common interests, on which it negotiates if it wants to reach a deal.[465] Iran still needs technology transfer from the West/Japan to Iran: Iran needs $100 billion to develop its oil and gas industry, which could be a major factor in normalizing its international relations in future.[466] Hojjat Al-Eslam Mesbahi-Moqaddam, head of the parliamentary Economic Development Scheme Commission, says the Iranian Central Bank has 'more than $100 billion'.[467] Iran is known to have huge reserves which would be best to exploit now, tax and encourage high production; Iran could then invest in industries *inside* Iran and develop its economy more effectively.[468] The pressure from sanctions may not be as great as the West would like it to be, but there is still great potential in renewing energy cooperation,[469] nuclear power cooperation, a regional security framework inclusive of Iran and a US security guarantee.[470]

Regional security inclusive of Iran will be a challenge if Iran continues to project more influence regionally and in South West Asia to undercut the US presence there.[471] Khamenei has also called the US and EU presence in the Persian Gulf 'detrimental and unwarranted'.[472] Therefore some moderation of Western intervention will be required. Finding common ground should start with Afghanistan. One senior British diplomat opined: 'I think Iran should be included in a regional security framework, and I think the way to start is to engage them over a regional framework over Afghanistan and then building out from there.'[473] Any political agreement with Iran will require the support of the IAEA, the UN, Iran's main trading partners and the USA.[474] The goals of the P5+1 – the USA, Russia, Germany, France, China and the UK – will always be to have high levels of assurance that Iran is not diverting nuclear material for military purposes and that it will contribute to regional security.[475] However, these relationships cannot be dominated by the nuclear issue alone, since distrust on the Iranian side will continue to build if communications and negotiations remain sterile.[476]

Iran has pointed to greater regionalism in Central Asia and the development of bilateral relations with a variety of other non-aligned actors from Ecuador to Turkmenistan to Zimbabwe in order to counter US- and UNSC-imposed sanctions. However, none of these relationships will be able to fill the void left by the loss of contracts with IOCs and FDI from the West. This is particularly the case as major oil and gas investment is needed to modernize South Pars LNG fields 1–11 to boost production and revenues.[477] Iran's 'axis of oil' with Venezuela is also in question which makes its options for balancing against Israel, the USA and other European powers almost non-existent.

Instead of sanctions and a possible military strike against Iran by the USA or Israel, the West should be able to not only illustrate, but demonstrate, to Khamenei, Ahmadinejad and the IRGC that it is in their interests to re-align with the West. This would mean Iran turns a page in its support of PIJ and Hezbollah, puts its enrichment programme into full compliance with the NPT or a revised treaty, and limits its irredentism and leverage of sectarian divides. For the West, it would mean the US government coming to terms with the 1979 embassy hostage crisis and making up for the common stance taken against Iran during the Iran–Iraq War. The best way to do this is by replicating Kennedy's policy with the Soviet Union using some moderated Helsinki Process, or Kissinger's policy of rapprochement with China (with some moderations since the USA and China were already nuclear powers).[478]

A new 'critical dialogue', involving many of the binding commitments in the Helsinki Process, across politico-military, environmental, economic and human aspects of security is required. A new TCA would fulfil the economic dimension of the process which could include facilitating oil payments and re-establishing trade links, renewing FDI and opening markets. This would serve to undermine the black markets controlled by the IRGC, their profits and the security threats from smuggled nuclear and dual-use goods. A TCA would also serve to broaden dialogue on a number of levels whereby each issue could promote modified foreign policy behaviour because it would be in Iran's national interest to do so.

Beyond a nuclear-based deal, Afghanistan holds part of the key to reintegrating Iran with the international community through a revised regional security agreement which could extend to include the GCC states. The US government has found Iranian overtures of a broad dialogue hard to reconcile with its own preference for a narrow dialogue and has reservations about dialogue in general. The lack of serious commitment from the US administration has had a serious knock-on effect in negotiations with the EU3 and yet such contact with full US support is increasingly the only positive option available as the US government tries to assuage Israeli national security fears, reduce its forces in Afghanistan and Iraq and endeavours to promote a successful conclusion to the MEPP and GWOT.

CHAPTER 5

THE TRIANGULATION OF US FOREIGN POLICY TOWARDS THE MIDDLE EAST

This chapter argues that the international community, notably the non-Western states of the UNSC, Russia and China, as well as non-aligned BRICS members such as India, all impinge on US foreign policy in the Middle East. Non-Western states will continue to gain strength from the relative decline in US hegemony, facilitated partly through the lack of a two-state solution, sectarian strife after the US-led invasion of Iraq and, in the case of Afghanistan, from early troop disengagement. However, the USA will continue to leverage its policies towards the Middle East through more dependent states such as Japan, which still require US security guarantees, and by impinging on the policies of its partners such as the EU3. The respective motivations and roles of the leading actors in the international community outlined in this chapter are increasingly important to the foreign policy calculations of the EU3 and the USA. The chapter concludes with foreign policy recommendations for the USA based on its existing foreign policy objectives and strategies, relative to the foreign policy performance of emerging powers.

Russia

The willingness of Russia to impinge on US foreign policies in the Middle East is a function of Russia's historical relationship with the

USA, Russia's status as a former great power and the spheres of influence created during the Cold War. Russian relations with the Middle East have continued to rest on Syria, which is a bulkhead against perceived western domination in the Middle East. Russian relations with Iran have also been important, but have tended to follow a more ad hoc pattern based on the convergence of their respective strategic national interests. Post-9/11, Russia has viewed increasing US and NATO operations in the Middle East, Caucasus and Central Asia with unease since large parts of these regions remain in Russia's sphere of influence. Russia and Iran therefore share the same strategic interests in pushing out third powers, such as the USA, from the region. Russia does have a basic framework of cooperation with Iran, laid out in the Treaty of Basic Principles of Cooperation, signed in 2001.[1] However, the combination of Russia's economy still being based on the exportation of raw materials and hydrocarbons, and the effect of sanctions against Iran, have limited bilateral trade and investment. Therefore, Russo-Iranian cooperation cannot expect to rival Russian relations with the USA, EU and Commonwealth of Independent States (CIS).

The Russo-Iranian bilateral relationship has been compromised mainly by the Iranian nuclear programme and Russia's diplomatic response to it. In particular, from 2000, the main barrier to improving Russia's relations with Iran was due to the Gore–Chernomyrdin Protocol. This negotiation between the USA and Russia was based on the US government trying to learn more about the conventional arms sales between Russia and Iran, and to circumscribe it. In exchange for cooperation, the US government did not seek to impose penalties (sanctions) against Russia for supplying arms to a US State Department-designated State Sponsor of Terrorism.[2] Russia did not end the arms transfers according to the Gore–Chernomyrdin timetable, and the agreement therefore became non-functioning. However, there has been cooperation from Russia, on a more ad hoc basis, regarding Russia's involvement in constructing the Bushehr nuclear facility in Iran. Russia was quite willing to delay development of the Bushehr nuclear reactor in pursuit of its wider interests with the USA and UNSC. As Katzman observed in Chapter 4, by delaying the development of the Bushehr reactor, Russia was able to allay US fears about uranium enrichment at the site and wider fears about the Iranian nuclear programme. In general, Russia appears to be against an Iranian nuclear weapons capability, primarily because it would change the balance of power in the region and lead to more assertive Iranian policies in Russia's traditional sphere of influence.

Putin, during his second term as President of Russia in 2007, labelled Iran as Russia's 'greatest national security threat' when speaking to then US Defence Secretary Robert Gates.[3] However, labels have not stopped Russia from supplying 70 per cent of Iranian arms, justifying them as defensive weapons.[4] The TOR-M1 short-range surface-to-air missile system deal (useful to Iran in countering US or Israeli airstrikes) was signed between Russia and Iran in December 2005 and completed in early 2007.[5] However, the more recent S-300 missile defence deal has been suspended by Dmitry Medvedev in an attempt to improve Russian relations with the USA.[6] This move is particularly significant because a missile defence system such as the S-300 could reduce the ability for Israel or the USA to conduct a pre-emptive aerial campaign to destroy Iran's underground nuclear facilities at Natanz and Fordo, near Qom.[7] Whether the incumbent president, Vladimir Putin, chooses to maintain, withdraw, or expand Russian economic interests in Iran remains to be seen. The Russian chief of the general staff, army general Nikolai Makarov, said in 2012 that based on Russian-US analysis and in the context of joint missile defence, Iran does represent a threat.[8] Iran could therefore give Russia and the USA a useful pretext for expanding military and missile defence cooperation, a persistent irritant in their bilateral relationship.

However, Russian-US cooperation may not be sustainable and there is evidence from Russia that penalties can be employed if it feels the USA is interfering in its sphere of influence. Russia began work again at the $1 billion Bushehr reactor in 2009 in response to US support of Georgia in its 2008 conflict with Russia.[9] The reactor was made operational in 2011.[10] The Russian rationale appears to be based on its view that Iranian rhetoric about its nuclear programme is simply bravado. Russian support of the Iranian civilian nuclear programme can also be attributed to the Russian elite wishing to increase their business interests in Iran with the support of the Kremlin. From 2009,

Medvedev and Obama have worked in closer cooperation to sanction Iran as Russia was more willing to compromise with the USA in order to further Russian global interests. Russia is also conscious that better relations between the USA and Iran must be limited by better relations between Russia and Iran if Russia is to maintain its dominant regional position. Russian foreign policy towards Iran will continue to be a function of its competing and converging national and international interests, and the Kremlin's choice to participate in UNSC resolutions as one of the easiest ways to pursue its global interests. For example, Russia is unlikely to support the strengthening of the US–EU oil embargo against Iran because, as an energy exporter, Russia wants to disassociate political motivations from energy exports.[11]

President Obama established a 'reset' policy with Russia in 2010, and although this has quickly been complicated by NATO missile defence, the renaissance in relations continues to be responsible for limiting some of Russia's relations with Iran.[12] Russia has always taken the view that unilateral sanctions against Iran were not justified and pushed for cooperation with Iran across various sectors including energy, high technology and culture. Russia's relations with Iran are based on pragmatism and opportunity, exploiting the withdrawal of Western investment and capital from the Iranian market within the confines of simultaneously pursuing a better partnership with the USA. The Russian policy towards Iran has sometimes sent mixed signals because it has competing foreign policy objectives towards the USA and Iran.

Russian foreign policy objectives towards the USA include elements of cooperation as outlined by the *Survey of the Foreign Policy of the Russian Federation*, a 2007 report issued by the Russian Ministry of Foreign Affairs.[13] Good relations with the USA were determined in the report to be vital in containing transnational threats such as terrorism and proliferation.[14] Advancing cooperation with the USA was also balanced with concerns against Western-led interference in Russian affairs, wider Western interests and military interventions.[15] Leading Western interests included NATO missile defence in Eastern Europe and Turkey, NATO operations in Afghanistan, western penetration in the Caucasus and Central Asia and trans-Caspian pipelines to Europe.

Meanwhile, Russia has been offering Iran substantial relief from international sanctions through cooperation with companies such as Rosneft, Gazprom and Tatneft exporting petrol, selling equipment to Iran's oil and gas industry and establishing new transport infrastructure projects.[16] The proposed Neka-Jask pipeline which would involve Gazprom and NIOC and link the Kazakh oil fields and those in the Caspian region with Oman is one potential joint venture.[17] There are also energy swap deals taking place between Russia, Iran and Turkmenistan so that Russia can continue to control competing oil and gas supplies to Europe. The failure of the Nabucco pipeline to link the EU to oil- and gas-producing states beyond Turkey can also be seen to be part of this Russian strategy of energy cooperation and control.[18] Talks between Russia and OPEC to coordinate production levels to keep prices high also confirm this policy, but underscore the missing supply and demand sides of energy cooperation that could contribute to a closer bilateral relationship.[19]

Russian banks may no longer be able to process payments from Iran, and other trade may be low level, but Iran could utilize what could be termed the 'India Model' by paying for trade in a local currency such as Russian roubles. This change could facilitate Iranian investments in the Russian market. The Russo-Iranian bilateral relationship remains a pragmatic one, built on the triangulation of decision-making expected from Russia by the USA. Triangulation is likely to be easier for Russia than China, since Russian diplomats are more experienced in negotiating with their US counterparts, especially during crises such as the Cold War. Keeping unnecessary irritants and aggravations between Russia and the West to a minimum are the principle attributes of Russian foreign policy in its dealings with Iran and other Middle East states. The Russian case shows the following factors to be important in Russian-US relations, with significant consequences for the Middle East. Firstly, compromise is possible over non-vital Russian and US interests. Conversely, Russia and the USA have clashed over their perceived vital interests in the Middle East, notably in Syria.

Whether or not the Syrian uprising will be successful at toppling the Al-Assad regime, a Russian ally, and whether or not the Free Syrian Army receives Western assistance will determine whether Russia chooses to ally itself with the West in the UNSC. Russian policy post-Assad could impact on its existing alliance with the USA, and it could have great consequences for future Western foreign policy in the Middle East. Russia has already lost its economic and political ties to Egypt, Iraq and Libya, and therefore supporting further Western interventions in the Middle East would be foolhardy, bordering on counterproductive. The only exemption to this would be if Russia could establish a quid pro quo with the West in a similar way to the alleged deal between Saudi Arabia and NATO regarding actions towards Libya and Bahrain outlined in Chapter 3.

Secondly, Russia has leverage against the USA, more than almost any other state. Russian WMD programmes and stocks of conventional weapons, membership in major multilateral organizations such as the UNSC and its status as a regional hegemon make it less susceptible to US pressure. Successive US administrations will need Russia in the pursuit of other foreign policies and particularly on geo-strategic and security-related issues. For example, Russia can leverage its primary interests with the USA through progressing or stalling on the ratification of the new START treaty.[20]

Russia is relatively free to conduct trade and investment with Iran under a US presidential waiver and pursue the most favourable terms of trade.[21] The Kremlin enjoys the kinds of benefits from its active dialogue with Iran that is recommended to the West in Chapter 4. There is bilateral cooperation on drug trafficking and in building economic ties, implementing measures against terrorism and attempting to stave off the commonly perceived threats from the 'colour' revolutions in the CIS and Balkan states.[22] However, Russian cooperation with Iran on arms sales and nuclear expertise has attracted alleged Saudi attempts to counter them through closer Saudi-Russian trade links and the offer of lucrative Saudi contracts.[23] Saudi Arabia relations with Russia will likely suffer from close Iranian-Russian relations, as illustrated by the $800 million cancelled Russian Railways contract in Saudi Arabia in 2008 due to its other business interests in Libya at the time, a state with which Saudi Arabia had difficult relations.[24] Saudi Arabia is also alleged to have directly interfered in the case of the Bushehr plant and handed out generous payments to Russian workers if they decided to quit and go home.²⁵ Generally though, Saudi-Russian relations will remain dominated by their respective stance on oil, whereby Saudi Arabia is pushing for lower prices and Russia and Iran are pushing for higher oil prices. As long as Russia continues to benefit from OPEC oil production cuts without cutting production itself, increasing friction will be apparent between Riyadh and Moscow until the Kremlin decides to join OPEC. The lack of coordination on oil policy has already extended to a lack of consultation on Syria before Russia employed its veto in the UNSC. As a consequence, Saudi Arabia has been forced to support the idea of helping to arm the Syrian Free Army.²⁶

Russia holds the keys for Iranian expansion of economic ties into the CIS region and continues to block Iranian accession to non-Western regional economic organizations such as the SCO (a potential energy axis). This is despite Iranian rhetoric supporting Russian policies towards Georgia, Abkazia and South Ossetia.²⁷ Russia understands that it must assert its interests with the USA but only on the points on which the USA is willing to compromise. If Russia does go through another period of resurgent nationalism, and this is translated into tougher negotiations with the USA, the Obama administration could find that its 'reset' policy towards Russia was premature. Even more damaging to the USA and EU3 would be if Russia were to renege on important security treaties or resist cooperation in the UNSC or G20 in response to changes in the Middle East dynamic.

China

Since China experienced its first oil deficit in 1993, it has pursued a policy of putting its economic relationship with the Gulf States ahead of politics.²⁸ China has also increased its oil imports from the Gulf dramatically, leading to an oil-based partnership since 1999 between Sinopec and Saudi Aramco, with the participation of ExxonMobil.²⁹ A rise in oil prices in the early 2000s has given Saudi Arabia the financial resources to invest in China at a time when China was opening up to Gulf investment after WTO accession. The bilateral relationship was also facilitated by 9/11 as Saudi Arabia felt it necessary to establish better relations with China as an alternative partner to the

USA. In contrast, China's relations with Iran have been less strategic than those with Saudi Arabia and more transactional, particularly since a deal between Sinopec and NIOC has dwindled from a $100 billion long-term contract in 2004 to a $2 billion contract by the time it was implemented in 2007.[30] In the Saudi and Iranian relationship with China, differences stem from Iran not being part of the WTO and coming under increasing pressure from international sanctions. China is cutting oil imports from Iran, which may be testament to Chinese cooperation with US sanctions and an unwillingness to accept US punitive measures, an opportunity to command a lower oil price from Iran[31] or simply differences over the terms of supply agreements that can easily be rectified.[32]

The Chinese approach to relations with Saudi Arabia, Iran and the wider Middle East has formed part of its calculations of its international relations with the USA, including China's emerging great power status, China's fears of US interference in its domestic politics (a point echoed by Russia) and the knock-on effects that the Arab Uprisings might have in Beijing. China's policy towards the Middle East and the USA is therefore not always explicitly stated, but signalled through its primary security, energy and economic policies. Energy policy is at the heart of current Chinese foreign policy because of its massive internal energy demands. China is also dependent on the USA for protection of much of the 7,000 miles of sea lanes between the Strait of Hormuz and the Strait of Malacca into the South China Sea. Energy policy has led China to build relations with states such as Syria, Iran and Iraq, which are less pro-Western and have significant oil reserves ready to export. However, this Chinese policy must be put into the broader context of the symbiotic relationship that now exists between China and the USA in the global economy. China remains economically dependent on the USA as an export market and the USA remains exposed to China through Beijing's ownership of US treasury bonds. Neither side is at the point of wanting to compromise its primary objectives over Middle East politics which have yet to be played out in full. Nevertheless, strategically and militarily, there are many irritants in the Sino-US relationship, including US arms sales to Taiwan, US military surveillance close to Chinese borders and strengthened

US security ties with China's neighbours such as India, Vietnam and, further afield, Australia.[33]

Politically, China is becoming a leading example of an alternative economic model which does not require democracy to thrive. China therefore undermines Western assertions that democracy provides a framework for economic reform which could lead every state to prosperity. China proves that what is important is integration into the world economy, not the importation of political systems from the West. China's unique political economy hybrid (a one-party state and market economy) could therefore be its biggest asset in the post-Arab Uprisings environment. China is also an attractive model versus the Western one because of its peaceful development and harmonious approach to international relations. This is known as China's 'multidimensional diplomacy' which was promoted by Jiang Zemin at the 16th Chinese People's Political Consultative Conference in 2002 and pursued under Hu Jintao.[34] China continues to veto UNSC resolutions that deal with the internal affairs of sovereign states in the Middle East. These non-intervention principles tend to hold unless there are circumstances which make intervention preferable, based on international security concerns or the possibility that China becomes unnecessarily isolated in the UNSC.[35]

China's position on the Middle East has been facilitated less by avoiding confrontation with the USA, than by Saudi Arabia and Iran seeking a strategic counterweight to the USA post-9/11. In response, Beijing has promoted multilateralism and the UN as the crucial actor with regard to reconstruction in Iraq. China has also favoured explicit end dates for US troop occupation there.[36] In 2002, Beijing dispatched its first Middle East peace envoy, Wang Shijie, to the region as an indication of China's more involved approach.[37] China, like Russia, has gained from active diplomatic engagement in the Middle East, but from a much lower starting point. China's rationale is largely based on signing new trade and investment deals which will secure its energy needs into the future. The challenge for China will be to garner new or deeper relationships in the Middle East that have been dominated by increasing inter-regionalism with the West (e.g. between the EU and GCC) and long-term arms deals. Although China's economic growth has been meteoric, what would be the implications for its trade deals with the Middle East states should that growth slow? Many Middle East states are very cautious about developing exclusive relationships, and therefore tend to focus on developing links with a number of powers in case such a situation arises.

Growing Sino-Saudi relations are met by Western fears of China securing access to energy supplies in the Middle East and beyond at the expense of the West. This could be particularly worrying for the West if China views its relationship with the USA as a 'long-term zero-sum game'.[38] The Brookings Institution cites Chinese policies on, or attitudes to, intellectual property theft, its RMB currency, constraints on FDI and rare earth metals to support its 'zero-sum' theory.[39] China has growing hard power options with the development of its blue water capability (including at the Pakistani deep water port of Gwadar, close to the Strait of Hormuz).[40] Consequently, China has a growing capability to counter the growing US presence in the Gulf and its bases in Central, South and West Asia.

China's foreign policy towards the Middle East will remain one which addresses possible causes of confrontation between China and the USA. China can also afford to take a more relaxed approach to the Middle East, as opposed to Russia for example, since it already has good relations with many Gulf States. China can afford to wait for the USA to continue to make missteps and facilitate its own departure from the region to become an 'over the horizon' power once again. However, multilaterally, China is tied into the P5+1 grouping which aims to exert pressure on Iran to abandon its uranium enrichment programme. Therefore, through membership of global organizations, China will increasingly be tied into global norms which have been at least partly developed or determined by US interests. For the time being China may have to tow the multilateral line, but increasingly China is acquiring the financial resources and influence which the USA is currently leveraging against its adversaries, such as freezing assets, cancelling commercial contracts and implementing sanctions. Should the USA continue to withdraw from its oil-related interests from the Middle East, China could be left to fill the void.

In the meantime, Russia and China will continue to monitor the Arab Uprisings for signs of US support for domestic opposition groups through its 'Freedom Agenda' in spreading US influence and for signs that the contagion of the uprisings has spread to their own capitals. Russia and China have experience of domestic unrest, from the period of transition from Communism to capitalism in Moscow in 1991, and the Tiananmen Square protests in Beijing in 1989. There have already been uprisings in the Russian sphere of influence of Eastern Europe, dubbed 'colour' revolutions, between 2003 and 2005. Like the Arab Uprisings, these have been attributed not to spontaneous revolutions but to the USA, through the 'democracy assistance' work of the United States Agency for International Development (USAID), the National Endowment for Democracy, the Open Society Institute, Freedom House and the International Center on Nonviolent Conflict.[41]

The mistrust therefore, between Russia, China and the USA, could lead Russia and China to adopt a countering strategy disproportionate to any US influence in the uprisings.[42] Russia and China have already responded robustly against Western-led intervention in Syria.[43] However, their respective positions may quickly be moderated by their exposure to the Gulf monarchies. For example, King Abdullah of Saudi Arabia spoke candidly on Saudi national television about his concerns regarding the sectarian nature of the conflict in Syria following the UNSC vote.[44]

India

India is a vital US partner in the Asian region because it is an emerging market and perceived bulkhead against Chinese expansionism. India is also a beacon of democracy and open society that the USA is trying to replicate in the wider Middle East. However, India cannot be described as pro-Western. India has a long history and leading role in the NAM and has more policy options apart from directly aligning with the West by being part of the BRICS group. Furthermore, India is not caving into US pressure to sanction Iran. India is one of Iran's top trade partners and unlike Western states, Iran has managed to work out a flexible solution for its payment problems with India. The solution, which involves Indian rupees to pay for 45 per cent of Iran's oil, could lead to increased trade ties with Iran and the opportunity for India to increase its influence across the Middle East as US foreign policy falters.[45] There are already signs that India has been able to use the BRICS alliance to promote its more independent foreign policies. For example, at the end of the fourth summit of the BRICS states in New Delhi in March 2012, the Indian Prime Minister, Manmohan Singh, said that: 'We agreed that a lasting solution in Syria and Iran can only be found through dialogue...'[46] This statement puts the emphasis of active engagement with Iran and Syria very much back on the foreign policy agenda of the EU3 and the USA.

Japan

Japan is the state that is the least likely to impinge on the foreign policy interests of the EU3 and the USA in the Middle East. This is due to a number of reasons: Japan has been dependent on US security guarantees since the end of the Second World War; Japan has no political stake in the Middle East and there are conflicting debates about what future role Japan should play abroad; and Japan has suffered from a series of domestic crises (earthquake, tsunami and civilian nuclear crisis) which have made it difficult for the state to engage in an active foreign policy.

Japan continues to lack a military profile of its own due to its postwar constitution, and this is becoming a source of tension in Japanese domestic politics. Japan therefore remains dependent on the USA for its security in the same way that it remains dependent on the Middle East for its energy needs. Energy dependency ensures a consistent level of Japanese political solidarity with the oil exporters, even if its direct intervention during periods of conflict has been confined to helping finance the Gulf War.[47] As a leading economy, Japan can offer more than solidarity to the Middle East. In the post-Arab Uprisings environment, Japanese economic assistance, planning and expertise in political transition could be vital to sustaining democratic projections. These are complimentary to US policy in support of the uprisings.

Japan is already trying to generate goodwill in the Middle East, mainly through large-scale development grants and loans to states such as Egypt.[48] Japan continues to build on these ties with training programmes for graduates in Tunisia and Egypt.[49] The paradox for future Japanese foreign policy-makers is the split approach between trying to fulfil Japanese energy needs through investing in energy projects from Iran through Central Asia, and keeping its commitment to the USA to maintain pressure on Iran.[50] Which course Japanese policy-makers choose in the future could have a dramatic bearing on Japanese engagement in the Middle East and its relations with the USA. Unfortunately for Japan, apart from the G20, its influence through multilateral organizations which could boost its engagement in the Middle East remain limited.

Without a major political stake in the Middle East, economic relations are far more important in maintaining Japanese foreign relations than they are for many of the other states in this chapter, except perhaps India. The Japanese policy of putting energy security before bilateral relations has further eroded Japan's relationship with major oil exporters. Although Japan is a major oil customer and a significant source of commercial opportunities and expertise for many Middle East states, including Iran, these linkages have been negatively impacted by Japan's dependence on the USA. The USA has therefore easily been able to convert Japan's military weakness into political concessions regarding its policies on the Middle East, and especially in cutting back Iranian oil imports.[51] The growing size of China and India as major oil customers with more independent bilateral and collective foreign policies is also likely to skew future Middle East relations in their favour.

The Convergence of Western Foreign Policies in the Middle East

The 'strategic triangle' between the USA, EU and pro-Western Middle East states such as Saudi Arabia was functioning long before 9/11, most notably against Iran during the Iran–Iraq War and against Iraq during the first Gulf War. However, the GWOT facilitated their closer cooperation and the EU has preferred to harmonize its positions with the USA. This is also true to some extent in the case of the EU's relationship with the UN and Russia through the Quartet which was set up in 2002 to support the MEPP and eventual Palestinian statehood, and comprises the UN, EU, the USA and Russia. An independent EU foreign policy has therefore proved elusive.[52] What started out as an ideologically compatible 'War on Terror' has given way to a new Western agenda of democratic and economic reform, which has been met with resistance both in the Middle East and, increasingly, from other permanent members of the UNSC.[53]

There are a number of systemic issues with the EU, which have led to dependence on the USA taking a policy lead in the Middle East. Firstly, the EU and the USA share a similar ideological outlook, which makes cooperation on democracy and reform in the Middle East relatively easy. US and EU policies have been compromised by their double standards regarding democracy promotion, which was apparent in their withdrawal of economic support following the electoral win of Hamas in Gaza in 2006. EU policy on economic reform has also been compromised through a lack of credibility after the global financial crisis in 2008 and Euro crisis in 2012.[54]

Secondly, the EU, having being conceived as a European economic community, has been predominantly concerned with economic policy as opposed to security policy, which makes it highly dependent on US hard power. The disintegration of the Balkans required US support through NATO and the EU must consult closely with the USA on the Iranian nuclear dossier through the P5+1 arrangement. The EU continues to invest in soft power; €12 billion through the European Neighbourhood Policy (ENP) to spread EU values.[55] However, it is hard power which is likely to count more in addressing a range of conventional and unconventional threats in the Middle East. EU NATO member defence spending of $270 billion is expected to be overtaken by the Asian states in 2012, marking a further erosion of relative European power.[56] Furthermore, whilst some European states have well-developed policies on the Middle East, others such as Germany have none beyond Israel and Iran.[57]

Given the shifting global balance of power against US and EU interests, their overlapping memberships in international organizations such as the UNSC and their long-term commitments to existing policies, the decoupling of the USA and EU is unlikely to happen soon.

US Policy in the Middle East and Policy Prescriptions

The USA needs to re-evaluate its policies on the Middle East since many of them have impinged on its own national interests. President Obama tried to herald a 'new beginning' in his Cairo speech despite maintaining focus on a democratization and reform agenda.[58] However, before the GMEI is adopted, concrete evidence of more positive US intentions in the Middle East needs to be established, such as a two-state solution to the Israel–Palestine conflict and the implementation of long-term economic measures outlined in the Barcelona Process.[59] An integral part of fulfilling these prerequisites is active engagement with the Middle East governments and peoples, and with allies and adversaries. The USA should recalibrate its policies towards the Middle East during the Arab Uprisings and allow Middle East states to define their own future, instead of contributing to the perception that the USA is pursuing its own interests through a 'Freedom Agenda'.[60] If uprisings fail based on popular support for the existing government or type of governance, then the USA should be more willing to work with governments which do not necessarily share its core values. The solution in that case is highlighted in Chapter 4 as being based on a robust and comprehensive diplomatic framework, focusing on state and regional issues, and the inclusion of associated actors or issues that are particularly challenging.

US engagement in the Gulf continues to form a big part of the challenge to activating a pan-regional security framework that would safeguard a new regional order, stability and peace. The USA is attempting to salvage its relationship with the GCC based on engagement mainly against the common threats of Iran and Syria, through the newly dubbed GCC–US Strategic Cooperation Forum.[61] However, Iran and Syria could be coupled with the Central Asian region for Western policy purposes because Central Asia is where the USA, EU3, Russia, China, India, Pakistan and the Middle East states have similar aims and objectives. The continuity of policy from Central Asia into the Middle East therefore represents a greater opportunity for extended cooperation. By engaging in foreign policy issues related to the wider region, Western governments could establish a Helsinki Process with relatively stable states (at least states which are far less geopolitically sensitive). This would give the rest of the Middle East states time to make critical decisions about their own futures.

In trying to shape the Middle East, the USA could learn from the Saudi policy outlined in Chapter 3, because when it matters most, during periods of conflict and uprisings, Saudi policy has targeted the 'hearts and minds' of the local population. That is not a euphemism for an ideological struggle or military intervention advocated by a Republican presidential candidate[62] or the American Israel Public Affairs Committee (AIPAC).[63] It literally advocates investing in the hearts and minds of the population through massive investments in healthcare and education. The USA, through the implementation of more humanitarian, trade and investment programmes would be more likely to succeed in achieving its democratization objectives through the better communication of a positive image of democracy that directly addresses local priorities.

CHAPTER 6

CONCLUSIONS: ECONOMIC FACTORS IN MIDDLE EAST FOREIGN POLICIES

This final chapter compares Saudi and Iranian foreign policy, and assesses the relative weight of economic and non-economic factors in Middle East FPA. A number of conclusions are drawn about economic factors in alliance-building and alliance-deconstruction in and between the pro-Western and 'resistance' alliances. The conclusions in this research are also applied to Syria, another member of the 'resistance axis' which is experiencing some of the same targeted, US-led sanctions as those imposed on Iran. Indicative factors outlined in the book are applied to hypotheses about the future of Middle East foreign policy-making and the future of FPA. The Saudi and Iranian cases illustrate the extent to which a combination of ideological, geo-strategic and economic resources have insulated the regimes against internal and external pressures and resulted in their dominance in the regional system.

The Relative Weight of Economic and Non-Economic Factors

This book covers a range of factors in foreign policy, such as ideology, geo-strategic concerns and objectives and economic issues. In practice, in the Saudi and Iranian cases, these have tended to galvanize around regional rivalries. The ideological factors which have been shown to be paramount in Saudi and Iranian foreign policies are:

1. The ideological rationales that underpin their foreign policy orientations and participation in the pro-Western alliance versus anti-systemic or anti-Western alliance;
2. Sectarianism as a source of conflict, alliance and legitimacy between and within states;
3. An emphasis on ideational resources in Iran, such as its ancient civilization and empire, which helps it to compete against the stronger Islamic and pan-Arab credentials of Saudi Arabia;
4. Increasing nationalism in Iran as part of a reflex against perceived Western domination and interference in domestic affairs;
5. The continued relevance of the occupied Palestinian territories as a pan-Arab cause from which the Iranian regime is able to draw support for its 'resistance' policies against Israel.

The geo-strategic factors which have been shown to be paramount in their foreign policies are:

1. Increasing US interventionist policies from the first Gulf War and its renewed influence across the wider Middle East, in Afghanistan, Iraq and in support of the Arab Uprisings;
2. The domestic and international security imperatives of Saudi Arabia through the GCC, notably in Bahrain;
3. The Iranian nuclear programme, which has led to tightening sanctions by the West and negative foreign policy responses by Iran in turn, such as threats to close the Strait of Hormuz.

The economic factors which have been shown to be paramount in their foreign policies are:

1. Oil revenues in contributing to the national budget and foreign reserves;
2. The use of oil pricing (within OPEC) and unilateral supply policies as a weapon used between major exporters, notably by Saudi Arabia;

3. Stable and secure energy markets (including deepening bilateral relations such as new strategic partnerships, based on energy supply and cooperation);
4. The short-term effectiveness of 'riyal politik' and cheap/free oil to encourage bandwagoning from ideologically compatible 'small states' or non-state actors without adequate access to economic resources during periods of crisis;
5. The use of large commercial contracts as leveraging mechanisms against suppliers through which states such as Saudi Arabia may attempt to exert influence on behalf of close allies (such as the USA) for more congruent Middle Eastern policies;
6. The multiple, and ultimately symbolic rather than material, trade and cooperation agreements signed between Iran and non-aligned or anti-Western members of the international community.

The continuation and emergence of new geo-strategic factors such as the Arab Uprisings have simply aggravated the decades-old regional rivalry between Iran and Saudi Arabia. Saudi Arabia has used its vast material resources not only as a weapon against oil price-sensitive adversaries such as Iran, but is simultaneously using the same resources to increase ties with strategic allies internationally. In contrast, economic factors in Iranian foreign policy are made less relevant by its overriding ideological and geo-strategic manifestations, interpretations and extrapolations. These include the primacy of its nuclear programme as a manifestation of regional leadership and security concerns; its support for proscribed groups and Shi'i communities in the Levant and the Gulf as leverage against ideological and sectarian rivals; and a lack of support for a two-state solution based on its 'resistance' perspective. Iran's foreign policies in this regard tend to lack an exclusive economic output. For example, payments to the Afghan government and to Hezbollah were accompanied by payments from other actors such as the USA and Syria respectively.

However, a second tier of Iranian foreign policies which aims to counter the impact of sanctions does have a significant economic dimension to it, which includes trade realignment, subsidy reform and new oil- and gas-based partnerships. Since sanctions against Iran are still some way off from creating a tipping point[1] towards greater pragmatism in Iranian foreign policy, the utilization of economic factors (and therefore the balance with non-economic factors) continues to be skewed according to its foremost national interests. Should economic conditions worsen in Iran, there could be an expectation that Iranian foreign policy might once again become more pragmatic and boost the fortunes of the Green movement or other reformists in Iran. The chance of this happening remains slim without a comprehensive oil embargo that includes Iran's top trade partners such as China, Russia, India, the UAE and Turkey. The greatest economic factor in Iran is therefore the central role of maintaining oil revenues to sustain the current regime and its 'revolutionary' foreign policy agenda.

Economic Factors in Alliance Building

Economic factors, with an emphasis on relationships dominated by oil, have been evident in a number of foreign policies that Saudi Arabia and Iran have pursued, and continue to pursue. The Saudi response to the Arab Uprisings has reflected the shock that the Saudis felt with the loss of a vital regional ally, President Mubarak in Egypt. Through Saudi Arabia losing its confidence in the USA, a more normalized era in Saudi–US relations has begun, and forced Saudi Arabia to establish a new modus operandi in its foreign policy.

Saudi strategic thinking in the growing multilateral platform of the GCC is becoming more important than at any time before, as the GCC is taking on a more vital role during the Arab Uprisings. The GCC is a reliable alliance of like-minded Sunni monarchies with closely aligned national interests, concentrated in a region dominated once again by common threats. Some of those threats come from the standoff between Shi'i minorities and the GCC states. This has been evident in Bahrain and Saudi Arabia, and although Iran has not intervened directly in the demonstrations so far, the rhetorical campaign in support of the uprisings continues to be an irritant and destabilizing factor which contributes to GCC cohesion. Since most oil and gas exporters in the region are also members of the GCC, Saudi interests appear assured. However, there is still considerable friction between

Saudi Arabia and Qatar in their foreign policy perspectives. Qatar's primary aim appears to create distance and autonomy for itself but within the GCC rubric. However, unless Iran is able to establish an alternative alliance with Russia or China and thereby provide an alternative grouping for Qatar to ally with, Qatar's status and interests within the Saudi-dominated GCC are set to continue.

The GCC is probably the only organization in the Middle East with the material resources to stabilize the Arab revolutionary agenda and neutralize any Iranian threat. The GCC aims to continue the pro-stability process through a combination of state consolidation, regional integration and expansion. Economic factors in this new formation include Saudi Arabia seeking to expand the Peninsular Shield Force (PSF) and develop an indigenous arms industry to supplement or supplant its huge arms deals with the USA, although how this could proceed whilst Saudi Arabia is tied into arms-for-military training offset agreements is unclear. Saudi willingness to cover the costs associated with funding the vital needs of new GCC members such as economic development and security illustrate the precarious situation that it finds itself in following the Arab Uprisings. Saudi Arabia has approached economic investments in other theatres such as the Levant on a more piecemeal basis, based on coordination with third parties such as Egypt and the PNA, mainly on humanitarian grounds, but still linked to its overall objectives of increasing its national security. To maintain partnerships with other Muslim states, such as Pakistan, oil is the lubricant in the engine of bilateral relations, driven mainly by ideological and defensive components. The latter have become paramount during the Arab Uprisings and in a regional environment dominated by uncertainty and a secondary threat, which is the support the USA is putting behind many of the revolutionary campaigns.

Economic Factors in Deconstructing Adversarial Alliances

Economic factors are far more evident in the attempted deconstruction of alliances between oil exporters. Saudi Arabia has attempted to use its economic muscle in the Middle East to limit and roll back Iranian influence. It is also attempting to leverage its relationships with other

CONCLUSIONS   161

key actors and coordinate policies in order to isolate Iran internationally and therefore try to influence its foreign and nuclear policy. This is evident in two main theatres: in OPEC and as part of the Western-imposed sanctions regime; and against members of the 'resistance axis' in the Levant and Gulf. Iran's countering measures have similarly focused on oil policy and OPEC, but lacking swing status, Iran is being forced to develop client–patron relationships which will supplement its deficiencies in major economic and political groupings.

In OPEC, Saudi Arabia tried and failed to secure agreement to drop international oil prices in order to put economic pressure on Iran. Failing this, Saudi Arabia has been forced to use its status as swing producer to try and force down prices unilaterally, not only as part of its Iran strategy but as part of its obligations to major customers in the global economy suffering from low economic growth and relatively high prices in the oil market. Had Saudi oil objectives been in line with the interests of the majority of other major oil-exporting states during a crucial OPEC meeting in 2011, Iran may have found less support for its oil price policy. The role of oil has been given new meaning due to the Western embargo placed on Iranian oil exports in 2012. Saudi Arabia is already working with its Western allies to fill the shortfall of exports, but since the embargo is perceived to be a declaration of economic war, Saudi Arabia could find its position facilitates a military response from Iran. The bilateral relations of the swing producer in times of crisis are thus enhanced and its policies served best when international oil prices are high and alternative suppliers (such as Iraq and Libya) are few.

Iran is able to counter Saudi oil policy in OPEC in two main ways. Firstly, OPEC is losing relevance: OPEC has rarely managed to control the international price of oil, which is a large part of its *raison d'être*. Secondly, Iran is countering Saudi downward pricing pressure by establishing an alliance of states with similar pricing policies and/or anti-Western sentiment, such as Venezuela. Iran is also trying to persuade members that changing oil payments from the US dollar to another currency or curriences would be in OPEC's interests, but which simply addresses Iran's primary payment concerns due to sanctions. At the same time, Iran is attempting to extract more gas from

South Pars gas fields which would enable it to compete with Qatar and Russia more effectively. China prefers to build supply relationships bilaterally, which would favour a closer oil-based relationship with Iran. This is something the USA is trying to discourage through a combination of direct lobbying and diplomatic appeals as part of its sanctions policy against the Iranian regime.

Saudi policy against Iran's nuclear programme is partly played out in its oil policy stated above and in the GCC. However, Saudi Arabia has been left to unilaterally target Iranian influence in some major theatres such as weak or conflict-ridden states including Lebanon, Palestine, Yemen, Bahrain, Iraq and now Syria. Saudi Arabia's use of economic resources and political influence will continue to focus on containing and deconstructing the 'resistance axis' in partnership with other states where possible. By concentrating on its existing allies and relationships within its broader sphere of influence, Saudi Arabia has at its disposal states in the Gulf, Central Asia and South East Asia which could contribute to its efforts. There is therefore a certain comparison to be drawn between the past Saudi–US approach to defeating Communism in the developing world and the current Saudi–GCC perspective on Iranian activities in the Middle East.

Saudi Arabia is also leveraging two states which Iran may have had cause to balance with, but which now appear to be generating strategic relations with Saudi Arabia instead. The Saudi–Pakistan relationship has developed over a long period and can be seen to play a leading role in Saudi Arabia's nuclear policy, since it enjoys a close defensive partnership, buttressed by aid and preferential oil supplies, and an alleged option to purchase nuclear weapons should the need arise. China, a state which Iran had the most reason to be most optimistic about, is also developing long-term relations with Saudi Arabia based on its huge oil exports. Apart from US pressure not to engage with Iran, China also appears open to a civil nuclear partnership with Saudi Arabia which could establish the foundations for a Saudi nuclear deterrence against Iran in future.

The perceived Shi'i and 'resistance axis' threat has taken on a new resonance in Saudi Arabia since the Arab Uprisings have begun, and therefore the scope of policies (its 'Iran Initiative') aimed at countering

CONCLUSIONS 163

Iran have multiplied into a greater number of targeted and coordinated internal and external policies. They range from suppressing Shi'i demonstrations mainly in and around Qatif in the eastern province, to leading the Peninsula Shield Force against the Shi'i uprising in Bahrain and taking a similar stance to the USA and UK against Bashar Al-Assad in Syria. Since Saudi Arabia has a big stake in the outcome of the uprising in Syria, its policies are likely to be open to exploring all options, including economic, in influencing its outcome within the parameters set for it by the engagement of the Arab League.

Iran's role in the 'resistance axis' is primarily based on ideological rather than economic foundations and it is therefore better able to battle against its adversaries such as Saudi Arabia and the West through symbolic actions and victories. Its role in deconstructing adversarial alliances lies mainly in undermining their fragile political economy, Islamic legitimacy and social cohesion. Iran has been able to leverage its place in OPEC, its proxies in the Levant (as seen in the 2006 Hezbollah attack against Israel) and Shi'i communities in the Gulf. The 'axis of oil' is a much more uncertain but potentially more profound set of strategic relationships that could create the necessary space for Iran to accentuate its freedom of action in future. Iranian relations with anti-Western states such as Venezuela and states with a historical alignment against the West, such as Russia, could provide the necessary economic opportunities to challenging the West in established organizations such as OPEC. Iran's relationship with Russia and China in particular, could also give Iran its greatest advantage against the West, through leveraging their respective membership of the UNSC.

Future Trends

The future of Middle East foreign policy orientation and traditional alliances has been thrown into flux by the Arab Uprisings of 2011 and this is likely to be the case for the foreseeable future. However, one can theorize that, pending the satisfactory outcome of the chief foreign policy priorities for Saudi Arabia or Iran, the region will take one of the two following courses. The first envisages a 'status quo' in regional relations whereby Saudi Arabia has stemmed the worst effects of the Arab Uprisings and secured Morocco, Jordan, Turkey, Egypt and Yemen in new GCC strategic partnerships. Saudi foreign policy will also continue to undergo a slow reorientation (including a deepening of energy, arms and defensive relations) towards the rising powers of India and China in Asia. Saudi Arabia (and others) could also establish a nuclear deterrent of some kind, whilst the West tries to implement its traditional balance of power and containment approach against the Iranian regime. That is consistent with continued conservative rule in Iran and Al-Assad rule in Syria, a moribund WMDFZ in the Middle East and a halt to the political changes sparked by the Arab Uprisings.

Whilst these cannot be guaranteed, the second possibility envisages a revolutionary change, not from Iran facing down Western sanctions and achieving nuclear threshold status, but resulting from US actions in Syria, Afghanistan, Pakistan or elsewhere in the Gulf. US warships are already patrolling in the Strait of Hormuz[2] and could precipitate Iranian defensive measures, which could then lead to a limited war and massive insurance costs for oil shipping.[3] A similar scenario would envisage Iran closing the Strait in response to successful attempts by Israel to threaten a pre-emptive strike if the West does not impose tougher sanctions akin to an 'economic war'.[4] Iran has limited capabilities for a conventional war, and an asymmetrical war strategy is suited to engagement in the Strait whilst it does its utmost to reach a nuclear threshold capability.[5] In this case, the Saudi alliance with the West is likely to become strengthened as Saudi Arabia would require the US security umbrella and the West would require Saudi cooperation to maintain manageable international oil prices.

The least likely scenario is that sanctions put so much pressure on the Iranian regime that it leads either to a rapprochement with the West or facilitates regime change and a new beginning in Iran–West relations. However, since the Ahmadinejad regime has not been pragmatic enough to engage a large proportion of Iranian society, the presidential elections of 2013 could put another reform-minded president in government or facilitate more demonstrations and a popular reformist movement.

The Implications of the Iran Case for Sanctions against Syria

At the time of writing, the Al-Assad regime, and to a lesser extent the Free Syria Army, are under increasing pressure to stop the bloody civil war which has so far claimed 93,000 lives across the country.[6] Although the Arab League has taken the lead on this issue, a UNSC resolution calling for Al-Assad to transfer political power has been vetoed by Russia and China.[7] According to Ban Ki-moon, the UN Secretary General, such non-resolutions are said to only play into the hands of Al-Assad.[8] Neither of the two UN Special envoys, Kofi Annan and Lakdar Brahimi (Joint UN/League of Arab States Special Representative for Syria), have been able to stem the violence between the two sides. Where Syria is concerned, splits in the UNSC appear starker than in the case of Iran because for Russia and China, Syria marks a further erosion of the principle of sovereignty defined in the Westphalia Treaty. Syria is also a strategic asset to Russia, one where Russian influence helps to contain jihadism in the Caucasus and western domination of the Levant. Russia is therefore sending more arms to the Al-Assad regime to secure the government's position.[9] This has only encouraged the Pentagon to provide five military options of its own, ranging from training and technical assistant to enforcing a no-fly zone.[10]

In contrast, the EU has imposed sanctions against the Al-Assad family to isolate it diplomatically, and yet the case of Iran highlights the ineffectiveness of sanctions to affect government policy.[11] Sanctions are a long-term tool, so utilizing them to tackle immediate human rights concerns in Syria is even less convincing than their use against the Iranian regime. Similar to the negative effect of western sanctions against the Iranian government, they could reinforce the positive bilateral diplomatic relationships with alternative powers such as Russia and China, especially if they continue to block UNSC resolutions against Al-Assad.

The same argument can be applied to Syria as that made in Chapter 4: active engagement between the members of the UNSC, members of the Arab League and Syria could have persuaded the Al-Assad regime to sign a treaty early on in the conflict which would have halted the bloodshed. Depending on how the deal was structured, active engagement could also have led Iran and Al-Assad's Syria to tolerate, rather than resist, a two-state solution. The precedent in establishing that active engagement might have worked with Syria is the secret Israel–Syria peace talks which involved negotiations on Israeli withdrawal from the Golan Heights.[12] Although the US-brokered talks were subsequently aborted due to the Arab Uprisings, and there were no guarantees they would have succeeded, the very idea of peace talks with the Syrian government is encouraging. However, the situation in Syria has quickly become complex because the dynamic includes integrated domestic, regional and international dimensions. The domestic opposition is fragmented and supported to different extents by regional and international donors. The conflict has also been internationalised through a geo-political stand-off between the US and Russia, made more bitter by a growing death toll and unfolding humanitarian crisis, as well as pre-emptive strikes on arms transfers and weapons facilities in Syria by Israel.[13]

If the West continues down the pressure track in Syria – at the time of writing the UK and France were already poised to arm the Syrian rebels[14] – Iran and Hezbollah will be more likely to risk an escalation of the Israeli-Palestinian conflict and greater involvement in Syria. US policy in Iraq is also having a bearing. Unconditional US support for Iraqi Prime Minister Nouri Al-Maliki during a security clampdown against Sunnis in Iraq is only likely to exacerbate the flow of Sunni Islamist fighters crossing over the border into Syria to fight alongside their brethren.[15]

Given the importance of Syria in sectarian terms, particularly as a conduit of arms to Hezbollah in Lebanon, Saudi Arabia and Qatar have quickly moved to help arm the Syrian rebels through close cooperation with Turkish intelligence and the Jordanian government.[16] Indeed, Qatar has provided funding to a range of groups, including extremists such as Jabhat al-Nusra, and has become the first state to open a new opposition-run Syrian Arab Republic embassy.[17] The initial expression of wanting to avoid more bloodshed, arming the wrong groups and preventing a sectarian war which could easily spill into their own countries, has given way to faciliating the demise of the Al-Assad regime amid deadlock between major powers in the UNSC. The solution, and prerequisite for active engagement to be implemented successfully in Syria is therefore a swifter, stronger and broader alliance between the 'Friends of Syria Group' which prevents unilateral decision making over Syria and pulls Syria back from becoming a penetrated failed state or 'sectarian democracy'. This approach should include members of the UNSC in establishing a diplomatic agreement, and a more active role for members of the Arab League and other stakeholders such as Iran, in implementing it.

Re-contextualizing Diplomatic Engagement in the Middle East

Diplomatic engagement in the Middle East is under intense pressure from the Arab Uprisings and the demonstrations have contributed to the growth of domestic variables that the ruling elites must consider in their foreign policy-making. The events of 2012 have, in some cases, changed the regimes themselves, in Tunisia, Egypt and possibly in Syria. Saudi Arabia is investing billions of dollars to ensure its vision for a broader, more integrated and consolidated Arab Gulf Union Council succeeds.[18] As argued in Chapter 3, Saudi Arabia has drawn influence from a widely defined series of alliances, including with Pakistan and China. The Saudi regime is even more comfortable in working with the like-minded Sunni regimes in Morocco, Egypt and Jordan even though they fall outside the traditional neighbourhood of the GCC. These states can aid stability and provide the much needed manpower for the growth of the PSF which is expected over the coming years. The challenge will be for these states to invest in their political association in ways which guarantee their long-term cooperation rather than a simple patron-client bargain.

As argued in Chapter 4, the only way to address the deadlock in diplomatic engagement between Iran and the West is through a fundamental rethinking of sanctions and dialogue. Diplomatic engagement across the Middle East has been consistently hampered by the ideological chasm between Iran and the West. US interventions in Afghanistan and Iraq have, combined with a network of military bases across the Gulf and Central Asia, made the USA a local power. Therefore, a new indigenous security framework that involves all the local actors is vital to the reinvigoration of trade and cooperation across the Middle East. The resistance axis, the Iranian nuclear programme and new sectarian conflicts are three major impediments to advancing such cooperation. Afghanistan could hold the key to aligning Western, Russian, GCC and Iranian national security interests and provide an opportunity and logic to building a Central Asian and wider Middle Eastern security architecture. Chapter 4 shows that there is much to learn in both the West and Iran about the kinds of diplomatic engagement which may prove to be most fruitful in building up to this, why some foreign policies are met only with resistance and how other policies were close to succeeding. The final two chapters illustrate that the biggest issues facing the Middle East will continue to be informed by domestic contestation, the geo-strategic imperatives of global powers and the strength of regional alliances.

The Future of FPA

The use of constructive-balancing as a conceptual model in this book drew out some of the most important perceptions in the West, Saudi Arabia, Iran and the international community, which continue to inform their respective foreign policies. The omni-balancing concept rightfully recognizes the necessity, particularly during the Arab Uprisings, to focus on the multi-level in order to account for all the possible factors in driving foreign policy.

Still, FPA has a long way to go. The Arab Uprisings have illustrated that the discipline needs to take a broader focus and cover all sorts of influences which don't initially appear to be directly related to foreign policy. The importance of a conceptual model which is led by empirics is therefore paramount. The Arab Uprisings have highlighted the difference between the instability of revolutions and reforms in republics as opposed to monarchies, and so there is space to explore the apparent linkage between domestic stability, hydrocarbon revenues and more assertive foreign policies from oil and gas exporters into the 2000s.

NOTES

Introduction

1. *Salafiyya* or Salafism 'refers to the movement that believes that Muslims should emulate the first three generations of Islam referred to as the pious forefathers (*al-salaf al-salih*) as much as possible in all areas of life'. Roel Meijer (ed.), 'Glossary', *Global Salafism: Islam's New Religious Movement* (New York: Columbia University Press, 2009), p. xiii.

Chapter 1. A Conceptual Framework

1. Richard Snyder, Henry Bruck and Burton Sapin, *Decision Making as an Approach to the Study of International Politics* (Princeton, NJ: Princeton University, 1954).
2. James Rosenau, 'Pre-Theories and Theories of Foreign Policy', in R. B. Farrell (ed.), *Approaches in Comparative and International Politics* (Evanston: Northwestern University Press, 1966).
3. Margaret and Harold Sprout, *Man-Milieu Relationship Hypotheses in the Context of International Politics* (Princeton, NJ: Princeton University, 1956).
4. Kenneth Waltz, *Theory of International Politics* (Reading, Massachusetts: Addison Wesley, 1979).
5. Stephen Walt, *The Origin of Alliances* (New York: Cornell University Press, 1987).
6. Gerd Nonneman, 'Analyzing the Foreign Policies of the Middle East and North Africa: A Conceptual Approach', in G. Nonneman (ed.), *Analyzing Middle East Foreign Policies: The Relationship with Europe* (Abingdon: Routledge, 2005), p. 7.

7. Raymond Hinnebusch, 'Introduction to the Politics of the Middle East', *The International Politics of the Middle East* (Manchester: Manchester University Press, 2003), p. 12.
8. F. Gregory Gause III, 'The Gulf War and the 1990s', *The International Relations of the Persian Gulf* (Cambridge: Cambridge University Press, 2010), pp. 102–103; p. 105.
9. Raymond Hinnebusch, 'Introduction: The Analytical Framework', in R. Hinnebusch & A. Ehteshami (eds.), *The Foreign Policies of Middle East States* (London: Lynne Rienner Publishers, Inc, 2002), p. 16.
10. James P. Piscatori, 'Islamic Values and National Interest: The Foreign Policy of Saudi Arabia', in Adeed Dawisha (ed.), *Islam in Foreign Policy* (Cambridge: Cambridge University Press, 1983), pp. 35–51.
11. Bahgat Korany and Ali E. Hillal Dessouki, in B. Korany & Ali E. Hillal Dessouki (eds.), 'A Literature Survey and a Framework for Analysis', *The Foreign Policies of Arab States* (Cairo: Westview Press, 1984), p. 7.
12. Ali Akbar Rezaei, 'Foreign Policy Theories: Implications for the Foreign Policy Analysis of Iran', in Anoushiravan Ehteshami and Mahjoob Zweiri (eds.), *Iran's Foreign Policy: From Khatami to Ahmadinejad* (Reading: Ithaca Press, 2008), p. 27.
13. Raymond Hinnebusch, 'Explaining International Politics in the Middle East: The Struggle of Regional Identity and Systemic Structure', in G. Nonneman (ed.), *Analyzing Middle East Foreign Policies: The Relationship with Europe*, p. 246
14. As discussed in Gerd Nonneman, 'Analyzing the Foreign Policies of the Middle East and North Africa: A Conceptual Framework', in G. Nonneman (ed.), *Analyzing Middle East Foreign Policies: The Relationship with Europe*, p. 10.
15. Ibid., p. 9.
16. Raymond Hinnebusch, 'Explaining International Politics in the Middle East: The Struggle of Regional Identity and Systemic Structure', in G. Nonneman (ed.), *Analyzing Middle East Foreign Policies: The Relationship with Europe*, p. 248.
17. As quoted in ibid., p. 246; Bassel F. Salloukh, 'Regime Autonomy and Regional Foreign Policy Choices in the Middle East: A Theoretical Exploration', *Persistent Permeability? Regionalism, Localism, and Globalisation in the Middle East* (Aldershot: Ashgate, 2004), p. 86.
18. Raymond Hinnebusch, 'Explaining International Politics in the Middle East: The Struggle of Regional Identity and Systemic Structure', in G. Nonneman (ed.), *Analyzing Middle East Foreign Policies: The Relationship with Europe*, p. 243.
19. Ibid., pp. 249–255.
20. Bassel F. Salloukh & Rex Brynen, 'Pondering Permeability: Some Introductory Explorations', *Persistent Permeability? Regionalism, Localism, and Globalisation in the Middle East*, p. 1.

21. Gerd Nonneman, 'Saudi-European Relations 1902–2001 – a Pragmatic Quest for Relative Autonomy', *International Affairs* 77/3, 2001, p. 654.
22. Raymond Hinnebusch, 'Introduction: The Analytical Framework', *The Foreign Policies of Middle East States*, p. 18.
23. Anoushiravan Ehteshami and Mahjoob Zweiri, 'Introduction', in A. Ehteshami and M. Zweirei (eds.), *Iran's Foreign Policy: From Khatami to Ahmadinejad*, p. xiii.
24. Ibid., p. 8.
25. Kal Holsti, *International Politics*, 7th ed. (Englewood Cliffs: Prentice Hall, 2004).
26. Baghat Korany and Ali E. Hillal Dessouki, 'Foreign Policy Approaches and Arab Countries: A Critical Evaluation and an Alternative Framework', *The Foreign Policies of Arab States: The Challenge of Globalization* (Cairo: The American University in Cairo Press, 2008), p. 39.
27. F. Gregory Gause III, 'The Gulf War and the 1990s', *The International Relations of the Persian Gulf*, pp. 102–103.
28. Bassel F. Salloukh & Rex Brynen, 'Pondering Permeability: Some Introductory Explorations', *Persistent Permeability? Regionalism, Localism, and Globalisation in the Middle East*, p. 1.
29. Ali Ansari, *Confronting Iran: the Failure of American Foreign Policy and the Roots of Mistrust*, (London: C. Hurst & Co., 2006).
30. Alexander Wendt, 'Anarchy is What States Make of it: the Social Construction of Power Politics', *International Organization* 46/2, 1992, pp. 391–425.
31. Raymond Hinnebusch, 'Explaining International Politics in the Middle East: The Struggle of Regional Identity and Systemic Structure', in G. Nonneman (ed.), *Analyzing Middle East Foreign Policies: The Relationship with Europe*, pp. 249–255.
32. As discussed in Bahgat Korany and Ali E. Hillal Dessouki, 'Introduction: Foreign Policies of Arab States', in Bahgat Korany and Ali E Hillal Dessouki (eds.), *The Foreign Policies of Arab States: The Challenge of Globalization*, p. 7; Raymond Hinnebusch, 'Introduction: The Analytical Framework', *The Foreign Policies of Middle East States*, p. 2.
33. As discussed in Raymond Hinnebusch, 'Introduction: The Analytical Framework', *The Foreign Policies of Middle East States*, p. 18.
34. Gerd Nonneman, 'Saudi-European Relations 1902–2001 – a Pragmatic Quest for Relative Autonomy', *International Affairs*, p. 654.
35. Christopher Clapham, 'The Domestic Politics of Foreign Policy Management', *Africa and the International System* (Cambridge: Cambridge University Press, 1996), p. 64.
36. Stephen M. Walt, 'Explaining Alliance Formation', *The Origins of Alliances*, p. 22.

37. Rory Miller, 'Conclusion', *The Politics of Trade and Diplomacy: Ireland's Evolving Relationship with the Muslim Middle East*, Irish Studies in International Affairs, 15, 2004, p. 144.
38. Stephen M. Walt, 'Introduction: Exploring Alliance Formation', *The Origins of Alliances*, p. 5.
39. Ibid., p. 29.
40. Robert Pranger, 'Foreign Policy Capacity in the Middle East', in J. Kipper & H. H. Saunders (eds.), *The Middle East in Global Perspective* (Oxford: Westview Press, 1991), p. 20.
41. Enabling or constraining factors might include the material and political resources available; competition between regional or global powers; and the location and concentration of their interests. Gerd Nonneman, 'Saudi-European Relations 1902–2001 – a Pragmatic Quest for Relative Autonomy', *International Affairs*, p. 635; Gerd Nonneman, 'Analyzing the Foreign Policies of the Middle East and North Africa: A Conceptual Framework', in G. Nonneman (ed.), *Analyzing Middle East Foreign Policies: The Relationship with Europe*, p. 16.
42. F. Gregory Gause III, 'Theory – System in Understanding Middle East International Politics: Rereading Paul Noble's "The Arab System: Pressures, Constraints and Opportunities"', in L. Bassel and F. Salloukh (eds.), *Persistent Permeability? Regionalism, Localism, and Globalisation in the Middle East*, p. 23.
43. Gerd Nonneman, 'Saudi-European Relations 1902–2001 – a Pragmatic Quest for Relative Autonomy', *International Affairs*, pp. 633–4.
44. Christopher Hill, 'Theories of Foreign Policy Making for the Developing Countries', in Christopher Clapham (ed.), *Foreign Policy Making in Developing States* (Westmead: Saxon House, 1977), pp. 1–17; Gerd Nonneman, 'Saudi-European Relations 1902–2001 – a Pragmatic Quest for Relative Autonomy', *International Affairs*, p. 634.
45. Gerd Nonneman, 'Analyzing the Foreign Policies of the Middle East and North Africa: A Conceptual Framework', in G. Nonneman (ed.), *Analyzing Middle East Foreign Policies: The Relationship with Europe*, p. 9.
46. Stephen David quoted in ibid., p. 19.
47. Ibid., p. 10.
48. Ibid., pp. 7–11.
49. Ibid., p. 9.
50. Raymond Hinnebusch, 'Introduction: The Analytical Framework', *The Foreign Policies of Middle East States*, p. 15.
51. Bassel F. Salloukh, 'Regime Autonomy and Regional Foreign Policy Choices in the Middle East: A Theoretical Exploration', *Persistent Permeability? Regionalism, Localism, and Globalisation in the Middle East*, p. 84.

52. Raymond Hinnebusch, 'Introduction: The Analytical Framework', *The Foreign Policies of Middle East States*, p. 93.
53. John Vasquez, *The Power of Power Politics: From Classical Realism to Neotraditionalism* (Cambridge: Cambridge University Press, 1998).

Chapter 2. The Shaping Factors of Regional Insecurity and Conflict in the Formulation of Contemporary Saudi and Iranian Foreign Policy

1. Raymond Hinnebusch, 'Explaining International Politics in the Middle East: The Struggle of Regional Identity and Systemic Structure', in G. Nonneman (ed.), *Analyzing Middle East Foreign Policies: The Relationship with Europe* (Abingdon: Routledge, 2005), p. 250; Nicholas Fallon, 'Background to the 1973/74 Oil Crisis', *Middle East Oil Money and its Future Expenditure* (London: Graham & Trotman Ltd, 1975), p. 6
2. Ibid.
3. Hans Mathias Kepplinger and Herbert Roth, 'Creating a Crisis: German Mass Media and Oil Supply in 1973–4', *The Public Opinion Quarterly* 43/3, Autumn 1979, p. 286.
4. Nicholas Fallon, 'Background to the 1973/74 Oil Crisis', *Middle East Oil Money and Its Future Expenditure*, p. 3.
5. Bruce A. Beaubouff, 'The First Oil Shock', *The Strategic Petroleum Reserve: US Energy Security and Oil Politics, 1975–2005*, (United States: Bruce A. Beaubouff, 2007), p. 17; Kamil Mahdi, 'Kuwait: History', *The Middle East and North Africa 2004*, 50th Edition (London: European Publications, 2004), p. 677.
6. Ibid.
7. Giacomo Luciani, 'Oil and Political Economy in the International Relations of the Middle East', in L. Fawcett (ed.), *International Relations of the Middle East* (Oxford: Oxford University Press, 2005), p. 92.
8. As defined by a series of concepts including: no taxation and political bargaining or representation, a dependence on external resources, the large role that the state plays in the national economy, the disconnect between state and citizen, the importance of ministry 'fiefdoms' and the role their 'executives' play in the management of state policy and the inability of rentier theory to distinguish between enabling and disabling factors of oil income. Steffen Hertog, 'Comparing the Case Studies: Comparing Saudi Arabia', *Princes, Brokers, and Bureaucrats: Oil and the State in Saudi Arabia* (Ithaca: Cornell University Press, 2010), pp. 264–275.

9. The USA had alleviated other Arab–European oil boycotts in 1956 and 1967 by putting more of its oil onto the market. Rachel Bronson, 'Understanding US – Saudi Relations', in G. Nonneman & P. Aarts (eds.), *Saudi Arabia in the Balance: Political Economy, Society, Foreign Affairs* (London: C. Hurst & Co., 2005), p. 380.
10. Keith McLachlan, 'The Oil Industry in the Middle East', in John I. Clarke & Howard Bowen-Jones (eds.), *Change and Development in the Middle East* (New York: Methuen & Co., 1981), p. 107.
11. King Faisal and Prince Sa'ud al-Faisal in Sheikh Rustum Ali, *Saudi Arabia and Oil Diplomacy* (New York: Praeger Publishers, 1976), p. 108.
12. Gerd Nonneman, 'Saudi-European Relations 1902–2001 – a Pragmatic Quest for Relative Autonomy', *International Affairs* 77/3, 2001, p. 647.
13. Bruce A. Beaubouff, *The Strategic Petroleum Reserve: US Energy Security and Oil Politics, 1975–2005*, p. 17; 'History', *The Middle East and North Africa 2004*, 50th Edition (London: European Publications, 2004), p. 677.
14. Gerd Nonneman, 'Saudi-European Relations 1902–2001 – a Pragmatic Quest for Relative Autonomy', *International Affairs*, p. 648.
15. Ibid.
16. Nicholas Fallon, 'Background to the 1973/74 Oil Crisis', *Middle East Oil Money and Its Future Expenditure*, p. 4.
17. Ibid.
18. Ray Hudson, David Rhind and Helen Mounsey, 'Community Policies and Funding', *An Atlas of EEC Affairs* (London: Methuen and Co., 1984), p. 13.
19. Nicholas Fallon, 'Background to the 1973/74 Oil Crisis', *Middle East Oil Money and Its Future Expenditure*, p. 5; Michael Graham Fry, Erik Goldstein and Richard Langthorne, 'Crises and Conferences, 1945 – 1990', *Guide to International Relations and Diplomacy* (London: Michael Graham Fry, Erik Goldstein and Richard Langthorne, 2002), p. 351.
20. Ibid., p. 52.
21. Ibid.
22. Ibid., p. 5.
23. King Faisal and Prince Sa'ud al-Faisal in Sheikh Rustum Ali, *Saudi Arabia and Oil Diplomacy* (New York: Praeger Publishers, 1976), p. 108.
24. Andrew Scott Cooper, 'Showdown at Doha: The Secret Oil Deal That Helped Sink the Shah of Iran', *The Middle East Journal* 62/4, Autumn 2008, pp. 570–572.
25. Higher oil prices would again lead to more active Saudi diplomacy in 2002 as discussed in Chapter 3.
26. Shireen Hunter, 'Channels of OPEC Aid', *OPEC and the Third World: the Politics of Aid* (Beckenham: Croom Helm, 1984), p. 253.

27. Sheikh Rustum Ali, *Saudi Arabia and Oil Diplomacy* (New York: Praeger Publishers, 1976), pp. 90–98.
28. Ibid.
29. Anthony H. Cordesman, 'The Impact of Saudi Aid and Capital', *Western Strategic Interests in Saudi Arabia* (Beckenham: Croom Helm, 1987), p. 39.
30. Sheikh Rustum Ali, *Saudi Arabia and Oil Diplomacy* (New York: Praeger Publishers, 1976), pp. 90–98.
31. $47.7 billion went to multilateral institutions and approximately $750 million went to Arab and Islamic institutions, whilst $424 million went to African institutions. Assa Abdulrahman Hussein, *Alliance Behaviour and the Foreign Policy of the Kingdom of Saudi Arabia, 1973–1991* (Ann Arbor: UMI Dissertation Services, 1995), p. 103.
32. Syria topped the Saudi donor list, receiving $12.3 billion, followed by Egypt and Jordan receiving $9.4 billion and $8.4 billion respectively, between 1973 and 1990. Ibid., p. 105.
33. Anthony H. Cordesman, 'The Impact of Saudi Aid and Capital', *Western Strategic Interests in Saudi Arabia*, p. 39.
34. Ibid.
35. Ibid.
36. Ibid., p. 143.
37. Rachel Bronson, 'We Support Some, They Support Some', *Thicker Than Oil: America's Uneasy Partnership with Saudi Arabia* (Oxford: Oxford University Press, 2006), p. 180.
38. Ibid.
39. Ibid.
40. Saudi Arabia was also concerned about Sudan's inability to prevent Libyan forces crossing its territory during the Libyan war with Chad. Ibid.
41. Ibid.
42. Assa Abdulrahman Hussein, *Alliance Behaviour and the Foreign Policy of the Kingdom of Saudi Arabia, 1973–1991*, (Ann Arbor: UMI Dissertation Services, 1995), p. 106
43. Saudi Arabia sent up to $32 million to the Contras at the request of the White House. Rachel Bronson, 'Understanding US–Saudi Relations', *Saudi Arabia in the Balance*, p. 383.
44. Ibid., p. 390.
45. R. K. Ramazani, 'Iran's Foreign Policy: Independence, Freedom and the Islamic Republic', in A. Ehteshami and M. Zweirei (eds.), *Iran's Foreign Policy: From Khatami to Ahmadinejad*, p. 1.
46. Vanessa Martin, 'The Political Situation, 1978–79', *Creating an Islamic State: Khomeini and the Making of a New Iran* (London: I.B.Tauris, 2000), p. 148.

47. Ray Takeyh, 'Relations with the "Great Satan"', *Guardians of the Revolution: Iran and the World in the Age of the Ayatollahs* (Oxford: Oxford University Press, 2009), p. 35.
48. Ibid., p. 39.
49. Ibid., p. 35.
50. Baqer Moin, 'Khomeini in Paris; The End of an Empire', *Khomeini: Life of the Ayatollah* (London: I.B.Tauris, 1999), p. 186.
51. John Limbert and Bruce Laingen, 'Limbert & Laingen: Iran Hostages: Thoughts 30 Years Later', *The Washington Times*, 28 January 2011, available at http://www.washingtontimes.com/news/2011/jan/28/iran-hostages-thoughts-30-years-later/, last accessed 23 April 2013.
52. Ray Takeyh, 'Relations with the "Great Satan"', *Guardians of the Revolution: Iran and the World in the Age of the Ayatollahs*, p. 35.
53. John Limbert and Bruce Laingen, 'Limbert & Laingen: Iran Hostages: Thoughts 30 Years Later', *The Washington Times*, 28 January 2011.
54. Congressional Record: Proceedings and Debates of the 109th Congress, First Session, United States of America Senate, 20 June 2005, Vol. 151, Pt 10, 13412.
55. Anoushiravan Ehteshami, 'Iran', in Tim Niblock and Emma Murphy (eds.), *Economic and Political Liberalization in the Middle East* (New York: British Academic Press, 1993), p. 219.
56. Ibid., p. 222.
57. Ibid.
58. The Council of Guardians was mainly representing the bazaar and landowners and therefore their objectives can best be seen in the light of protecting their interests. Anoushiravan Ehteshami, 'Iran', *Economic and Political Liberalization in the Middle East*, p. 222.
59. Anoushiravan Ehteshami, 'Iran', Economic and Political Liberalization in the Middle East, p. 224.
60. Ibid.
61. Ibid.
62. Containment was first outlined by George Kennan, then Director of the US State Department's new Policy Planning Staff, in a 1946 *Foreign Affairs* article entitled 'The Sources of Soviet Conduct', discussed here: John Lewis Gaddis, 'Reconsiderations: Containment: A Reassessment', *Foreign Affairs*, July 1977, available at http://www.foreignaffairs.com/articles/27903/john-lewis-gaddis/reconsiderations-containment-a-reassessment, last accessed 23 April 2013.
63. Wayne White, Middle East Institute, 'Re: Mousavian: A Package to Resolve the Nuclear Impasse with Iran', email sent to the Gulf2000 List, 2 April 2011.

64. Kenneth M. Pollack, 'At War with the World', *The Persian Puzzle* (New York: Random House, 2004), p. 184.
65. Rob Johnson, 'The Iran–Iraq War in Retrospect', *The Iran–Iraq War* (Palgrave Macmillan: New York, 2011), pp. 185–186.
66. Ibid., p. 179.
67. Lawrence G. Potter and Gary G. Sick, 'Introduction' in Lawrence G. Potter and Gary G. Sick (eds.), *Iran, Iraq, and the Legacies of War* (New York: Palgrave Macmillan, 2004), p. 8.
68. Rob Johnson, 'The Iran–Iraq War in Retrospect', *The Iran–Iraq War*, p. 179.
69. Ibid.
70. Richard L. Russell, 'China's Strategic Prongs: Saudi Arabia, Iran and Pakistan', *Weapons Proliferation and War in the Greater Middle East* (Abingdon: Routledge, 2005), p. 130.
71. Trita Parsi, *Treacherous Alliance: The Secret Dealings of Israel, Iran, and the US* (New Haven & London: Yale University Press, 2007), p. 105.
72. Maximilian Terhalle, 'Understanding the Limits of Power: America's Middle East Experience', *Review of International Studies* 37/2, April 2011, p. 635.
73. Rob Johnson, 'The Iran–Iraq War in Retrospect', *The Iran–Iraq War*, p. 182.
74. Iran could not engage with overtures from the USSR since it supported the mujahidin against Soviet troops in Afghanistan during the 1980s.
75. Arshin Adib-Moghaddam, SOAS, 'The United States and Saddam (Adib-Moghaddam)', email sent to 5 April 2011 to the Gulf2000 List
76. Ibid.
77. Ibid.
78. John Towers et al., 'Arms Transfer to Iran', *Excerpts From the Tower Commission Report*, available at http://www.presidency.ucsb.edu/PS157/assignment per cent20files per cent20public/TOWER per cent20EXCERPTS.htm#PartIII, accessed 9 March 2012
79. *The New York Times*, 'The Iran-Contra Report: "Steering to Failure"', 19 November 1987, http:/www.nytimes.com/1987/11/19/world/the-iran-contra-report-steering-to-failure.html, last accessed 12 April 2013
80. Rob Johnson, 'The Iran–Iraq War in Retrospect', *The Iran–Iraq War*, p. 180.
81. Christin Marschall, *Iran's Persian Gulf Policy: From Khomeini to Khatami* (London: Routledge Curzon, 2003), p. 188.
82. David Albright and Andrea Stricker, 'Iran's Nuclear Program', *The Iran Primer*, United States Institute of Peace, available at http://iranprimer.usip.org/resource/irans-nuclear-program, last accessed 23 April 2013.

83. Saddam Hussein sent Rafsanjani a letter requesting Iranian participation in the invasion of Kuwait. Interview with Ali Biniaz, Director, Centre for Energy and International Economy, Institute for Political and International Studies (IPIS), Tehran, 27 February 2011.
84. Lionel Beehner, 'Timeline: US–Iran Contacts', Council of Foreign Relations, 9 March 2007, available at http://www.cfr.org/iran/timeline-us-iran-contacts/p12806#p3, last accessed 23 April 2013.
85. The 'resistance axis' comprises Syria, Hamas and Hezbollah. Mohamad Bazzi, 'Expect More Adventurism from Iran', Council on Foreign Relations, available at http://www.cfr.org/iran/expect-more-adventurism-iran/p20064, last accessed 23 April 2013.
86. Richard N. Haass, 'The George H.W. Bush Administration', *The Iran Primer*, United States Institute of Peace, available at http://iranprimer.usip.org/resource/george-hw-bush-administration, last accessed 23 April 2013.
87. Arshin Adib-Moghaddam, 'Westphalia and the Anarchic Gulf Society: the Second Persian Gulf War and its Aftermath', *The International Politics of the Persian Gulf: A Cultural Genealogy* (Abingdon: Routledge, 2006), p. 75.
88. Ibid.
89. Oman was calling for greater GCC engagement with Iran through establishing a regional security forum which would make Iran part of the solution regionally and help normalize its relations internationally. Joseph A. Kechichian, *Oman and the World: The Emergence of an Independent Foreign Policy* (Santa Monica: RAND, 1995), p. 10; Marc J. O'Reilly, 'Omnibalancing: Oman Confronts an Uncertain Future', *Middle East Journal* 52/1, Winter 1998, p. 75; Majid Al-Khalili, 'Oman's Foreign Policy (1990–2004)', *Oman's Foreign Policy* (Westport, United States: Praeger Security International, 2009), p. 97.
90. Christin Marschall, *Iran's Persian Gulf Policy: From Khomeini to Khatami*, p. 154.
91. Joseph A. Kechichian, 'Key Future Gulf Security Issues', *Political Dynamics and Security in the Arabian Peninsula Through the 1990s* (Santa Monica: RAND, 1993), p. 90.
92. Ibid., p. 170.
93. Ibid.
94. Ibid., p. 5.
95. Vahe Petrossian, 'Reformers Set for Victory', *Middle East Economic Digest* (hereafter *MEED*), 18 February 2000, p. 2.
96. Ibid.
97. Michael Axworthy, 'Diplomatic Relations Between Iran and the United Kingdom in the Early Reform Period, 1997–2000', in A. Ehteshami and M. Zweirei (eds.), *Iran's Foreign Policy: From Khatami to Ahmadinejad*, p. 105.

98. Gulf States Newsletter (hereafter *GSN*), 'Politics and Defence: A US-Iranian Collision?', 20/509, 17 April 1995, p. 2
99. Kenneth Pollack and Ray Takeyh, 'Taking on Tehran', *Foreign Affairs* 84/2, March/April 2005, p. 20
100. Thomas Hegghammer, 'Deconstructing the Myth about al-Qa'ida and Khobar', Combatting Terrorism Center at West Point, 15 February 2008, available at http://www.ctc.usma.edu/posts/deconstructing-the-myth-about-al-qaida-and-khobar, last accessed 23 April 2013.
101. *GSN*, 'Politics and Defence: The End of Dual Containment?', 23/595, 21 September 1998, p. 2.
102. F. Gregory Gause III, 'The Illogical of Dual Containment', *Foreign Affairs* 73/2, March/April 1994, available at http://www.foreignaffairs.com/articles/49686/f-gregory-gause-iii/the-illogic-of-dual-containment, last accessed 23 April 2013.
103. Anoushiravan Ehteshami, 'The Foreign Policy of Iran', *The Foreign Policies of Middle East States*, p. 291.
104. Kenneth Katzman, *The Iran-Libya Sanctions Act (ILSA)*, CRS Report for Congress, Congressional Research Service, 26 April 2006, 1, available at http://fpc.state.gov/documents/organization/66441.pdf, last accessed 23 April 2013.
105. Richard Dalton et al., 'Iran: Breaking the Nuclear Deadlock', Chatham House Report, 2008, p. 13.
106. Gawdat Bahgat, *American Oil Diplomacy in the Persian Gulf and the Caspian Sea* (Gainesville: University Press Florida, 2003), p. 119.
107. Ibid.
108. *GSN*, 'Politics and Defence: Balancing Acts', 23/581, 9 March 1998, p. 3.
109. Ibid.
110. Ibid.
111. *GSN*, 'Politics and Defence: A US-Iranian Collision?', 17 April 1995, 20/509, p. 2.
112. Ibid.
113. *GSN*, 'Politics and Defence: America and Iran', 23/577, 12 January 1998, p. 2.
114. Abdullah Baabood, *EU-Gulf Political and Economic Relations: Assessment and Policy Recommendations* (Dubai: Gulf Research Center, 2006), p. 12.
115. *GSN*, 'Politics and Defence: America and Iran', 23/577, 12 January 1998, p. 2.
116. Ibid., p. 9.
117. Ibid., p. 9.

118. Ali Khamenei, speech, 23 March 2004, available at http://farsi.khamenei.ir/speech-content?id=3236&q, last accessed 23 April 2013.
119. Ibid.
120. Ibid.
121. *GSN*, 'Politics and Defence: America and Iran', 23/577, 12 January 1998, p. 2.
122. Ibid.
123. *GSN*, 'Politics and Defence: Football and Politics', 23/589, 29 June 1998, p. 2.
124. Ibid.
125. Shayerah Ilias, *Iran's Economic Conditions: U.S Policy Issues*, CRS Report for Congress, Congressional Research Service, p. 14.
126. *GSN*, 'Politics and Defence: Iran–EU Meeting', 23/587, 1 June 1998, p. 6.
127. Abdullah Baabood, *EU-Gulf Political and Economic Relations*, p. 14.
128. Ibid.
129. Ziba Moshaver, 'Revolution, Theocratic Leadership and Iran's Foreign Policy: Implications for Iran-EU Relations', in G. Nonneman (ed.), *Analyzing Middle East Foreign Policies*, p. 187
130. Ibid.
131. *GSN*, 'Politics and Defence: Balancing Acts', 23/581, 9 March 1998, p. 3.
132. *GSN*, 'Politics and Defence: Iran – Fatwa Statement', 23/596, 5 October 1998, p. 4; British Embassy Tehran, 'Embassy History', available at http://ukiniran.fco.gov.uk/en/about-us/our-embassy/embassy-history/.
133. *Middle East Economic Survey*, 'Iran and UK Debate Investment Framework as UK Oil Firms Wait on Contracts Awards', XLIII/3, 17 January 2000.
134. Secretary of State Madeleine K. Albright, 'Remarks before the American–Iranian Council', 17 March 2000, Washington D.C., available at http://www.mideastinfo.com/documents/iranspeech.htm, last accessed 23 April 2013.
135. Anoushiravan Ehteshami, 'Iran's Assessment of the Iraq Crisis and the Post-9/11 International Order', in Ramesh Thakur and Waheguru Pal Singh Sidhu (eds.), *The Iraq Crisis and World Order: Structural, Normative and Institutional Change* (Tokyo: United Nations University Press, 2006), p. 139.
136. Ibid., p. 140.
137. David Butter, 'Iran: a Force for Stability', *MEED*, 5 October 2001, p. 5.
138. *GSN*, 'Politics and Defence: Saudi Arabia – Tiff with Washington', 20/510, 8 May 1995, p. 5.
139. Joseph S. Nye, 'Conflicts After the Cold War', *Power in the Global Information Age: From Realism to Globalisation* (Abingdon: Routledge, 2005), p. 43.

140. Ibid.
141. Tim Niblock with Monica Malik, 'Constrained Development 1985–2000', *The Political Economy of Saudi Arabia* (London: Routledge, 2007), p. 102.
142. Ibid.
143. Rachel Bronson, 'Understanding US–Saudi Relations', *Saudi Arabia in the Balance*, p. 389.

Chapter 3. Saudi Foreign Policy: Oil, Wahabism and 'Riyal Politik'

1. These are discussed in Robert Mason, 'From Wellhead to Wire: Diversification and Its Challenges in Saudi Arabia', *Instituto de Empresa International Relations Blog*, 14 June 2010, available at http://ir.blogs.ie.edu/2011/06/14/from-wellhead-to-wire-diversification-and-its-challenges-in-saudi-arabia/, last accessed 23 April 2013.
2. A 'rentier economy' is defined as one 'where rent situations predominate', 'relies on substantial *external* rent' and in the 'Rentier State', 'only few are engaged in the generation of this rent (wealth), the majority being only involved in the distribution or utilisation of it; which translates into the government being the principal recipient of the rent. Hazem Beblawi, 'The Rentier State in the Arab World' in Giacomo Luciani (ed.), *The Arab State* (Berkeley: University of California Press, 1990), pp. 87–88.
3. Nawaf E. Obaid, 'Reducing Dependence on Oil Income', *The Oil Kingdom at 100 – Petroleum Policymaking in Saudi Arabia* (Washington D.C.: Washington Institute for Near East Policy, 2000), p. 67.
4. The GCC absorbed $36 billion out of the total cost of $61 billion of the Gulf War, along with around 50 per cent of the cost of the US forward presence in the Gulf. *GSN*, 'New US National Defence Strategy Signals Shift to Lighter "Footprint" in the Gulf States', 29/755, 15 April 2005, p. 9.
5. Tim Niblock with Monica Malik, 'Constrained development 1985–2000', *The Political Economy of Saudi Arabia* (London: Routledge, 2007), p. 99.
6. CIA World Fact Book, 'Saudi Arabia', available at https://www.cia.gov/library/publications/the-world-factbook/geos/sa.html, last accessed 23 April 2013.
7. Tom Everett-Heath, 'Push and Pull', *MEED*, 11 January 2002, p. 4.
8. Bruce Maddy-Weitzman, 'Riyalpolitik', *Mideast Monitor*, available at http://www.dayan.org/pdfim/2908JREP26.pdf, accessed 30 August 2011.
9. *MEED*, 'Oil Price Brings Budget Surplus', 15 September 2000, p. 28.

10. Edmund O'Sullivan, 'The Rise and Fall of Saudi Arabia's Great Gas Initiative', *MEED*, 27 June 2003, p. 4.
11. Gawdat Bahgat, *American Oil Diplomacy in the Persian Gulf and the Caspian Sea* (Gainesville: University Press Florida, 2003), p. 64.
12. Ibid.
13. Interview with Sir Sherard Cowper-Coles, former British Ambassador to Saudi Arabia and UK Special Envoy to Afghanistan, London, 4 June 2010.
14. *MEED*, 'Special Report: Saudi Arabia', 30 June 2000, p. 20.
15. *MEED*, 'Cover Story: Prince Alwaleed', 23–29 April 2004, p. 6.
16. *GSN*, 'Close at Last for First Saudi IWPP', 29/770, 25 November 2005, p. 11.
17. *MEED*, 'Special Report: Saudi Arabia', 17–23 February 2006, p. 44.
18. *The Economist*, 'Join the Club', 1 May 2008, available at http://www.economist.com/node/11294279, last accessed 23 April 2013.
19. *Reuters*, 'Saudi Gov't Approves New State-Owned Investment Firm', 24 March 2009, available at http://www.arabianbusiness.com/saudi-gov-t-approves-new-state-owned-investment-firm-40966.html, last accessed 23 April 2013.
20. *Reuters*, 'Saudi to Launch $5bn Investment Firm', 28 April 2009, available at http://www.emirates247.com/2.266/investment/saudi-to-launch-5bn-investment-firm-2009-04-28-1.96034, last accessed 23 April 2013.
21. Angus McDowall, 'Seizing the Initiative', *MEED*, 15 February 2002, p. 4.
22. Remarks from Prince Turki Al-Faisal, 'Address at the Gulf Research Meeting Opening Ceremony', University of Cambridge, 6 July 2011; Royal Embassy of Saudi Arabia, Washington D.C., 'White House Welcomes Expansion of Saudi Women's Political Participation', 25 September 2011, available at http://www.saudiembassy.net/latest_news/news09251101.aspx, last accessed 23 April 2013.
23. Anthony H. Cordesman, *Saudi Arabia Enters the Twenty-First Century* (Westport: Center for Strategic and International Studies, 2003), p. 278.
24. Angus McDowall, 'Cover Story: Saudi Arabia', *MEED*, 1 March 2002.
25. *MEED*, 'Special Report: US', 6 April 2001, p. 25; *MEED*, 'Special Report: US', 28 February 2003, p. 26.
26. Leonardo Maugeri, *The Age of Oil: The Mythology, History, and Future of the World's Most Controversial Resource* (Westport: Praeger, 2006), p. 262.
27. *GSN*, 'Politics and Security: Saudi Arabia', 29/759, 10 June 2005, p. 4.
28. Ibid.
29. This is a form of *Wasta*, an Arabic word that is associated with favouritism through connections and influence, mainly with royal connections in the

case of Saudi Arabia, rather than merit. Pascal Menoret, *The Saudi Enigma: A History* (Beirut: World Book Publishing, 2005), p. 86.
30. Digby Lidstone, 'Digging Deep', *MEED*, 6 December 2002, p. 7.
31. Pascal Menoret, 'Conclusion', *The Saudi Enigma: A History* (Beirut: World Book Publishing, 2005), p. 216.
32. Mai Yamani, 'The Two Faces of Saudi Arabia', *Survival* 50/1, February–March 2008, p. 145.
33. *GSN*, 'Saudi/U.S.: Rice in Riyadh as Dissidents Appeal', 29/760, 24 June 2006, p. 6.
34. Email interview with Roberto Toscani, former Italian Ambassador to Iran, 13 August 2011.
35. Remarks from Prince Turki Al-Faisal, 'Address at the Gulf Research Meeting Opening Ceremony', University of Cambridge, 6 July 2011.
36. Abdul Ilah Muhammad Jadaa, 'Local Press: Who Did Not Benefit from 2-Month Salary?', 5 April 2011, *Arab News.com*, available at http://arabnews.com/saudiarabia/article345612.ece?comments=all, accessed 1 June 2011.
37. Remarks from Prince Turki Al-Faisal, University of Exeter, 16 March 2011.
38. Ibid.
39. Remarks from Prince Turki Al-Faisal, 'Address at the Gulf Research Meeting Opening Ceremony', University of Cambridge, 6 July 2011.
40. *Al Jazeera*, 'Saudi Arabia's #Women2Drive', 16 June 2011, available at http://stream.aljazeera.com/story/saudi-women-drivers, last accessed 23 April 2013.
41. Remarks from Prince Turki Al-Faisal, 'Address at the Gulf Research Meeting Opening Ceremony', University of Cambridge, 6 July 2011.
42. Nawaf E. Obaid, 'Introduction', *The Oil Kingdom at 100 – Petroleum Policymaking in Saudi Arabia*, p. 13.
43. *MEED*, 'Special Report: Defence', 28 January–3 February 2005, p. 26.
44. Nawaf Obaid, 'The Day of Saudi Collapse is Not Near', *Foreign Policy*, 13 April 2011, available at http://oilandglory.foreignpolicy.com/posts/2011/04/13/the_day_of_saudi_collapse_is_not_near (registration required), last accessed 23 April 2013.
45. Toby Matthiesen, 'Saudi Arabia: the Middle East's Most Under Reported Conflict', *The Guardian*, 23 January 2012, available at http://www.guardian.co.uk/commentisfree/2012/jan/23/saudi-arabia-shia-protesters, last accessed 23 April 2013.
46. Epitomized by the derogatory term '*rawafid*' or '*rafidi*', meaning 'rejectionists'. Email remarks from Henry Precht, former Chief of Iran Desk in US State Department 1978–1980, G2000 Project, 6 October 2011.

47. Michael Peel, 'Shia Attack Riyadh's Crackdown Pledge', *FT*, 5 October 2011, available at http://www.ft.com/intl/cms/s/0/54036a36-ef68-11e0-bc88-00144feab49a.html#axzz1aWMBSfVG (registration required), last accessed 23 April 2013.
48. Anna Fifield and Najmeh Bozorgmehr, 'US Accuses Iran of Saudi Envoy Death Plot', *FT*, 11 October 2011, available at http://www.ft.com/intl/cms/s/0/185fa35c-f439-11e0-bdea-00144feab49a.html#axzz1aWMBSfVG (registration required), last accessed 23 April 2013.
49. Nawaf Obaid, 'The Day of Saudi Collapse is Not Near', *Foreign Policy*.
50. Ibid.
51. *MEED*, 'Guarding the Lifelines', 31 March–6 April 2006, p. 5.
52. The so-called 'resistance axis' includes Iran, Syria, Hezbollah and Hamas. International Crisis Group, 'Drums of War: Israel and the "Axis of Resistance"', 2 August 2010, available at http://www.crisisgroup.org/en/regions/middle-east-north-africa/iraq-syria-lebanon/lebanon/097-drums-of-war-israel-and-the-axis-of-resistance.aspx, accessed 6 August 2010.
53. Although some European states such as the UK thought it a step back from existing Israeli-Palestinian negotiations and placed more emphasis on Jordan and Egypt which have borders with Israel. Interview with a UK government analyst who asked not to be named, London, 13 May 2010.
54. Interview with a former Saudi minister who asked not to be named, Cambridge, 8 July 2011.
55. Martin Indyk, 'Dual Containment and the Peace Process', *Innocent Abroad* (New York: Simon and Schuster, 2009), p. 173.
56. Royal Embassy of Saudi Arabia, Washington D.C., 'Press Release: Saudi Arabia Announces Massive Aid Package to Lebanon, Palestine to Help Relief Efforts', 26 July 2006, available at http://www.saudiembassy.net/archive/2006/press/page3.aspx, last accessed 23 April 2013.
57. Ewen MacAskill, 'Wikileaks Cables: Saudis Proposed Arab Force to Invade Lebanon', *The Guardian*, 7 December 2010, available at http://www.guardian.co.uk/world/2010/dec/07/wikileaks-saudi-arab-invasion-lebanon, last accessed 23 April 2013.
58. Hezbollah can raise funds through varied forms of in-kind and cash support from Iran and, to a lesser extent, Syria for its mix of terrorist, guerrilla, political and social-welfare operations which spans up to 40 countries on five different continents. Other sources of funding are said to include expatriate remittances, charities, front organizations and criminal enterprises including alleged drug trafficking across the Lebanon-Israel border and in Europe. Both Hamas and Hezbollah are also said to have received between $50 million and $500 million between 1999 and 2001 from Arab

expatriates in Brazil through Paraguayan financial institutions. Matthew Levitt, 'Hezbollah Finances: Funding the Party of God', *The Washington Institute for Near East Policy*, February 2005, available at http://www.washingtoninstitute.org/templateC06.php?CID=772, last accessed 23 April 2013; Assaf Uni, 'Report: Hezbollah Funded by Drug Trade in Europe', *Haaretz*, 9 January 2010, available at http://www.haaretz.com/news/report-hezbollah-funded-by-drug-trade-in-europe-1.261091, last accessed 23 April 2013; Curtis C. Connell, *Terrorist and Organized Crime Groups in the Tri-Border Area (TBA) of South America*, The Library of Congress, Federal Research Division, July 2003, p. 2–4; Ilan Berman, *Hezbollah in the Western Hemisphere*, Statement before the US House of Representatives Committee on Homeland Security/Subcommittee on Counterterrorism and Intelligence, American Foreign Policy Council, 7 July 2011.

59. *The Economist*, 'How Iran Fits In', 17 January 2009, available at http://www.economist.com/node/12959539, last accessed 23 April 2013.
60. Interview with a former Saudi minister who asked not to be named, Cambridge, 8 July 2011.
61. Remarks from Prince Turki Al Faisal, University of Exeter, 16 March 2011.
62. Telephone interview with Martin Indyk, former US Ambassador to Israel and Special Assistant to President Bill Clinton for Near East and South Asian Affairs at the National Security Council, 1 November 2011.
63. *Saudi in Focus*, 'Gulf States Offer $10 Billion to Israel in Exchange for a Palestinian State', available at http://www.saudiinfocus.com/ar/forum/showthread.php?36862, last accessed 23 April 2013.
64. Yemen currently has observer status in the GCC and could potentially join the GCC which would mean turning the GCC into the Arab Peninsula Cooperation Council. Remarks from Prince Turki Al-Faisal, University of Exeter, 16 March 2011.
65. *MEED*, 'Free Trade – with Strings Attached', 29 August 2003, p. 22; *MEED*, 'Special Report: Saudi Arabia', 17–23 February 2006, p. 42.
66. Sultan Sooud Al Qassemi, 'How Saudi Arabia and Qatar Became Friends Again', *Foreign Policy*, 21 July 2011, available at http://www.foreignpolicy.com/articles/2011/07/21/how_saudi_arabia_and_qatar_became_friends_again?page=full (registration required), last accessed 23 April 2013.
67. *Islam Times*, 'Qatari Prime Minister: The Saudi Regime Will Inevitably Fall by Our Hands', 25 December 2011, available at http://www.islamtimes.org/vdcawmn6e49nuw1.tgk4.html, last accessed 23 April 2013.
68. 'Prince Talal bin Abdul Aziz, the Brother of the King of Saudi Arabia Warns of Qatar's Scheme to Divide Saudi Arabia and to Hit Syria, as a Service to the Zionist Entity', 4 December 2011, available at http://

tunisianquestfortruth.wordpress.com/2011/12/04/prince-talal-bin-abdulaziz-the-brother-of-the-king-of-saudi-arabia-warns-of-qatars-scheme-to-divide-saudi-arabia-and-to-hit-syria-as-a-service-to-the-zionist-entity/ as published in Arabic at http://www.libanonchat.org/?p=13176, last accessed 23 April 2013.
69. James M. Dorsey, 'Saudi Arabia Embraces Salafism: Countering the Arab Uprising? – Analysis', *Eurasia Review*, 13 January 2012, available at http://www.eurasiareview.com/13012012-saudi-arabia-embraces-salafism-countering-the-arab-uprising-analysis/, last accessed 23 April 2013.
70. Ian Black, 'CIA Using Saudi Base for Drone Assassinations in Yemen', *The Guardian*, 6 February 2013, available at http://www.guardian.co.uk/world/2013/feb/06/cia-using-saudi-base-drone-yemen, last accessed 23 April 2013.
71. Obaid, Nawaf. 'A Saudi Perspective on the Arab Uprisings', *CNN*, 22 November 2009, available at http://globalpublicsquare.blogs.cnn.com/2011/06/08/a-saudi-perspective-on-the-arab-uprisings/, last accessed 23 April 2013.
72. Further discussion about Arab–Israeli trade can be found in Robert Mason, 'Arab–Israeli Trade: A Distant, Yet Transformative, Prospect', *Instituto de Empresa International Relations Blog*, 10 February 2010, available at http://ir.blogs.ie.edu/2011/02/10/arab-%E2%80%93-israeli-trade-a-distant-yet-transformative-prospect/, last accessed 12 April 2013.
73. *GSN*, 'After the GCC's Muscat Summit, Currency Plan Credibility Hangs on Acts, Not Words', 845, 16 January 2009, available at http://www.gsnonline.com/HTML/Public/GSNs_World/Free_Content/Free_content_70.html, accessed 12 March 2009.
74. Remarks of Prince Turki Al-Faisal, University of Exeter, 16 March 2011.
75. *GSN*, 'Air Force Modernisation', 27/23, 27 June 2003, p. 13.
76. Kristian Coates Ulrichsen, 'Challenges of Transition in the Gulf Cooperation Council States', *Global Affairs*, 24 September 2011, available at http://eng.globalaffairs.ru/number/Approaching-a-Post-Oil-Era-15328, last accessed 23 April 2013.
77. Carole A. O'Leary and Nicholas A. Heras, 'Saudi Arabia's "Iran Initiative" and Arab Tribalism: Emerging Forces Converge in the Arab World', *The Jamestown Foundation*, 21 October 2011, available at http://www.jamestown.org/single/?no_cache=1&tx_ttnews per cent5Btt_news per cent5D=38555&tx_ttnews per cent5BbackPid per cent5D=7&cHash=80812bf625d6ca0316fc61874cab6961, accessed 4 January 2012.
78. Nawaf Obaid, 'A Saudi Perspective on the Arab Uprisings', *CNN*, 22 November 2009.

79. *Al Arabiya*, 'Economic Implications of Jordan and Morocco Joining GCC', 12 May 2011, available at http://www.alarabiya.net/articles/2011/05/12/148876.html, last accessed 23 April 2013.
80. *Arab News*, '$4 Billion Saudi Aid for Egypt', 21 May 2011, available at http://www.arabnews.com/saudiarabia/article420017.ece, accessed 29 May 2011; although as of January 2012, only between $500 million-$1.5 billion has been disbursed with indications that the USA may be putting pressure on Saudi Arabia to withhold funding in order to get Egypt to talk to the IMF first. Emails from Philip McCrum, Editorial Director of the Economist and Issandr El Amrani, Arabist Research, to the G2K List, 18 January 2012.
81. Remarks from Prince Turki Al-Faisal, 'Address at the Gulf Research Meeting Opening Ceremony', University of Cambridge, 6 July 2011.
82. 'Islamic Awakening' was a common expression used by the media in Iran, discovered by this author during field research in Tehran, March 2011; *BBC News*, 'Bahrain Expels Iranian Diplomat Over "Spy Ring"', 26 April 2011, available at http://www.bbc.co.uk/news/world-middle-east-13195541, last accessed 23 April 2013.
83. Nawaf Obaid, 'Amid the Arab Spring, a US–Saudi Split', *The Washington Post*, 16 May 2011, available at http://www.washingtonpost.com/opinions/amid-the-arab-spring-a-us-saudi-split/2011/05/13/AFMy8Q4G_story.html, last accessed 23 April 2013.
84. Ibid.
85. Remarks from Prince Turki Al-Faisal, University of Exeter, 16 March 2011.
86. *BBC News*, 'Arab League Backs Libya No-Fly Zone', 12 March 2011, available at http://www.bbc.co.uk/news/world-africa-12723554, last accessed 23 April 2013.
87. *Reuters*, 'Obama, Cameron and Saudi King Urge Syria End Violence', 13 August 2011, available at http://uk.reuters.com/article/2011/08/13/uk-syria-obama-saudi-idUKTRE77C19X20110813, last accessed 23 April 2013; Khaled Yacoub Oweis, 'Syria's Assad Says Military Stops, Shooting Reported', *Reuters*, 18 August 2011, available at http://uk.reuters.com/article/2011/08/18/idINIndia-58841020110818, accessed 18 August 2011.
88. Ali Al-Ahmad, Director, Gulf Institute, Washington D.C., 'Saudi Arabia Throws its Weight Behind Syrian Opposition', Email sent to the G2K List, 25 August 2011.
89. Farid Mirbagheri, 'Narrowing the Gap or Camouflaging the Divide: An Analysis of Mohammad Khatami's "Dialogue of Civilisations"', *British Journal of Middle Eastern Studies* 34/3, December 2007, p. 305.

90. Will Fulton, Ariel Farrar-Wellman and Robert Frasco, 'Saudi Arabia – Iran Foreign Relations', *Iran Tracker*, 1 August 2011, available at http://www.irantracker.org/foreign-relations/saudi-arabia-iran-foreign-relations, last accessed 23 April 2013.
91. *The Guardian*, 'US Embassy Cables: Saudis Fear "Shia Triangle" of Iran, Iraq and Pakistan', 3 December 2010, available at http://www.guardian.co.uk/world/us-embassy-cables-documents/201549, last accessed 23 April 2013.
92. Saudi Arabia will not improve economic relations with Iran until this issue is resolved. Remarks from Prince Turki Al-Faisal, University of Exeter, 16 March 2011.
93. In addition to holding 25 per cent of the world's oil capacity and 70 per cent of spare capacity, Saudi Arabia is also planning to invest $100 billion in 16 nuclear power plants and also in solar energy which is expected to boost short-term domestic needs. Nawaf Obaid, 'A Saudi Perspective on the Arab Uprisings', 22 November 2009.
94. Danial Anas Kaysi, 'The Saudis go to Baghdad', *The National Interest*, 19 October 2011, available at http://nationalinterest.org/commentary/saudis-baghdad-3639, last accessed 23 April 2013.
95. Nawaf Obaid, 'Stepping into Iraq', *The Washington Post*, 29 November 2006, available at http://www.washingtonpost.com/wp-dyn/content/article/2006/11/28/AR2006112801277.html, last accessed 23 April 2013.
96. *MEED*, 'Manning the Borders', 31 March–6 April 2006, p. 4.
97. As stated by Bandar al-Aiban, former chairman of the foreign affairs committee of the Majlis Al-Shura. *MEED*, 'Cover Story: Prince Sa'ud al-Faisal', p. 6.
98. *GSN*, 'Defence Pointers', 29/766, 30 September 2005, p. 7.
99. Ross Colvin, '"Cut Off Head of Snake" Saudis Told US on Iran', *Reuters*, 29 November 2010, available at http://www.reuters.com/article/2010/11/29/us-wikileaks-iran-saudis-idUSTRE6AS02B20101129, last accessed 23 April 2013.
100. Remarks from Prince Turki Al-Faisal, University of Exeter, 16 March 2011.
101. Jay Solomon, 'Saudi Suggests "Squeezing" Iran Over Nuclear Ambitions', *The Wall Street Journal*, 22 June 2011, available at http://online.wsj.com/article/SB10001424052702304887904576400083811644642.html?mod=WSJEUROPE_hpp_MIDDLESecondNews, last accessed 23 April 2013.
102. Flynt Leverett and Hillary Mann Leverett, 'Oil and the Iranian–Saudi "Cold War"', *Race for Iran*, 12 July 2011, available at http://www.raceforiran.com/oil-and-the-iranian-saudi- per centE2 per cent80 per cent9Ccold-war per centE2 per cent80 per cent9D, accessed 12 July 2011.

103. Shaimaa Fayed, 'Saudi Shows Who's Boss, To Pump 10 Mln bpd', *Reuters*, 10 June 2011, available at http://in.reuters.com/article/2011/06/10/idINIndia-57632320110610, last accessed 23 April 2013.
104. Matthew R. Simmons, *Twilight in the Desert: The Coming Saudi Oil Shock and the World Economy* (New Jersey: John Wiley and Sons, 2005), p. 269.
105. Downstream refining capacity is becoming a bottleneck which is adding to pressure on pricing, so Saudi Arabia has to invest in both upstream and downstream projects whilst maintaining manageable prices.
106. Interview with Dr Leo Drollas, Chief Economist, Center for Global Energy Studies, 26 January 2011, London.
107. Ibid.
108. Jason Burke, 'Riyadh Will Build Nuclear Weapons if Iran Gets Them, Saudi Prince Warns', *The Guardian*, 29 June 2011, available at http://www.guardian.co.uk/world/2011/jun/29/saudi-build-nuclear-weapons-iran, last accessed 23 April 2013.
109. Dealings with Iran started out on the wrong foot through the E3 of France, Germany and the UK which made public its use of both the stick and carrot approach to negotiations. Remarks by Prince Turki Al-Faisal, University of Exeter, 16 March 2011.
110. Jeremy Pelofsky and Basil Katz, 'Iranians Charged in US Over Assassination Plot', *Reuters*, 11 October 2011, available at http://uk.reuters.com/article/2011/10/11/uk-usa-security-iran-idUKTRE79A5BQ20111011, last accessed 23 April 2013.
111. Joshua Teitelbaum, 'Saudi Arabia's Shi'i Opposition: Background and Analysis', The Washington Institute for Near East Policy, 14 November 1996, available at http://www.washingtoninstitute.org/templateC05.php?CID=1104, last accessed 23 April 2013.
112. Email remarks from Walter Posch, SWP Berlin, to the G2K list, 12 October 2011; Email remarks from Kenneth Katzman, Congressional Research Service, to the G2K list, 12 October 2011; Joby Warrick and Thomas Erdbrink, 'Assassination Plot was so Clumsy, Officials at First Doubted Iran's Role', *The Washington Post*, 13 October 2011, available at http://www.washingtonpost.com/world/national-security/us-investigators-initially-doubted-iran-link-to-assassination-plot/2011/10/12/gIQAnWgpfL_story.html, last accessed 23 April 2013.
113. A full list is available at http://www.oic-oci.org/member_states.asp, last accessed 23 April 2013.
114. Evidence of this can be found in Petronas, the Malaysian NOC, which operates in 32 countries outside of Malaysia. Daniel Yergin, 'Epilogue', *The*

Prize: The Epic Quest for Oil, Money and Power (New York: Free Press, 2008), p. 770.
115. Interview with H.E. Professor Dato' Syed Omar Al Saggaf, Malaysian Ambassador to Saudi Arabia, 5 June 2011.
116. Ibid.
117. Interview with a former Saudi minister who asked not to be named, Cambridge, 8 July 2011.
118. *BBC News*, 'Saudis Boost Aid to Wave Victims', 7 January 2005, available at http://news.bbc.co.uk/1/hi/world/middle_east/4151241.stm, last accessed 23 April 2013.
119. See projects in Africa and Asia, *Annual Report*, The Saudi Fund for Development, available at http://www.sfd.gov.sa/, last accessed 23 April 2013.
120. Oliver Bloom, 'Saudi Arabia's Nuclear Program', *Center for Strategic and International Studies*, 17 May 2010, available at http://csis.org/blog/saudi-arabias-nuclear-program, last accessed 23 April 2013.
121. Bruce Riedel, *Saudi Arabia: Nervously Watching Pakistan*, Brookings Institution, 28 January 2008, available at http://www.brookings.edu/research/opinions/2008/01/28-saudi-arabia-riedel, last accessed 23 April 2012.
122. Elsa Walsh, 'The Prince: How the Saudi Ambassador Became Washington's Indispensable Operator', *The New Yorker*, 24 March 2003, p. 60, available at http://www.saudiembassy.net/files/PDF/03-ST-Bandar-0324-NewYorker.pdf, last accessed 23 April 2013.
123. *GSN*, 'Saudi Arabia and Bahrain', 32/840, 10 November 2008, p. 4.
124. *MEED*, 'Special Report: Saudi Arabia', 21–27 April 2006, p. 46.
125. *GSN*, 'Politics', 32/840, 10 November 2008, p. 4.
126. Oliver Bloom, 'Saudi Arabia's Nuclear Program', *Center for Strategic and International Studies*, 17 May 2010.
127. *The Guardian*, 'US Embassy Cables: Saudis Fear "Shia Triangle" of Iran, Iraq and Pakistan', 3 December 2010.
128. Rachel Bronson, 'September 11 and Beyond', *Thicker Than Oil: America's Uneasy Partnership with Saudi Arabia* (Oxford: Oxford University Press, 2006), p. 232.
129. Israel received more than $2 billion in military aid alone in 2002. *MEED*, 'Pax Americana', 28 February 2003, p. 22.
130. *MEED*, 'Special Report: Saudi Arabia', 22 March 2002, p. 26.
131. Ibid.
132. *MEED*, 'Pax Americana', 28 February 2003, p. 22.
133. Although Citigroup said the sale of its 20 per cent in Samba Financial Group was conducted on business grounds, many analysts feel that

post-9/11 issues such as the *Patriot Act* and threats of future class actions were part of the equation. 'Others Go Where Citigroup Has Been', *GSN*, 28/736, 11 June 2004, p. 12.

134. President Bush vowed to make the USA less dependent on Middle East oil in his State of the Union Speech given on 31 January 2006. George W. Bush, 'Text of Bush's State of the Union Speech', *CNN.com*, available at http://edition.cnn.com/2006/POLITICS/01/31/sotu.transcript/, last accessed 23 April 2013. This policy was confirmed by President Obama's statement on becoming a 'major customer' of Brazilian oil when production climbs at new fields. The White House, 'Remarks by President Obama and President Rousseff of Brazil in Brasilia, Brazil', 19 March 2011, available at http://www.whitehouse.gov/the-press-office/2011/03/19/remarks-president-obama-and-president-rousseff-brazil-brasilia-brazil, last accessed 23 April 2013.
135. *MEED*, 'Losing the Sense of Balance', 28 February 2003, p. 25.
136. *MEED*, 'Saudi Arabia: Special Report', 17–23 February 2006, p. 40.
137. Sam Hakim, 'Gulf Cooperation Council Stock Markets Since September 11', *Middle East Policy* 15/1 (Spring 2008), p. 73.
138. Adam Porter, 'How Much Oil Do We Really Have?', *BBC News*, 15 July 2005, available at http://news.bbc.co.uk/1/hi/business/4681935.stm, last accessed 23 April 2013.
139. Matthew R. Simmons, *Twilight in the Desert*, p. 285
140. Ibid.
141. Ibid.
142. Ibid.
143. Daniel Yergin, 'Epilogue', *The Prize: The Epic Quest for Oil, Money and Power*, p. 770.
144. Julian Borger, 'Saudi Royals Face Trillion-Dollar Lawsuit Over September 11', *The Guardian*, 16 August 2002, available at http://www.guardian.co.uk/world/2002/aug/16/saudiarabia.usa, last accessed 23 April 2013.
145. Flynt Leverett, 'Reengaging Riyadh', in Flynt Leverett and Martin Indyk (eds.), *The Road Ahead: Middle East Policy in the Bush Administration's Second Term* (Washington D.C.: Brookings Institution, 2005), p. 97.
146. Rachel Bronson, *Thicker Than Oil*, pp. 235–238.
147. Ibid.
148. Tom Everett-Heath, 'Push and Pull', *MEED*, 11 January 2002, p. 4.
149. Rachel Bronson, *Thicker Than Oil*, pp. 235–238.
150. Ibid.
151. Edmund O'Sullivan, 'Pushing a New Agenda', *MEED*, 19 September 2003, p. 5.

152. Marina Ottaway and Thomas Carothers, *The Greater Middle East Initiative: Off to a False Start*, Carnegie Endowment, 29 March 2004, available at http://carnegieendowment.org/files/Policybrief29.pdf, last accessed 23 December 2013.
153. Ibid.
154. Suzanne Maloney, 'The Alliance that Dare not Speak its Name', *Brookings*, 20 May 2011, available at http://www.brookings.edu/opinions/2011/0520_obama_middle_east_maloney.aspx, last accessed 23 April 2013.
155. Rachel Bronson, *Thicker Than Oil*, p. 238.
156. 'Friends in High Places', *MEED*, 23–29 June 2006, 38
157. Remarks from Prince Turki Al-Faisal, University of Exeter, 16 March 2011.
158. Interview with a former Saudi minister who asked not to be named, Cambridge, 8 July 2011.
159. The plan echoed the 1981 King Fahd plan based loosely on UNSCR 242 and 338, offering a complete peace to Israel in return for a total withdrawal to its pre-1967 borders and the establishment of a Palestinian state. Angus McDowall, 'The Power of Speech', *MEED*, 22 March 2002, p. 25.
160. *MEED*, 'Special Report: Saudi Arabia', 22 March 2002, p. 26.
161. Ibid., pp. 237–239.
162. Ibid., p. 237
163. *MEED*, 'Special Report: Saudi Arabia', 28 March 2003, p. 22.
164. On 20 April 2002 Iran and Iraq proposed a Muslim oil embargo against the USA which Prince Sa'ud Al-Faisal, the Saudi Foreign Minister, promised he would not support. *MEED*, 'Special Report: Saudi Arabia', 21 June 2002, p. 25.
165. US Vice President Dick Cheney found this to be the case during his visit to the Middle East in March 2003. Rachel Bronson, *Thicker Than Oil*, p. 239.
166. *MEED*, 'Cover Story: Arab Summit', 29 March 2002, p. 5.
167. CIA World Factbook, 'Economy – Overview – Saudi Arabia', September 2009, available at https://www.cia.gov/library/publications/the-world-factbook/geos/sa.html, last accessed 23 April 2013.
168. *MEED*, 'Special Report: Saudi Arabia', 28 March 2003, p. 25.
169. *MEED*, 'Bursting with Wealth', 17–23 February 2006, p. 43.
170. Mai Yamani, 'Terminal Decline?', *The World Today*, Chatham House, 60/7, July 2004, p. 11.
171. Ibid.
172. *GSN*, 'Imposing Discipline Abroad, King Sets Foreign Policy Line', 32/823, 18 February 2008, p. 1.
173. Michel Cousins, 'Turki al-Faisal Calls on Obama to Push for Middle East Settlement', *Arab News*, 15 May 2010, available at http://arabnews.com/saudiarabia/article54062.ece.

174. Arab Revolutions, 'Prince Talal bin Abdul Aziz, the Brother of the King of Saudi Arabia Warns of Qatar's Scheme to Divide Saudi Arabia and to Hit Syria, as a Service to the Zionist Entity', 4 December 2011.
175. *GSN*, 'Focus', 28/748, 22 December 2004, p. 2.
176. Martin Indyk, *Innocent Abroad*, p. 155.
177. Interview with Sherard Cowper-Coles, London, 4 June 2010.
178. Anthony H. Cordesman, 'Iranian and Saudi Competition in the Gulf', *United States Institute of Peace: The Iran Primer*, 27 April 2011, available at http://iranprimer.usip.org/blog/2011/apr/27/iranian-and-saudi-competition-gulf, last accessed 23 April 2013.
179. Prince Turki, 'Failed Favouritism Towards Israel', *The Washington Post*, 10 June 2011, available at http://www.washingtonpost.com/opinions/palestinian-rights-wont-be-denied-by-the-united-states-and-israel/2011/06/07/AGmnK2OH_story.html, last accessed 23 April 2013.
180. Roger Hardy, 'Saudi-US Relations Strained Over Afghanistan', *BBC News*, 15 November 2001, available at http://news.bbc.co.uk/1/hi/world/middle_east/1657721.stm, last accessed 23 April 2013.
181. *BBC News*, 'Saudi: US Presence Illegal', 29 March 2007, available at http://news.bbc.co.uk/1/hi/world/middle_east/6505803.stm, last accessed 23 April 2013.
182. Bruce W. Jentleson, 'Metternich of Arabia', *The National Interest*, 29 June 2011, available at http://nationalinterest.org/commentary/metternich-arabia-5543, last accessed 23 April 2013.
183. Matthew Rosenberg, Jay Solomon, and Margaret Coker, 'Saudi Bid to Curb Iran Worries US', *The Wall Street Journal*, 27 May 2011, available at http://online.wsj.com/article/SB10001424052702303654804576347282491615962.html, last accessed 23 April 2013.
184. *GSN*, 'Politics and Security', 29/759, 10 June 2005, p. 5.
185. Ibid.
186. *GSN*, 'Focus: Saudi Foreign Policy', 32/823, 18 February 2008, p. 3.
187. Adam Entous, 'Saudi Arms Deal Advances', *The Wall Street Journal*, 12 September 2010, available at http://online.wsj.com/article/SB10001424052748704621204575488361149625050.html, last accessed 23 April 2013.
188. Ibid.
189. Joshua Teitelbaum, 'Empty Words: Saudi Blustering and US – Saudi Realities', *Perspectives Papers on Current Affairs 147*, The Begin-Sadat Center for Strategic Studies, 17 July 2011, available at http://www.biu.ac.il/Besa/perspectives147.html, last accessed 23 April 2013.
190. One which Saudi Arabia was not willing to risk by lobbying China on the issue of not blocking renewed sanctions against Iran. Georja Calvin-Smith,

'Riyadh Unwilling to Lobby China Over Iran Sanctions', *France 24*, 16 February 2010, available at http://www.france24.com/en/20100216-riyadh-unwilling-lobby-china-over-iran-sanctions, last accessed 23 April 2013.
191. Grant Smith and Christian Schmollinger, 'China Passes US as World's Biggest Energy Consumer, IEA Says', *Bloomberg*, 20 July 2010, available at http://www.bloomberg.com/news/2010-07-19/china-passes-u-s-as-biggest-energy-consumer-as-oil-imports-jump-iea-says.html, last accessed 23 April 2013.
192. Madelaine Bunting, 'The Saudi Intervention in Bahrain will Fuel Sectarianism, not Stifle it', *The Guardian*, 20 March 2011, available at http://www.guardian.co.uk/commentisfree/2011/mar/20/bahrain-saudi-intervention-religious-divide, last accessed 23 April 2013.
193. Angus McDowall, 'Courage of Convictions', *MEED*, 20 September 2002, p. 25.
194. *MEED*, 'The View from the Top', 2 May 2003, p. 5.
195. *MEED*, 'Special Report: Saudi Arabia', 31 January 2003, p. 30.
196. Email interview with a European diplomat who asked not to be named, 1 April 2011.
197. Ibid.
198. European Commission Directorate-General for Energy, 'Registration of Crude Oil Imports and Deliveries into the European Union (EU27)', 1 December 2009, p. 1, available at http://ec.europa.eu/energy/observatory/oil/import_export_en.htm, last accessed 23 April 2013.
199. Richard Youngs and Ana Echague, 'Europe and the Gulf: Strategic Neglect?', *Studia Diplomatica*, Vol LX/1, 2007, p. 29.
200. Interview with a UK government analyst who asked not to be named, London, 13 May 2010.
201. Gerd Nonneman, 'Saudi-European Relations 1902–2001 – a Pragmatic Quest for Relative Autonomy', *International Affairs* 77/3, 2001, p. 652.
202. Interview with a UK government analyst who asked not to be named, London, 13 May 2010.
203. Interview with Sherard Cowper-Coles, London, 4 June 2010.
204. Ibid.
205. David Robertson and Alex Spence, 'Six Year BAE Investigation Ends with Minor Accountancy Charges', *The Times*, 6 February 2010, available at http://business.timesonline.co.uk/tol/business/industry_sectors/industrials/article7016732.ece (subscription required).
206. *Death of a Princess* is a film about the great-niece of the Saudi king who confessed to adultery and was publicly executed in Saudi Arabia, along

with her lover. The film was the first time Shari'a law had been examined by the West as it pertained to Saudi Arabia, but was nevertheless unwelcome attention paid to Saudi culture and the behaviour of the ruling regime. Thomas White and Gladys Ganley, 'The "Death of a Princess" Controversy', *PBS*, available at http://www.pbs.org/wgbh/pages/frontline/shows/princess/reflect/harvard.html, last accessed 23 April 2013.
207. Interview with Sherard Cowper-Coles, London, 4 June 2010.
208. Rosemary Hollis, 'Europe and Gulf Security: A Competitive Business', in David E. Long and Christian Koch (eds.), *Gulf Security in the Twenty-First Century* (Abu Dhabi: The Emirates Center for Strategic Studies and Research, 1997), p. 82.
209. Gerd Nonneman, 'Saudi-European Relations 1902–2001 – a Pragmatic Quest for Relative Autonomy', *International Affairs*, p. 650.
210. *GSN*, 'Economy and Trade: The United Kingdom and the Gulf', 19 September 1994, 19/495, p. 7.
211. *GSN*, 'Politics and Defence: Saudi Arabia's Illusory Security', 3 October 1994, 19/496, p. 3.
212. *MEED*, 'Extending the Deal', 28 January–3 February 2005, p. 29.
213. Ibid.
214. Interview with Chris Innes-Hopkins, Director of UK Trade and Investment, British Embassy, Riyadh, 7 June 2011.
215. Ibid.
216. Ibid.
217. David Robertson, 'BAE Poised to Clinch £20bn Saudi Eurofighter Deal', *The Times*, 7 September 2007, available at http://business.timesonline.co.uk/tol/business/industry_sectors/engineering/article2402913.ece (subscription required); Eurofighter Typhoon, 'Consortium Structure', available at http://www.eurofighter.com/eurofighter-typhoon/programme-organisation/consortium-structure.html, last accessed 23 April 2013.
218. Ibid.
219. Interview with Chris Innes-Hopkins, Riyadh, 7 June 2011.
220. Oliver Klaus, 'Friends Reunited', *MEED*, 21–27 October 2005, p. 4.
221. Ibid.
222. Ibid.
223. Interview with Sherard Cowper-Coles, London, 4 June 2010.
224. Ibid.
225. Ibid.
226. Interview with Sherard Cowper-Coles, London, 4 June 2010.
227. J.E. Hartshorn, 'Pause or Plateau', in Chris Hope and Jim Skea (eds.), *Oil Trade, Politics and Prospects* (Cambridge: Cambridge University Press, 1993), p. 1.

228. Elisabeth Rosenthal, 'Gulf Oil States Seeking a Lead in Clean Energy', *The New York Times*, 12 January 2009, available at http://www.nytimes.com/2009/01/13/world/middleeast/13greengulf.html?pagewanted=all, last accessed 23 April 2013; Bertelsmann Siftung, 'Europe and the Gulf Region – Towards a New Horizon', Discussion Paper Presented at the 12th Kronberg Talks, 11–12 May 2009, Riyadh, p. 24.
229. Gordon Brown's visit to the Gulf in November 2008 was for precisely this reason. Richard Youngs, *Impasse in Euro-Gulf Relations*, FRIDE Working Paper, April 2009, p. 1.
230. Ibid.
231. Bertelsmann Siftung, 'Europe and the Gulf Region – Towards a New Horizon', p. 8.
232. *Global Security*, 'Mecca', available at http://www.globalsecurity.org/military/world/gulf/mecca.htm, last accessed 23 April 2013.
233. Banque Saude Fransi, 'Trade Notes: Saudi Arabia', 17 November 2009, available at www.alfransi.com.sa/en/general/download/file/456 (file download), last accessed 23 April 2013.
234. Ibid.
235. Ibid.
236. *Saudi-US Relations Information Service* (hereafter *SUSRIS*), 'Franco-Saudi State Visit: President Chirac in Riyadh', 10 March 2006, available at http://www.susris.com/articles/2006/nid/060310-chirac-visit.html.
237. *GSN*, 'Saudi Defence: Will France Reap Rewards for Riyadh Connection?', 29/756, 29 April 2005, p. 5.
238. Ibid.
239. *GSN*, 'With French Deal, Abdullah's National Guard Strengthens its Status as the "Second Saudi Army"', 32/829, 19 May 2008, p. 6.
240. Elsa Walsh, 'The Prince: How the Saudi Ambassador Became Washington's Indispensable Operator', *The New Yorker*, p. 63.
241. *GSN*, 'Partnership Back in Vogue as State Regains the Initiative in Washington', 28/739, 23 July 2004, p. 7.
242. *GSN*, 'Focus', 31/809, 6 July 2007, pp. 2–3.
243. John Sfakianakis, 'Saudi-Germany Relations', *SAAB Notes*, 8 November 2007, available at http://www.gulfinthemedia.com/files/article_en/356522.pdf, last accessed 23 April 2013.
244. Ibid.
245. Ibid.
246. Discussion on this topic will follow the next government report on arms exports which will also include reference to the Arab Uprisings, Israel and Yemen. Interview with Ruprecht Polenz, Member of the German

Bundestag and Chairman of the Committee on Foreign Affairs, Berlin, 22 September 2011; Stephen Evans, 'German Parliament to Debate Sale of 200 Tanks to Saudis', *BBC News*, 6 July 2011, available at http://www.bbc.co.uk/news/world-europe-14043668, last accessed 23 April 2013.

247. Digby Lidstone, 'Trade Routes', *MEED*, 7–13 July 2006, p. 4.
248. James Gavin, 'The Sun Sets for Japan', *MEED*, 25 February 2000, p. 4.
249. Gerd Nonneman, 'Determinants and Patterns of Saudi Foreign Policy: "Omnibalancing" and "Relative Autonomy" in Multiple Environments', in P. Aarts and G. Nonneman, *Saudi Arabia in the Balance: Political Economy, Society, Foreign Affairs* (London: C. Hurst & Co., 2006), p. 344.
250. *GSN*, 'USA Takes Fright, as China's Vision Becomes Clearer in Relations with Iran and Saudi Arabia', 30/786, 21 July 2006, p. 9.
251. Expo 2010, 'Saudi–Chinese Relations', available at http://www.saudiexpo2010.com/index.php/en/saudi-chinese-relations, last accessed 23 April 2013.
252. Contemporary Sino-Saudi relations only go back to Saudi recognition of the PRC in 1990, which is now the most important China-Arab or China-Gulf relationship. Tim Niblock, *China and Saudi Arabia: the Shaping of the Relationship*, paper delivered at the Gulf Research Meeting, University of Cambridge, 7 July 2010.
253. India's links to the GCC go back centuries and were primarily based on the old silk routes from Xian in China to the Mediterranean, which has turned into a new twenty-first century silk route comprising the massive movements of energy products, goods, investments and peoples across Asia. H.E. Talmiz Ahmad, Indian Ambassador to the Kingdom of Saudi Arabia, *Investments and Joint Ventures in India-GCC Economic Ties: Opportunities and Challenges*, paper delivered at Gulf Research Meeting, University of Cambridge, 8 July 2011.
254. *MEED*, 'Friends in High Places', 23–29 June 2006, p. 38.
255. *GSN*, 'USA Takes Fright, as China's Vision Becomes Clearer in Relations with Iran and Saudi Arabia', 30/786, 21 July 2006, p. 8.
256. World Trade Organization, 'China and the WTO', available at http://www.wto.org/english/thewto_e/countries_e/china_e.htm, last accessed 23 April 2013.
257. Henry Mayer, 'China and Saudi Arabia Form Stronger Trade Ties', *The New York Times*, 20 April 2010, available at http://www.nytimes.com/2010/04/21/business/global/21energy.html, last accessed 23 April 2013.
258. Ibid.
259. Ibid.

260. Henry Mayer, 'China and Saudi Arabia Form Stronger Trade Ties', *The New York Times*.
261. Ed Blanche, 'The Insatiable Dragon', *The Middle East*, Issue 422, May 2011, p. 14.
262. International Energy Agency, 'World Energy Outlook 2007: China and India Insights', 45, available at http://www.worldenergyoutlook.org/media/weowebsite/2008-1994/weo_2007.pdf, last accesed 23 April 2013.
263. Email interview with a Chinese Professor of Middle East Studies who asked not to be named, 8 October 2011.
264. *BBC News*, 'China to Build Mecca Rail System', 11 February 2009, available at http://news.bbc.co.uk/1/hi/7883182.stm, last accessed 23 April 2013.
265. *IPS*, 'Saudi Arabia and Iran Spar Over Oil Embargo', 16 January 2012.
266. Ibid.
267. Summer Said, 'Saudi Arabia, China Sign Nuclear Cooperation Pact', *The Wall Street Journal*, 16 January 2012, available at http://online.wsj.com/article/SB10001424052970204468004577164742025285500.html?mod=googlenews_wsj, last accessed 23 April 2013.
268. Email interview with a Chinese Professor of Middle Eastern Studies who asked not to be named, 8 October 2011.
269. New oil fields are being found, explored and drilled in Brazil, Colombia and Argentina. Venezuela alone is said to have bigger oil reserves than Saudi Arabia. Simon Romero, 'New Fields May Propel Americas to Top of Oil Companies' Lists', *The New York Times*, 19 September 2011, available at http://www.nytimes.com/2011/09/20/world/americas/recent-discoveries-put-americas-back-in-oil-companies-sights.html, last accessed 23 April 2013.
270. For a discussion on the Indo-Saudi 'strategic partnership' see Robert Mason, *Realizing the Indo-Saudi 'Strategic Partnership': An Analysis of the Leading Drivers*, paper delivered at the Gulf Research Meeting, University of Cambridge, 8 July 2011.
271. Interview with Talmiz Ahmad, Riyadh, 4 June 2011.
272. Indian Ministry of External Affairs, 'Indo-Saudi Relations', available at http://meaindia.nic.in/meaxpsite/foreignrelation/saudi.pdf, last accessed 23 April 2013.
273. Walid Mazi, 'GCC-India FTA "On Right Track"', *Arabnews.com*, 26 February 2011, available at http://www.arabnews.com/node/369394, last accessed 23 April 2013.
274. Ajay N. Jha, 'The Balance Sheet: Need for a Fresh Perspective', *India's Economic Diplomacy in the Gulf* (New Delhi: ABC Publishing House, 1988), p. 175.

275. *MEED*, 'Cover Story: Saudi Arabia', 1 March 2002, p. 1.
276. Interview with a former Saudi minister who asked not to be named, Cambridge, 8 July 2011.
277. Abeer Tayel and Mustapha Ajbailim, 'Iran, Egypt Renewing Ties?', *Al Arabiya*, 18 April 2011, available at http://www.alarabiya.net/articles/2011/04/18/145906.html, last accessed 23 April 2013.
278. Nawaf Obaid, 'Is Riyadh Ready to "Recalibrate the Partnership"?', 15 May 2011, *SUSRIS*, available at http://www.susris.com/2011/05/15/is-riyadh-ready-to-recalibrate-the-partnership/, last accessed 23 April 2013.

Chapter 4. Iranian Foreign Policy: The Politics of Civilization, Security and Economy

1. The broad and contested term (due to its pre-Islamic origins) used to describe Iran's sense of identity, culture, purpose and place in the modern world.
2. The author would like to thank the British Institute of Persian Studies (BIPS) for the travel award to Iran which made possible some of the research contained in this chapter.
3. Shayerah Ilias, *Iran's Economic Conditions: U.S Policy Issues*, CRS Report for Congress, Congressional Research Service, p. 34.
4. Remarks by US National Security Advisor Tom Donilon, prepared by the Office of the Press Secretary, the White House, 22 November 2011, sent by email to the G2K List.
5. Kenneth Katzman, *Iran Sanctions*, CRS Report for Congress, Congressional Research Service, 13 October 2011, 1, available at http://www.fas.org/sgp/crs/mideast/RS20871.pdf, last accessed 23 April 2013.
6. An impasse has been apparent in nuclear negotiations, a track which has been blocked and called 'sterile'; interview with Sir Richard Dalton, former British Ambassador to Iran, London, 26 January 2011. Human rights negotiations are said to be 'going nowhere'; interview with a European diplomat who asked not to be named, Tehran, 24 February 2011.
7. David E. Thaler and Alireza Nader, 'Deep Seated Entanglements: the Web of Iranian Leadership Can be Negotiated, Not Unravelled', *RAND Review*, available at http://www.rand.org/publications/randreview/issues/spring2010/iran.html, last accessed 23 April 2013.
8. Interview with Ali Biniaz, Director, Center for Energy and International Economy, Institute for Political and International Studies (IPIS), Tehran, 27 February 2011.
9. Maziar Behrooz, 'Factionalism in Iran Under Khomeini', *Middle Eastern Studies* 27/4, 1991, p. 601.

10. Mehdi Moslem, *Factional Politics in Post-Khomeini Iran* (Syracuse: Syracuse University Press, 2002).
11. Asghar Schirazi, 'The Genesis of the Constitution', *The Constitution of Iran: Politics and the State in the Islamic Republic* (London: I.B.Tauris, 1997), p. 33.
12. Ibid., p. 598.
13. Ibid., p. 599.
14. Robin Wright, 'The Challenge of Iran', *The Iran Primer*, available at http://iranprimer.usip.org/resource/challenge-iran, last accessed 23 April 2013.
15. Maziar Behrooz, 'Factionalism in Iran Under Khomeini', *Middle Eastern Studies*, p. 607.
16. *GSN*, 'Politics and Security – Faced by Strategic Encirclement, Iran Develops the full Spectrum of Deterrence', 732, 16 April 2004, p. 7.
17. Ali Alfoneh, 'The Basij Resistance Force', *The Iran Primer*, United States Institute of Peace, available at http://iranprimer.usip.org/resource/basij-resistance-force, last accessed 23 April 2013.
18. Ibid.
19. *GSN*, 'Politics and Defence: Khatami's Long Game', 23/585, 4 May 1998, p. 2.
20. Vahe Petrossian, 'Khatami's Test', *MEED*, 24 November 2000, p. 5.
21. David Butter, 'Iran: a Force for Stability', *MEED*, 5 October 2001, p. 5.
22. Islamic *mardumsalari* (democracy) is an evolving concept in Iranian political discourse, but can be generally defined as 'government for the people' which is inclusive and takes into account Islam, a constitution, values and principles. It is inconsistent with the principle of *velayat-e faqih* (autocratic rule of God) and is less democratic than the principle 'government by the people'. Shabnam Jane Holliday, 'Islamist-Iranian Discourse of National Identity: Khatami's State Counter-Discourse', *Discourses and Counter-Discourses of Iranian National Identity During Khatami's Presidency (1997–2005)* (PhD book), November 2007, p. 141.
23. Shabnam Holliday, 'Khatami's Islamist-Iranian Discourse of National Identity: A Discourse of Resistance', *British Journal of Middle Eastern Studies* 37/1, 2, April 2010, p. 13.
24. *The Economist*, 'Khatami's Last Stand, Perhaps', 14 November 2002, available at http://www.economist.com/node/1446624, last accessed 23 April 2013.
25. Ali Gheissari and Vali Nasr, 'The Conservative Consolidation in Iran', *Survival* 47/2, Summer 2005, pp. 178–181.
26. Ibid.
27. Ibid., p. 175.
28. Ibid.

NOTES TO PAGES 88–90　　　　　201

29. Richard Dalton, 'Iran: Election or Coup?', Chatham House, 15 June 2009, available at http://www.chathamhouse.org/media/comment/view/163683, last accessed 23 April 2013.
30. Ali Gheissari and Vali Nasr, 'The Conservative Consolidation in Iran', *Survival*, p. 178.
31. Kenneth Katzman, 'Introduction', *Iran's Islamic Revolutionary Guard Corps: Radical Ideology Despite Institutionalization in the Islamic Republic*, PhD book (UMI), 1991, p. 1.
32. Ali Gheissari and Vali Nasr, 'The Conservative Consolidation in Iran', *Survival*, p. 178.
33. Kenneth Katzman, 'Conclusions and Prospects', *Iran's Islamic Revolutionary Guard Corps: Radical Ideology Despite Institutionalization in the Islamic Republic*, p. 373.
34. Ibid.
35. Ali Gheissari and Vali Nasr, 'The Conservative Consolidation in Iran', *Survival*, p. 180.
36. Ibid.
37. Ibid., p. 181.
38. Kenneth Katzman, *Iran: US Concerns and Policy Responses*, CRS Report for Congress, Congressional Research Service, 8 August 2011, 27, available at http://www.fas.org/sgp/crs/mideast/RL32048.pdf, last accessed 23 April 2013.
39. Ibid., pp. 181–182.
40. Interview with a foreign government representative who asked not to be named, London, 3 June 2010.
41. Ibid.
42. Fareed Mohamedi, 'The Oil and Gas Industry', *The Iran Primer*, United States Institute of Peace, available at http://iranprimer.usip.org/resource/oil-and-gas-industry, last accessed 23 April 2013.
43. Ibid.
44. Kenneth Katzman, *Iran: US Concerns and Policy Responses*, CRS Report for Congress, p. 27.
45. Ibid.; Remarks by Roberto Toscano at the University of Exeter, 23 November 2011.
46. Ibid.
47. Email interview with Roberto Toscano, former Italian Ambassador to Iran, 12 August 2011.
48. Ali Gheissari and Vali Nasr, 'The Conservative Consolidation in Iran', *Survival*, p. 178.
49. Email interview with Roberto Toscano, former Italian Ambassador to Iran, 12 August 2011.

50. Amy Kellogg, 'Wikileaks: Iran President Ahmadinejad Slapped by Head of Revolutionary Guard', *Fox News*, 4 January 2011, available at http://www.foxnews.com/world/2011/01/04/wikileaks-iran-president-ahmadinejad-slapped-head-revolutionary-guard/, last accessed 23 April 2013.
51. Ibid.; Richard Dalton, 'Uneasy Stability', *The World Today*, Chatham House, April 2010, p. 7.
52. Henner Fürtig, 'Conflict and Cooperation in the Persian Gulf: The Interregional Order and US Policy', *Middle East Journal* 61/4, Spring 2007, p. 629.
53. As argued in Ali M. Ansari, *Crisis of Authority: Iran's 2009 Presidential Election* (London: Chatham House, 2010).
54. Remarks by Roberto Toscano at the University of Exeter, 23 November 2011.
55. US Embassy Bern, 'Swiss Ambassador to Iran Comments on Assisting US Citizens and Dealing with Post-Election Tehran', *Wikileaks*, 1 September 2009, available at http://wikileaks.org/cable/2009/09/09BERN363.html, last accessed 23 April 2013.
56. *The Economist*, 'Still Sitting Pretty', 12 June 2010, p. 65.
57. Eva Rakel, 'Conglomerates in Iran: the Political Economy of Islamic Foundations', in Alex. E Fernandez and Jilberto and Barbara Hogenboom (eds.), *Big Business and Economic Development: Conglomerates and Economic Groups in Developing Countries and Transition Economies Under Globalisation* (Abingdon: Routledge, 2007), p. 111.
58. Anthony H. Cordesman, 'Paramilitary, Internal Security, and Intelligence Forces', *Iran's Revolutionary Guards, the Al Quds Force, and Other Intelligence and Paramilitary Forces*, Center for Strategic and International Studies, 16 August 2007, p. 12, available at http://csis.org/files/media/csis/pubs/070816_cordesman_report.pdf, last accessed 23 April 2013.
59. Arshin Adib-Moghaddam, 'Islamic Utopian Romanticism and the Foreign Policy Culture of Iran', *Iran in World Politics* (London: C. Hurst and Co., 2007), p. 71.
60. Lionel Beehner, 'Iran's Multifaceted Foreign Policy', Council on Foreign Relations, 7 April 2006, available at http://www.cfr.org/iran/irans-multifaceted-foreign-policy/p10396#p2, last accessed 23 April 2013.
61. Ibid.
62. Ali Gheissari and Vali Nasr, 'The Conservative Consolidation in Iran', *Survival*, p. 180
63. Lionel Beehner, 'Iran's Multifaceted Foreign Policy', Council on Foreign Relations, 7 April 2006, available at http://www.cfr.org/iran/irans-multifaceted-foreign-policy/p10396, last accessed 23 April 2013.

64. Eva Rakel, 'Conglomerates in Iran: the Political Economy of Islamic Foundations', p. 111.
65. Ibid., p. 115.
66. *The Economist*, 'Still Sitting Pretty', 12 June 2010, p. 65.
67. Vahe Petrossian, 'It's the Economy', *MEED*, 30 June 2000, p. 5.
68. Ali A. Saeidi, 'Iran Para-Governmental Organizations (Bonyads)', *Payvand*, 27 February 2009, available at http://www.payvand.com/news/09/feb/1327.html, last accessed 23 April 2013.
69. Shayerah Ilias, 'Iran's Economy', *CRS Report for Congress*, Congressional Research Service, p. 9.
70. Ibid.
71. Ibid.
72. Ibid.
73. Open Source Center Report, 'Iran: Mostzafan va Janzaban Supports Veterans, Covert Activities', 2 May 2006.
74. The Qods forces also operate as 'corps' in Iraq, Jordan, Afghanistan, Pakistan, India, Turkey, the Arabian Peninsula, Central Asia, Europe, North America and North Africa including Egypt, Tunisia, Algeria, Sudan and Morocco. Anthony H. Cordesman, 'The Quds (Qods, or Jerusalem) forces', *Iran's Revolutionary Guards, the Al Quds Force, and Other Intelligence and Paramilitary Forces*, Center for Strategic and International Studies, 16 August 2007, pp. 8–9.
75. Kenneth Katzman, *Iran: US Concerns and Policy Responses*, CRS Report for Congress, Congressional Research Service, 8 August 2011, p. 27.
76. Ibid.
77. Rachel Brandenburg, 'Iran and the Palestinians', *The Iran Primer*, United States Institute of Peace, available at http://iranprimer.usip.org/resource/iran-and-palestinians, last accessed 23 April 2013.
78. Amjad Atallah, 'What do Arabs Really Think About Iran?', *Foreign Policy*, 11 August 2010, available at http://mideast.foreignpolicy.com/posts/2010/08/11/what_do_arabs_really_think_about_iran?sms_ss=facebook (registration required), last accessed 23 April 2013.
79. In response to a query by Rabbi Hershel Gluck about a missing Israeli Defence Force (IDF) soldier believed to be held by Hamas to senior IRGC figure Ayatollah Syed Salman Safavi in London, the latter said: 'there can be no agreement after Gaza'. *Wikileaks*, 'Iran/Israel: Regime Insider Reportedly Passes Tough Message on Israeli Hostages', *Wikileaks*, 7 April 2009, available at http://www.cablegatesearch.net/cable.php?id=09LONDON837&q=safavi per cent20salma, last accessed 23 April 2013.
80. Interview with a foreign government representative who asked not to be named, London, 3 June 2010.

81. Telephone interview with Martin Indyk, 1 November 2011.
82. Ahmed Eleiba, 'Revolution Warms Egyptian-Iranian Relations', *Al-Ahram Online*, 5 April 2011, available at http://english.ahram.org.eg/NewsContent/1/64/9243/Egypt/Politics-/Revolution-warms-EgyptianIranian-relations.aspx, last accessed 23 April 2013.
83. Ahmed Seyoufi, 'Iranian Official in Cairo: Tehran is Ready to Help Egypt', *Al-Ahram Daily*, 11 February 2012, available at http://digital.ahram.org.eg/Policy.aspx?Serial=796369, last accessed 23 April 2013.
84. Magdi Abdelhadi, 'Spat Over Iranian Film on Sadat', *BBC News*, 24 July 2008, available at http://news.bbc.co.uk/1/hi/world/middle_east/7523967.stm, last accessed 23 April 2013.
85. Anthony H. Cordesman, 'The Egyptian Military and the Arab-Israeli Military Balance', Center for Strategic and International Studies, 10 February 2011, available at http://csis.org/publication/egyptian-military-and-arab-israeli-military-balance, last accessed 23 April 2013.
86. Interview with Ali Biniaz, Tehran, 27 February 2011.
87. *The Washington Post*, 'Clinton Tells Egyptian Foreign Minister that US Aid Threatened by NGO Dispute', 4 February 2012, available at http://www.washingtonpost.com/world/middle-east/clinton-tells-egyptian-foreign-minister-that-us-aid-threatened-by-ngo-dispute/2012/02/04/gIQAwDnjpQ_story.html.
88. Ibid.
89. Ibid.
90. *Reuters*, 'Syria's Brotherhood Rejected Iran-Mediated Deal', 18 January 2012, available at http://www.reuters.com/article/2012/01/18/us-syria-brotherhood-iran-idUSTRE80H1AD20120118, last accessed 23 April 2013.
91. Telephone interview with Martin Indyk, 1 November 2011.
92. Interview with Richard Dalton, London, 26 January 2011.
93. Ibid.
94. *GSN*, 'Economy and Trade: Iran Reaches Across the Gulf', 23/591, 27 July 1998, p. 10.
95. Ibid.
96. *Iran, Its Neighbours and the Regional Crises*, Chatham House Report, p. 6, available at http://www.chathamhouse.org/sites/default/files/public/Research/Middle%20East/iran0806.pdf, last accessed 23 April 2013.
97. *GSN*, 'Politics and Defence: Gulf Security', 23/591, 27 July 1998, p. 4; Alireza Nader, 'Iran and a Nuclear-Weapon-Free Middle East', Arms Control Association, September 2011, available at http://www.armscontrol.org/print/5013, last accessed 23 April 2013.
98. *GSN*, 'Politics and Defence: A US-Iranian Collision?', 17 April 1995, 20/509, p. 2.

NOTES TO PAGES 97–99   205

99. Interview with Ruprecht Polenz, Berlin, 22 September 2011.
100. Gawdat Bahgat, 'Security in the Persian Gulf: Perils and Opportunities', *Contemporary Security Policy*, p. 312.
101. Interview with Ruprecht Polenz, Berlin, 22 September 2011.
102. *BBC News*, 'Islamic Solidarity Games Cancelled Over Gulf Dispute', 18 January 2010, available at http://news.bbc.co.uk/1/hi/8465235.stm, last accessed 23 April 2013.
103. Mehran Kamrava, 'Iran's Regional and Foreign Security Policies in the Persian Gulf', *International Relations of the Gulf Working Group Summary Report*, Center for International and Regional Studies, Georgetown University School of Foreign Service in Qatar, 2009, p. 14.
104. Ibid.
105. *Wikileaks*, 'Saudi–Iranian Tensions Evident In Counter Accusations Over Yemen, Pilgrimages and Islamic Games', 19 January 2010, available at http://wikileaks.org/cable/2010/01/10RIYADH93.html, last accessed 23 April 2013.
106. Interview with Ali Biniaz, Tehran, 27 February 2011.
107. IMF, 'Regional Economic Outlook: Middle East and Central Asia', *World Economic and Financial Surveys*, May 2008, p. 49, available at http://www.imf.org/external/pubs/ft/reo/2008/mcd/eng/mreo0508.pdf, last accessed 23 April 2013.
108. *Iran News*, 'Iran Keen to Expand All-Out Ties With Kuwait', 26 February 2011, p. 15.
109. Gawdat Bahgat, 'Security in the Persian Gulf: Perils and Opportunities', *Contemporary Security Policy*, p. 312.
110. Ibid.
111. Remarks by Prince Turki al-Faisal, University of Exeter, 16 March 2011.
112. Fred Pals, Grant Smith and Ola Galal, 'OPEC's "Worst Meeting" Ends Without Agreement, Boosting Prices', *Bloomberg Businessweek*, 9 June 2011, available at http://www.businessweek.com/news/2011-06-09/opec-s-worst-meeting-ends-without-agreement-boosting-prices.html, last accessed 23 April 2013.
113. Interview with Dr Leo Drollas, Chief Economist, Centre for Global Energy Studies, London, 26 January 2011.
114. Ibid.
115. Ibid.
116. Iran has the world's third-largest proven reserves of oil and second-largest proven reserves of gas. BP, 'BP Statistical Energy Review', June 2011, available at http://www.bp.com/assets/bp_internet/globalbp/globalbp_uk_english/reports_and_publications/statistical_energy_review_2011/STAGING/

local_assets/pdf/statistical_review_of_world_energy_full_report_2011. pdf, last accessed 23 April 2013.
117. Richard Dalton (ed.), 'Iran: Breaking the Nuclear Deadlock', Chatham House Report, 2008, p. 15.
118. Claude Mandil, 'Russia Must Act to Avert a Gas Supply Crisis', *FT*, 22 March 2006, available at http://www.ft.com/cms/s/0/9d8a635a-b948-11da-b57d-0000779e2340.html#axzz1Hcfpoavq, last accessed 23 April 2013.
119. Interview with Ali Biniaz, Tehran, 27 February 2011.
120. Kayhan Barzegar, 'Iran's Foreign Policy in Post-Invasion Iraq', *Middle East Policy* XV/4, Winter 2008, p. 51.
121. Interview with Ruprecht Polenz, Berlin, 22 September 2011.
122. Kayhan Barzegar, 'Iran's Foreign Policy in Post-Invasion Iraq', *Middle East Policy* XV/4, Winter 2008, p. 51.
123. Ibid., p. 49.
124. Ibid., p. 50.
125. Kayhan Barzegar, 'Iran's Foreign Policy in Post-Invasion Iraq', *Middle East Policy* XV/4, Winter 2008, p. 48.
126. *Iran News*, 'Iran Ready to Boost Iraq Oil Exports', 24 February 2011, p. 2.
127. Kenneth Katzman, *Iran: US Concerns and Policy Responses*, Congressional Research Service, p. 30.
128. Ibid.
129. Ibid., p. 31.
130. Ibid.
131. Telephone interview with Martin Indyk, 1 November 2011.
132. Ibid.
133. United States of America Mission to the International Organizations in Vienna, 'Statement by China, France, Germany, the Russian Federation, the United Kingdom, and the United States of America', 9 March 2011, available at http://vienna.usmission.gov/110309p51.html, last accessed 23 April 2013.
134. Richard Dalton, 'A New Approach is Needed to Tackle Iranian Nuclear Debate', *The Telegraph*, 18 December 2008, available at http://www.telegraph.co.uk/comment/3832240/A-new-approach-is-needed-to-tackle-Iranian-nuclear-debate.html, last accessed 23 April 2013.
135. Ibid.
136. Interview with Ruprecht Polenz, Berlin, 22 September 2011.
137. US Mission UNVIE Vienna, 'Austrian Diplomat Shares Iranian President's Claim', *Wikileaks*, 8 February 2010, available at http://wikileaks.org/cable/2010/02/10UNVIEVIENNA40.html, last accessed 23 April 2013.
138. Chatham House, *Iran, Its Neighbours and the Regional Crises*, p. 13.

139. Ibid.
140. Roman D. Ortiz, 'Iran in Mexico and the Caribbean: Building a Strategic a Strategic Trampoline Towards the US', *HACER Latin American News*; Saeed Kamali Dehghan, 'Iran Demands Apology from US Over Saudi Ambassador "Assassination Plot"', *The Guardian*, 31 October 2011, available at http://www.guardian.co.uk/world/2011/oct/31/iran-demands-apology-assassination-plot, last accessed 23 April 2013.
141. The potential for fresh international sanctions after what has been called the 'high water mark' of sanctions in 2010 is debated by Suzanne Maloney, 'Progress of the Obama Administration's Policy Toward Iran', *Brookings*, 15 November 2011, available at http://www.brookings.edu/testimony/2011/1115_iran_policy_maloney.aspx, last accessed 23 April 2013.
142. Andrew Parasiliti, 'Iran: Diplomacy and Deterrence', *Survival* 51/5, October–November 2009, p. 7.
143. Interview with Ruprecht Polenz, Berlin, 22 September 2011.
144. President Sarkozy has also proposed sanctioning Iran's central bank to ratchet up pressure on the Iranian regime. Fiona Shaikh and Arshad Mohammed, 'Western States Step Up Sanctions on Iran', *Reuters*, 21 November 2011, available at http://www.reuters.com/article/2011/11/21/us-iran-sanctions-idUSTRE7AK27D20111121, last accessed 23 April 2013; Patrick Clawson and Simon Henderson, 'Impact of Sanctioning Iran's Central Bank', *PolicyWatch 1877*, The Washington Institute for Near East Policy, 29 November 2011, available at http://www.washingtoninstitute.org/templateC05.php?CID=3428, last accessed 23 April 2013.
145. Saeed Kamali Dehghan, 'Iran's Parliament Votes to Expel British Ambassador', *The Guardian*, 27 November 2011, available at http://www.guardian.co.uk/world/2011/nov/27/iran-votes-expel-british-ambassador, last accessed 23 April 2013.
146. *The Guardian*, 'Iran Protestors Attack UK Embassy in Tehran – Tuesday 29 November', 29 November 2011, available at http://www.guardian.co.uk/world/blog/2011/nov/29/iran-protesters-attack-uk-embassy-tehran-live, last accessed 23 April 2013.
147. The sanctions are expected to come into effect six months from January 2012, since this will allow the USA and foreign governments time to find alternative oil exporters to buy from or find workarounds to continue paying for Iranian oil. Suzanne Maloney, 'Obama's Counterproductive New Iran Sanctions', *Foreign Affairs*, 5 January 2012, available at http://www.foreignaffairs.com/ARTICLES/137011/suzanne-maloney/obamas-counterproductive-new-iran-sanctions?page=show, last accessed 23 April 2013.

148. Yochi J. Dreazen, 'The US and Iran Are Already Locked in Economic War', *The Atlantic*, 5 January 2012, available at http://www.theatlantic.com/international/archive/2012/01/the-us-and-iran-are-already-locked-in-economic-war/250872/, last accessed 23 April 2013.
149. Roshanak Taghavi, 'Why Iran's Currency Dropped to Worst Low in Two Decades', *The Christian Science Monitor*, 3 January 2012, available at http://www.csmonitor.com/World/Middle-East/2012/0103/Why-Iran-s-currency-dropped-to-worst-low-in-two-decades, last accessed 23 April 2013.
150. David E. Sanger, 'Iran Threatens to Block Oil Shipments, as US Prepares Sanctions', *The New York Times*, 27 December 2011, available at http://www.nytimes.com/2011/12/28/world/middleeast/iran-threatens-to-block-oil-route-if-embargo-is-imposed.html?_r=2&hp, last accessed 23 April 2013.
151. Gary Sick, 'Sick: Iran's Real Weapon of Mass Destruction', *Le Monde Diplomatique*, 2 March 2012.
152. As argued by Farideh Farhi in an email to the G2K List, 25 January 2012.
153. Richard Dalton, email to the G2K List, 25 January 2012.
154. Email interview with Roberto Toscano, 12 August 2011; interview with a European diplomat who asked not to be named, Tehran, 24 February 2011.
155. Shayerah Ilias, 'Iran's Economy', *CRS Report for Congress*, Congressional Research Service, p. 4.
156. Telephone interview with Martin Indyk, 1 November 2011.
157. Interview with Leo Drollas, London, 26 January 2011.
158. Interview with Richard Dalton, London, 26 January 2011.
159. Richard Dalton et al., 'Iran: Breaking the Nuclear Deadlock', Chatham House Report, 2008, p. 13.
160. Interview with Leo Drollas, London, 26 January 2011.
161. Flynt Leverett and Hillary Mann Leverett, 'Oil and the Iranian – Saudi "Cold War"', *Race for Iran*, 12 July 2011, available at http://www.raceforiran.com/oil-and-the-iranian-saudi- per centE2 per cent80 per cent9Ccold-war per centE2 per cent80 per cent9D, accessed 12 July 2011.
162. The Arab Uprisings have ensured oil prices remain above $100 per barrel. *ABC News*, 'Iran's Economy: A Political Battleground, But Could it Undo the Islamic Republic', 5 July 2011, available at http://abcnews.go.com/blogs/headlines/2011/07/irans-economy-a-political-battleground-but-could-it-undo-the-islamic-republic/, last accessed 23 April 2013.
163. Ibid.
164. Interview with Richard Dalton, London, 26 January 2011; Ramin Mostaghim and Ned Parker, 'Iran's Supreme Leader Backs Ahmadinejad',

Los Angeles Times, 30 May 2011, available at http://articles.latimes.com/2011/may/30/world/la-fg-iran-khamenei-20110530, last accessed 23 April 2013.
165. Najmeh Bozorgmehr, 'Iran Fires Central Banker', *FT*, 21 September 2008, available at http://www.ft.com/cms/s/0/54c007b6-8825-11dd-b114-0000779fd18c.html#axzz1X5XvwtDH (registration required), last accessed 23 April 2013.
166. Ibid.
167. *The Economist*, 'Getting a Grip in Iran', 14 August 2007, available at http://www.economist.com/node/9642293, last accessed 23 April 2013.
168. *The Telegraph*, 'Mahmoud Ahmadinejad Fires Foreign Minister', 13 December 2010, available at http://www.telegraph.co.uk/news/worldnews/middleeast/iran/8199460/Mahmoud-Ahmadinejad-fires-foreign-minister.html, last accessed 23 April 2013.
169. Barbara Slavin, 'The Incredible Shrinking Ahmadinejad', *Foreign Policy*, 25 May 2011, available at http://www.foreignpolicy.com/articles/2011/05/25/the_incredible_shrinking_ahmadinejad (registration required), last accessed 23 April 2013.
170. Clifford Krauss, 'Ahmadinejad Backs Out of Key Role at OPEC', *The New York Times*, 24 May 2011, available at http://www.nytimes.com/2011/05/25/world/middleeast/25opec.html, last accessed 23 April 2013.
171. Barbara Slavin, 'The Incredible Shrinking Ahmadinejad', *Foreign Policy*, 25 May 2011.
172. Najmeh Bozorgmehr, 'Amhadi-Nejad Drawn into Funds Scandal', *FT*, 19 September 2011, available at http://www.ft.com/intl/cms/s/0/f0e0ccf4-df82-11e0-845a-00144feabdc0.html#ixzz1YWZuLBNW (registration required), last accessed 23 April 2013.
173. Reza Marashi and Sahar Namazikhah, 'Khamenei's Power Consolidation Gambit', *Al Jazeera*, 11 November 2011, available at http://www.aljazeera.com/indepth/opinion/2011/11/20111110103232754325.html, last accessed 23 April 2013.
174. Kevan Harris, 'Iran's Massive Banking Scandal', *The Iran Primer*, United States Institute of Peace, 16 October 2011, available at http://iranprimer.usip.org/blog/2011/oct/16/iran per centE2 per cent80 per cent99s-massive-banking-scandal, accessed 16 October 2011.
175. Jay Solomon and Farnaz Fassihi, 'Iran Redistributes Wealth in a Bid to Fight Sanctions', *The Wall Street Journal*, 27 July 2011, available at http://online.wsj.com/article/SB10001424052702304223804576448203609699930.html?mod=WSJEUROPE_hpp_MIDDLETopNews#printMode, last accessed 23 April 2013.
176. Ibid.

177. IMF, 'Statement by IMF Article IV Mission to the Islamic Republic of Iran', Press Release No. 11/228, 13 June 2011, available at http://www.imf.org/external/np/sec/pr/2011/pr11228.htm, last accessed 23 April 2013.
178. Jay Solomon and Farnaz Fassihi, 'Iran Redistributes Wealth in a Bid to Fight Sanctions', *The Wall Street Journal*, 27 July 2011.
179. Iran RPO Dubai, 'Iran: Bazaari Protests Highlight Resistance to Economic Policies', *Wikileaks*, 23 October 2008, available at http://wikileaks.org/cable/2008/10/08IRANRPODUBAI50.html, last accessed 23 April 2013.
180. Ibid.
181. William Yong, 'Iran Embarks on Sweeping Changes in its Economy', *International Herald Tribune*, 17 January 2011, p. 1.
182. Ibid., p. 21.
183. Ibid.
184. For example, Hezbollah's activities – including smuggling, extortion and narcotics trafficking – amount to $20 million annually in the so-called 'Tri-Border Region' (the lawless area between Argentina, Paraguay and Brazil). Ilan Berman, *Hezbollah in the Western Hemisphere*, Statement before the US House of Representatives Committee on Homeland Security/Subcommittee on Counterterrorism and Intelligence, American Foreign Policy Council, 7 July 2011.
185. Bolivia has since become more circumspect about the influence that an Iran–Venezuela axis could have. Steven Heydemann, 'Iran's Alternative Allies', *The Iran Primer*, United States Institute of Peace; *The Economist*, 'Ayatollahs in the Backyard', 26 November 2009, available at http://www.economist.com/node/14969124, last accessed 23 April 2013.
186. *Iran News*, 'Iran, Ecuador Discuss Medical Cooperation', 23 February, 2011, p. 3.
187. *The Economist*, 'Ayatollahs in the Backyard', 26 November 2009.
188. Anthony H. Cordesman, 'The Quds (Qods, or Jerusalem) forces', *Iran's Revolutionary Guards, the Al Quds Force, and Other Intelligence and Paramilitary Forces*, Center for Strategic and International Studies, 16 August 2007, p. 8.
189. Emily Schmall, 'Deal Reached for Inquiry on Bombing in Argentina', *The New York Times*, 27 January 2013, available at http://www.nytimes.com/2013/01/28/world/americas/argentina-and-iran-to-investigate-jewish-center-bombing.html, last accessed 23 April 2013.
190. *Associated Press*, 'Iran Ends Voluntary Cooperation with the IAEA', 2 May 2006, available at http://www.msnbc.msn.com/id/11105378/ns/world_news-mideast_n_africa/t/iran-ends-voluntary-cooperation-iaea/#.Tsk2crKa9Ic, last accessed 23 April 2013.

191. Ed Crooks and Javier Blas, 'OPEC to Study Effects of Falling Dollar', *FT*, 18 November 2007, available at http://www.ft.com/intl/cms/s/0/99951144-960c-11dc-b7ec-0000779fd2ac.html#axzz1eFOgbnlG (registration required), last accessed 23 April 2013; Linda Pressly, 'The "Axis of Annoyance"', *BBC News*, 13 August 2009, available at http://news.bbc.co.uk/1/hi/8195581.stm, last accessed 23 April 2013.
192. Steven Heydemann, 'Iran's Alternative Allies', *The Iran Primer*, United States Institute of Peace, available at http://iranprimer.usip.org/resource/irans-alternative-allies, last accessed 23 April 2013.
193. Ibid.
194. *BBC Hardtalk*, 'Chavez: US "Military Imperialism" in Latin America', 14 June 2010, available at http://news.bbc.co.uk/1/hi/programmes/hardtalk/8731623.stm, last accessed 23 April 2013; Ariel Farrar-Wellman, 'Brazil–Iran Foreign Relations', *Iran Tracker*, 10 May 2010, available at http://www.irantracker.org/foreign-relations/brazil-iran-foreign-relations, last accessed 23 April 2013.
195. Shubhajit Roy, 'India with NAM in Slamming IAEA report on Iran', *Indian Express*, 17 September 2010, available at http://www.indianexpress.com/news/India-with-NAM-in-slamming-IAEA-report-on-Iran/682728, last accessed 23 April 2013.
196. *Iran News*, 'Trade Delegation Visits Zimbabwe', 23 February, 2011, p. 12.
197. *Iran News*, 'Japanese Envoy Acknowledges Growth of Tehran–Tokyo Cooperation', 23 February, 2011, p. 3.
198. Ibid.
199. Steven Heydemann, 'Iran's Alternative Allies', *The Iran Primer*.
200. Ibid.
201. Ibid., pp. 167–183.
202. Iran RPO Dubai, 'Iran Regional Presence Office Dubai: Window on Iran', *Wikileaks*, 28 May 2009, available at http://wikileaks.org/cable/2009/05/09RPODUBAI223.html.
203. Ibid.
204. Ibid.
205. M. D. Rasooldeen, 'Riyadh Declaration Cements Ties', *Arab News*, 1 March 2010, available at http://arabnews.com/saudiarabia/article24178.ece, accessed 1 March 2010.
206. Interview with Richard Dalton, London, 26 January 2011.
207. Ibid.
208. Interview with Abbas Maleki, Director of the International Institute for Caspian Studies and former Iranian Deputy Foreign Minister, Tehran, 23 February 2011.

209. Ibid.
210. Interview with Professor Abbas Maleki, Tehran, 23 February 2011.
211. Ibid.
212. Interview with a European diplomat who asked not to be named, Tehran, 24 February 2011.
213. Ibid.
214. *The Economist*, 'A Step Away from the Bomb', 12–18 June 2010, p. 17.
215. Ibid.
216. Sebnem Arsu, 'Turkey Pursues Kurdish Rebels After 24 Soldiers Are Killed Near Iraq', *The New York Times*, 19 October 2011, available at http://www.nytimes.com/2011/10/20/world/europe/dozens-dead-in-attacks-on-turkish-forces.html, last accessed 23 April 2013.
217. Telephone interview with Martin Indyk, 1 November 2011.
218. Interview with Ruprecht Polenz, Berlin, 22 September 2011.
219. The White House, 'Remarks by the President at the New Economic School Graduation', Moscow, 7 July 2009, available at http://www.whitehouse.gov/the_press_office/Remarks-By-The-President-At-The-New-Economic-School-Graduation/, last accessed 23 April 2013.
220. *Iran News*, 'IKCO, Turkish Firm to Manufacture New Brand of Car', 23 February, 2011, p. 12.
221. Interview with a European diplomat who asked not to be named, Tehran, 24 February 2011.
222. Ibid.
223. Ibid.
224. Ibid.
225. Fareed Mohamedi, 'The Oil and Gas Industry', *The Iran Primer*, United States Institute of Peace, available at http://iranprimer.usip.org/resource/oil-and-gas-industry, last accessed 23 April 2013.
226. *Iran News*, 'Further Ties With Turkmenistan Sought', 23 February, 2011, p. 12.
227. *Wikileaks*, 'Iran Regional Presence Office Dubai: Window on Iran', 28 May 2009.
228. *BBC News*, 'Iran and Pakistan Sign "Historic" Pipeline Deal', 17 March 2010, available at http://news.bbc.co.uk/1/hi/8572267.stm, last accessed 23 April 2013.
229. Ibid.
230. Gawdat Bahgat, *American Oil Diplomacy in the Persian Gulf and the Caspian Sea*, p. 119.
231. Remarks from a foreign diplomat who asked not to be named, 8 July 2011, Cambridge.

232. Interview with Ali Biniaz, Tehran, 27 February 2011.
233. Ibid.
234. *Reuters*, 'Pakistan, Iran Begins Work on Oil Pipeline', 11 March 2013, available at http://gulfnews.com/business/economy/pakistan-iran-begins-work-on-oil-pipeline-1.1156915, last accessed 23 April 2013.
235. Interview with Ali Biniaz, Tehran, 27 February 2011.
236. *The Economist*, 'Getting a Grip in Iran', 14 August 2007, available at http://www.economist.com/node/9642293.
237. Clifford Krauss, 'Ahmadinejad Backs Out of Key Role at OPEC', 24 May 2011, *The New York Times*.
238. Total maintains a representative office in Tehran in order to recoup debt from previous contracts. Interview with a European diplomat who asked not to be named, Tehran, 24 February 2011; Energy Information Administration, 'Iran', US Department of Energy, January 2010, available at http://www.eia.gov/cabs/Iran/Full.html, last accessed 23 April 2013.
239. Interview with Richard Dalton, London, 26 January 2011.
240. Ibid.
241. Cho Mee-Young and Yoo Choonsik, 'Exclusive: Sanctions Trap Billions of Iran petrodollars in Korea', *Reuters*, 3 August 2011, available at http://www.reuters.com/article/2011/08/03/us-iran-korea-idUSTRE77228Q20110803, last accessed 23 April 2013.
242. Interview with a European diplomat who asked not to be named, Tehran, 24 February 2011; Mark N. Katz, 'The Russia and China Factors in Sanctions', *The Iran Primer*, United States Institute of Peace, 28 November 2011, available at http://iranprimer.usip.org/blog/2011/nov/28/russia-and-china-factors-sanctions, last accessed 23 April 2013.
243. Interview with Richard Dalton, London, 26 January 2011.
244. Pratish Narayanan, 'Iran Receives $100 Million in Oil Payments From India, PTI Says', *Bloomberg*, 2 August 2011, available at http://www.bloomberg.com/news/2011-08-02/iran-receives-100-million-in-oil-payments-from-india-pti-says.html, last accessed 23 April 2013.
245. Remarks from a foreign diplomat who asked not to be named, 8 July 2011, Cambridge.
246. Richard Dalton et al., 'Iran: Breaking the Nuclear Deadlock', Chatham House Report, 2008, p. 13.
247. Fareed Mohamedi, 'Rising Oil Prices Create Political Cushion for Iran', *Iran Primer*, United States Institute of Peace, 7 March 2011, available at http://iranprimer.usip.org/blog/2011/mar/07/rising-oil-prices-create-political-cushion-iran, last accessed 23 April 2013.
248. Ibid.

249. Interview with Ali Biniaz, Tehran, 27 February 2011.
250. Ibid.
251. Interview with Talmiz Ahmad, Riyadh, 4 June 2011.
252. Ibid.
253. Interview with Ali Biniaz, Tehran, 27 February 2011.
254. Interview with an Iranian diplomat who asked not to be named, Tehran, 27 February 2011.
255. For details, see the Economic Cooperation Organization: http://www.ecosecretariat.org/, last accessed 23 April 2013.
256. Interview with an Iranian diplomat who asked not to be named, Tehran, 27 February 2011.
257. *Wikileaks*, 'Iranian Tourism: An Opportunity for Leverage?', 3 November 2008, available at http://wikileaks.org/cable/2008/11/08ISTANBUL557.html, last accessed 23 April 2013.
258. Telephone interview with Martin Indyk, 1 November 2011.
259. Abbas Maleki, 'Iran', Central Asia-Caucasus Institute, 167, available at http://www.silkroadstudies.org/new/docs/publications/GCA/GCAPUB-06.pdf, last accessed 23 April 2013.
260. Interview with Richard Dalton, London, 26 January 2011.
261. Ibid.
262. Olivia Bosch, 'Iran and the Traffickers', *The World Today*, Chatham House, May 2006, p. 7.
263. *Rianovosti*, 'Countries Under UN Sanctions Cannot Join SCO – Medvedev', 11 June 2010, available at http://en.rian.ru/world/20100611/159390139.html, last accessed 23 April 2013.
264. *GSN*, 'Politics and Defence: A US-Iranian Collision?', 20/509, 17 April 1995, p. 2.
265. *The Economist*, 'Still Sitting Pretty', 12 June 2010, p. 66.
266. *GSN*, 'Politics and Defence: A US-Iranian Collision?', 17 April 1995, p. 2.
267. The Washington Institute for Near East Policy, Taskforce on Iranian Proliferation, Regional Security and US Policy, 'Preventing a Cascade of Instability: US Engagement to Check Iranian Nuclear Progress', March 2009, p. 5.
268. Joby Warrick, 'Russian Scientist Vyacheslav Danilenko's Aid to Iran Offers Peak at Nuclear Program', *The Washington Post*, 14 November 2011, available at http://www.washingtonpost.com/world/national-security/russian-scientist-vyacheslav-danilenkos-aid-to-iran-offers-peek-at-nuclear-program/2011/11/12/gIQAeuiCJN_print.html, last accessed 23 April 2013.
269. Mark N. Katz, 'The Russia and China Factors in Sanctions', *The Iran Primer*, United States Institute of Peace, 28 November 2011.

270. *JTA*, 'Senators Press Obama on China – Iran', 14 March 2011, available at http://www.jta.org/news/article/2011/03/14/3086409/senators-press-obama-on-china-iran, last accessed 23 April 2013.
271. *Commodity Online*, 'China and UAE Ditch US Dollar, Will Use Yuan for Oil Trade', 24 January 2012, available at http://www.commodityonline.com/news/china-and-uae-ditch-us-dollar-will-use-yuan-for-oil-trade-45444-3-1.html, last accessed 23 April 2013.
272. Flynt Leverett, 'The New Axis of Oil', *New America Foundation*, July 2006, available at http://www.newamerica.net/publications/articles/2006/the_new_axis_of_oil, last accessed 23 April 2013.
273. Melanie Lee, 'Exclusive: How US Trying to Wean China off Iranian Oil', *Reuters*, 2 May 2011, available at http://www.reuters.com/article/2011/05/02/businesspro-us-china-iran-nuclear-idUSTRE7411QG20110502, last accessed 23 April 2013.
274. John M. Glionna, 'US Presses China, Japan, South Korea, to Trim Iran Oil Imports', *Los Angeles Times*, 10 January 2012, available at http://articles.latimes.com/2012/jan/10/world/la-fg-japan-korea-iran-20120110, last accessed 23 April 2013.
275. Interview with a European diplomat who asked not to be named, Tehran, 24 February 2011.
276. Nicholas Watt, 'Tony Blair Calls for Regime Change in Iran and Syria', *The Guardian*, 9 September 2011, available at http://www.guardian.co.uk/politics/2011/sep/09/tony-blair-regime-change-iran-syria, last accessed 23 April 2013; Ramazani quotes Blair as saying that 'what makes a nuclear Iran dangerous "is the nature of the regime itself"'. R. K. Ramazani, 'Khamenei's Nuclear Narrative', *Middle East Online*, 20 February 2012, available at http://www.middle-east-online.com/english/?id=50742, last accessed 23 April 2013.
277. Interview with Ruprecht Polenz, Berlin, 22 September 2011.
278. Kenneth Pollack and Ray Takeyh, 'Taking on Tehran', *Foreign Affairs* 84/2, March–April 2005, p. 21.
279. Interview with Richard Dalton, London, 26 January 2011.
280. Pierre Terzian, *OPEC: the Inside Story* (London: Zed Books, 1985).
281. *GSN*, 'USA Edges Towards a More Pragmatic Iran Policy', 30/790, 29 September 2006, p. 4.
282. Ziba Moshaver, 'Revolution, Theocratic Leadership and Iran's Foreign Policy: Implications for Iran–EU Relations', in G. Nonneman (ed.), *Analyzing Middle East Foreign Policies and the Relationship with Europe*, p. 183.
283. Interview with a European diplomat who asked not to be named, Tehran, 24 February 2011.

284. Mahmoud Ahmadinejad was involved in covert operations; Akbar Hashemi Rafsanjani was responsible for post-war reconstruction and regional ties throughout his Presidency; Mir Hossein Mousavi was still praised for his handling of the wartime economy despite his position of Prime Minister having been abolished; Mehdi Karroubi was head of the Imam Khomeini Relief Committee and Martyr's Foundation and Chairman of the Parliament after the war; and Mohsen Rezaei was a top commander in the IRGC during the war. *FT*, 'Profiles of Iran's Presidential Candidates', 4 June 2009, available at http://www.ft.com/intl/cms/s/0/99fb422a-5050-11de-9530-00144feabdc0.html#axzz1X5XvwtDH (registration required), last accessed 23 April 2013; interview with a European diplomat who asked not to be named, Tehran, 24 February 2011.
285. Lawrence G. Potter and Gary G. Sick, 'Introduction' in Lawrence G. Potter and Gary G. Sick (eds.), *Iran, Iraq, and the Legacies of War*, p. 8.
286. Interview with a foreign government representative who asked not to be named, London, 3 June 2010.
287. Interview with Ali Biniaz, Tehran, 27 February 2011.
288. Suzanne Maloney, 'Progress of the Obama Administration's Policy Toward Iran', *Brookings*, p. 15 November 2011, available at http://www.brookings.edu/testimony/2011/1115_iran_policy_maloney.aspx, last accessed 23 April 2013.
289. Interview with Ali Biniaz, Tehran, 27 February 2011.
290. Interview with Abbas Maleki, Tehran, 23 February 2011.
291. Interview with Ruprecht Polenz, Berlin, 22 September 2011.
292. Interview with Abbas Maleki, Tehran, 23 February 2011.
293. Interview with Ruprecht Polenz, Berlin, 22 September 2011.
294. Email interview with Roberto Toscano, 12 August 2011.
295. Ibid.
296. Ziba Moshaver, 'Revolution, Theocratic Leadership and Iran's Foreign Policy: Implications for Iran–EU Relations', in G. Nonneman (ed.), *Analyzing Middle East Foreign Policies*, p. 186.
297. Remarks from Prince Turki Al-Faisal, University of Exeter, 16 March 2011.
298. Morteza Behrouzifar and Homayoon Nassimi, 'US Sanctions and Global Energy Markets', *Journal of Middle Eastern Geopolitics* 1/4, April–June 2006, p. 346.
299. The 'Geneva Group' was one of the non-UN initiatives formed in 2000 with a membership of Italy, Germany, Iran and the USA which failed to mediate a political transition in Afghanistan. Kenneth Katzman, *Afghanistan: Post Taliban Governance, and US Policy*, CRS Report for Congress, Congressional Research Service, 18 June 2009, pp. 9, 55.

300. Apart from being close geographically, Iranians and Tajiks share the same religion and ethnicity and the Tajik language is part of the Persian/Farsi family. International Crisis Group, 'Central Asia: Fault Lines in the New Security Map', 2001, available at http://www.crisisgroup.org/en/regions/asia/central-asia/020-central-asia-fault-lines-in-the-new-security-map.aspx, last accessed 23 April 2013, p. 209.
301. Morteza Behrouzifar and Homayoon Nassimi, 'US Sanctions and Global Energy Markets', *Journal of Middle Eastern Geopolitics*, p. 347.
302. Interview with Ruprecht Polenz, Berlin, 22 September 2011.
303. Interview with a senior British diplomat who asked not to be named, London, 4 June 2011.
304. Interview with Ali Biniaz, Tehran, 27 February 2011.
305. Barbara Slavin, 'Post-9/11 Rebuffs Set US – Iran Relations on Downward Spiral', *IPS*, 7 September 2011, available at http://ipsnews.net/news.asp?idnews=105019, last accessed 23 April 2013.
306. Gary Sick, 'A Selective Partnership: Getting US–Iranian Relations Right', *Foreign Affairs* 85/6, November–December 2006, p. 142.
307. Christopher Rundle, 'Iran–United Kingdom Relations Since the Revolution: Opening Doors', in *Iran's Foreign Policy*, p. 99.
308. Email from Bill Beeman, University of Minnesota, to the G2K List, 14 November 2011.
309. *BBC News*, 'Bush's "Evil Axis" Comment Stirs Critics', 2 February 2002, available at http://news.bbc.co.uk/1/hi/world/americas/1796034.stm, last accessed 23 April 2013; Gawdat Bahgat, 'Security in the Persian Gulf: Perils and Opportunities', *Contemporary Security Policy*, p. 303.
310. Ali Ansari, 'Nuclear Poker', *The World Today*, Chatham House, May 2006, p. 5.
311. Iran's Permanent Mission to the UN. 'An Unnecessary Crisis: Setting the Record Straight about Iran's Nuclear Programme', *Payvand*, 18 November 2005, available at http://www.payvand.com/news/05/nov/1211.html, last accessed 23 April 2013.
312. Ibid.
313. These can be altered or reversed depending on circumstances and are only as strong as the leader who issues them, Khamenei being drastically weakened since the late-2000s. Michael Eisenstadt and Mehdi Khalaji, 'Nuclear Fatwa: Religion and Politics in Iran's Proliferation Strategy', *Policy Focus #115*, The Washington Institute for Near East Policy, September 2011, p. 10; Kenneth Katzman, *Iran: US Concerns and Policy Responses*, Congressional Research Service, p. 27.
314. Ibid.

315. Barbara Slavin, *Bitter Friends, Bosom Enemies*, p. 212.
316. Ibid.
317. Ibid.
318. Ibid.
319. Gary Sick, 'A Selective Partnership: Getting US–Iranian Relations Right', *Foreign Affairs* 85/6, November–December 2006, p. 142.
320. Office of the President of the United States, 'The National Security Strategy of the United States of America – 2006', March 2006, available at http://www.isn.ethz.ch/isn/Digital-Library/Publications/Detail/?ord588=grp2&ots591=0c54e3b3–1e9c-be1e-2c24-a6a8c7060233&lng=en&id=15462, last accessed 23 April 2013.
321. Matthew Green, 'Karzai Says Iran Gave "Bags" of Cash as Aid', *FT*, 25 October 2010, available at http://www.ft.com/intl/cms/s/0/73d83fa0-e058-11df-99a3-00144feabdc0.html#axzz1lbi8znLX (registration required), last accessed 23 April 2013.
322. Interview with Ruprecht Polenz, Berlin, 22 September 2011.
323. *BBC News*, 'Iran's Illegal Arms Trade: "Hypocritical and Dangerous"', 7 June 2010, available at http://www.bbc.co.uk/news/world-13545621, last accessed 23 April 2013.
324. Telephone interview with Martin Indyk, 1 November 2011.
325. Interview with Richard Dalton, London, 26 January 2011.
326. Ibid.
327. Ibid.
328. Ibid.
329. Gareth Smyth, 'Iranian–Saudi Tensions Play Out in Beirut, Tripoli', *PBS*, 24 March 2012, available at http://www.pbs.org/wgbh/pages/frontline/tehranbureau/2012/03/region-flashpoint-lebanon-iranian-saudi-tensions-play-out-in-beirut-tripoli.html.
330. Ibid.
331. Scott Lucas, 'Wikileaks and Iran 2007: Brother of Revolutionary Guards Commander Safavi Offers Co-operation to US', *EA World View*, 29 December 2010, available at http://www.enduringamerica.com/home/2010/12/29/wikileaks-and-iran-2007-brother-of-revolutionary-guards-comm.html, last accessed 23 April 2013.
332. Interview with a European diplomat who asked not to be named, Tehran, 24 February 2011.
333. Anthony H. Cordesman, 'The Quds (Qods, or Jerusalem) forces', *Iran's Revolutionary Guards, the Al Quds Force, and Other Intelligence and Paramilitary Forces*, Center for Strategic and International Studies, 16 August 2007, p. 9.
334. Iran could have delivered AQ operatives to the West or any Muslim state to show positive intentions towards, and its position on, counterterrorism.

However, in a conversation between Roberto Toscano and an Iranian foreign ministry official, the issue of reciprocity came up because Iran would expect MEK operatives to be delivered to Iran in turn. There was also the possibility that AQ would retaliate in Iran, most likely against Western embassies. The AQ issue in Iran is thus divided into a bargaining chip with the West and its concern about terrorism which keeps Iranian policy ambiguous. Roberto Toscano, email to the G2K List, 29 July 2011; N. K. Gvosdev and Ray Takeyh, 'Pragmatism in the Midst of Iranian Turmoil', *The Washington Quarterly* 27, p. 39.

335. Kayhan Barzegar, 'Iran's Foreign Policy in Post-Invasion Iraq', *Middle East Policy* XV/4, Winter 2008, p. 56.
336. Barbara Slavin, *Bitter Friends, Bosom Enemies*, p. 211.
337. Kayhan Barzegar, 'Iran's Foreign Policy in Post-Invasion Iraq', *Middle East Policy* XV/4, Winter 2008, p. 47.
338. The Washington Institute for Near East Policy, Taskforce on Iranian Proliferation, Regional Security and US Policy, 'Preventing a Cascade of Instability: US Engagement to Check Iranian Nuclear Progress', March 2009, p. 1.
339. Barbara Slavin, *Bitter Friends, Bosom Enemies*, p. 216.
340. Iran's Permanent Mission to the UN, 'An Unnecessary Crisis: Setting the Record Straight about Iran's Nuclear Programme', *Payvand*.
341. Kenneth Katzman, *Iran: US Concerns and Policy Responses*, Congressional Research Service, p. 28.
342. Ibid.
343. Interview with Richard Dalton, London, 26 January 2011.
344. Ibid.
345. Anoushiravan Ehteshami, 'Iran's Assessment of the Iraq Crisis and the Post-9/11 International Order', *The Iraq Crisis and World Order*, p. 138.
346. Interview with a foreign government representative who asked not to be named, London, 3 June 2010.
347. Morteza Behrouzifar and Homayoon Nassimi, 'US Sanctions and Global Energy Markets', *Journal of Middle Eastern Geopolitics* 1/4, April–June 2006, p. 98.
348. Ibid., p. 344.
349. Anoushiravan Ehteshami, 'Iran's Assessment of the Iraq Crisis and the Post-9/11 International Order', *The Iraq Crisis and World Order*, p. 138.
350. *CNN*, 'Rafsanjani: US Must Do More', 15 June 2005, available at http://edition.cnn.com/2005/WORLD/meast/06/14/iran.rafsanjani/index.html, last accessed 23 April 2013.
351. Kenneth Katzman, *Iran: US Concerns and Policy Responses*, Congressional Research Service, p. 29.

352. European Commission, 'Iran', available at http://ec.europa.eu/trade/creating-opportunities/bilateral-relations/countries/iran/, last accessed 23 April 2013; interview with Abbas Maleki, Tehran, 23 February 2011.
353. Mark Hibbs and Andreas Persbo, *The ElBaradei Legacy*, Bulletin of the Atomic Scientists, p. 14.
354. Shahriar Sabet-Saeidi, 'Iranian–European Relations: A Strategic Partnership', *Iran's Foreign Policy*, p. 65.
355. Ibid.
356. *Tehran Times*, 'Iran Provides 20 Answers to Clarify Ambiguities About its Nuclear Program', 9 November 2011, available at http://tehrantimes.com/politics/4362-iran-provides-20-answers-to-clarify-ambiguities-about-its-nuclear-program, last accessed 23 April 2013.
357. *GSN*, 'USA Edges Towards a More Pragmatic Iran Policy', 30/790, 29 September 2006, p. 4.
358. Interview with Richard Dalton, London, 26 January 2011.
359. Ibid.
360. Ibid.
361. Ibid.
362. 'Great Satan' is normally used to describe the United States whilst 'Little Satan' is used to describe Israel. However, the 'Great Satan' has also been used to refer to the UK after violent clashes following the disputed 2009 presidential election. William O. Beeman, *The 'Great Satan' vs. the 'Mad Mullahs'*, (Chicago: The University of Chicago Press, 2005), p. 130; Adam Smith, 'Has Britain Replaced the US as Iran's Little Satan', *Time*, 26 June 2009, available at: http://www.time.com/time/world/article/0,8599,1907066,00.html, last accessed 23 April 2013.
363. Ibid.
364. Ewen MacAskill and Chris McGreal, 'Israel Should be Wiped Off Map, Says Iran's President', *The Guardian*, 27 October 2005, available at http://www.guardian.co.uk/world/2005/oct/27/israel.iran, last accessed 23 April 2013.
365. Remarks by Roberto Toscano at the University of Exeter, 23 November 2011.
366. A pre-emptive attack would go against US interests in stabilizing Afghanistan and Iraq and 'Russia's stranglehold over Europe would be almost complete if a US attack on Iran precipitated the expected closing of the Straits of Hormuz'. However, Israel and the USA have worked together on a pre-emptive strike against a suspected plutonium production reactor at Al Kibar in Syria in September 2007. Amjad Atallah, 'What do Arabs Really Think About Iran?', *Foreign Policy*, 11 August 2010; *The*

Economist, 'The Riddle of Iran', 19 July 2007, http://www.economist.com/node/9514293, last accessed 23 April 2013; *UPI*, 'Israel Defence Chief: Iran Our Main Threat', 31 October 2011, available at http://www.upi.com/Top_News/Special/2011/10/31/Israel-defense-chief-Iran-our-main-threat/UPI-76471320081019/, last accessed 23 April 2013; Mark Hibbs and Andreas Persbo, *The ElBaradei Legacy*, Bulletin of the Atomic Scientists, pp. 16–17, available at http://www.carnegieendowment.org/static/npp/pdf/elbaradei-legacy.pdf, accessed 1 November 2011; telephone interview with Martin Indyk, 1 November 2011.

367. This virus knocked out 1,000 (about one fifth) of Iran's centrifuges and was successful partly because Israel uses similar centrifuges itself, some of which it used for testing the virus. Michael Joseph Gross, 'A Declaration of Cyber War', *Vanity Fair*, April 2011, available at http://www.vanityfair.com/culture/features/2011/04/stuxnet-201104, last accessed 23 April 2013; William J. Broad, John Markoff and David E. Sanger, 'Israeli Test on Worm Called Crucial in Iran Nuclear Delay', *The New York Times*, 15 January 2011, available at http://www.nytimes.com/2011/01/16/world/middleeast/16stuxnet.html?pagewanted=all, last accessed 23 April 2013.

368. Scott Peterson, 'Did Israel Assassinate Iran's "Missile King"?', *The Christian Science Monitor*, 14 November 2011, available at http://www.csmonitor.com/World/Middle-East/2011/1114/Did-Israel-assassinate-Iran-s-missile-king, last accessed 23 April 2013.

369. US Department of State, 'Foreign Terrorist Organizations', 15 September 2011, available at http://www.state.gov/s/ct/rls/other/des/123085.htm, accessed 20 October 2011.

370. A possibility advanced by some US Republican presidential candidates during the 2012 elections' debate on foreign policy. Seymour M. Hersh, 'Iran and the IAEA', *The New Yorker*, 18 November 2011, available at http://www.newyorker.com/online/blogs/comment/2011/11/iran-and-the-iaea.html, last accessed 23 April 2013.

371. Andrew R.C. Marshall and Peter Apps, 'Iran "Shadow War" Intensifies, Crosses Borders', *News Daily*, 16 February 2012, available at http://www.newsdaily.com/stories/tre81f1e7-us-iran-israel-security/, accessed 3 March 2012.

372. Ibid.

373. Richard Dalton et al., 'Iran: Breaking the Nuclear Deadlock', Chatham House Report, p. 13.

374. Ibid., p. 15.

375. Interview with Richard Dalton, London, 26 January 2011.

376. *Iran News*, 'China to Import 23,500bpd Iran Gas', 24 February 2011, p. 4.

377. Ibid.
378. Behzad Shahandeh, *Sino–Iranian Relations: A Marriage of Convenience*, paper presented at the Gulf Research Meeting, University of Cambridge, 7–10 July 2010, p. 2.
379. Ibid.
380. Ibid., p. 11.
381. Ibid., p. 12.
382. Interview with Leo Drollas, London, 26 January 2011.
383. Interview with Richard Dalton, London, 26 January 2011.
384. Chen Aizhu and Chris Buckley, 'Exclusive – China Curbs Iran Energy Work Under Shadow of US Sanctions', *Reuters*, 2 September 2011, available at http://in.reuters.com/article/2011/09/02/idINIndia-59109420110902, last accessed 23 April 2013.
385. Interview with a European diplomat who asked not to be named, Tehran, 24 February 2011.
386. Anoushiravan Ehteshami and Mahjoob Zweiri, 'Introduction', *Iran's Foreign Policy*, p. xiv.
387. Michael Eisenstadt and Mehdi Khalaji, 'Nuclear Fatwa: Religion and Politics in Iran's Proliferation Strategy', *Policy Focus #115*, The Washington Institute for Near East Policy, September 2011, p. 10; Kenneth Katzman, *Iran: US Concerns and Policy Responses*, Congressional Research Service, p. 27.
388. Ibid.
389. Interview with Ali Biniaz, Tehran, 27 February 2011.
390. Interview with a European diplomat who asked not to be named, Tehran, 24 February 2011.
391. Ibid.
392. Interview with Ruprecht Polenz, Berlin, 22 September 2011.
393. Kenneth Katzman, *Iran: US Concerns and Policy Responses*, Congressional Research Service, p. 32.
394. Ibid.
395. Ibid., p. 28.
396. Ibid.
397. US Mission UNVIE Vienna, 'Austrian Diplomat Shares Iranian President's Claim', *Wikileaks*, 8 February 2010, available at http://wikileaks.org/cable/2010/02/10UNVIEVIENNA40.html, last accessed 23 April 2013.
398. Ibid.
399. Ibid.
400. Ibid.
401. It is important to note different stances regarding different issues. For example Larijani is actually more internationalist than his peers, stating that

'We should not have what I would call an obstinate policy towards the world.' Kenneth Pollack and Ray Takeyh, 'Taking on Tehran', *Foreign Affairs*, p. 22.
402. Ibid.
403. Ibid.
404. Ibid.
405. Ali Vaez and Charles D. Ferguson, 'An Iranian Offer Worth Considering', *The New York Times*, 29 September 2011, available at http://www.nytimes.com/2011/09/30/opinion/30iht-edvaez30.html?_r=3&ref=global, last accessed 23 April 2013.
406. Interview with a European diplomat who asked not to be named, Tehran, 24 February 2011.
407. Interview with Richard Dalton, London, 26 January 2011.
408. Interview with Ruprecht Polenz, Berlin, 22 September 2011; Kaveh L. Afrasiabi, 'Small US–Iran Step on Long Road', *Asia Times*, 5 November 2011, available at http://www.atimes.com/atimes/Middle_East/MK05Ak01.html, last accessed 23 April 2013.
409. Ibid.
410. *Iran News*, 'Moscow Ready to Sign Radioactive Isotope Contract with Tehran', 24 February 2011, p. 15.
411. Interview with Ruprecht Polenz, Berlin, 22 September 2011.
412. Between 2000 and 2005 there was cooperation on drugs between Iran and the UK. Interview with Richard Dalton, London, 26 January 2011.
413. Richard Dalton et al., 'Iran: Breaking the Nuclear Deadlock', Chatham House Report, 2008, p. 6.
414. *Daily Star*, 'Snap Checks Not Part of Inspections Offer, Iran Nuclear Chief Clarifies', 7 September 2011, available at http://www.dailystar.com.lb/News/Middle-East/2011/Sep-07/148092-snap-checks-not-part-of-inspections-offer-iran-nuclear-chief-clarifies.ashx#axzz1X9R9OJh3, last accessed 23 April 2013.
415. Interview with a European diplomat who asked not to be named, Tehran, 24 February 2011.
416. Ibid.
417. P. K. Kerr, 'Has Iran Violated the NPT', *Iran's Nuclear Program: Tehran's Compliance with International Obligations*, Congressional Research Service, p. 8, available at http://www.fas.org/sgp/crs/nuke/R40094.pdf, accessed 4 October 2012; Semira N. Nikou, 'Timeline of Iran's Nuclear Activities', *The Iran Primer*, USIP, available at http://iranprimer.usip.org/resource/timeline-irans-nuclear-activities, last accessed 23 April 2013.
418. Ali Ansari, 'Nuclear Poker', *The World Today*, Chatham House, May 2006, p. 5.

419. Kenneth Katzman, *Iran: US Concerns and Policy Responses*, Congressional Research Service, p. 28.
420. Interview with a European diplomat who asked not to be named, Tehran, 24 February 2011.
421. Suzanne Maloney, 'Progress of the Obama Administration's Policy Toward Iran', *Brookings*, 15 November 2011.
422. Interview with Ruprecht Polenz, Berlin, 22 September 2011.
423. Interview with Ali Biniaz, Tehran, 27 February 2011.
424. Ibid.
425. *The Economist*, 'Can the Bush Doctrine Last?', 27 May 2008, available at http://www.economist.com/node/10873479, last accessed 23 April 2013.
426. Remarks from Prince Turki Al-Faisal, University of Exeter, 16 March 2011.
427. Interview with Ruprecht Polenz, Berlin, 22 September 2011.
428. Ibid.
429. Interview with Richard Dalton, London, 26 January 2011.
430. Alfred Nurja, 'WMD-Free Middle East Proposal at a Glance', Arms Control Association, available at http://www.armscontrol.org/factsheets/mewmdfz, last accessed 23 April 2013.
431. Remarks from Prince Turki Al-Faisal, University of Exeter, 16 March 2011.
432. Gawdat Bahgat, 'Security in the Persian Gulf: Perils and Opportunities', *Contemporary Security Policy* 29/2, August 2008, p. 306.
433. Interview with Ruprecht Polenz, Berlin, 22 September 2011.
434. Email interview with Roberto Toscano, 12 August 2011.
435. Interview with Ruprecht Polenz, Berlin, 22 September 2011.
436. Remarks from Prince Turki Al-Faisal, University of Exeter, 16 March 2011.
437. Arms Control Association, 'Nuclear Weapons: Who Has What at a Glance', available at http://www.armscontrol.org/factsheets/Nuclearweaponswhohaswhat, last accessed 23 April 2013.
438. Interview with Ruprecht Polenz, Berlin, 22 September 2011.
439. Ibid.
440. Gary Sick, 'A Selective Partnership: Getting US–Iranian Relations Right', *Foreign Affairs* 85/6, November–December 2006, p. 145.
441. Interview with Ruprecht Polenz, Berlin, 22 September 2011.
442. Alireza Nader, 'Is Regime Change in Iran the Only Solution?', *Foreign Policy*, 26 January 2012, available at http://mideast.foreignpolicy.com/posts/2012/01/26/is_regime_change_in_iran_the_only_solution (registration required), last accessed 23 April 2013.

443. Admiral Mullen, Chairman of the Joint Chiefs of Staff in the USA, said he had concerns about the lack of direct contact between the USA and Iran, noting that even in the Cold War the USA could still talk to the Soviet Union. Jim Garamore, 'Chairman Concerned Over Lack of US–Iran Contact', US Department of Defence, 14 September 2011, available at http://www.defense.gov/news/newsarticle.aspx?id=65334, last accessed 23 April 2013.
444. During containment against the Soviet threat, it was deemed necessary for the USA to negotiate from strength. Melvyn P. Leffler, 'Remembering George Kennan: Lessons for Today', *USIP*, available at http://www.usip.org/files/resources/SRdec06.pdf, last accessed 23 April 2013.
445. Kayhan Barzegar, 'Sanctions Won't End Iran's Nuclear Programme', *Foreign Affairs*, 9 February 2012, available at http://www.foreignaffairs.com/features/letters-from/sanctions-wont-end-irans-nuclear-program, last accessed 23 April 2013.
446. Shirin Shafaie, 'Diplomatic Miscalculations and the Threat of War: Part 1', *Fair Observer*, 22 February 2012.
447. Telephone interview with Martin Indyk, 1 November 2011; confirmed in an email interview with Roberto Toscano, 12 August 2011.
448. Although far less than the stated objective of 50,000 centrifuges. Ali Vaez, 'Seyed Hossein Mousavian: The West is Pushing Iran in the Wrong Direction', *Bulletin of the Atomic Scientists*, 18 November 2011, available at http://thebulletin.org/web-edition/features/seyed-hossein-mousavian-the-west-pushing-iran-the-wrong-direction, last accessed 23 April 2013.
449. Ibid.
450. Tim Niblock, 'Conclusion', *"Pariah States" & Sanctions in the Middle East: Iraq, Libya, Sudan* (Boulder, CO: Lynne Rienner, 2001), p. 93.
451. Ibid., p. 213.
452. Tucker Reals, 'Would Israel Attack Iran, or is Netanyahu "Bluffing"?', *CBS News*, 1 April 2009, available at http://www.cbsnews.com/8301-503543_162-4908619-503543.html, last accessed 23 April 2013.
453. IAEA reports such as the *Implementation of the NPT Safeguards Agreement and Relevent Provisions of Security Council Resolutions in the Islamic Republic of Iran*, IAEA, 8 November 2011, available at http://isis-online.org/uploads/isis-reports/documents/IAEA_Iran_8Nov2011.pdf, last accessed 23 April 2013.
454. Aaron David Miller, 'Trouble Over Tehran', *Foreign Policy*, 8 November 2011, available at http://www.foreignpolicy.com/articles/2011/11/07/trouble_over_tehran (registration required), last accessed 23 April 2013; International Campaign for Human Rights in Iran, 'Raising Their Voices',

available at http://www.iranhumanrights.org/wp-content/uploads/raising-their-voices-final.pdf, last accessed 23 April 2013.
455. Andrew Parasiliti, 'Iran: Diplomacy and Deterrence', *Survival*, p. 5.
456. Barbara Slavin, 'EU-Iran New Sanctions Aimed at Averting Wider Conflict', *IPS*, 25 January 2012, available at http://ipsnews.net/news.asp?idnews=106549, last accessed 23 April 2013.
457. Telephone interview with Martin Indyk, 1 November 2011.
458. Interview with Ali Biniaz, Tehran, 27 February 2011.
459. Ibid.
460. Email interview with Roberto Toscano, 12 August 2011.
461. Ibid.
462. Interview with Ruprecht Polenz, Berlin, 22 September 2011.
463. Email interview with Roberto Toscano, 12 August 2011.
464. 'Possible Military Dimensions', *Implementation of the NPT Safeguards Agreement and Relevant Provisions of Security Council Resolutions in the Islamic Republic of Iran*, IAEA, p. 7.
465. Email interview with Roberto Toscano, 12 August 2011; confirmed by Richard Dalton, 'Relations Will Only Improve When it Benefits Tehran', *The Independent*, 30 December 2009.
466. Interview with a European diplomat who asked not to be named, Tehran, 24 February 2011.
467. Richard Dalton, Email to the G2K List, 25 January 2012.
468. Interview with Leo Drollas, London, 26 January 2011.
469. Iran is trying to export gas to Western Europe through the Nabucco pipeline project which includes negotiations between Iran, Turkey and Austria. Kenneth Katzman, 'European Gas Pipeline Routes', *Iran Sanctions*, Congressional Research Service, 9 November 2010, p. 8.
470. Interview with Ruprecht Polenz, Berlin, 22 September 2011; email interview with Roberto Toscano, 12 August 2011.
471. *Radio Free Europe*, 'Iran's Naval-Gazing More Political Than Military', 29 September 2011, available at http://www.rferl.org/content/iran_navy_/24334129.html, last accessed 23 April 2013.
472. Ibid.
473. Interview with a senior British diplomat who asked not to be named, London, 4 June 2011.
474. Richard Dalton, 'Does Tehran Have a Plan C?', *The Guardian*, 27 September 2009, available at http://www.guardian.co.uk/commentisfree/2009/sep/27/iran-nuclear-weapon-plan-c, last accessed 23 April 2013.
475. Ibid.
476. Ibid.

477. Interview with Leo Drollas, Centre for Global Energy Studies, London, 26 January 2011.
478. Barbara Slavin, *Bitter Friends, Bosom Enemies*, p. 226.

Chapter 5. The Triangulation of US Foreign Policy towards the Middle East

1. *Pravda*, 'Russian State Duma Has Ratified Treaty on Cooperation With Iran', 19 December 2001, available at http://english.pravda.ru/news/world/19-12-2001/24746-0/, last accessed 23 April 2013.
2. John M. Broder, 'Despite a Secret Pact by Gore in '95, Russian Arms Sales to Iran Go On', *The New York Times*, 13 October 2000, available at http://www.nytimes.com/2000/10/13/world/despite-a-secret-pact-by-gore-in-95-russian-arms-sales-to-iran-go-on.html?pagewanted=all&src=pm, last accessed 23 April 2013.
3. Flynt Leverett and Hilary Mann Leverett, 'Dr Gates on Russia's "Schizophrenic" Iran Policy', *Race for Iran*, 18 June 2010, available at http://www.raceforiran.com/dr-gates-on-russia per centE2 per cent80 per cent99s-per centE2 per cent80 per cent9Cschizophrenic per centE2 per cent80 per cent9D-iran-policy, accessed 18 June 2010.
4. Alla Kassianova, 'Russian-Iranian Defence Cooperation vs. US Sanctions', *Russian Weapon Sales to Iran: Why they are Unlikely to Stop*, PONARS Policy Memo 427, December 2006, pp. 1–2, available at http://csis.org/files/media/csis/pubs/pm_0427.pdf, last accessed 23 April 2013.
5. *Rianovosti*, 'Iran Successfully Tests Russian TOR-M1 Missiles', 7 February 2007, available at http://en.rian.ru/russia/20070207/60358702.html, last accessed 23 April 2013.
6. Nikolay A. Kozhanov, *Possible Changes in Russo-Iranian Relations after the Presidential Elections of 2012 in Russia*, BRISMES Annual Conference 2012 paper, London School of Economics, 26–28 March 2012.
7. The closure of the Fordo facility is one of Israel's top conditions for Iran–West talks. Yaakov Katz, 'Barak Reveals Israel's Conditions for Iran–West Talks', *The Jerusalem Post*, 4 April 2012, available at http://www.jpost.com/IranianThreat/News/Article.aspx?id=264839, last accessed 23 April 2013.
8. *Rianovosti*, 'Russian Military Concedes Iran, N. Korea Nuclear Threat', 24 April 2012, available at http://en.rian.ru/russia/20120424/173017423.html, last accessed 23 April 2013.
9. Philip P. Pan, 'Biden Says Russia Used "Pretext" to Invade Georgia in 2008', *The Washington Post*, 24 July 2009, available at http://www.washingtonpost.com/wp-dyn/content/article/2009/07/23/AR2009072301541.html, last accessed 23 April 2013.

10. *UPI*, 'Iran: Bushehr Nuclear Plant Operational', 18 May 2011, available at http://www.upi.com/Top_News/World-News/2011/05/18/Iran-Bushehr-nuclear-plant-operational/UPI-39011305717766/, last accessed 23 April 2013.
11. Paul Stevens, *An Embargo on Iranian Crude Oil Exports: How Likely and With What Impact?*, Chatham House EEDP Programme Paper, January 2012, p. 4.
12. Avnish Patel, 'Taking Forward NATO-Russia Missile Defence Cooperation', *Royal United Services Institute* (hereafter *RUSI*), available at http://www.rusi.org/analysis/commentary/ref:C4D886D88718D2/, last accessed 23 April 2013.
13. Olga Oliker et al., *Russian Foreign Policy: Sources and Implications* (Santa Monica: RAND, 2009), p. 83, available at http://www.rand.org/content/dam/rand/pubs/monographs/2009/RAND_MG768.pdf, last accessed 23 April 2013.
14. Ibid., p. 83.
15. Ibid., p. 85.
16. Nikolay A. Kozhanov, *Possible Changes in Russo-Iranian Relations after the Presidential Elections of 2012 in Russia*, BRISMES Annual Conference 2012 paper, London School of Economics, 26–28 March 2012.
17. AEI Iran Tracker, 'Global Business in Iran Database: Gazprom – OOC – NIOC, Neka – Jask Pipeline', available at http://www.irantracker.org/global-business-in-iran/projects/gazprom-ooc-nioc-neka-jask-pipeline, last accessed 23 April 2013.
18. Nabucco Pipeline, 'Route', available at http://www.nabucco-pipeline.com/portal/page/portal/en/pipeline/route, last accessed 23 April 2013.
19. *Reuters*, 'Russia's Putin Pledges Coordination with OPEC', 17 September 2010, available at http://uk.reuters.com/article/2010/09/17/uk-russia-opec-idUKTRE68G2W720100917, last accessed 23 April 2013.
20. Anna Newby, *Russia Continued Relevance in US Policy, World Affairs*, Center for Strategic and International Studies, 20 August 2010, available at http://csis.org/blog/russia-continued-relevance-us-policy-world-affairs, last accessed 23 April 2013.
21. Andrew E. Kramer, 'Russia Plan to Help Iran Challenges Sanctions', *The New York Times*, 14 July 2010, available at http://www.nytimes.com/2010/07/15/world/europe/15russia.html, last accessed 23 April 2013.
22. Anna Newby, 'Russia Continued Relevance in US Policy, World Affairs', Center for Strategic and International Studies, 20 August 2010.
23. Mark N. Katz, 'Saudi-Russian Relations since the Abdullah-Putin Summit', Middle East Policy Council, available at http://www.mepc.org/journal/middle-east-policy-archives/saudi-russian-relations-abdullah-putin-summit, last accessed 23 April 2013.

24. Ibid.
25. Ibid.
26. *Al Arabiya*, 'Saudi Arabia Urges Russia to "Advise" Syria to End Bloodshed Ahead of Medvedev Meeting', 5 March 2012, available at http://english.alarabiya.net/articles/2012/03/05/198625.html, last accessed 23 April 2013.
27. Anna Newby, 'Russia Continued Relevance in US Policy, World Affairs', Center for Strategic and International Studies, 20 August 2010.
28. Tim Niblock, 'China's Growing Involvement in the Gulf: the Geopolitical Significance', in S. Shen and J. Blanchard (eds.), *Multidimensional Diplomacy of Contemporary China* (Boulder: Lexington Books, 2010), pp. 207–233.
29. Ibid.
30. Ibid.
31. Mark Landler and Steven Lee Myers, 'US Sees Positive Signs from China on Security Issues', *The New York Times*, 26 April 2012, available at http://www.nytimes.com/2012/04/27/world/asia/us-is-seeing-positive-signs-from-chinese.html?_r=2&hpw&pagewanted=all, last accessed 23 April 2013.
32. Mayne Ma, 'Chain Oil Imports from Iran Rebound', *The Wall Street Journal*, 21 May 2012, available at http://online.wsj.com/article/SB10001424052702303610504577417803213035894.html, last accessed 23 April 2013.
33. Kenneth Lieberthal and Wang Jisi, 'Understanding Strategic Distrust: the Chinese Side', *Addressing US-China Strategic Distrust*, John L. Thornton China Center Monograph Series #4, March 2012, Brookings, p. 14, available at http://www.brookings.edu/~/media/Files/rc/papers/2012/0330_china_lieberthal/0330_china_lieberthal.pdf, last accessed 23 April 2013.
34. Tim Niblock, 'China's Growing Involvement in the Gulf: the Geopolitical Significance', in S. Shen and J. Blanchard (eds.), *Multidimensional Diplomacy of Contemporary China*, (Boulder: Lexington Books, 2010), pp. 207–233.
35. China backs sanctions against Iran due to its nuclear programme, not human rights abuses, and took the step to sanction Libya probably based on the unanimity of its Middle East trading partners against Qaddafi. CS Monitor, 'Libya Sanctions: China's New Role at the UN', 28 February 2011, available at http://www.csmonitor.com/Commentary/the-monitors-view/2011/0228/Libya-sanctions-China-s-new-role-at-the-UN, last accessed 23 April 2013.
36. Chunlong Lu and Jie Chen, 'China's Middle East Policy Since the Post-Mao Reform', in Jack Covarrubias and Tom Lansford (eds.), *Strategic Interests in the Middle East: Opposition or Support for US Foreign Policy* (Aldershot: Ashgate, 2007), p. 93.
37. Ibid.

38. Kenneth Lieberthal and Wang Jisi, 'Understanding Strategic Distrust: the US Side', *Addressing US-China Strategic Distrust*, John L. Thornton China Center Monograph Series #4, March 2012, Brookings, pp. 28–29.
39. Ibid.
40. Tarique Niazi, 'Gwadar: China's Naval Outpost in the Indian Ocean', *China Brief* 5/4, The Jamestown Foundation, available at http://www.jamestown.org/single/?tx_ttnews%5Btt_news%5D=3718, last accessed 23 April 2013.
41. Gerald Sussman and Sascha Krader, 'Template Revolutions: Marketing US Regime Change in Eastern Europe', *Westminster Papers in Communication and Culture* 5/3, 2008, University of Westminster, available at http://www.westminster.ac.uk/__data/assets/pdf_file/0011/20009/006WPCC-Vol5-No3-Gerald_Sussman_Sascha_Krader.pdf, last accessed 23 April 2013.
42. Fiona Hill, 'How Russia and China See the Egyptian Revolution', *Foreign Policy*, 15 February 2011, available at http://www.foreignpolicy.com/articles/2011/02/15/how_russia_and_china_see_the_egyptian_revolution?page=full (registration required), last accessed 23 April 2013.
43. BBC News, 'US "Disgust" as Russia and China Veto UN Syria Resolution', 4 February 2012, available at http://www.bbc.co.uk/news/world-middle-east-16890434, last accessed 23 April 2013.
44. Rick Gladstone, 'In Rare, Blunt Speech, Saudi King Criticizes Syria Vetoes', *The New York Times*, 10 February 2012, available at http://www.nytimes.com/2012/02/11/world/middleeast/in-rare-blunt-speech-saudi-king-criticizes-syria-vetoes.html?_r=1, last accessed 23 April 2013.
45. P. R. Kumaraswamy, 'India Defies Oil Sanctions on Iran', BESA Ceter Perspectives Paper 168, 19 March 2012, available at http://www.biu.ac.il/SOC/besa/docs/perspectives168.pdf, last accessed 23 April 2013.
46. *Macau Daily Times*, 'BRICS Summit Insists on Dialogue for Syria, Iran', 30 March 2012, available at http://www.macaudailytimes.com.mo/world/34890-BRICS-summit-insists-dialogue-for-Syria-Iran.html, last accessed 23 April 2013.
47. Yukiko Miyagi, *Japan and the Arab Uprisings*, BRISMES Annual Conference 2012, LSE, 26–28 March 2012.
48. Mike Elkin, 'Loans to Egypt Hinge on Democracy Issues', *The New York Times*, 29 February 2012, available at http://www.nytimes.com/2012/03/01/world/middleeast/01iht-m01-egypt-aid.html?pagewanted=all, last accessed 23 April 2013.
49. Yukiko Miyagi, *Japan and the Arab Uprisings*, BRISMES Annual Conference 2012, LSE, 26–28 March 2012.
50. Sachiko Sakamaki and Andy Sharp, 'US Envoy Einhorn Says Japan Agrees on Need to Increase Pressure on Iran', *Bloomberg*, 18 January 2012, available

at http://www.bloomberg.com/news/2012-01-18/u-s-envoy-turns-to-japan-after-pushing-south-korea-on-iran-oil-sanctions.html, last accessed 23 April 2013.
51. *Al Arabiya*, 'US Wins Japan's Consent to Cut Iran's Oil Imports but India Stays in as an Importer', 12 January 2012, available at http://www.alarabiya.net/articles/2012/01/12/187852.html, last accessed 23 April 2013.
52. Rosemary Hollis, 'No Friend of Democratization: Europe's Role in the Genesis of the "Arab Spring"', *International Affairs* 88/1, 2012, p. 94.
53. Ibid.
54. Ibid.
55. European Commission, 'European Neighbourhood Policy', available at http://ec.europa.eu/world/enp/funding_en.htm, last accessed 23 April 2013.
56. *FT*, 'Asia Defence Spending to Overtake Europe', 7 March 2012, available at http://www.ft.com/cms/s/0/0aab435c-6846-11e1-a6cc-00144feabdc0.html#axzz1v8aiR5Dq (registration required), last accessed 23 April 2013.
57. Herman Gröhe et al., 'Even Handed, Not Neutral: Points of Reference for a German Middle East Policy', in Volker Perthes (ed.), *Germany and the Middle East: Interest and Options* (Berlin: Heinrich-Böll-Stiftung and Stiftung Wissenschaft und Politik, 2002), 11, available at http://www.swp-berlin.org/fileadmin/contents/products/fachpublikationen/GermanyAndTheMiddleEast_mitKopierschutz.pdf, last accessed 23 April 2013.
58. *The Guardian*, 'Full Text: Barack Obama's Cairo Speech', 4 June 2009, available at http://www.guardian.co.uk/world/2009/jun/04/barack-obama-keynote-speech-egypt, last accessed 23 April 2013.
59. Tamara Cofman Wittes, 'A New US Proposal for a Greater Middle East Initiative: An Evaluation', *Brookings*, 10 May 2004, available at http://www.brookings.edu/papers/2004/0510middleeast_wittes.aspx, last accessed 23 April 2013.
60. This position is supported in the USA by Greg Gause who advocates that the US government do nothing since there is no immediate threat to any American vital national interest. By following an interventionist policy, the exact opposite effect may be achieved. Greg Gause, 'Don't Just do Something, Stand There!', *Foreign Policy*, 21 December 2011, available at http://www.foreignpolicy.com/articles/2011/12/21/america_arab_spring_do_nothing (registration required), last accessed 23 April 2013.
61. *SUSRIS*, 'US, Saudi, GCC Leaders to Talk on Iran, Syria Crisis', 29 March 2012.
62. Helene Cooper, '"Loose Talk of War" Only Helps Iran, President Says', *The New York Times*, 4 March 2012, available at http://www.nytimes.

com/2012/03/05/world/middleeast/in-aipac-speech-obama-warns-against-loose-talk-of-war.html, last accessed 23 April 2013.
63. Ibid.

Chapter 6. Conclusions: Economic Factors in Middle East Foreign Policies

1. There is some debate as to what the true figure of Iran's reserves is: the figure is estimated to be between $79 billion and $120 billion. IMF, 'IMF Executive Board Concludes 2011 Article IV Consultation with Islamic Republic of Iran', 3 August 2011, available at http://www.imf.org/external/np/sec/pn/2011/pn11107.htm, last accessed 23 April 2013; *Payvand Iran News*, 'Iran Reserves: $120 Billion in Cash, 907 Tons of Gold', 2 January 2012, available at http://www.payvand.com/news/12/feb/1009.html, last accessed 23 April 2013.
2. At the time of writing, there were two strike groups patrolling in the Persian Gulf (during a period of overlap), led by two aircraft carriers: the USS *Abraham Lincoln* and the USS *Carl Vinson*. Simon Henderson, 'Danger Zone', *Foreign Policy*, 27 March 2012, available at http://www.foreignpolicy.com/articles/2012/03/27/danger_zone?page=0,0, last accessed 23 April 2013.
3. Scott Peterson, 'How Iran Could Beat Up On America's Superior Military', *The Christian Science Monitor*, 26 January 2012, available at http://www.csmonitor.com/World/Middle-East/2012/0126/How-Iran-could-beat-up-on-America-s-superior-military, last accessed 23 April 2013.
4. Gary Sick, 'Will Israel Really Attack Iran?', 29 January 2012, available at http://garysick.tumblr.com/.
5. Ibid.
6. David Jolly, 'Death Toll in Syrian Civil War Near 93,000 U.N. Says', *The New York Times*, 13 June 2013, available at http://www.nytimes.com/2013/06/14/world/middleeast/un-syria-death-toll.html?adxnnl=1&adxnnlx=1374688871-Xzn+7RnudKql3UMb2km45g, last accessed 24 July 2013.
7. Geoff Dyer et al., 'US "Disgusted" with Syria Peace Plan Veto', *FT*, 5 February 2012, available at http://www.ft.com/intl/cms/s/0/2b019f4e-4-f1d-11e1-bc30–00144feabdc0.html#axzz1lsxJ5uRc, last accessed 23 April 2013.
8. *Emirates 24/7*, 'Arab League Mission to Return to Syria', 9 February 2012, available at http://www.emirates247.com/news/region/arab-league-mission-to-return-to-syria-2012-02-09-1.442078, last accessed 23 April 2013.

NOTES TO PAGES 165–167 233

9. BBC News, 'Syria Crisis: US Rues Russian Missiles Sent to Damascus', 18 May 2013, available at http://www.bbc.co.uk/news/world-middle-east-22578673, accessed 19 May 2013
10. Mark Landler, 'Pentagon Lays Out Options for U.S. Military Effort in Syria', *The New York Times,* 22 July 2013, available at http://www.nytimes.com/2013/07/23/world/middleeast/pentagon-outlining-options-to-congress-suggests-syria-campaign-would-be-costly.html?nl=todaysheadlines&emc=edit_th_20130723&_r=1&, last accessed 24 July 2013.
11. Bruno Waterfield, 'EU Imposes Syria Sanctions Targeting Assad Luxury Lifestyle', *The Telegraph,* 23 April 2012, available at http://www.telegraph.co.uk/news/worldnews/middleeast/syria/9221551/EU-imposes-Syrian-sanctions-targeting-Assad-luxury-lifestyle.html, last accessed 23 April 2013.
12. Isabel Kerchner, 'Secret Israel-Syria Peace Talks Involved Golan Heights Exit', *The New York Times,* 12 October 2012, available at http://www.nytimes.com/2012/10/13/world/middleeast/secret-israel-syria-peace-talks-involved-golan-heights-exit.html?_r=0, last accessed 23 April 2013.
13. Mark Landler, 'Israel Hints at New Strikes, Warning Syria Not to Hit Back', *The New York Times,* 15 May 2013, available at http://www.nytimes.com/2013/05/16/world/middleeast/israeli-official-signals-possibility-of-more-syria-strikes.html?_r=0, accessed 19 May 2013.
14. Joshua Chaffin, 'UK and France Push to Arm Syria Rebels', *FT,* 15 March 2013, available at http://www.ft.com/intl/cms/s/0/8f4fd6f4-8cd5-11e2-8-ee0-00144feabdc0.html#axzz2NpIJVVbW, last accessed 23 April 2013.
15. UPI, 'In Syrian Shadow, Iraq Jihadists Resurgent', 19 March 2013, available at http://www.upi.com/Top_News/Special/2013/03/19/In-Syrian-shadow-Iraq-jihadists-resurgent/UPI-61371363717849/, last accessed 24 July 2013.
16. Roula Khalaf and Abigail Fielding-Smith, 'How Qatar Seized Control of the Syrian Revolution', *FT,* 17 May 2013, available at http://www.ft.com/cms/s/2/f2d9bbc8-bdbc-11e2-890a-00144feab7de.html#axzz2TjRbGiN2, accessed 19 May 2013; Roula Khalaf and Abigail Fielding-Smith, 'Qatar bankrolls Syrian Revolt with Cash and Arms', *FT,* 16 May 2013, available at http://www.ft.com/cms/s/0/86e3f28e-be3a-11e2-bb35-00144feab7de.html#axzz2TjRbGiN2, accessed 19 May 2013.
17. Ibid.; James Longman, 'Gulf States at Odds Over Syria War', BBC News, 1 July 2013, available at http://www.bbc.co.uk/news/world-middle-east-23125629, last accessed 24 July 2013.
18. *SUSRIS,* 'Arab Gulf Union Council – What's in a Name', 8 March 2012, available at http://www.susrisblog.com/2012/03/08/arab-gulf-union-council-whats-in-a-name/, last accessed 23 April 2013.

BIBLIOGRAPHY

ABC News. 'Iran's Economy: A Political Battleground, But Could it Undo the Islamic Republic', 5 July 2011, available at http://abcnews.go.com/blogs/headlines/2011/07/irans-economy-a-political-battleground-but-could-it-undo-the-islamic-republic/, last accessed 23 April 2013

Abdelhadi, Magdi. 'Spat over Iranian Film on Sadat', *BBC News*, 24 July 2008, available at http://news.bbc.co.uk/1/hi/world/middle_east/7523967.stm, last accessed 23 April 2013

Adib-Moghaddam, Arshin. 'Westphalia and the Anarchic Gulf Society: the Second Persian Gulf War and its Aftermath', *The International Politics of the Persian Gulf: A Cultural Genealogy*. Abingdon: Routledge, 2006, 52–81

Adib-Moghaddam, Arshin. 'Islamic Utopian Romanticism and the Foreign Policy Culture of Iran', *Iran in World Politics*. London: C. Hurst & Co., 2007, 31–83

Adib-Moghaddam, Arshin. SOAS, 'The United States and Saddam (Adib-Moghaddam)', email sent 5 April 2011 to the Gulf2000 List

AEI Iran Tracker. 'Global Business in Iran Database: Gazprom – OOC – NIOC, Neka – Jask Pipeline', available at http://www.irantracker.org/global-business-in-iran/projects/gazprom-ooc-nioc-neka-jask-pipeline, last accessed 23 April 2013

Afrasiabi, Kaveh L. 'Small US – Iran Step on Long Road', *Asia Times*, 5 November 2011, available at http://www.atimes.com/atimes/Middle_East/MK05Ak01.html, last accessed 23 April 2013

Ahmad, Talmiz. Interview, Riyadh, 4 June 2011

Ahmad, Talmiz. *Investments and Joint Ventures in India-GCC Economic Ties: Opportunities and Challenges*. Paper delivered at Gulf Research Meeting, University of Cambridge, 8 July 2011

Aizhu, Chen, and Chris Buckley. 'Exclusive – China Curbs Iran Energy Work Under Shadow of US Sanctions', *Reuters*, 2 September 2011, available at http://in.reuters.com/article/2011/09/02/idINIndia-59109420110902, last accessed 23 April 2013

BIBLIOGRAPHY

Alani, Mustafa. *Saudi Policy Predicament in Yemen*, Gulf Research Center, 21 July 2011, available at http://grc.kcorp.net/?frm_action=view_newsletter_web&sec_code=grccommentary&frm_module=contents&show_web_list_link=1&int_content_id=74808, last accessed 23 April 2013

Al Arabiya. 'Economic Implications of Jordan and Morocco Joining GCC', 12 May 2011, available at http://www.alarabiya.net/articles/2011/05/12/148876.html, last accessed 23 April 2013

Al Arabiya. 'US Wins Japan's Consent to Cut Iran's Oil Imports but India Stays in as an Importer', 12 January 2012, available at http://www.alarabiya.net/articles/2012/01/12/187852.html, last accessed 23 April 2013

Al Arabiya. 'Saudi Arabia Urges Russia to "Advise" Syria to End Bloodshed Ahead of Medvedev Meeting', 5 March 2012, available at http://english.alarabiya.net/articles/2012/03/05/198625.html, last accessed 23 April 2013

Albright, David, and Andrea Stricker. 'Iran's Nuclear Program', *The Iran Primer*, United States Institute of Peace, available at http://iranprimer.usip.org/resource/irans-nuclear-program, last accessed 23 April 2013

Albright, Madeleine K. 'Remarks before the American–Iranian Council', 17 March 2000, Washington D.C., available at http://www.mideastinfo.com/documents/iranspeech.htm, last accessed 23 April 2010

Al-Faisal, Turki. University of Exeter, 16 March 2011

Al-Faisal, Turki. 'Address at the Gulf Research Meeting Opening Ceremony', University of Cambridge, 6 July 2011

Al Faisal, Turki. 'Failed Favouritism towards Israel', *The Washington Post*, 10 June 2011, available at http://www.washingtonpost.com/opinions/palestinian-rights-wont-be-denied-by-the-united-states-and-israel/2011/06/07/AGmnK2OH_story.html, last accessed 23 April 2013

Alfoneh, Ali. 'The Basij Resistance Force', *The Iran Primer*, United States Institute of Peace, available at http://iranprimer.usip.org/resource/basij-resistance-force, last accessed 23 April 2013

Ali, Rustam, *Saudi Arabia and Oil Diplomacy*, New York: Praeger Publishers, 1976

Al Jazeera. 'Saudi Arabia's #Women2Drive', 16 June 2011, available at http://stream.aljazeera.com/story/saudi-women-drivers, last accessed 23 April 2013

Al-Khalili, Majid. 'Oman's Foreign Policy (1990–2004)', *Oman's Foreign Policy*. Westport: Praeger Security International, 2009, 95–125

Al Saggaf, Dato' Syed Omar. Interview, Riyadh 5 June 2011.

Ali Khamenei. 'Speech', 23 March 2004, available at http://farsi.khamenei.ir/speech-content?id=3236&q=, last accessed 23 April 2013

Al Qassemi, Sultan Sooud. 'How Saudi Arabia and Qatar Became Friends Again', *Foreign Policy*, 21 July 2011, available at http://www.foreignpolicy.com/articles/2011/07/21/how_saudi_arabia_and_qatar_became_friends_again?page=full (registration required), last accessed 23 April 2013

Al-Saheil, Turki. 'Khalid Sheikh Mohammed Implicated during Riyadh Compound Bombing Trial', *Asharq Alawsat*, 6 July 2011, available at http://www.asharq-e.com/news.asp?section=1&id=25782, last accessed 23 April 2013.

Amanpour, Christiane. '1979 Hostage Crisis Still Casts Pall on US – Iran Relations', *CNN*, 4 November 2009, available at http://edition.cnn.com/2009/WORLD/meast/11/04/iran.hostage.anniversary/index.html, last accessed 23 April 2013

Ansari, Ali. *Confronting Iran: the Failure of American Foreign Policy and the Roots of Mistrust*, London: C. Hurst & Co., 2006

Ansari, Ali. 'Nuclear Poker', *The World Today*, Chatham House, April 2006

Ansari, Ali M. *Crisis of Authority: Iran's 2009 Presidential Election*. London: Chatham House, 2010

Arab News. '$4 Billion Saudi Aid for Egypt', 21 May 2011, available at http://www.arabnews.com/saudiarabia/article420017.ece, last accessed 26 July 2011

Arab News. 'Morocco, Jordan Inch Closer to GCC', 11 September 2011, available at http://www.arabnews.com/saudiarabia/article500539.ece, last accessed 1 December 2011

Arango, Tim. 'Vacuum is Feared as US Quits Iraq, but Iran's Deep Influence May not Fill It', *The New York Times*, 8 October 2011, available at http://www.nytimes.com/2011/10/09/world/middleeast/if-united-states-leaves-vacuum-in-iraq-disliked-iran-may-not-fill-it.html?_r=2&hp=&pagewanted=all, last accessed 23 April 2010

Arms Control Association. 'Nuclear Weapons: Who Has What at a Glance', available at http://www.armscontrol.org/factsheets/Nuclearweaponswhohaswhat, last accessed 23 April 2010

Arsu, Sebnem. 'Turkey Pursues Kurdish Rebels after 24 Soldiers Are Killed Near Iraq', *The New York Times*, 19 October 2011, available at http://www.nytimes.com/2011/10/20/world/europe/dozens-dead-in-attacks-on-turkish-forces.html, last accessed 23 April 2010

Associated Press. 'Iran Ends Voluntary Cooperation with the IAEA', 2 May 2006, available at http://www.msnbc.msn.com/id/11105378/ns/world_news-mideast_n_africa/t/iran-ends-voluntary-cooperation-iaea/#.Tsk2crKa9Ic, last accessed 23 April 2010

Atallah, Amjad. 'What do Arabs Really Think About Iran?', *Foreign Policy*, 11 August 2010, available at http://mideast.foreignpolicy.com/posts/2010/08/11/what_do_arabs_really_think_about_iran?sms_ss=facebook (registration required), last accessed 23 April 2010

Ayoob, Mohammed. *Regional Security in the Third World: Case Studies from South East Asia and the Middle East*. Boulder, Colorado: Westview Press, 1986

Baabood, Abdullah. *EU-Gulf Political and Economic Relations: Assessment and Policy Recommendations*. Dubai: Gulf Research Center, 2006

Bahgat, Gawdat. *American Oil Diplomacy in the Persian Gulf and the Caspian Sea*. Gainesville: University Press Florida, 2003

Bahgat, Gawdat. 'Security in the Persian Gulf: Perils and Opportunities', *Contemporary Security Policy* 29/2, August 2008, 303–321

Bakhash, Shaul. *Reign of the Ayatollahs: Iran and the Islamic Revolution.* New York: Basic Books, 1984

Bakr, Amenam and Emma Farge. 'OPEC Oil Talks Collapse, No Output Deal', *Reuters*, 8 June 2011, available at http://www.reuters.com/article/2011/06/08/us-opec-idUSTRE75715L20110608, last accessed 23 April 2013

Baktiari, Bahman. *Parliamentary Politics in Revolutionary Iran: The Institutionalisation of Factional Politics.* Gainsville: University Press Florida, 1996

Banque Saudi Fransi. 'Trade Notes: Saudi Arabia', 17 November 2009, available at www.alfransi.com.sa/en/general/download/file/456 (file download), last accessed 23 April 2013

Barzegar, Kayhan. 'Iran's Foreign Policy in Post-Invasion Iraq', *Middle East Policy* XV/4, Winter 2008, 47–58

Barzegar, Kayhan. 'Sanctions Won't End Iran's Nuclear Programme', *Foreign Affairs* 9 February 2012, available at http://www.foreignaffairs.com/features/letters-from/sanctions-wont-end-irans-nuclear-program, last accessed 23 April 2013

Bazzi, Mohamad. 'Expect More Adventurism from Iran', Council on Foreign Relations, available at http://www.cfr.org/iran/expect-more-adventurism-iran/p20064, last accessed 23 April 2013

BBC Hardtalk. 'Chavez: US "Military Imperialism" in Latin America', 14 June 2010, available at http://news.bbc.co.uk/1/hi/programmes/hardtalk/8731623.stm, last accessed 23 April 2013

BBC News. 'Bush's "Evil Axis" Comment Stirs Critics', 2 February 2002, available at http://news.bbc.co.uk/1/hi/world/americas/1796034.stm, last accessed 23 April 2013

BBC News. 'Saudis Boost Aid to Wave Victims', 7 January 2005, available at http://news.bbc.co.uk/1/hi/world/middle_east/4151241.stm, last accessed 23 April 2013

BBC News. 'Saudi: US Presence Illegal', 29 March 2007, available at http://news.bbc.co.uk/1/hi/world/middle_east/6505803.stm, last accessed 23 April 2013

BBC News. 'China to Build Mecca Rail System', 11 February 2009, available at http://news.bbc.co.uk/1/hi/7883182.stm, last accessed 23 April 2013

BBC News. 'Islamic Solidarity Games Cancelled Over Gulf Dispute', 18 January 2010, available at http://news.bbc.co.uk/1/hi/8465235.stm, last accessed 23 April 2013

BBC News. 'Iran and Pakistan Sign "Historic" Pipeline Deal', 17 March 2010, available at http://news.bbc.co.uk/1/hi/8572267.stm, last accessed 23 April 2013

BBC News. 'Iran's Illegal Arms Trade: "Hypocritical and Dangerous"', 7 June 2010, available at http://www.bbc.co.uk/news/world-13545621, last accessed 23 April 2013

BBC News. 'Arab League Backs Libya No-Fly Zone', 12 March 2011, available at http://www.bbc.co.uk/news/world-africa-12723554, last accessed 23 April 2013

BBC News. 'Bahrain Expels Iranian Diplomat Over "Spy Ring"', 26 April 2011, available at http://www.bbc.co.uk/news/world-middle-east-13195541, last accessed 23 April 2013

BBC News. 'US "Disgust" as Russia and China Veto UN Syria Resolution', 4 February 2012, available at http://www.bbc.co.uk/news/world-middle-east-16890434, last accessed 23 April 2013

Beaubouff, Bruce A. 'The Energy Crisis Begins: 1970–75', *The Strategic Petroleum Reserve: US Energy Security and Oil Politics, 1975–2005*. United States: Bruce A. Beaubouff, 2007, 8–41

Beblawi, Hazem. 'The Rentier State in the Arab World' in Giacomo Luciani (ed.), *The Arab State*. Berkeley: University of California Press, 1990, 85–99

Beehner, Lionel. 'Iran's Multifaceted Foreign Policy', Council on Foreign Relations, 7 April 2006, available at http://www.cfr.org/iran/irans-multifaceted-foreign-policy/p10396#p2, last accessed 23 April 2013

Beehner, Lionel. 'Timeline: US–Iran Contacts', Council of Foreign Relations, 9 March 2007, available at http://www.cfr.org/iran/timeline-us-iran-contacts/p12806#p3, last accessed 23 April 2013

Beeman, William O. *The 'Great Satan' vs. the 'Mad Mullahs'*. Chicago: The University of Chicago Press, 2005

Beeman, William O. University of Minnesota, Email to the G2K List, 14 November 2011

Behrooz, Maziar. 'Factionalism in Iran Under Khomeini', *Middle Eastern Studies* 27/4 (1991), 597–614

Behrouzifar, Morteza and Homayoon Nassimi, 'US Sanctions and Global Energy Markets', *Journal of Middle Eastern Geopolitics* 1/4, April–June 2006, 83–102

Berman, Ilan. *Hezbollah in the Western Hemisphere*. Statement before the US House of Representatives Committee on Homeland Security/Subcommittee on Counterterrorism and Intelligence, American Foreign Policy Council, 7 July 2011

Bertelsmann Siftung, *Europe and the Gulf Region – Towards a New Horizon*, Discussion Paper Presented at the 12th Kronberg Talks, 11–12 May 2009, Riyadh

Biniaz, Ali. Interview, Tehran, 27 February 2011

Black, Ian. 'CIA Using Saudi Base for Drone Assassinations in Yemen', *The Guardian*, 6 February 2013, available at http://www.guardian.co.uk/world/2013/feb/06/cia-using-saudi-base-drone-yemen, last accessed 23 April 2013

Blanche, Ed. 'The Insatiable Dragon', *The Middle East* 422, May 2011, 12–18

Blomfield, Adrian. 'Syria Unrest; Saudi Arabia Calls on "Killing Machine" to Stop', *The Telegraph*, 8 August 2011, available at http://www.telegraph.co.uk/

news/worldnews/middleeast/syria/8687912/Syria-unrest-Saudi-Arabia-calls-on-killing-machine-to-stop.html, last accessed 23 April 2013

Bloom, Oliver. 'Saudi Arabia's Nuclear Program', *Center for Strategic and International Studies*, 17 May 2010, available at http://csis.org/blog/saudi-arabias-nuclear-program, last accessed 23 April 2013

Borger, Julian. 'Saudi Royals Face Trillion-Dollar Lawsuit Over September 11', *The Guardian*, 16 August 2002, available at http://www.guardian.co.uk/world/2002/aug/16/saudiarabia.usa, last accessed 23 April 2013

Borger, Julian. 'Western Powers Agree to Resume Iran Talks over Nuclear Programme', *The Guardian*, 6 March 2012, available at http://www.guardian.co.uk/world/2012/mar/06/west-iran-talks-nuclear-programme, last accessed 23 April 2013

Bosch, Olivia. 'Iran and the Traffickers', *The World Today*, Chatham House, May 2006

Bozorgmehr, Najmeh. 'Iran Fires Central Banker', *Financial Times*, 21 September 2008, available at http://www.ft.com/cms/s/0/54c007b6–8825–11dd-b114–0000779fd18c.html#axzz1X5XvwtDH (registration required), last accessed 23 April 2013

Bozorgmehr, Najmeh. 'Amhadi-Nejad Drawn into Funds Scandal', *Financial Times*, 19 September 2011, available at http://www.ft.com/intl/cms/s/0/f0e0ccf4-df82–11e0–845a-00144feabdc0.html#ixzz1YWZuLBNW (registration required), last accessed 23 April 2013

BP. 'BP Statistical Energy Review', June 2011, available at http://www.bp.com/assets/bp_internet/globalbp/globalbp_uk_english/reports_and_publications/statistical_energy_review_2011/STAGING/local_assets/pdf/statistical_review_of_world_energy_full_report_2011.pdf, last accessed 23 April 2013

Brandenburg, Rachel. 'Iran and the Palestinians', *The Iran Primer*, United States Institute of Peace, available at http://iranprimer.usip.org/resource/iran-and-palestinians, last accessed 23 April 2013

British Embassy Tehran. 'Embassy History', available at http://ukiniran.fco.gov.uk/en/about-us/our-embassy/embassy-history/, accessed 25 May 2011

Broad, William J. John Markoff and David E. Sanger. 'Israeli Test on Worm Called Crucial in Iran Nuclear Delay', *The New York Times*, 15 January 2011, available at http://www.nytimes.com/2011/01/16/world/middleeast/16stuxnet.html?pagewanted=all, last accessed 23 April 2013

Broder, John M. 'Despite a Secret Pact by Gore in '95, Russian Arms Sales to Iran Go On', *The New York Times*, 13 October 2000, available at http://www.nytimes.com/2000/10/13/world/despite-a-secret-pact-by-gore-in-95-russian-arms-sales-to-iran-go-on.html?pagewanted=all&src=pm, last accessed 23 April 2013

Bronson, Rachel. 'Understanding US–Saudi Relations', *Saudi Arabia in the Balance: Political Economy, Society, Foreign Affairs*. London: C. Hurst & Co., 2005, 372–399

Bronson, Rachel. *Thicker Than Oil: America's Uneasy Partnership with Saudi Arabia*. Oxford: Oxford University Press, 2006

Buchta, Wilfried. *Who Rules Iran?: The Structure of Power in the Islamic Republic*. Washington D.C.: Washington Institute for Near East Policy and the Konrad Adenauer Stiftung, 2000

Bunting, Madelaine. 'The Saudi Intervention in Bahrain will Fuel Sectarianism, not Stifle it', *The Guardian*, 20 March 2011, available at http://www.guardian.co.uk/commentisfree/2011/mar/20/bahrain-saudi-intervention-religious-divide, last accessed 23 April 2013

Burke, Jason. 'Riyadh Will Build Nuclear Weapons if Iran Gets Them, Saudi Prince Warns', *The Guardian*, 29 June 2011, available at http://www.guardian.co.uk/world/2011/jun/29/saudi-build-nuclear-weapons-iran, last accessed 23 April 2013

Butter, David. 'Iran: a Force for Stability', *Middle East Economic Digest*, 5 October 2001, 5

Bush, G. W. 'Text of Bush's State of the Union Speech', *CNN*, available at http://edition.cnn.com/2006/POLITICS/01/31/sotu.transcript/, last accessed 23 April 2013

Calvin-Smith, Georja. 'Riyadh Unwilling to Lobby China Over Iran Sanctions', *France 24*, 16 February 2010, available at http://www.france24.com/en/20100216-riyadh-unwilling-lobby-china-over-iran-sanctions, last accessed 23 April 2013

Chaffin, Joshua. 'UK and France Push to Arm Syria Rebels', *Financial Times*, 15 March 2013, available at http://www.ft.com/intl/cms/s/0/8f4fd6f4-8cd5-11e2-8ee0-00144feabdc0.html#axzz2NpIJVVbW (registration required), last accessed 23 April 2013

The Christian Science Monitor. 'Libya Sanctions: China's New Role at the UN', 28 February 2011, available at http://www.csmonitor.com/Commentary/the-monitors-view/2011/0228/Libya-sanctions-China-s-new-role-at-the-UN, last accessed 23 April 2013

CIA World Fact Book. 'Saudi Arabia', available at https://www.cia.gov/library/publications/the-world-factbook/geos/sa.html, last accessed 23 April 2013

Clapham, Christopher. 'The Domestic Politics of Foreign Policy Management', *Africa and the International System*. Cambridge: Cambridge University Press, 1996, 62–67

Clawson, Patrick, and Simon Henderson. 'Impact of Sanctioning Iran's Central Bank', *PolicyWatch 1877*, The Washington Institute for Near East Policy, 29 November 2011, available at http://www.washingtoninstitute.org/templateC05.php?CID=3428, last accessed 23 April 2013

CNN. 'Rafsanjani: US Must Do More', 15 June 2005, available at http://edition.cnn.com/2005/WORLD/meast/06/14/iran.rafsanjani/index.html, last accessed 23 April 2013

Colvin, Ross. '"Cut off Head of Snake" Saudis Told US on Iran', *Reuters*, 29 November 2010, available at http://www.reuters.com/article/2010/11/29/

Bibliography

us-wikileaks-iran-saudis-idUSTRE6AS02B20101129, last accessed 23 April 2013

Commodity Online. 'China and UAE Ditch US Dollar, Will Use Yuan for Oil Trade', 24 January 2012, available at http://www.commodityonline.com/news/china-and-uae-ditch-us-dollar-will-use-yuan-for-oil-trade-45444-3-1.html, last accessed 23 April 2013

Connell, Curtis C. *Terrorist and Organized Crime Groups in the Tri-Border Area (TBA) of South America*. The Library of Congress, Federal Research Division, July 2003

Cooper, Andrew Scott. 'Showdown at Doha: The Secret Oil Deal That Helped Sink the Shah of Iran', *The Middle East Journal* 62/4, Autumn 2008, 567–591

Cooper, Helene. '"Loose Talk of War" Only Helps Iran, President Says', *The New York Times*, 4 March 2012, available at http://www.nytimes.com/2012/03/05/world/middleeast/in-aipac-speech-obama-warns-against-loose-talk-of-war.html, last accessed 23 April 2010

Cordesman, Anthony H. 'The Impact of Saudi Aid and Capital', *Western Strategic Interests in Saudi Arabia*. Beckenham: Croom Helm, 1987, 39–40

Cordesman, Anthony H. *Saudi Arabia Enters the Twenty-First Century*. Westport: Center for Strategic and International Studies, 2003

Cordesman, Anthony H. and Nawaf Obaid. 'The New Balance of Threats in the Gulf Region', *National Security in Saudi Arabia: Threats, Responses, and Challenges*. Westport: Praeger Security International, 2005, 1–104

Cordesman, Anthony H. 'Paramilitary, Internal Security, and Intelligence Forces', *Iran's Revolutionary Guards, the Al Quds Force, and Other Intelligence and Paramilitary Forces*, Center for Strategic and International Studies, 16 August 2007, available at http://csis.org/files/media/csis/pubs/070816_cordesman_report.pdf, last accessed 23 April 2013

Cordesman, Anthony H. 'The Egyptian Military and the Arab-Israeli Military Balance', Center for Strategic and International Studies, 10 February 2011, available at http://csis.org/publication/egyptian-military-and-arab-israeli-military-balance, last accessed 23 April 2013

Cordesman, Anthony H. 'Iranian and Saudi Competition in the Gulf', *United States Institute of Peace: The Iran Primer*, 27 April 2011, available at http://iranprimer.usip.org/blog/2011/apr/27/iranian-and-saudi-competition-gulf, last accessed 23 April 2013

Cowper-Coles, Sherard. Interview, London, 4 June 2010

Chatham House. *Iran, Its Neighbours and the Regional Crises*, p. 6, available at http://www.chathamhouse.org/sites/default/files/public/Research/Middle%20East/iran0806.pdf, last accessed 23 April 2013

Council on Foreign Relations. 'Backgrounder: Profile Osama bin Laden', September 2007, available at http://www.cfr.org/terrorist-leaders/profile-osama-bin-laden/p9951#p11, last accessed 23 April 2013

Cousins, Michel. 'Turki al-Faisal Calls on Obama to Push for Middle East Settlement', *Arab News*, 15 May 2010, available at http://arabnews.com/saudiarabia/article54062.ece, accessed 17 May 2010

Crooks, Ed, and Javier Blas. 'OPEC to Study Effects of Falling Dollar', *Financial Times*, 18 November 2007, available at http://www.ft.com/intl/cms/s/0/99951144-960c-11dc-b7ec-0000779fd2ac.html#axzz1eFOgbnlG (registration required), last accessed 23 April 2013

Daily Star. 'Snap Checks Not Part of Inspections Offer, Iran Nuclear Chief Clarifies', 7 September 2011, available at http://www.dailystar.com.lb/News/Middle-East/2011/Sep-07/148092-snap-checks-not-part-of-inspections-offer-iran-nuclear-chief-clarifies.ashx#axzz1X9R9OJh3, last accessed 23 April 2013

Dalton, Richard (ed.). *Iran: Breaking the Nuclear Deadlock*, A Chatham House Report, 2008, available at http://www.chathamhouse.org/sites/default/files/public/Research/Middle%20East/bp1208iran.pdf, last accessed 23 April 2013

Dalton, Richard. 'A New Approach is Needed to Tackle Iranian Nuclear Debate', *The Telegraph*, 18 December 2008, available at http://www.telegraph.co.uk/comment/3832240/A-new-approach-is-needed-to-tackle-Iranian-nuclear-debate.html, last accessed 23 April 2013

Dalton, Richard. 'Iran: Election or Coup?', *Chatham House*, 15 June 2009, available at http://www.chathamhouse.org/media/comment/view/163683, last accessed 23 April 2013

Dalton, Richard. 'Does Tehran Have a Plan C?', *The Guardian*, 27 September 2009, available at http://www.guardian.co.uk/commentisfree/2009/sep/27/iran-nuclear-weapon-plan-c, last accessed 23 April 2013

Dalton, Richard. 'Relations Will Only Improve When it Benefits Tehran', *The Independent*, 30 December 2009

Dalton, Richard. 'Uneasy Stability', *The World Today* 66/4, Chatham House, March 2010

Dalton, Richard. Interview, London, 26 January 2011.

Dalton, Richard. Email to the G2K List, 25 January 2012

Dehghan, Saeed Kamali. 'Iran Demands Apology from US Over Saudi Ambassador "Assassination Plot"', *The Guardian*, 31 October 2011, available at http://www.guardian.co.uk/world/2011/oct/31/iran-demands-apology-assassination-plot, last accessed 23 April 2013

Dehghan, Saeed Kamali. 'Iran's Parliament Votes to Expel British Ambassador', *The Guardian*, 27 November 2011, available at http://www.guardian.co.uk/world/2011/nov/27/iran-votes-expel-british-ambassador, last accessed 23 April 2013

Diplomat. 'Ahmadinejad in Riyadh', 6 March 2007, 4, available at http://www.ids.gov.sa/IDS_PDF/DIP/pdf/Diplomat6.pdf, accessed 3 January 2010

Donilon, Tom. Remarks by US National Security Advisor prepared by the Office of the Press Secretary, the White House, 22 November 2011, sent by email to the G2K List.

BIBLIOGRAPHY

Dorsey, James M. 'Saudi Arabia Embraces Salafism: Countering the Arab Uprising? – Analysis', *Eurasia Review*, 13 January 2012, available at http://www.eurasiareview.com/13012012-saudi-arabia-embraces-salafism-countering-the-arab-uprising-analysis/, last accessed 23 April 2013

Dreazen, Yochi J. 'The US and Iran Are Already Locked in Economic War', *The Atlantic*, 5 January 2012, available at http://www.theatlantic.com/international/archive/2012/01/the-us-and-iran-are-already-locked-in-economic-war/250872/, last accessed 23 April 2013

Drollas, Leo. Interview, London, 26 January 2011

Dyer, Geoff, et al. 'US "Disgusted" with Syria Peace Plan Veto', *Financial Times*, 5 February 2012, available at http://www.ft.com/intl/cms/s/0/2b019f4e-4f1d-11e1-bc30-00144feabdc0.html#axzz1lsxJ5uRc (registration required), last accessed 23 April 2013

Economic Cooperation Organization: http://www.ecosecretariat.org/, last accessed 23 April 2013

The Economist. 'Khatami's Last Stand, Perhaps', 14 November 2002, available at http://www.economist.com/node/1446624 , last accessed 23 April 2013

The Economist. 'The Riddle of Iran', 19 July 2007, available at http://www.economist.com/node/9514293, last accessed 23 April 2013

The Economist. 'Getting a Grip in Iran', 14 August 2007, available at http://www.economist.com/node/9642293 , last accessed 23 April 2013

The Economist. 'Join the Club', 1 May 2008, available at http://www.economist.com/node/11294279, last accessed 23 April 2013

The Economist. 'Can the Bush Doctrine Last?', 27 May 2008, available at http://www.economist.com/node/10873479, last accessed 23 April 2013

The Economist. 'How Iran Fits In', 17 January 2009, available at http://www.economist.com/node/12959539, last accessed 23 April 2013

The Economist. 'Ayatollahs in the Backyard', 26 November 2009, available at http://www.economist.com/node/14969124, last accessed 23 April 2013

The Economist. 'Still Sitting Pretty', 10 June 2010, available at http://www.economist.com/node/16319793, last accessed 23 April 2013

The Economist. 'A Step Away from the Bomb', 10 June 2010, available at http://www.economist.com/node/16321536, last accessed 23 April 2013

Ehteshami, Anoushiravan. *After Khomeini: The Iranian Second Republic*. London: Routledge, 1995

Ehteshami, Anoushiravan. 'Iran's Assessment of the Iraq Crisis and the Post-9/11 International Order' in Thakur, Ramesh, Sidhu and Waheguru Pal Singh (eds.), *The Iraq Crisis and World Order: Structural, Institutional and Normative Change*. Tokyo: United Nations University Press, 2006, 134–161

Ehteshami, Anoushiravan, and Mahjoob Zweiri (eds.). *Iran's Foreign Policy: From Khatami to Ahmadinejad*. Reading: Ithaca Press, 2008

Ehteshami, Anoushiravan. 'Iran', in Tim Niblock and Emma Murphy (eds.), *Economic and Political Liberalization in the Middle East*. New York, British Academic Press, 1993, 214–236

Eisenstadt, Michael, and Mehdi Khalaji. 'Nuclear Fatwa: Religion and Politics in Iran's Proliferation Strategy', *Policy Focus #115*, The Washington Institute for Near East Policy, September 2011

Eleiba, Ahmed. 'Revolution Warms Egyptian-Iranian Relations', *Al-Ahram Online*, 5 April 2011, available at http://english.ahram.org.eg/NewsContent/1/64/9243/Egypt/Politics-/Revolution-warms-EgyptianIranian-relations.aspx, last accessed 23 April 2013

Elkin, Mike. 'Loans to Egypt Hinge on Democracy Issues', *The New York Times*, 29 February 2012 available at http://www.nytimes.com/2012/03/01/world/middleeast/01iht-m01-egypt-aid.html?pagewanted=all, last accessed 23 April 2013

Emirates 24/7. 'Arab League Mission to Return to Syria', 9 February 2012, available at http://www.emirates247.com/news/region/arab-league-mission-to-return-to-syria-2012-02-09-1.442078, last accessed 23 April 2013

Energy Information Administration, US Department of Energy. 'Iran', January 2010, available at http://www.eia.gov/cabs/Iran/Full.html, last accessed 23 April 2013

England, Andrew. 'Cautious Saudis Step into SWF Arena', *Financial Times*, 28 April 2008, available at http://www.ft.com/cms/s/0/5d19b7d8-1564-11dd-996c-0000779fd2ac.html (registration required), last accessed 23 April 2013

Entous, Adam. 'Saudi Arms Deal Advances', *The Wall Street Journal*, 12 September 2010, available at http://online.wsj.com/article/SB10001424052748704621204575488361149625050.html, last accessed 23 April 2013

Eurofighter Typhoon. 'Consortium Structure', available at http://www.eurofighter.com/eurofighter-typhoon/programme-organisation/consortium-structure.html, last accessed 23 April 2013

European Commission. 'European Neighbourhood Policy', available at http://ec.europa.eu/world/enp/funding_en.htm, last accessed 23 April 2013

European Commission. 'Iran', available at http://ec.europa.eu/trade/creating-opportunities/bilateral-relations/countries/iran/, last accessed 23 April 2013

European Commission Directorate-General for Energy. 'Registration of Crude Oil Imports and Deliveries into the European Union (EU27)', 1 December 2009, available at http://ec.europa.eu/energy/observatory/oil/import_export_en.htm, last accessed 23 April 2013

Evans, Stephen. 'German Parliament to Debate Sale of 200 Tanks to Saudis', *BBC News*, 6 July 2011, available at http://www.bbc.co.uk/news/world-europe-14043668, last accessed 23 April 2013

Everett-Heath, Tom. 'Push and Pull', *Middle East Economic Digest*, 11 January 2002, 4

Fallon, Nicholas. 'Background to the 1973/74 Oil Crisis', *Middle East Oil Money and its Future Expenditure*. London: Graham & Trotman Ltd, 1975, 7–9

Farhi, Farideh. Email to the G2K List, 25 January 2012

Farrar-Wellman, Ariel. 'Brazil–Iran Foreign Relations', *Iran Tracker*, 10 May 2010, available at http://www.irantracker.org/foreign-relations/brazil-iran-foreign-relations, last accessed 23 April 2013

FAS Intelligence Resource Program. 'Saudi Arabia', available at http://www.fas.org/irp/threat/missile/saudi.htm, last accessed 23 April 2013

Fayed, Shaimaa. 'Saudi Shows Who's Boss, To Pump 10 Mln bpd', *Reuters*, 10 June 2011, available at http://in.reuters.com/article/2011/06/10/idINIndia-57632320110610, last accessed 23 April 2013

Fifield, Anna, and Najmeh Bozorgmehr. 'US Accuses Iran of Saudi Envoy Death Plot', *Financial Times*, 11 October 2011, available at http://www.ft.com/intl/cms/s/0/185fa35c-f439-11e0-bdea-00144feab49a.html#axzz1aWMBSfVG (registration required), last accessed 23 April 2013

Financial Times. 'Profiles of Iran's Presidential Candidates', 4 June 2009, available at http://www.ft.com/intl/cms/s/0/99fb422a-5050-11de-9530-00144feabdc0.html#axzz1X5XvwtDH (registration required), last accessed 23 April 2013

Financial Times. 'Asia Defence Spending to Overtake Europe', 7 March 2012, available at http://www.ft.com/cms/s/0/0aab435c-6846-11e1-a6cc-00144feabdc0.html#axzz1v8aiR5Dq (registration required), last accessed 23 April 2013

France 24. 'Anti-Christian Violence Sparks Fears of Rising Salafi Influence', 12 May 2011, available at http://www.france24.com/en/20110512-egypt-christian-muslim-violence-sparks-fears-rising-salafi-influence, last accessed 23 April 2013

Fry, Michael Graham, Erik Goldstein and Richard Langthorne. 'Crises and Conferences, 1945–1990', *Guide to International Relations and Diplomacy*. London: Michael Graham Fry, Erik Goldstein and Richard Langthorne, 2002, 292–362

Fulton, Will, Ariel Farrar-Wellman and Robert Frasco. 'Saudi Arabia–Iran Foreign Relations', *Iran Tracker*, 1 August 2011, available at http://www.irantracker.org/foreign-relations/saudi-arabia-iran-foreign-relations, last accessed 23 April 2013

Fürtig, Henner. 'Conflict and Cooperation in the Persian Gulf: The Interregional Order and US Policy', *Middle East Journal* 61/4, Spring 2007, 627–640

Gaddis, John Lewis. 'Reconsiderations: Containment: A Reassessment', *Foreign Affairs*, July 1977, available at http://www.foreignaffairs.com/articles/27903/john-lewis-gaddis/reconsiderations-containment-a-reassessment, last accessed 23 April 2013

Garamore, Jim. 'Chairman Concerned Over Lack of US – Iran Contact', US Department of Defence, 14 September 2011, available at http://www.defense.gov/news/newsarticle.aspx?id=65334, last accessed 23 April 2013

Gause, F. Gregory. 'The Gulf War and the 1990s', *The International Relations of the Persian Gulf*. Cambridge: Cambridge University Press, 2010, 88–136

Gause, F. Gregory. 'The Illogic of Dual Containment, *Foreign Affairs* 73/2, March/April 1994, available at http://www.foreignaffairs.com/articles/49686/f-gregory-gause-iii/the-illogic-of-dual-containment, last accessed 23 April 2013

Gause, F. Gregory. 'Don't Just do Something, Stand There!', *Foreign Policy*, 21 December 2011, available at http://www.foreignpolicy.com/articles/2011/12/21/america_arab_spring_do_nothing (registration required), last accessed 23 April 2013

Gavin, James. 'The Sun Sets for Japan', *Middle East Economic Digest*, 25 February 2000, 4

Gheissari, Ali, and Vali Nasr. 'The Conservative Consolidation in Iran', *Survival* 47/2, Summer 2005, 175–190

Glionna, John M. 'US Presses China, Japan, South Korea, to Trim Iran Oil Imports', *Los Angeles Times*, 10 January 2012, available at http://articles.latimes.com/2012/jan/10/world/la-fg-japan-korea-iran-20120110, last accessed 23 April 2013

Gladstone, Rick. 'In Rare, Blunt Speech, Saudi King Criticizes Syria Vetoes', *The New York Times*, 10 February 2012, available at http://www.nytimes.com/2012/02/11/world/middleeast/in-rare-blunt-speech-saudi-king-criticizes-syria-vetoes.html?_r=1, last accessed 23 April 2013

Global Security. 'Hamas Funding', available at http://www.globalsecurity.org/military/world/para/hamas-funds.htm, last accessed 23 April 2013

Global Security. 'Mecca', available at http://www.globalsecurity.org/military/world/gulf/mecca.htm, last accessed 23 April 2013

Green, Matthew. 'Karzai Says Iran Gave "Bags" of Cash as Aid', *Financial Times*, 25 October 2010, available at http://www.ft.com/intl/cms/s/0/73d83fa0-e058-11df-99a3-00144feabdc0.html#axzz1lbi8znLX (registration required), last accessed 23 April 2013

Gröhe, Herman, et al. 'Even Handed, Not Neutral: Points of Reference for a German Middle East Policy', in Volker Perthes (ed.), *Germany and the Middle East: Interest and Options*, Berlin: Heinrich-Böll-Stiftung and Stiftung Wissenschaft und Politik, 2002, 11, available at http://www.swp-berlin.org/fileadmin/contents/products/fachpublikationen/GermanyAndTheMiddleEast_mitKopierschutz.pdf, last accessed 23 April 2013

Gross, Michael Joseph. 'A Declaration of Cyber War', *Vanity Fair*, April 2011, available at http://www.vanityfair.com/culture/features/2011/04/stuxnet-201104, last accessed 23 April 2013

The Guardian. 'Full Text: Barack Obama's Cairo Speech', 4 June 2009, available at http://www.guardian.co.uk/world/2009/jun/04/barack-obama-keynote-speech-egypt, last accessed 23 April 2013

The Guardian. 'US Embassy Cables: Saudis Fear "Shia Triangle" of Iran, Iraq and Pakistan', 3 December 2010, available at http://www.guardian.co.uk/world/us-embassy-cables-documents/201549, last accessed 23 April 2013

BIBLIOGRAPHY 247

The Guardian. 'Iran Protestors Attack UK Embassy in Tehran – Tuesday 29 November', 29 November 2011, available at http://www.guardian.co.uk/world/blog/2011/nov/29/iran-protesters-attack-uk-embassy-tehran-live, last accessed 23 April 2013
Gulf States Newsletter. 'Economy and Trade: The United Kingdom and the Gulf', 19 September 1994, 19/495
Gulf States Newsletter. 'Politics and Defence: Saudi Arabia's Illusory Security', 19/496, 3 October 1994
Gulf States Newsletter. 'Politics and Defence: Iran – US Blocks Oil Deal', 20/507, 27 March 1995
Gulf States Newsletter. 'Politics and Defence: A US-Iranian Collision?', 20/509, 17 April 1995
Gulf States Newsletter. 'Politics and Defence: in Brief', 20/510, 8 May 1995
Gulf States Newsletter. 'Politics and Defence: America and Iran', 23/577, 12 January 1998
Gulf States Newsletter. 'Centre Piece: Khatami 1, Clinton 0', 23/578, 26 January 1998
Gulf States Newsletter. 'Politics and Defence: Balancing Acts', 23/581, 9 March 1998
Gulf States Newsletter. 'Centrepiece: Europe and the Middle East', 23/582, 23 March 1998
Gulf States Newsletter. 'Politics and Defence: Khatami's Long Game', 23/585, 4 May 1998
Gulf States Newsletter. 'Politics and Defence: Iran–EU Meeting', 23/587, 1 June 1998
Gulf States Newsletter. 'Politics and Defence: Football and Politics', 23/589, 29 June 1998
Gulf States Newsletter. 'Economy and Trade: Iran Reaches Across the Gulf', 23/591, 27 July 1998
Gulf States Newsletter. 'Politics and Defence: The End of Dual Containment?', 23/595, 21 September 1998
Gulf States Newsletter. 'Politics and Defence: Iran – Fatwa Statement', *GSN*, 23/596, 5 October 1998
Gulf States Newsletter. 'Air Force Modernisation', 27/23, 27 June 2003
Gulf States Newsletter. 'Politics and Security – Faced by Strategic Encirclement, Iran Develops the full Spectrum of Deterrence', 732, 16 April 2004
Gulf States Newsletter. 'Others Go In Where Citigroup Has Been', 28/736, 11 June 2004
Gulf States Newsletter. 'Partnership Back in Vogue as State Regains the Initiative in Washington', 28/739, 23 July 2004
Gulf States Newsletter. 'Focus', 28/748, 22 December 2004
Gulf States Newsletter. 'New US National Defence Strategy Signals Shift to Lighter "Footprint" in the Gulf States', 29/755, 15 April 2005

Gulf States Newsletter. 'Saudi Defence: Will France Reap Rewards for Riyadh Connection?', 29/756, 29 April 2005
Gulf States Newsletter. 'Politics and Security: Saudi Arabia', 29/759, 10 June 2005
Gulf States Newsletter. 'Saudi/US: Rice in Riyadh as Dissidents Appeal', 29/760, 24 June 2005
Gulf States Newsletter. 'Defence Pointers', 29/766, 30 September 2005
Gulf States Newsletter. 'Busy Times for Saudi Kremlinologists as King Abdullah Consolidates', 5/768, 28 October 2005
Gulf States Newsletter. 'Close at Last for First Saudi IWPP', 29/770, 25 November 2005
Gulf States Newsletter. 'USA Takes Fright, as China's Vision Becomes Clearer in Relations with Iran and Saudi Arabia', 30/786, 21 July 2006
Gulf States Newsletter. 'USA Edges Towards a More Pragmatic Iran Policy', 30/790, 29 September 2006
Gulf States Newsletter. 'Focus', 31/809, 6 July 2007
Gulf States Newsletter. 'Imposing Discipline Abroad, King Sets Foreign Policy Line', 32/823, 18 February 2008
Gulf States Newsletter. 'With French Deal, Abdullah's National Guard Strengthens its Status as the "Second Saudi Army"', 32/829, 19 May 2008
Gulf States Newsletter. 'Saudi Arabia and Bahrain', 32/840, 10 November 2008
Gulf States Newsletter, 'After the GCC's Muscat Summit, Currency Plan Credibility Hangs on Acts, Not Words', 845, 16 January 2009, available at http://www.gsn-online.com/HTML/Public/GSNs_World/Free_Content/Free_content_70.html, accessed 12 March 2009
Gupta, Grish. 'Hugo Chavez Tries to Silence Health Rumours With His Usual Flair', *Christian Science Monitor,* 30 September 2011, available at http://www.csmonitor.com/World/Americas/Latin-America-Monitor/2011/0930/Hugo-Chavez-tries-to-silence-health-rumors-with-his-usual-flair, last accessed 23 April 2013
Gvosdev, N. K. and Ray Takeyh. 'Pragmatism in the Midst of Iranian Turmoil', *The Washington Quarterly,* Autumn 2004, 33–56
Haass, Richard N. 'The George H.W. Bush Administration', *The Iran Primer,* United States Institute of Peace, available at http://iranprimer.usip.org/resource/george-hw-bush-administration, last accessed 23 April 2013
Hardy, Roger. 'Saudi-US Relations Strained Over Afghanistan', *BBC News,* 15 November 2001, available at http://news.bbc.co.uk/1/hi/world/middle_east/1657721.stm, last accessed 23 April 2013
Hartshorn, J. E. 'Governments in the Oil Business', in Chris Hope and Jim Skea (eds.), *Oil Trade, Politics and Prospects.* Cambridge: Cambridge University Press, 1993.
Hakim, Sam. 'Gulf Cooperation Council Stock Markets since September 11', *Middle East Policy* 15/1, Spring 2008, 70–81
Harris, Kevan. 'Iran's Massive Banking Scandal', *The Iran Primer,* United States Institute of Peace, 16 October 2011, available at http://iranprimer.usip.org/

blog/2011/oct/16/iran per centE2 per cent80 per cent99s-massive-banking-scandal, accessed 16 October 2011

Hechikopf, Kevin. 'Panetta: Iran Cannot Develop Nukes, Block Strait', *CBS News*, 8 January 2012, available at http://www.cbsnews.com/8301-3460_162-57354645/panetta-iran-cannot-develop-nukes-block-strait/, last accessed 23 April 2013

Henderson, Simon. 'Danger Zone', *Foreign Policy*, 27 March 2012, available at http://www.foreignpolicy.com/articles/2012/03/27/danger_zone?page=0,0, last accessed 23 April 2013

Hersh, Seymour M. 'Iran and the IAEA', *The New Yorker*, 18 November 2011, available at http://www.newyorker.com/online/blogs/comment/2011/11/iran-and-the-iaea.html, last accessed 23 April 2013

Hertog, Steffen. 'Comparing the Case Studies: Comparing Saudi Arabia', *Princes, Brokers, and Bureaucrats: Oil and the State in Saudi Arabia*. Ithaca: Cornell University Press, 2010, 246–277

Hibbs, Mark, and Andreas Persbo. *The ElBaradei legacy, Bulletin of the Atomic Scientists*, 16–17, available at http://www.carnegieendowment.org/static/npp/pdf/elbaradei-legacy.pdf, accessed 1 November 2011

Hill, Christopher. in Christopher Clapham (ed.) 'Theories of Foreign Policy Making for the Developing Countries', *Foreign Policy Making in Developing States*. Westmead: Saxon House, 1977, 1–17

Hill, Fiona. 'How Russia and China See the Egyptian Revolution', *Foreign Policy*, 15 February 2011, available at http://www.foreignpolicy.com/articles/2011/02/15/how_russia_and_china_see_the_egyptian_revolution?page=full (registration required), last accessed 23 April 2013

Hinnebusch, Raymond. 'Introduction to the Politics of the Middle East', *The International Politics of the Middle East*. Manchester: Manchester University Press, 2003, 1–14

Hinnebusch, Raymond. 'Introduction: The Analytical Framework', in R. Hinnebusch & A. Ehteshami (eds.), *The Foreign Policies of Middle East States*. London: Lynne Rienner Publishers Inc, 2002, 1–29

Hiro, Dilip. *The Longest War: The Iran–Iraq Military Conflict*. London: Grafton, 1989

Holliday, Shabnam Jane. 'Islamist-Iranian Discourse of National Identity: Khatami's State Counter-Discourse', *Discourses and Counter-Discourses of Iranian National Identity During Khatami's Presidency (1997–2005)*, (PhD book), November 2007

Hollis, Rosemary. 'Europe and Gulf Security: A Competitive Business', in David E. Long and Christian Koch (eds.), *Gulf Security in the Twenty-First Century*. Abu Dhabi: The Emirates Center for Strategic Studies and Research, 1997, 75–90

Rosemary Hollis. 'No Friend of Democratization: Europe's Role in the Genesis of the "Arab Spring"', *International Affairs* 88/1, 2012, 81–94

Holsti, Kal. *International Politics*, 7th ed. Englewood Cliffs: Prentice Hall, 2004

Houghton, David Patrick. 'The Origins of the Crisis', *US Foreign Policy and the Iran Hostage Crisis*. Cambridge: Cambridge University Press, 2001, 46–75

Hudson, Ray, David Rhind and Helen Mounsey. 'Community Policies and Funding', *An Atlas of EEC Affairs*. London: Methuen and Co., 1984, 10–19

Hudson, Valerie. *Foreign Policy Analysis: Classical and Contemporary Theory*. Boulder, Colorado: Rowman and Littlefield, 2007

Hussein, Assa Abdulrahman. *Alliance Behaviour and the Foreign Policy of the Kingdom of Saudi Arabia, 1973–1991*. Ann Arbor: UMI Dissertation Services, 1995

Hunter, Shireen. 'Channels of OPEC Aid', *OPEC and the Third World: the Politics of Aid*. Beckenham: Croom Helm, 1984, 192–264

Hegghammer, Thomas. 'Deconstructing the Myth about al-Qa'ida and Khobar', Combatting Terrorism Center at West Point, 15 February 2008, available at http://www.ctc.usma.edu/posts/deconstructing-the-myth-about-al-qaida-and-khobar, last accessed 23 April 2013

Heydemann, Steven. 'Iran's Alternative Allies', *Iran Primer*, United States Institute of Peace, available at http://iranprimer.usip.org/resource/irans-alternative-allies, last accessed 23 April 2013

IAEA. *Implementation of the NPT Safeguards Agreement and Relevant Provisions of Security Council Resolutions in the Islamic Republic of Iran*, 8 November 2011, available at http://isis-online.org/uploads/isis-reports/documents/IAEA_Iran_8Nov2011.pdf, last accessed 23 April 2013

Ilias, Shayerah. *Iran's Economic Conditions: U.S Policy Issues*, CRS Report for Congress, Congressional Research Service

IMF. 'Regional Economic Outlook: Middle East and Central Asia', *World Economic and Financial Surveys*, May 2008, available at http://www.imf.org/external/pubs/ft/reo/2008/mcd/eng/mreo0508.pdf, last accessed 23 April 2013

IMF. 'Statement by IMF Article IV Mission to the Islamic Republic of Iran', Press Release No. 11/228, 13 June 2011, available at http://www.imf.org/external/np/sec/pr/2011/pr11228.htm, last accessed 23 April 2013

IMF. 'IMF Executive Board Concludes 2011 Article IV Consultation with Islamic Republic of Iran', 3 August 2011, available at http://www.imf.org/external/np/sec/pn/2011/pn11107.htm, last accessed 23 April 2013

Indian Ministry of External Affairs. 'Indo-Saudi Relations', available at http://meaindia.nic.in/meaxpsite/foreignrelation/saudi.pdf, last accessed 23 April 2013

Indyk, Martin. 'Dual Containment and the Peace Process', *Innocent Abroad*. New York: Simon and Schuster, 2009, 149–167

Indyk, Martin. Telephone interview, 1 November 2011

Innes-Hopkins, Chris. Interview, Riyadh, 7 June 201.

International Campaign for Human Rights in Iran. 'Raising Their Voices', available at http://www.iranhumanrights.org/wp-content/uploads/raising-their-voices-final.pdf, last accessed 23 April 2013

BIBLIOGRAPHY 251

International Crisis Group. 'Central Asia: Fault Lines in the New Security Map', 2001, available at http://www.crisisgroup.org/en/regions/asia/central-asia/020-central-asia-fault-lines-in-the-new-security-map.aspx, last accessed 23 April 2013

International Crisis Group. 'Drums of War: Israel and the "Axis of Resistance"', 2 August 2010, available at http://www.crisisgroup.org/en/regions/middle-east-north-africa/iraq-syria-lebanon/lebanon/097-drums-of-war-israel-and-the-axis-of-resistance.aspx, accessed 6 August 2010

International Energy Agency, 'World Energy Outlook 2007: China and India Insights', 45, available at http://www.worldenergyoutlook.org/media/weowebsite/2008-1994/weo_2007.pdf, last accesed 23 April 2013

Inter Press Services. 'Saudi Arabia and Iran Spar Over Oil Embargo', 16 January 2012

Iran News. 'Iran, Ecuador Discuss Medical Cooperation', 23 February 2011

Iran News. 'IKCO, Turkish Firm to Manufacture New Brand of Car', 23 February 2011

Iran News. 'Further Ties With Turkmenistan Sought', 23 February 2011

Iran News. 'Trade Delegation Visits Zimbabwe', 23 February 2011

Iran News. 'Japanese Envoy Acknowledges Growth of Tehran – Tokyo Cooperation', 23 February 2011

Iran News. 'China to Import 23,500bpd Iran Gas', 24 February 2011

Iran News. 'Moscow Ready to Sign Radioactive Isotope Contract with Tehran', 24 February 2011

Iran News. 'Iran Ready to Boost Iraq Oil Exports', 24 February 2011

Iran News. 'Iran Keen to Expand All-Out Ties with Kuwait', 26 February 2011

Iran's Permanent Mission to the UN. 'An Unnecessary Crisis: Setting the Record Straight about Iran's Nuclear Programme', *Payvand*, 18 November 2005, available at http://www.payvand.com/news/05/nov/1211.html, last accessed 23 April 2013

Iran RPO Dubai. 'Iran Regional Presence Office Dubai: Window on Iran', *Wikileaks*, 28 May 2009, available at http://wikileaks.org/cable/2009/05/09RPODUBAI223.html, last accessed 23 April 2013

Iran RPO Dubai. 'Iran: Bazaari Protests Highlight Resistance to Economic Policies', *Wikileaks*, 23 October 2008, available at http://wikileaks.org/cable/2008/10/08IRANRPODUBAI50.html, last accessed 23 April 2013

Islam Times. 'Qatari Prime Minister: The Saudi Regime Will Inevitably Fall by Our Hands', 25 December 2011, available at http://www.islamtimes.org/vdcawmn6e49nuw1.tgk4.html, last accessed 23 April 2013

Jadaa, Abdul Ilah Muhammad. 'Local Press: Who Did Not Benefit from 2-Month Salary?', 5 April 2011, *Arab News.com*, available at http://arabnews.com/saudiarabia/article345612.ece?comments=all, accessed 1 June 2011

Jentleson, Bruce W. 'Metternich of Arabia', *The National Interest*, 29 June 2011, available at http://nationalinterest.org/commentary/metternich-arabia-5543, last accessed 23 April 2013

Jha, Ajay N. 'The Balance Sheet: Need for a Fresh Perspective', *India's Economic Diplomacy in the Gulf*. New Delhi: ABC Publishing House, 1988, 175–227

Johnson, Rob. 'The Iran–Iraq War in Retrospect', *The Iran–Iraq War*. Palgrave Macmillan: New York, 2011, 179–195

Johnson, Simon. 'The Rise of Sovereign Wealth Funds', *Finance and Development*, International Monetary Fund, September 2007, 44/3, available at http://www.imf.org/external/pubs/ft/fandd/2007/09/straight.htm, last accessed 23 April 2013

JTA. 'Senators Press Obama on China – Iran', 14 March 2011, available at http://www.jta.org/news/article/2011/03/14/3086409/senators-press-obama-on-china-iran, last accessed 23 April 2013

Kamrava, Mehran. 'Iran's Regional and Foreign Security Policies in the Persian Gulf', *International Relations of the Gulf Working Group Summary Report*, Center for International and Regional Studies, Georgetown University School of Foreign Service in Qatar, 2009

Kassianova, Alla. 'Russian-Iranian Defence Cooperation vs. US Sanctions', *Russian Weapon Sales to Iran: Why they are Unlikely to Stop*, PONARS Policy Memo 427, December 2006, 1–2, available at http://csis.org/files/media/csis/pubs/pm_0427.pdf, last accessed 23 April 2013

Katz, Mark N. 'The Russia and China Factors in Sanctions', *The Iran Primer*, United States Institute of Peace, 28 November 2011, available at http://iranprimer.usip.org/blog/2011/nov/28/russia-and-china-factors-sanctions, last accessed 23 April 2013

Katz, Mark N. 'Saudi-Russian Relations since the Abdullah-Putin Summit', Middle East Policy Council, available at http://www.mepc.org/journal/middle-east-policy-archives/saudi-russian-relations-abdullah-putin-summit, last accessed 23 April 2013

Katz, Yaakov. 'Barak Reveals Israel's Conditions for Iran – West Talks', *The Jerusalem Post*, 4 April 2012, available at http://www.jpost.com/IranianThreat/News/Article.aspx?id=264839, last accessed 23 April 2013.

Katzman, Kenneth. *Iran's Islamic Revolutionary Guard Corps: Radical Ideology Despite Institutionalization in the Islamic Republic* (PhD book), UMI, 1991

Katzman, Kenneth. *The Iran-Libya Sanctions Act (ILSA)*, CRS Report for Congress, Congressional Research Service, 26 April 2006, 1, available at http://fpc.state.gov/documents/organization/66441.pdf , last accessed 23 April 2013

Katzman, Kenneth. *Afghanistan: Post Taliban Governance, and US Policy*, CRS Report for Congress, Congressional Research Service, 18 June 2009

Katzman, Kenneth. *Iran Sanctions*, Congressional Research Service, 9 November 2010, available at http://fpc.state.gov/documents/organization/151979.pdf, last accessed 23 April 2013

Katzman, Kenneth. *Iran: US Concerns and Policy Responses*, CRS Report for Congress, Congressional Research Service, 8 August 2011, 27, available at http://www.fas.org/sgp/crs/mideast/RL32048.pdf, last accessed 23 April 2013

Katzman, Kenneth. *Iran Sanctions*, CRS Report for Congress, Congressional Research Service, 13 October 2011, 1, available at http://www.fas.org/sgp/crs/mideast/RS20871.pdf, last accessed 23 April 2013

Kaysi, Danial Anas. 'The Saudis go to Baghdad', *The National Interest*, 19 October 2011, available at http://nationalinterest.org/commentary/saudis-baghdad-3639, last accessed 23 April 2013

Kechichian, Joseph A. *Oman and the World: The Emergence of an Independent Foreign Policy*. Santa Monica: RAND, 1995

Kechichian, Joseph A. 'Key Future Gulf Security Issues', *Political Dynamics and Security in the Arabian Peninsula through the 1990s*. Santa Monica: RAND, 1993, 101–110

Kellogg, Amy. 'Wikileaks: Iran President Ahmadinejad Slapped by Head of Revolutionary Guard', *Fox News*, 4 January 2011, available at http://www.foxnews.com/world/2011/01/04/wikileaks-iran-president-ahmadinejad-slapped-head-revolutionary-guard/, last accessed 23 April 2013

Kepplinger, Hans Mathias and Herbert Roth, 'Creating a Crisis: German Mass Media and Oil Supply in 1973–4', *The Public Opinion Quarterly* 43/3, Autumn 1979, 258–296

Kerchner, Isabel. 'Secret Israel-Syria Peace Talks Involved Golan Heights Exit', *The New York Times*, 12 October 2012, available at http://www.nytimes.com/2012/10/13/world/middleeast/secret-israel-syria-peace-talks-involved-golan-heights-exit.html?_r=0, last accessed 23 April 2013

Kerr, P. K. 'Has Iran Violated the NPT', *Iran's Nuclear Program: Tehran's Compliance with International Obligations*, Congressional Research Service, available at http://www.fas.org/sgp/crs/nuke/R40094.pdf, accessed 4 October 2012

Khamenei, Ali. Speech, 23 March 2004, available at http://farsi.khamenei.ir/speech-content?id=3236&q, last accessed 23 April 2013

Khazaee, Mohammad. 'Iran's Letter to U.N. on US Allegations', *The Wall Street Journal*, 11 October 2011, available at http://blogs.wsj.com/dispatch/2011/10/11/irans-letter-to-u-n-on-u-s-allegations/, last accessed 23 April 2013

Klaus, Oliver. 'Sultans of Swing', *Middle East Economic Digest*, 6–12 May 2005

Klaus, Oliver. 'Friends Reunited', *Middle East Economic Digest*, 21–27 October 2005

Knickmeyer, Ellen, and Nour Malas. 'Gulf States Deny Arms to Syria Rebels', *The Wall Street Journal*, 4 March 2012, available at http://online.wsj.com/article/SB10001424052970204276304577261341366601000.html, last accessed 23 April 2013

Korany, Bahgat and Ali E Hillal Dessouki, in B Korany & Ali E. Hillal Dessouki (eds.). 'A Literature Survey and a Framework for Analysis', *The Foreign Policies of Arab States*. Cairo: Westview Press, 1984, 5–9

Kozhanov, Nikolay A. *Possible Changes in Russo-Iranian Relations after the Presidential Elections of 2012 in Russia*, BRISMES Annual Conference 2012 paper, London School of Economics, 26–28 March 2012

Kramer, Andrew E. 'Russia Plan to Help Iran Challenges Sanctions', *The New York Times*, 14 July 2010, available at http://www.nytimes.com/2010/07/15/world/europe/15russia.html, last accessed 23 April 2013

Krauss, Clifford. 'Ahmadinejad Backs Out of Key Role at OPEC', *The New York Times*, 24 May 2011, available at http://www.nytimes.com/2011/05/25/world/middleeast/25opec.html, last accessed 23 April 2013

Kumaraswamy, P. R. 'India Defies Oil Sanctions on Iran', BESA Center Perspectives Paper 168, 19 March 2012, available at http://www.biu.ac.il/SOC/besa/docs/perspectives168.pdf, last accessed 23 April 2013

Landler, Mark, and Steven Lee Myers. 'US Sees Positive Signs from China on Security Issues', *The New York Times*, 26 April 2012, available at http://www.nytimes.com/2012/04/27/world/asia/us-is-seeing-positive-signs-from-chinese.html?_r=2&hpw&pagewanted=all, last accessed 23 April 2013

Lee, Melanie. 'Exclusive: How US Trying to Wean China off Iranian Oil', *Reuters*, 2 May 2011, available at http://www.reuters.com/article/2011/05/02/businesspro-us-china-iran-nuclear-idUSTRE7411QG20110502, last accessed 23 April 2013

Leffler, Melvyn P. 'Remembering George Kennan: Lessons for Today', *United States Institute of Peace*, available at http://www.usip.org/files/resources/SRdec06.pdf, last accessed 23 April 2013

Leverett, Flynt. 'Reengaging Riyadh', in Flynt Leverett and Martin Indyk (eds.), *The Road Ahead: Middle East Policy in the Bush Administration's Second Term*. Washington D.C.: Brookings Institution, 2005, 95–107

Leverett, Flynt. 'The New Axis of Oil', *New America Foundation*, July 2006, available at http://www.newamerica.net/publications/articles/2006/the_new_axis_of_oil, last accessed 23 April 2013

Leverett, Flynt, and Hilary Mann Leverett. 'Dr Gates on Russia's "Schizophrenic" Iran Policy', *Race for Iran*, 18 June 2010, available at http://www.raceforiran.com/dr-gates-on-russia per centE2 per cent80 per cent99s- per centE2 per cent80 per cent9Cschizophrenic per centE2 per cent80 per cent9D-iran-policy, accessed 18 June 2010

Leverett, Flynt, and Hillary Mann Leverett. 'Oil and the Iranian–Saudi "Cold War"', *Race for Iran*, 12 July 2011, available at http://www.raceforiran.com/oil-and-the-iranian-saudi- per centE2 per cent80 per cent9Ccold-war per centE2 per cent80 per cent9D, accessed 12 July 2011

Levitt, Matthew. 'Hezbollah Finances: Funding the Party of God', *The Washington Institute for Near East Policy*, February 2005, available at http://www.washingtoninstitute.org/templateC06.php?CID=772, last accessed 23 April 2013

Lidstone, Digby. 'Digging Deep', *Middle East Economic Digest*, 6 December 2002

Lidstone, Digby. 'Trade Routes', *Middle East Economic Digest*, 7–13 July 2006

Lieberthal, Kenneth, and Wang Jisi. 'Understanding Strategic Distrust: the Chinese Side', *Addressing US-China Strategic Distrust*, John L. Thornton China Center Monograph Series #4, March 2012, Brookings, available at

BIBLIOGRAPHY 255

http://www.brookings.edu/~/media/Files/rc/papers/2012/0330_china_lieberthal/0330_china_lieberthal.pdf, last accessed 23 April 2013

Limbert, John, and Bruce Laingen. 'Limbert & Laingen: Iran Hostages: Thoughts 30 Years Later', *The Washington Times*, January 28 2011, available at http://www.washingtontimes.com/news/2011/jan/28/iran-hostages-thoughts-30-years-later/, last accessed 23 April 2013

Lu, Chunlong, and Jie Chen. 'China's Middle East Policy Since the Post-Mao Reform', in Jack Covarrubias and Tom Lansford (eds.), *Strategic Interests in the Middle East: Opposition or Support for US Foreign Policy*. Aldershot: Ashgate, 2007, 81–97

Lucas, Scott. 'Wikileaks and Iran 2007: Brother of Revolutionary Guards Commander Safavi Offers Co-operation to US', *EA World View*, 29 December 2010, available at http://www.enduringamerica.com/home/2010/12/29/wikileaks-and-iran-2007-brother-of-revolutionary-guards-comm.html, last accessed 23 April 2013

Luciani, Giacomo. 'Oil and Political Economy in the International Relations of the Middle East', in Louise Fawcett (ed.), *International Relations of the Middle East*. Oxford: Oxford University Press, 2005, 79–102

Lunn, Jon. 'Saudi Arabia: History', *The Middle East and North Africa: Volume 50*. London: Europa Publications Limited, 2004, 959–971

Ma, Mayne. 'Chain Oil Imports from Iran Rebound', *The Wall Street Journal*, 21 May 2012, available at http://online.wsj.com/article/SB10001424052702303610504577417803213035894.html, last accessed 23 April 2013

MacAskill, Ewen. 'Wikileaks Cables: Saudis Proposed Arab Force to Invade Lebanon', *The Guardian*, 7 December 2010, available at http://www.guardian.co.uk/world/2010/dec/07/wikileaks-saudi-arab-invasion-lebanon, last accessed 23 April 2013

Maddy-Weitzman, Bruce. 'Riyalpolitik', *Mideast Monitor*, available at http://www.dayan.org/pdfim/2908JREP26.pdf, accessed 30 August 2011

MacAskill, Ewen, and Chris McGreal. 'Israel Should be Wiped off Map, Says Iran's President', *The Guardian*, 27 October 2005, available at http://www.guardian.co.uk/world/2005/oct/27/israel.iran, last accessed 23 April 2013

Macau Daily Times. 'BRICS Summit Insists on Dialogue for Syria, Iran', 30 March 2012, available at http://www.macaudailytimes.com.mo/world/34890-BRICS-summit-insists-dialogue-for-Syria-Iran.html, last accessed 23 April 2013

Mahdi, Kamil. 'Kuwait: History', *The Middle East and North Africa 2004, 50th Edition*. London: European Publications, 2004, 675–686

Maleki, Abbas. Inerview with the Director of the International Institute for Caspian Studies and former Iranian Deputy Foreign Minister, Tehran, 23 February 2011

Maleki, Abbas. 'Iran', Central Asia-Caucasus Institute, 167, available at http://www.silkroadstudies.org/new/docs/publications/GCA/GCAPUB-06.pdf, last accessed 23 April 2013

Maloney, Suzanne. 'The Alliance that Dare not Speak its Name', *Brookings*, 20 May 2011, available at http://www.brookings.edu/opinions/2011/0520_obama_middle_east_maloney.aspx, last accessed 23 April 2013

Maloney, Suzanne. 'Progress of the Obama Administration's Policy toward Iran', *Brookings*, 15 November 2011, available at http://www.brookings.edu/testimony/2011/1115_iran_policy_maloney.aspx, last accessed 23 April 2013

Maloney, Suzanne. 'Obama's Counterproductive New Iran Sanctions', *Foreign Affairs,* 5 January 2012, available at http://www.foreignaffairs.com/ARTICLES/137011/suzanne-maloney/obamas-counterproductive-new-iran-sanctions?page=show, last accessed 23 April 2013

Mandil, Claude. 'Russia Must Act to Avert a Gas Supply Crisis', *Financial Times*, 22 March 2006, available at http://www.ft.com/cms/s/0/9d8a635a-b948-11da-b57d-0000779e2340.html#axzz1Hcfpoavq (registration required), last accessed 23 April 2013

Marashi, Reza, and Sahar Namazikhah. 'Khamenei's Power Consolidation Gambit', *Al Jazeera*, 11 November 2011, available at http://www.aljazeera.com/indepth/opinion/2011/11/20111110103232754325.html, last accessed 23 April 2013

Marschall, Christin. *Iran's Persian Gulf Policy: From Khomeini to Khatami*. London: Routledge Curzon, 2003

Marshall, Andrew R.C, and Peter Apps. 'Iran "Shadow War" Intensifies, Crosses Borders', *News Daily*, 16 February 2012, available at available at http://www.newsdaily.com/stories/tre81f1e7-us-iran-israel-security/, accessed 3 March 2012

Martin, Vanessa. 'The Establishment of the Islamic State', *Creating an Islamic State: Khomeini and the Making of a New Iran*. London: I.B.Tauris, 2000, 147–174

Mason, Robert. 'Arab-Israeli Trade: A Distant, Yet Transformative, Prospect', *Instituto de Empresa International Relations Blog*, 10 February 2010, available at http://ir.blogs.ie.edu/2011/02/10/arab-%E2%80%93-israeli-trade-a-distant-yet-transformative-prospect/, last accessed 12 April 2013

Mason, Robert. 'From Wellhead to Wire: Diversification and Its Challenges in Saudi Arabia', *Instituto de Empresa International Relations Blog*, 14 June 2010, available at http://ir.blogs.ie.edu/2011/06/14/from-wellhead-to-wire-diversification-and-its-challenges-in-saudi-arabia/, last accessed 23 April 2013

Mason, Robert. *Realizing the Indo-Saudi 'Strategic Partnership': An Analysis of the Leading Drivers*, paper delivered at the Gulf Research Meeting, University of Cambridge, 8 July 2011

Matthiesen, Toby. 'Saudi Arabia: the Middle East's Most Under Reported Conflict', *The Guardian*, 23 January 2012, available at http://www.guardian.co.uk/commentisfree/2012/jan/23/saudi-arabia-shia-protesters, last accessed 23 April 2013

Maugeri, Leonardo. *The Age of Oil: The Mythology, History, and Future of the World's Most Controversial Resource*. Westport: Praeger, 2006

Mayer, Henry. 'China and Saudi Arabia Form Stronger Trade Ties', *The New York Times*, 20 April 2010, available at http://www.nytimes.com/2010/04/21/business/global/21energy.html, last accessed 23 April 2013

Mazi, Walid. 'GCC-India FTA "On Right Track"', *Arabnews.com*, 26 February 2011, available at http://www.arabnews.com/node/369394, last accessed 23 April 2013

McDowall, Angus. 'Seizing the Initiative', *Middle East Economic Digest*, 15 February 2002

McDowall, Angus. 'Cover Story: Saudi Arabia', *Middle East Economic Digest*, 1 March 2002

McDowall, Angus. 'The Power of Speech', *Middle East Economic Digest*, 22 March 2002

McDowall, Angus. 'Courage of Convictions', *Middle East Economic Digest*, 20 September 2002

McLachlan, Keith. 'The Oil Industry in the Middle East', in John I. Clarke and Howard Bowen-Jones (eds.), *Change and Development in the Middle East*. New York: Methuen & Co., 1981, 95–113

Mee-Young, Cho, and Yoo Choonsik. 'Exclusive: Sanctions Trap Billions of Iran petrodollars in Korea', *Reuters*, 3 August 2011, available at http://www.reuters.com/article/2011/08/03/us-iran-korea-idUSTRE77228Q20110803, last accessed 23 April 2013

Meijer, Roel (ed.). *Global Salafism: Islam's New Religious Movement*. New York: Columbia University Press, 2009

Menoret, Pascal. *The Saudi Enigma: A History*. Beirut: World Book Publishing, 2005

Middle East Economic Digest. 'Special Report: Saudi Arabia', 30 June 2000

Middle East Economic Digest. 'Oil Price Brings Budget Surplus', 15 September 2000

Middle East Economic Digest. 'Cover Story: Saudi Arabia', 1 March 2002

Middle East Economic Digest. 'Special Report: Saudi Arabia', 22 March 2002

Middle East Economic Digest. 'Cover Story: Arab Summit', 29 March 2002

Middle East Economic Digest. 'Special Report: US', 6 April 2001

Middle East Economic Digest. 'Special Report: Saudi Arabia', 21 June 2002

Middle East Economic Digest. 'Special Report: Saudi Arabia', 31 January 2003

Middle East Economic Digest. 'Pax Americana', 28 February 2003

Middle East Economic Digest. 'Special Report: Saudi Arabia', 28 March 2003

Middle East Economic Digest. 'The View from the Top', 2 May 2003

Middle East Economic Digest. 'Free Trade – with Strings Attached', 29 August 2003

Middle East Economic Digest. 'Cover Story: Prince Alwaleed', 23–29 April 2004

Middle East Economic Digest. 'Special Report: Defence', 28 January–3 February 2005

Middle East Economic Digest. 'Special Report: Saudi Arabia', 17–23 February 2006

Middle East Economic Digest. 'Guarding the Lifelines', 31 March–6 April 2006

Middle East Economic Digest. 'Special Report: Saudi Arabia', 21–27 April 2006

Middle East Economic Digest. 'Friends in High Places', 23–29 June 2006

Middle East Economic Digest. 'Cover Story: Prince Sa'udal-Faisal', 9–15 November 2007

Middle East Economic Survey. 'Iran and UK Debate Investment Framework as UK Oil Firms Wait on Contracts Awards', XLIII/3, 17 January 2000

Middle East Economic Survey. 'Iran Boosts Non-Oil Exports to $3.1 Billion', XLIII/15, 10 April 2000

Miller, Aaron David. 'Trouble over Tehran', *Foreign Policy*, 8 November 2011, available at http://www.foreignpolicy.com/articles/2011/11/07/trouble_over_tehran (registration required), last accessed 23 April 2013

Miller, Rory. 'The Politics of Trade and Diplomacy: Ireland's Evolving Relationship with the Muslim Middle East', *Irish Studies in International Affairs* 15, 2004, 123–145

Mirbagheri, Farid. 'Narrowing the Gap or Camouflaging the Divide: An Analysis of Mohammad Khatami's "Dialogue of Civilisations"', *British Journal of Middle Eastern Studies* 34/3, December 2007, 305–316

Miyagi, Yukiko. *Japan and the Arab Uprisings*, BRISMES Annual Conference 2012, LSE, 26–28 March 2012

Mohamedi, Fareed. 'The Oil and Gas Industry', *The Iran Primer*, United States Institute of Peace, available at http://iranprimer.usip.org/resource/oil-and-gas-industry, last accessed 23 April 2013

Mohamedi, Fareed. 'Rising Oil Prices Create Political Cushion for Iran', *The Iran Primer*, United States Institute of Peace, 7 March 2011, available at http://iranprimer.usip.org/blog/2011/mar/07/rising-oil-prices-create-political-cushion-iran, last accessed 23 April 2013

Moin, Baqer. 'Khomeini in Paris: The End of an Empire', *Khomeini: Life of the Ayatollah*. London: I.B.Tauris, 1999, 182–199

Monk, Ashby. 'Saudi New SWFs are "Stuck"', *Oxford SWF Project*, 22 July 2010, available at http://oxfordswfproject.com/2010/07/22/saudi per centE2 per cent80 per cent99s-new-swfs-are- per centE2 per cent80 per cent9Cstuck per centE2 per cent80 per cent9D/, accessed 10 August 2010

Moslem, Mehdi. *Factional Politics in Post-Khomeini Iran*. Syracuse: Syracuse University Press, 2002

Mostaghim, Ramin, and Ned Parker. 'Iran's Supreme Leader Backs Ahmadinejad', *Los Angeles Times*, 30 May 2011, available at http://articles.latimes.com/2011/may/30/world/la-fg-iran-khamenei-20110530, last accessed 23 April 2013

Mroue, Bassem. 'EU Threatens New Sanctions on Syria', *Time*, 8 February 2012, available at http://www.time.com/time/world/article/0,8599,2106369,00.html, accessed 10 February 2012

BIBLIOGRAPHY

Murphy, Jarrett. 'US and Iraq Go Way Back', *CBS News*, 31 December 2002, available at http://www.cbsnews.com/stories/2002/12/31/world/main 534798.shtml, last accessed 23 April 2013

Nader, Alireza. 'Iran and a Nuclear-Weapon-Free Middle East', Arms Control Association, September 2011, available at http://www.armscontrol.org/print/5013, last accessed 23 April 2013

Nader, Alireza. 'Is Regime Change in Iran the Only Solution?', *Foreign Policy*, 26 January 2012, available http://mideast.foreignpolicy.com/posts/2012/01/26/is_regime_change_in_iran_the_only_solution (registration required), last accessed 23 April 2013

Narayanan, Pratish. 'Iran Receives $100 Million in Oil Payments From India, PTI Says', *Bloomberg*, 2 August 2011, available at http://www.bloomberg.com/news/2011-08-02/iran-receives-100-million-in-oil-payments-from-india-pti-says.html, last accessed 23 April 2013

Nabucco Pipeline, 'Route', available at http://www.nabucco-pipeline.com/portal/page/portal/en/pipeline/route, last accessed 23 April 2013

Newby, Anna. *Russia Continued Relevance in US Policy, World Affairs*, Center for Strategic and International Studies, 20 August 2010, available at http://csis.org/blog/russia-continued-relevance-us-policy-world-affairs, last accessed 23 April 2013

The New York Times. 'The Iran–Contra Report; "Steering to Failure"', November 19, 1987, http://www.nytimes.com/1987/11/19/world/the-iran-contra-report-steering-to-failure.html, last accessed 23 April 2013

Niazi, Tarique. 'Gwadar: China's Naval Outpost in the Indian Ocean', *China Brief* 5/4, The Jamestown Foundation, available at http://www.jamestown.org/single/?tx_ttnews%5Btt_news%5D=3718, last accessed 23 April 2013

Niblock, Tim. 'The Case of Libya: Conclusion', *"Pariah States" & Sanctions in the Middle East: Iraq, Libya, Sudan*. Boulder: Lynne Rienner, 2001, 93–97

Niblock, Tim, with Monica Malik. 'Constrained Development 1985–2000', *The Political Economy of Saudi Arabia*. London: Routledge, 2007, 94–143

Niblock, Tim. *China and Saudi Arabia: the Shaping of the Relationship*, paper delivered at the Gulf Research Meeting, University of Cambridge, 7 July 2010

Niblock, Tim. 'China's Growing Involvement in the Gulf: the Geopolitical Significance', in S. Shen and J. Blanchard (eds.), *Multidimensional Diplomacy of Contemporary China*. Boulder: Lexington Books, 2010, 207–233

Nikou, Semira N. 'Timeline of Iran's Nuclear Activities', *The Iran Primer*, United States Institute of Peace, available at http://iranprimer.usip.org/resource/timeline-irans-nuclear-activities, last accessed 23 April 2013

Nonneman, Gerd. 'Saudi-European Relations 1902–2001 – a Pragmatic Quest for Relative Autonomy', *International Affairs* 77/3, 2001, 633–654

Nonneman, Gerd (ed.). *Analyzing Middle East Foreign Policies: The Relationship with Europe*. Abingdon: Routledge, 2005

Norell, Magnus. 'Executive Summary', *A Victory for Islamism? The Second Lebanon War and Its Repurcussions*, The Washington Institute for Near East Policy, November 2009, available at http://www.washingtoninstitute.org/pubPDFs/PolicyFocus98.pdf, accessed 10 December 2009

Nurja, Alfred. 'WMD-Free Middle East Proposal at a Glance', Arms Control Association, available at http://www.armscontrol.org/factsheets/mewmdfz, last accessed 23 April 2013

Nye, Joseph S. 'Conflicts after the Cold War', *Power in the Global Information Age: From Realism to Globalisation*, Abingdon: Routledge, 2005, 35–51

Obaid, Nawaf E. *The Oil Kingdom at 100 – Petroleum Policymaking in Saudi Arabia*. Washington D.C.: Washington Institute for Near East Policy, 2000

Obaid, Nawaf. 'Stepping into Iraq', *The Washington Post*, 29 November 2006, available at http://www.washingtonpost.com/wp-dyn/content/article/2006/11/28/AR2006112801277.html, last accessed 23 April 2013

Obaid, Nawaf. 'A Saudi Perspective on the Arab Uprisings', *CNN*, 22 November 2009

Obaid, Nawaf. 'A Saudi Perspective on the Arab Uprisings', *CNN*, 22 November 2009, available at http://globalpublicsquare.blogs.cnn.com/2011/06/08/a-saudi-perspective-on-the-arab-uprisings/, last accessed 23 April 2013

Obaid, Nawaf. 'The Day of Saudi Collapse is not Near', *Foreign Policy*, 13 April 2011, available at http://oilandglory.foreignpolicy.com/posts/2011/04/13/the_day_of_saudi_collapse_is_not_near (registration required), last accessed 23 April 2013

Obaid, Nawaf. 'Is Riyadh Ready to "Recalibrate the Partnership"?', 15 May 2011, *Saudi-US Relations Information Service*, available at http://www.susris.com/2011/05/15/is-riyadh-ready-to-recalibrate-the-partnership/, last accessed 23 April 2013

Obaid, Nawaf. 'Amid the Arab Spring, a US–Saudi Split', *The Washington Post*, 16 May 2011, available at http://www.washingtonpost.com/opinions/amid-the-arab-spring-a-us-saudi-split/2011/05/13/AFMy8Q4G_story.html, last accessed 23 April 2013

Office of the President of the United States. 'The National Security Strategy of the United States of America – 2006', March 2006, available at http://www.isn.ethz.ch/isn/Digital-Library/Publications/Detail/?ord588=grp2&ots591=0c54e3b3–1e9c-be1e-2c24-a6a8c7060233&lng=en&id=15462, last accessed 23 April 2013

O'Leary, Carole A, and Nicholas A. Heras, 'Saudi Arabia's "Iran Initiative" and Arab Tribalism: Emerging Forces Converge in the Arab World', *The Jamestown Foundation*, 21 October 2011, available at http://www.jamestown.org/single/?no_cache=1&tx_ttnews per cent5Btt_news per cent5D=38555&tx_ttnews per cent5BbackPid per cent5D=7&cHash=808 12bf625d6ca0316fc61874cab6961, accessed 4 January 2012

Oliker, Olga, et al. *Russian Foreign Policy: Sources and Implications*. Santa Monica: RAND, 2009, 83, available at http://www.rand.org/content/dam/rand/

pubs/monographs/2009/RAND_MG768.pdf, last accessed 23 April 2013

Open Source Center Report. 'Iran: Mostzafan va Janzaban Supports Veterans, Covert Activities', 2 May 2006

O'Reilly, Marc J. 'Omnibalancing: Oman Confronts an Uncertain Future', *Middle East Journal* 52/1, Winter 1998, 70–84

Organization of Arab Petroleum Exporting Countries. 'OAPEC Establishment', available at http://www.oapecorg.org/en/aboutus/establishment.htm, accessed 14 May 2010

Ortiz, Roman D. 'Iran in Mexico and the Caribbean: Building a Strategic a Strategic Trampoline Towards the US', *HACER Latin American News*, 27 October 2011, available at http://www.hacer.org/latam/?p=11611, last accessed 23 April 2013

O'Sullivan, Edmund. 'The Rise and Fall of Saudi Arabia's Great Gas Initiative', *Middle East Economic Digest*, 27 June 2003

O'Sullivan, Edmund. 'Pushing a New Agenda', *Middle East Economic Digest*, 19 September 2003

Ottaway, Marina, and Thomas Carothers. 'The Greater Middle East Initiative: Off to a False Start', *Carnegie Endowment: Policy Brief*, 29 March 2004, available at http://carnegieendowment.org/files/Policybrief29.pdf, last accessed 23 April 2013

Oweis, Khaled Yacoub. 'Syria's Assad Says Military Stops, Shooting Reported', *Reuters*, 18 August 2011, available at http://uk.reuters.com/article/2011/08/18/idINIndia-58841020110818, accessed 18 August 2011

Pals, Fred, Grant Smith and Ola Galal. 'OPEC's "Worst Meeting" Ends Without Agreement, Boosting Prices', *Bloomberg Businessweek*, 9 June 2011, available at http://www.businessweek.com/news/2011-06-09/opec-s-worst-meeting-ends-without-agreement-boosting-prices.html, last accessed 23 April 2013

Pan, Philip P. 'Biden Says Russia Used "Pretext" to Invade Georgia in 2008', *The Washington Post*, 24 July 2009, available at http://www.washingtonpost.com/wp-dyn/content/article/2009/07/23/AR2009072301541.html, last accessed 23 April 2013.

Parasiliti, Andrew. 'Iran: Diplomacy and Deterrence', *Survival* 51/5, October – November 2009, 5–13

Parsi, Trita. *Treacherous Alliance: The Secret Dealings of Israel, Iran, and the US*. New Haven & London: Yale University Press, 2007

Patel, Avnish. 'Taking Forward NATO-Russia Missile Defence Cooperation', *Royal United Services Institute*, available at http://www.rusi.org/analysis/commentary/ref:C4D886D88718D2/, last accessed 23 April 2013

Payvand Iran News. 'Iran Reserves: $120 Billion in Cash, 907 Tons of Gold', 2 January 2012, available at http://www.payvand.com/news/12/feb/1009.html, last accessed 23 April 2013

Peel, Michael. 'Shia Attack Riyadh's Crackdown Pledge', *Financial Times*, 5 October 2011, available at http://www.ft.com/intl/cms/s/0/54036a36-

ef68–11e0-bc88–00144feab49a.html#axzz1aWMBSfVG (registration required), last accessed 23 April 2013
Pelofsky, Jeremy, and Basil Katz. 'Iranians Charged in US Over Assassination Plot', *Reuters*, 11 October 2011, available at http://uk.reuters.com/article/2011/10/11/uk-usa-security-iran-idUKTRE79A5BQ20111011, last accessed 23 April 2013
Peterson, Scott. 'Did Israel Assassinate Iran's "Missile King"?', *The Christian Science Monitor*, 14 November 2011, available at http://www.csmonitor.com/World/Middle-East/2011/1114/Did-Israel-assassinate-Iran-s-missile-king, last accessed 23 April 2013
Peterson, Scott. 'How Iran Could Beat Up On America's Superior Military', *The Christian Science Monitor*, 26 January 2012, available at http://www.csmonitor.com/World/Middle-East/2012/0126/How-Iran-could-beat-up-on-America-s-superior-military, last accessed 23 April 2013
Petrossian, Vahe. 'Reformers Set for Victory', *Middle East Economic Digest*, 18 February 2000
Petrossian, Vahe. 'It's the Economy', *Middle East Economic Digest*, 30 June 2000
Petrossian, Vahe. 'Khatami's Test', *Middle East Economic Digest*, 24 November 2000
Piscatori, James P. 'Islamic Values and National Interest: The Foreign Policy of Saudi Arabia', in Adeed Dawisha (ed.), *Islam in Foreign Policy*. Cambridge: Cambridge University Press, 1983, 35–51
Polenz, Ruprecht. Interview, Berlin, 22 September 2011
Pollack, Kenneth M. 'At War with the World', *The Persian Puzzle*. New York: Random House, 2004
Pollack, Kenneth, and Ray Takeyh. 'Taking on Tehran', *Foreign Affairs* 84/2, March–April 2005, available at http://www.foreignaffairs.com/articles/60619/kenneth-pollack-and-ray-takeyh/taking-on-tehran, last accessed 23 April 2013
Porter, Adam. 'How Much Oil Do We Really Have?', *BBC News*, 15 July 2005, available at http://news.bbc.co.uk/1/hi/business/4681935.stm, last accessed 23 April 2013
Potter, Lawrence G. and Gary G. Sick. 'Introduction' in Lawrence G. Potter and Gary G. Sick (eds.), *Iran, Iraq, and the Legacies of War*. New York: Palgrave Macmillan, 2004, 1–11
Pranger, Robert. 'Foreign Policy Capacity in the Middle East', in J Kipper & H. H. Saunders (eds.), *The Middle East in Global Perspective*. Oxford: Westview Press, 1991, 19–38
Pravda. 'Russian State Duma has Ratified Treaty on Cooperation with Iran', 19 December 2001, available at http://english.pravda.ru/news/world/19–12–2001/24746–0/, last accessed 23 April 2013
Pressly, Linda. 'The "Axis of Annoyance"', *BBC News*, 13 August 2009, available at http://news.bbc.co.uk/1/hi/8195581.stm, last accessed 23 April 2013
Quandt, William B. 'The Superpower Rivalry', *Saudi Arabia in the 1980s: Foreign Policy, Security and Oil*. Washington D.C.: The Brookings Institution, 1981, 47–79

Radio Free Europe. 'Iran's Naval-Gazing More Political Than Military', 29 September 2011, available at http://www.rferl.org/content/iran_navy_/24334129.html, last accessed 23 April 2013

Rakel, Eva. 'Conglomerates in Iran: the Political Economy of Islamic Foundations', in Alex. E Fernandez and Jilberto and Barbara Hogenboom (eds.), *Big Business and Economic Development: Conglomerates and Economic Groups in Developing Countries and Transition Economies Under Globalisation*. Abingdon: Routledge, 2007, 109–133

Ramazani, R. K. 'Khamenei's Nuclear Narrative', *Middle East Online*, 20 February 2012, available at http://www.middle-east-online.com/english/?id=50742, last accessed 23 April 2013

Rasooldeen, M. D. 'Riyadh Declaration Cements Ties', *Arab News*, 1 March 2010, available at http://arabnews.com/saudiarabia/article24178.ece, accessed 25 March 2010

Reals, Tucker. 'Would Israel Attack Iran, or is Netanyahu "Bluffing"?', *CBS News*, 1 April 2009, available at http://www.cbsnews.com/8301-503543_162-4908619-503543.html, last accessed 23 April 2013

Reuters. 'Saudi Gov't Approves New State-Owned Investment Firm', 24 March 2009, available at http://www.arabianbusiness.com/saudi-gov-t-approves-new-state-owned-investment-firm-40966.html, last accessed 23 April 2013

Reuters. 'Saudi to Launch $5bn Investment Firm', 28 April 2009, available at http://www.emirates247.com/2.266/investment/saudi-to-launch-5bn-investment-firm-2009-04-28-1.96034, last accessed 23 April 2013

Reuters. 'Russia's Putin Pledges Coordination with OPEC', 17 September 2010, available at http://uk.reuters.com/article/2010/09/17/uk-russia-opec-idUK-TRE68G2W720100917, last accessed 23 April 2013

Reuters. 'Obama, Cameron and Saudi King Urge Syria End Violence', 13 August 2011, available at http://uk.reuters.com/article/2011/08/13/uk-syria-obama-saudi-idUKTRE77C19X20110813, last accessed 23 April 2013

Reuters. 'Syria Crackdown Toll Rises despite Arab Peace Deal: U.N.', 8 November 2011, available at http://www.reuters.com/article/2011/11/08/us-syria-idUS-TRE7A62Z520111108, last accessed 23 April 2013

Reuters. 'Syria's Brotherhood Rejected Iran-Mediated Deal', 18 January 2012, available at http://www.reuters.com/article/2012/01/18/us-syria-brotherhood-iran-idUSTRE80H1AD20120118, last accessed 23 April 2013

Reuters. 'Pakistan, Iran Begins Work on Oil Pipeline', 11 March 2013, available at http://gulfnews.com/business/economy/pakistan-iran-begins-work-on-oil-pipeline-1.1156915, last accessed 23 April 2013

Rianovosti. 'Iran Successfully Tests Russian TOR-M1 Missiles', 7 February 2007, available at http://en.rian.ru/russia/20070207/60358702.html, last accessed 23 April 2013

Rianovosti. 'Countries under UN Sanctions Cannot Join SCO – Medvedev', 11 June 2010, available at http://en.rian.ru/world/20100611/159390139.html, last accessed 23 April 2013

Rianovosti. 'Russia, China Seek Cooperation with Arab League on Syria', 9 February 2012, available at http://en.ria.ru/russia/20120209/171232225. html, last accessed 23 April 2013

Rianovosti. 'Russian Military Concedes Iran, N. Korea Nuclear Threat', 24 April 2012, available at http://en.rian.ru/russia/20120424/173017423.html, last accessed 23 April 2013

Riedel, Bruce. 'Saudi Arabia: Nervously Watching Pakistan', Brookings, Brookings Institution, 28 January 2008, available at http://www.brookings.edu/opinions/2008/0128_saudi_arabia_riedel.aspx, last accessed 23 April 2013

Robertson, David. 'BAE Poised to Clinch £20bn Saudi Eurofighter Deal', *The Times*, 7 September 2007, available at http://business.timesonline.co.uk/tol/business/industry_sectors/engineering/article2402913.ece (subscription required), last accessed 23 April 2013

Robertson, David, and Alex Spence. 'Six Year BAE Investigation Ends with Minor Accountancy Charges', *The Times*, 6 February 2010, available at http://business.timesonline.co.uk/tol/business/industry_sectors/industrials/article7016732.ece (subscription required), last accessed 23 April 2013

Robson, Colin. 'Interviews', *Real World Research: A Resource for Social Scientists and Practitioner – Researchers, 2nd edition.* Oxford: Blackwell Publishing, 2002, 269–292

Romero, Simon. 'New Fields May Propel Americas to Top of Oil Companies' Lists', *The New York Times*, 19 September 2011, available at http://www.nytimes.com/2011/09/20/world/americas/recent-discoveries-put-americas-back-in-oil-companies-sights.html, last accessed 23 April 2013

Rosenau, James. 'Pre-Theories and Theories of Foreign Policy', in R. B. Farrell (ed.), *Approaches in Comparative and International Politics.* Evanston: Northwestern University Press, 1966, 27–92

Rosenberg, Matthew, Jay Solomon, and Margaret Coker. 'Saudi Bid to Curb Iran Worries US', *The Wall Street Journal*, 27 May 2011, available at http://online.wsj.com/article/SB10001424052702303654804576347282491615962.html, last accessed 23 April 2013

Rosenthal, Elisabeth. 'Gulf Oil States Seeking a Lead in Clean Energy', *The New York Times*, 12 January 2009, available at http://www.nytimes.com/2009/01/13/world/middleeast/13greengulf.html?pagewanted=all, last accessed 23 April 2013

Roy, Shubhajit. 'India with NAM in Slamming IAEA report on Iran', *Indian Express,* 17 September 2010, available at http://www.indianexpress.com/news/India-with-NAM-in-slamming-IAEA-report-on-Iran/682728, last accessed 23 April 2013

Royal Embassy of Saudi Arabia, Washington D.C. 'Press Release: Saudi Arabia Announces Massive Aid Package to Lebanon, Palestine to Help Relief Efforts', 26 July 2006, available at http://www.saudiembassy.net/archive/2006/press/page3.aspx, last accessed 23 April 2013

BIBLIOGRAPHY

Royal Embassy of Saudi Arabia, Washington D.C. 'White House Welcomes Expansion of Saudi Women's Political Participation', 25 September 2011, available at http://www.saudiembassy.net/latest_news/news09251101.aspx, last accessed 23 April 2013

Russell, Richard L. 'China's Strategic Prongs: Saudi Arabia, Iran and Pakistan', *Weapons Proliferation and War in the Greater Middle East*. Abingdon: Routledge, 2005, 120–136

Saeidi, Ali A. 'Iran Para-Governmental Organizations (Bonyads)', *Payvand*, 27 February 2009, available at http://www.payvand.com/news/09/feb/1327.html, last accessed 23 April 2013

Safran, Nadav. *Saudi Arabia: The Ceaseless Quest for Security*. Ithaca: Cornell University Press, 1988

Said, Summer. 'Saudi Arabia, China Sign Nuclear Cooperation Pact', *The Wall Street Journal*, 16 January 2012, available at http://online.wsj.com/article/SB10001424052970204468004577164742025285500.html?mod=googlenews_wsj, last accessed 23 April 2013

Sakamaki, Sachiko, and Andy Sharp. 'US Envoy Einhorn Says Japan Agrees on Need to Increase Pressure on Iran', *Bloomberg*, 18 January 2012, available at http://www.bloomberg.com/news/2012-01-18/u-s-envoy-turns-to-japan-after-pushing-south-korea-on-iran-oil-sanctions.html, last accessed 23 April 2013

Salloukh, Bassel F. 'Regime Autonomy and Regional Foreign Policy Choices in the Middle East: A Theoretical Exploration', *Persistent Permeability? Regionalism, Localism, and Globalisation in the Middle East*. Aldershot: Ashgate, 2004, 81–105

Samore, Gary. *Royal Family Politics in Saudi Arabia (1953–1982)*. Unpublished PhD Dissertation, Harvard University, 1983

Sanger, David E. 'Iran Threatens to Block Oil Shipments, as US Prepares Sanctions', *The New York Times*, 27 December 2011, available at http://www.nytimes.com/2011/12/28/world/middleeast/iran-threatens-to-block-oil-route-if-embargo-is-imposed.html?_r=2&hp, last accessed 23 April 2013

Saudi Expo 2010. 'Saudi–Chinese Relations', available at http://www.saudiexpo2010.com/index.php/en/saudi-chinese-relations, last accessed 23 April 2010

Saudi Fund for Development. *Annual Report*, available at http://www.sfd.gov.sa/, last accessed 23 April 2010

Saudi in Focus. 'Gulf States Offer $10 Billion to Israel in Exchange for a Palestinian State, available at http://www.saudiinfocus.com/ar/forum/showthread.php?36862, last accessed 23 April 2013

Schirazi, Asghar. 'The Genesis of the Constitution', *The Constitution of Iran: Politics and the State in the Islamic Republic*, London: I.B.Tauris, 1997, 22–45

Schmall, Emily. 'Deal Reached for Inquiry on Bombing in Argentina', *The New York Times*, 27 January 2013, available at http://www.nytimes.

com/2013/01/28/world/americas/argentina-and-iran-to-investigate-jewish-center-bombing.html, last accessed 23 April 2013

Seyoufi, Ahmed. 'Iranian Official in Cairo: Tehran is Ready to Help Egypt', *Al-Ahram Daily*, 11 February 2012, available at http://digital.ahram.org.eg/Policy.aspx?Serial=796369, last accessed 23 April 2013

Sfakianakis, John. 'Saudi-Germany Relations', *SAAB Notes*, 8 November 2007, available at http://www.gulfinthemedia.com/files/article_en/356522.pdf, last accessed 23 April 2013

Shafaie, Shirin. 'Diplomatic Miscalculations and the Threat of War: Part 1', *Fair Observer*, 22 February 2012

Shahandeh, Behzad. *Sino–Iranian Relations: A Marriage of Convenience*, paper presented at the Gulf Research Meeting, University of Cambridge, 7–10 July 2010

Shaikh, Fiona, and Arshad Mohammed. 'Western States Step up Sanctions on Iran', *Reuters*, 21 November 2011, available at http://www.reuters.com/article/2011/11/21/us-iran-sanctions-idUSTRE7AK27D20111121, last accessed 23 April 2013

Sick, Gary. 'A Selective Partnership: Getting US–Iranian Relations Right', *Foreign Affairs* 85/6, November–December 2006, available at http://www.foreignaffairs.com/articles/62105/gary-sick/a-selective-partnership-getting-u-s-iranian-relations-right, last accessed 23 April 2013

Sick, Gary. 'Will Israel Really Attack Iran?', 29 January 2012, available at http://garysick.tumblr.com/post/16718681764/will-israel-really-attack-iran, accessed 29 January 2012

Sick, Gary. 'Sick: Iran's Real Weapon of Mass Destruction', *Le Monde Diplomatique*, 2 March 2012

Simmons, Matthew R. *Twilight in the Desert: The Coming Saudi Oil Shock and the World Economy*. New Jersey: John Wiley and Sons, 2005

Slavin, Barbara. 'The Incredible Shrinking Ahmadinejad', *Foreign Policy*, 25 May 2011, available at http://www.foreignpolicy.com/articles/2011/05/25/the_incredible_shrinking_ahmadinejad (registration required), last accessed 23 April 2013

Slavin, Barbara. 'Tensions Mount Over Iraq, Nuke Sanctions', *Inter Press Service*, 12 July 2011, available at http://ipsnews.net/news.asp?idnews=56451, last accessed 23 April 2013

Slavin, Barbara. 'Post-9/11 Rebuffs Set US – Iran Relations on Downward Spiral', *Inter Press Service*, 7 September 2011, available at http://ipsnews.net/news.asp?idnews=105019, last accessed 23 April 2013

Slavin, Barbara. 'EU-Iran New Sanctions Aimed at Averting Wider Conflict', *Inter Press Service*, 25 January 2012, available at http://ipsnews.net/news.asp?idnews=106549, last accessed 23 April 2013

Smith, Adam. 'Has Britain Replaced the US as Iran's "Little Satan"?', *Time*, 26 June 2009, available at http://www.time.com/time/world/article/0,8599,1907066,00.html, last accessed 23 April 2013

Smith, Grant, and Christian Schmollinger. 'China Passes US as World's Biggest Energy Consumer, IEA Says', *Bloomberg*, 20 July 2010, available at http://www.bloomberg.com/news/2010-07-19/china-passes-u-s-as-biggest-energy-consumer-as-oil-imports-jump-iea-says.html, last accessed 23 April 2013

Snyder, Richard, Henry Bruck and Burton Sapin. *Decision Making as an Approach to the Study of International Politics*. Princeton, NJ: Prince University, 1954

Sokolski, Henry, and Patrick Clawson. *Getting Ready for a Nuclear-Ready Iran*, Strategic Studies Institute, US Army, October 2005, available at http://www.strategicstudiesinstitute.army.mil/pdffiles/pub629.pdf, last accessed 23 April 2013

Solomon, Jay. 'Saudi Suggests "Squeezing" Iran Over Nuclear Ambitions', *The Wall Street Journal*, 22 June 2011, available at http://online.wsj.com/article/SB10001424052702304887904576400083811644642.html?mod=WSJEUROPE_hpp_MIDDLESecondNews, last accessed 23 April 2013

Solomon, Jay, and Farnaz Fassihi. 'Iran Redistributes Wealth in a Bid to Fight Sanctions', *The Wall Street Journal*, 27 July 2011, available at http://online.wsj.com/article/SB10001424052702304223804576448203609699930.html?mod=WSJEUROPE_hpp_MIDDLETopNews#printMode, last accessed 23 April 2013

Spencer, Richard. 'Wikileaks: How Iran Devised New Suicide Vest for Al-Qaeda to Use in Iraq', *The Telegraph*, 23 October 2010, available at http://www.telegraph.co.uk/news/worldnews/middleeast/iraq/8083016/Wikileaks-how-Iran-devised-new-suicide-vest-for-al-Qaeda-to-use-in-Iraq.html, last accessed 23 April 2013

Sprout, Margaret and Harold. *Man-Milieu Relationship Hypotheses in the Context of International Politics*. Princeton, NJ: Princeton University, 1956

Stevens, Paul. *An Embargo on Iranian Crude Oil Exports: How Likely and With What Impact?*, Chatham House EEDP Programme Paper, January 2012

Saudi-US Relations Information Service. 'Franco-Saudi State Visit: President Chirac in Riyadh', 10 March 2006, available at http://www.susris.com/articles/2006/nid/060310-chirac-visit.html, last accessed 23 April 2013

Saudi-US Relations Information Service. 'Arab Gulf Union Council – What's in a Name', 8 March 2012, available at http://www.susrisblog.com/2012/03/08/arab-gulf-union-council-whats-in-a-name/, last accessed 23 April 2013

Saudi-US Relations Information Service. 'US, Saudi, GCC Leaders to Talk on Iran, Syria Crisis', 29 March 2012, available at http://www.susris.com/2012/03/29/us-saudi-gcc-leaders-to-talk-on-iran-syria-crises/, last accessed 23 April 2013

Sussman, Gerald, and Sascha Krader. 'Template Revolutions: Marketing US Regime Change in Eastern Europe', *Westminster Papers in Communication and Culture* 5/3, 2008, University of Westminster, available at http://www.westminster.ac.uk/__data/assets/pdf_file/0011/20009/006WPCC-Vol5-No3-Gerald_Sussman_Sascha_Krader.pdf, last accessed 23 April 2013

Taghavi, Roshanak. 'Why Iran's Currency Dropped to Worst Low in Two Decades', *The Christian Science Monitor*, 3 January 2012, available at http://

www.csmonitor.com/World/Middle-East/2012/0103/Why-Iran-s-currency-dropped-to-worst-low-in-two-decades, last accessed 23 April 2013

Takeyh, Ray. 'Relations with the "Great Satan"', *Guardians of the Revolution: Iran and the World in the Age of the Ayatollahs.* Oxford: Oxford University Press, 2009, 35–61

Tayel, Abeer, and Mustapha Ajbailim. 'Iran, Egypt Renewing Ties?', *Al Arabiya*, 18 April 2011, available at http://www.alarabiya.net/articles/2011/04/18/145906.html, last accessed 23 April 2013

Tehran Times. 'Iran Provides 20 Answers to Clarify Ambiguities About its Nuclear Program', 9 November 2011, available at http://tehrantimes.com/politics/4362-iran-provides-20-answers-to-clarify-ambiguities-about-its-nuclear-program, last accessed 23 April 2013

Teitelbaum, Joshua. 'Saudi Arabia's Shi'i Opposition: Background and Analysis', The Washington Institute for Near East Policy, 14 November 1996, available at http://www.washingtoninstitute.org/templateC05.php?CID=1104, last accessed 23 April 2013

Teitelbaum, Joshua. 'Empty Words: Saudi Blustering and US – Saudi Realities', *Perspectives Papers on Current Affairs 147*, The Begin-Sadat Center for Strategic Studies, 17 July 2011, available at http://www.biu.ac.il/Besa/perspectives147.html, last accessed 23 April 2013

Terhalle, Maximilian. 'Understanding the Limits of Power: America's Middle East Experience', *Review of International Studies* 37/2, April 2011, 631–640

Terzian, Pierre. *OPEC: the Inside Story.* London: Zed Books, 1985

Teslik, Lee Hudson. 'Sovereign Wealth Funds', Council on Foreign Relations, 28 January 2009, available at http://www.cfr.org/publication/15251/#p5, last accessed 23 April 2013

Thaler, David E., and Alireza Nader, 'Deep Seated Entanglements: the Web of Iranian Leadership Can be Negotiated, Not Unravelled', *RAND Review*, available at http://www.rand.org/publications/randreview/issues/spring2010/iran.html, last accessed 23 April 2013

The Telegraph. 'Mahmoud Ahmadinejad Fires Foreign Minister', 13 December 2010, available at http://www.telegraph.co.uk/news/worldnews/middleeast/iran/8199460/Mahmoud-Ahmadinejad-fires-foreign-minister.html, last accessed 23 April 2013

The Telegraph. 'Iran to be "Held Accountable" for Assassination Plot, Says Joe Biden', 12 October 2011, available at http://www.telegraph.co.uk/news/worldnews/northamerica/usa/8822267/Iran-to-be-held-accountable-for-assassination-plot-says-Joe-Biden.html, last accessed 23 April 2013

Thompson, Richard. 'Returning to Form', *Middle East Economic Digest*, 27 January – 2 February 2006

Toscano, Roberto. Email interview, 12 August 2011.

Toscano, Roberto. Remarks by, at the University of Exeter, 23 November 2011

Towers, John, et al. 'Arms Transfer to Iran', *Excerpts From the Tower Commission Report*, available at http://www.presidency.ucsb.edu/PS157/assignment per cent20files per cent20public/TOWER per cent20EXCERPTS.htm#PartIII, accessed 9 March 2012

Ulrichsen, Kristian Coates. 'Challenges of Transition in the Gulf Cooperation Council States', *Global Affairs*, 24 September 2011, available at http://eng.globalaffairs.ru/number/Approaching-a-Post-Oil-Era-15328, last accessed 23 April 2013

Uni, Assaf. 'Report: Hezbollah Funded by Drug Trade in Europe', *Haaretz*, 9 January 2010, available at http://www.haaretz.com/news/report-hezbollah-funded-by-drug-trade-in-europe-1.261091, last accessed 23 April 2013

United States of America Mission to the International Organizations in Vienna. 'Statement by China, France, Germany, the Russian Federation, the United Kingdom, and the United States of America, 9 March 2011, available at http://vienna.usmission.gov/110309p51.html, last accessed 23 April 2013

United States of America Senate, *Congressional Record: Proceedings and Debates of the 109th Congress, First Session*, 20 June 2005, Vol. 151, Pt 10, 13412

UPI. 'Iran: Bushehr Nuclear Plant Operational', 18 May 2011, available at http://www.upi.com/Top_News/World-News/2011/05/18/Iran-Bushehr-nuclear-plant-operational/UPI-39011305717766/, last accessed 23 April 2013

UPI. 'Israel Defence Chief: Iran Our Main Threat', 31 October 2011, available at http://www.upi.com/Top_News/Special/2011/10/31/Israel-defense-chief-Iran-our-main-threat/UPI-76471320081019/, last accessed 23 April 2013

US Department of State. 'Foreign Terrorist Organizations', 15 September 2011, available at http://www.state.gov/s/ct/rls/other/des/123085.htm, accessed 15 September 2011

US Embassy Bern. 'Swiss Ambassador to Iran Comments on Assisting US Citizens and Dealing with Post-Election Tehran', *Wikileaks*, 1 September 2009, available at http://wikileaks.org/cable/2009/09/09BERN363.html, last accessed 23 April 2013

US Mission UNVIE Vienna. 'Austrian Diplomat Shares Iranian President's Claim', *Wikileaks*, 8 February 2010, available at http://wikileaks.org/cable/2010/02/10UNVIEVIENNA40.html, last accessed 23 April 2013

US Energy Information Administration, *Country Profile: Saudi Arabia*, available at http://www.eia.gov/countries/country-data.cfm?fips=sa, last accessed 23 April 2013

Vaez, Ali, and Charles D. Ferguson. 'An Iranian Offer Worth Considering', *The New York Times*, 29 September 2011, available at http://www.nytimes.com/2011/09/30/opinion/30iht-edvaez30.html?_r=3&ref=global, last accessed 23 April 2013

Vaez, Ali. 'Seyed Hossein Mousavian: The West is Pushing Iran in the Wrong Direction', *Bulletin of the Atomic Scientists*, 18 November 2011, available at http://thebulletin.org/web-edition/features/seyed-hossein-mousavian-the-west-pushing-iran-the-wrong-direction, last accessed 23 April 2013

Vasquez, John. *The Power of Power Politics: From Classical Realism to Neotraditionalism*. Cambridge: Cambridge University Press, 1998

Vassiliev, Alexei. *The History of Saudi Arabia*. London: Saqi Books, 1998

Vidal, John. 'Wikileaks Cables: Saudi Arabia Cannot Pump Enough Oil to Keep a Lid on Prices', *The Guardian*, 8 February 2011, available at http://www.guardian.co.uk/business/2011/feb/08/saudi-oil-reserves-overstated-wikileaks, last accessed 23 April 2013

Walsh, Elsa. 'The Prince: How the Saudi Ambassador Became Washington's Indispensable Operator', *The New Yorker*, 24 March 2003, p. 60, available at http://www.saudiembassy.net/files/PDF/03-ST-Bandar-0324-NewYorker.pdf, last accessed 23 April 2013

Walt, Stephen. *The Origin of Alliances*. New York: Cornell University Press, 1987

Waltz, Kenneth. *Theory of International Politics*. Reading, Massachusetts: Addison Wesley, 1979

Warrick, Joby, and Thomas Erdbrink. 'Assassination Plot was so Clumsy, Officials at First Doubted Iran's Role', *The Washington Post*, 13 October 2011, available at http://www.washingtonpost.com/world/national-security/us-investigators-initially-doubted-iran-link-to-assassination-plot/2011/10/12/gIQAnWgpfL_story.html, last accessed 23 April 2013

Warrick, Joby. 'Russian Scientist Vyacheslav Danilenko's Aid to Iran Offers Peak at Nuclear Program', *The Washington Post*, 14 November 2011, available at http://www.washingtonpost.com/world/national-security/russian-scientist-vyacheslav-danilenkos-aid-to-iran-offers-peek-at-nuclear-program/2011/11/12/gIQAeuiCJN_print.html, last accessed 23 April 2013

The Washington Institute for Near East Policy. 'Preventing a Cascade of Instability: US Engagement to Check Iranian Nuclear Progress', Taskforce on Iranian Proliferation, Regional Security and US Policy, March 2009

The Washington Post. 'Clinton Tells Egyptian Foreign Minister that US Aid Threatened by NGO Dispute', 4 February 2012, available at http://www.washingtonpost.com/world/middle-east/clinton-tells-egyptian-foreign-minister-that-us-aid-threatened-by-ngo-dispute/2012/02/04/gIQAwDnjpQ_story.html, accessed 4 February 2012

The White House. 'Remarks by the President at the New Economic School Graduation', Moscow, 7 July 2009, available at http://www.whitehouse.gov/the_press_office/Remarks-By-The-President-At-The-New-Economic-School-Graduation/, last accessed 23 April 2013

The White House. 'Remarks by President Obama and President Rousseff of Brazil in Brasilia, Brazil', 19 March 2011, available at http://www.whitehouse.gov/the-press-office/2011/03/19/remarks-president-obama-and-president-rousseff-brazil-brasilia-brazil, last accessed 23 April 2013

Waterfield, Bruno. 'EU Imposes Syria Sanctions Targeting Assad Luxury Lifestyle', *The Telegraph*, 23 April 2012, available at http://www.telegraph.

co.uk/news/worldnews/middleeast/syria/9221551/EU-imposes-Syrian-sanctions-targeting-Assad-luxury-lifestyle.html, last accessed 23 April 2013

Watt, Nicholas. 'Tony Blair Calls for Regime Change in Iran and Syria', *The Guardian*, 9 September 2011, available at http://www.guardian.co.uk/politics/2011/sep/09/tony-blair-regime-change-iran-syria, last accessed 23 April 2013

Wehrey, Frederic, et al. 'Sectarianism and Ideology in the Saudi–Iranian Relationship', *Saudi–Iranian Relations since the fall of Saddam*. Santa Monica: RAND, 2009, 11–45

Wendt, Alexander. 'Anarchy is What States Make of it: the Social Construction of Power Politics', *International Organization* 46/2, 1992, 391–425

White, Thomas, and Gladys Ganley. 'The "Death of a Princess" Controversy', PBS, available at http://www.pbs.org/wgbh/pages/frontline/shows/princess/reflect/harvard.html, last accessed 23 April 2013

White, Wayne. 'Re: Mousavian: A Package to Resolve the Nuclear Impasse with Iran'. Email sent to the Gulf2000 List, 2 April 2011.

Wikileaks. 'Iranian Tourism: An Opportunity for Leverage?', 3 November 2008, available at http://wikileaks.org/cable/2008/11/08ISTANBUL557.html, last accessed 23 April 2013

Wikileaks. 'Iran/Israel: Regime Insider Reportedly Passes Tough Message on Israeli Hostages', 7 April 2009, available at http://www.cablegatesearch.net/cable.php?id=09LONDON837&q=safavi per cent20salma, last accessed 23 April 2013

Wikileaks. 'Saudi–Iranian Tensions Evident In Counter Accusations Over Yemen, Pilgrimages and Islamic Games', 19 January 2010, available at http://wikileaks.org/cable/2010/01/10RIYADH93.html, last accessed 23 April 2013

Wittes, Tamara Cofman. 'A New US Proposal for a Greater Middle East Initiative: An Evaluation', *Brookings*, 10 May 2004, available at http://www.brookings.edu/papers/2004/0510middleeast_wittes.aspx, last accessed 23 April 2013

Wolf, Julie. 'The Iran–Contra Affair', *PBS*, available at http://www.pbs.org/wgbh/amex/reagan/peopleevents/pande08.html, last accessed 23 April 2013

World Trade Organization. 'China and the WTO', available at http://www.wto.org/english/thewto_e/countries_e/china_e.htm, last accessed 23 April 2013

Wright, Robert. 'Introduction', *Nonzero: History, Evolution & Human Cooperation*. London: Abacus, 2000, 3–13

Wright, Robin. 'The Challenge of Iran', *The Iran Primer*, available at http://iranprimer.usip.org/resource/challenge-iran, last accessed 23 April 2013

Yamani, Mai. 'Terminal Decline?', *The World Today*, Chatham House, 60/7, July 2004

Yamani, Mai. 'The Two Faces of Saudi Arabia', *Survival*, International Institute for Strategic Studies, 50/1, February-March 2008, 143–156

Yergin, Daniel. 'Epilogue', *The Prize: The Epic Quest for Oil, Money and Power*. New York: Free Press, 2008, 763–775

Yong, William. 'Iran Embarks on Sweeping Changes in its Economy', *International Herald Tribune*, 17 January 2011

Youngs, Richard, and Ana Echague, 'Europe and the Gulf: Strategic Neglect?', *Studia Diplomatica*, Vol LX/1, 2007, 29–41

Youngs, Richard. *Impasse in Euro-Gulf Relations*, FRIDE Working Paper, April 2009

INDEX

Abdulaziz, Bandar Bin Sultan Bin, 60, 66, 78
'Active Engagement', 85, 133, 135, 151, 154, 165–166
Afghanistan, 16, 32–33, 61, 110, 120, 122–123, 137, 139
Ahmadinejad, Mahmoud, 84, 92, 106, 126
Aid
   Iranian, 123
   Military, during Iran - Iraq War, 20
   Saudi, 14–16, 46–49, 51, 53, 58–59, 63–65, 162
   US, 95, 150
   WMDFZ in the Middle East and, 134
Alliances 1, 8, 159
Al-Qaeda, 27, 45, 55, 71, 120, 124
Al-Yamamah contract, 71–72, 75
Arab Peace Initiative, 47, 49, 65
Arab Uprisings, 35, 51–52, 64, 67–68, 105, 119, 147–151, 154, 158, 160, 162–164, 168
   See also Iran, Arab Uprisings and, and Saudi Arabia, Arab Uprisings, response to
As-Salaam contract, 72
Ayatollah, *see* Supreme Leader
'Axis of evil', 121

BAE Systems, 71–72
Basij, 87–88, 93
Blair, Cherie, 73
Blair, Tony, 71, 118
Bonyads - *see* Iran, political economy of
British Petroleum (BP), 72–73, 89
Bush, George W., 49, 60, 64–65, 75, 121–122
   administration of, 68, 125, 129, 132
   doctrine, 132
Bushehr, 116, 132, 141–142, 145

Carter Doctrine, *see* US Containment Policy
Central Bank of Iran, 103, 106, 137
Chirac, Jacques, 76, 118
Communism, 15–16, 33, 150, 162
Constructivism 6, 7, 10
Council of Guardians, 19

Expediency Council, 27, 91–92, 116

Al-Faisal, Sa'ud, 48, 61, 65–66, 79
Al-Faisal, Turki, 44, 57, 67
Foreign Policy Analysis 1–11, 156
   Economic factors in, 157–158, 160–163
   Future of, 168

Geo-strategic factors in, 157
Ideological factors in, 157

G20, 74, 146, 152
Global War on Terror (GWOT), 47, 61, 153
Gulf Cooperation Council (GCC), 2, 50–51
  Enlargement of, 52
Gulf War (1991) 5, 24–26

Hamas, 48–49, 94–95, 134–135
Hezbollah, 94–95, 134–135
HSBC, 73, 89

International Atomic Energy Agency (IAEA), 85, 99, 109, 122, 126–127, 130, 131, 136–137,
International Monetary Fund (IMF), 15, 37, 53, 74, 107
  Special Oil Facility of the, 15
International Oil Companies (IOCs), 12
Islamic Revolution, 1, 16, 17
Islamic Revolutionary Guards Corps (IRGC), 24, 87–91, 93, 106
Iran
  9/11 and, 31–32, 120–121, 124
  Arab Uprisings and, 53, 98, 100, 107, 114, 119, 132, 158
  Bahrain and, 97
  Central Asia and, 109–112, 138
  China and, 85, 128–129, 147
  Dialogues with, 28, 29, 30
  Economic Cooperation Organization (ECO) and, 115
  Egypt and, 95
  European relations with, 30–31, 104, 117–119, 125–127, 132–133
  Foreign Direct Investment (FDI), 84, 105
  Foreign policy of, 84, 91–139, 158
  Green Movement in, 91, 159
  Gulf Cooperation Council (GCC) states and, 98–100, 115

India and, 114
Iraq and, 101
Israel and, 21, 94–95, 127–128, 135–136
Latin America and, 108–109, 138
Political economy of, 18, 19, 26, 86, 92–93, 100, 106–107, 135, 137–138
Regional trade and, 111–117
Russia and, 85, 114, 116, 132, 141–146,
Sanctions against, 2, 85, 101, 103, 105, 110, 114, 116, 132, 135–136
Saudi Arabia and, 96–99
Shanghai Cooperation Organization (SCO) and, 115–116, 146
Trade and Cooperation Agreement (TCA) and, 30–31, 126, 138–139
Turkey and, 102, 111–112, 114, 130–131, 159
UAE and, 24, 55, 84, 97, 159
UK and, 31, 104, 127
US hostage crisis and, 17–18
USA and, 20, 22, 26, 27–28, 103, 117, 120–132, 139
See also Iranian nuclear programme
Iran - Contra Affair, 16, 22, 122
Iran - Iraq War, 20–24
Iran - Libya Sanctions Act (ILSA), 27, 84
Iran - Pakistan - India Pipeline (IPI), 112–114
Iran Sanctions Act (ISA), 132
Iranian nuclear programme, 93, 102, 105, 126, 129–138
Istanbul Cooperation Initiative (ICI), 55

Khamenei, Sayyid Ali, 31, 91, 103–106, 121, 126, 129, 137–138
Khatami, Sayyid Mohammad, 28–32, 87–88, 97
Khomeini, Ruhollah, 17–19, 21–22, 23, 86
See also Valayat-e faqih

INDEX

Larijani, Ali, 130
Liquefied Natural Gas (LNG), 128, 138
Loans, 15, 24, 33, 44, 59, 151

Majlis, of Iran, 26, 86, 87–88, 92
Majlis al-Shura, of Saudi Arabia, 69, 76
Makkah Accords, 48–49
Mashaie, Esfandiar, 130
Middle East
   China and the, 1, 3, 146–150
   Diplomatic engagement in the, 167–168
   Europe and the, 153
   Future trends in the, 163–164
   India and the, 150–151
   Japan and the, 151–152
   Russia and the, 140–146
   USA and the, 140–146, 152–155

National Iranian Oil Company (NIOC), 90, 144, 147
Non-Proliferation Treaty (NPT), 109, 121, 131–133, 136–138
   Additional Protocol of the, 125–127, 129, 131, 137
North Atlantic Treaty Organization (NATO), 13, 53, 81, 96–97, 141, 153
   Istanbul Cooperation Initiative (ICI), 55

Obama, Barack, 143, 154,
   administration, 95, 103, 117, 122, 129, 132, 146
Oil crisis (1973), 11, 12
   King Faisal role in, 13
   OAPEC involvement in, 11, 12, 13
   Palestine and the, 13
   and the USA, 14
OPEC, 11, 27, 105, 163
Operation *Eagle Claw*, see US hostage crisis
Organization of the Islamic Conference, 57

Palestinian Islamic Jihad (PIJ), 94
Palestinian National Authority (PNA), 48–49, 134, 160
Pan-Arabism, 6
Peninsular Shield Force (PSF), 160
Permeated region, 8
Petrochemicals, 33, 39, 80, 103

Qods Force, 94

Rafsanjani, Hashemi, 28, 86, 92
Ramadan War/Yom Kippur War, 11
   Kissinger, Henry and, 12
Relative Autonomy 9
Rentier States, 12
'Resistance axis', 93–96, 100, 107
Rice, Condoleeza, 60, 122, 124
Rowhani, Hassan, 98, 130

Sabic, 41–42
Salafism, 2
Sarkozy, Nicholas, 76, 118
Al-Saud, Abdullah bin Abdulaziz, 40, 42–43, 45, 48–49, 55, 61, 69
   Meetings with IOCs, 39
   Meetings with world leaders, 64–65, 68, 75
   National dialogue, 42
   Syria and, 150
   Tour of Asia, 78, 80
Saudi Arabia
   9/11 and, 32, 34, 39, 43–44, 47, 59, 60–66, 70–71, 146
   Aid, 15
   Arab Uprisings, response to, 43–44, 53, 159–160, 162
   China and, 60, 78–80, 146, 149
   Counterterrorism and, 35, 58, 64, 66, 71, 74, 81, 83
   Employment issues in, 41–42, 81
   Europe and, 70
   Foreign Direct Investment (FDI), 36, 38–41, 81

Foreign policy of, 11, 35–83, 158, 160–163
France and, 74–76
Germany and, 76
Human rights, *see* 'Riyadh Spring'
India and, 80
Iran and, 54–57
Japan and, 77
Malaysia and, 58
Middle East Peace Process (MEPP) and, 60, 81, 83
National security, 45
OPEC and, 35
Pakistan and, 58–59
Political economy, 36–42
Qatar and, 51
'Riyadh Spring', 42–43
'Riyal Politik', 15, 52
Shi'a community, 45, 48, 51
Sovereign Wealth Fund (SWF), 40
UK and, 71–74
USA and, 15–16, 32–34, 60–70, 78
Yemen and, 51
Saudi Aramco, 11, 39, 41–42, 56, 62, 73, 75, 146
Saudi Gas Initiative (SGI), 36, 39, 40
Saudi Arabian National Guard (SANG), 32, 42
Shell, 39, 72, 89, 114
Sinopec, 79, 128, 146–147
South Pars, 90, 128, 138, 162

Strait of Hormuz, 21, 23, 104, 147, 149, 157, 164,
Supreme Leader, 86–91, 93, 103, 106, 113,
Supreme National Security Council (SNSC), of Iran, 91–92, 99
Syria, 165–167
European sanctions against, 165

'Tehran Declaration', 102, 131
Tehran Research Reactor (TRR), 129, 131
Terrorism 21, 25, 28,
Iran and, 29–32, 110, 121, 124
Threat Perception 8

United Nations Security Council, 3, 85, 132, 134–135, 143, 146, 148, 163, 165, 167,
Sanctions against Iran by, *see* Iran, Sanctions against

Valayat-e faqih, 86, 91

Weapons of Mass Destruction (WMD) 8, 164
Free Zone in the Middle East (WMDFZME), 133
World Bank, 23, 37
World Trade Organization (WTO), 38, 73, 76, 78, 122, 146–147

CPSIA information can be obtained
at www.ICGtesting.com
Printed in the USA
LVHW042233300922
729678LV00006B/626